Naval Power in the Twenty-first Century

A *Naval War College Review* Reader

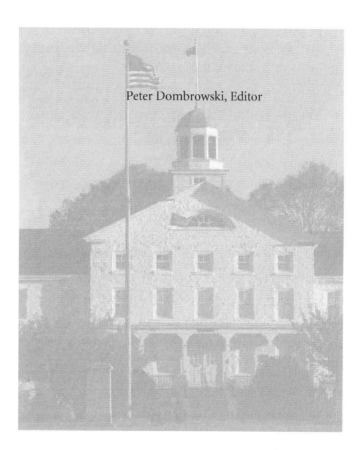

Peter Dombrowski, Editor

NAVAL WAR COLLEGE PRESS
Newport, Rhode Island

Naval War College

Newport, Rhode Island
Center for Naval Warfare Studies
Newport Paper Twenty-four
July 2005

President, Naval War College
Rear Admiral Jacob L. Shuford, U.S. Navy

Provost/Dean of Academics
Professor James F. Giblin, Jr.

Dean of Naval Warfare Studies
Dr. Kenneth H. Watman

Naval War College Press

Editor: Dr. Peter Dombrowski
Managing Editor: Pelham G. Boyer

Telephone: 401.841.2236
Fax: 401.841.1071
DSN exchange: 948
E-mail: press@nwc.navy.mil
Web: www.nwc.navy.mil/press

The Newport Papers are extended research projects that the Editor, the Dean of Naval Warfare Studies, and the President of the Naval War College consider of particular interest to policy makers, scholars, and analysts.

The views expressed in the Newport Papers are those of the authors and do not necessarily reflect the opinions of the Naval War College or the Department of the Navy.

Correspondence concerning the Newport Papers may be addressed to the Editor of the Naval War College Press. To request additional copies, back copies, or subscriptions to the series, please either write the President (Code 32S), Naval War College, 686 Cushing Road, Newport, RI 02841-1207, or contact the Press staff at the telephone, fax, or e-mail addresses given.

Contents

Foreword, *by Peter Dombrowski*   v

U.S. Naval Strategy in the Twenty-first Century
A Brief Introduction, *by Peter Dombrowski*   1

THE CHANGING NATIONAL SECURITY ENVIRONMENT

CHAPTER ONE   The Challenges of American
Imperial Power   9
by Michael Ignatieff

CHAPTER TWO   American Primacy:
Its Prospects and Pitfalls   19
by Stephen M. Walt

CHAPTER THREE   Has It Worked? The Goldwater-Nichols
Reorganization Act   39
by James R. Locher III

CHAPTER FOUR   The Erosion of Civilian Control of the
Military in the United States Today   61
by Richard H. Kohn

CHAPTER FIVE   "9/11" and After: A British View   111
by Sir Michael Howard

NAVAL STRATEGY

CHAPTER SIX   Fighting at and from the Sea: A Second
Opinion   123
by Frank Uhlig, Jr.

CHAPTER SEVEN   ". . . From the Sea" and Back Again: Naval
Power in the Second American Century   139
by Edward Rhodes

CHAPTER EIGHT   The Tyranny of Forward Presence   179
by Daniel Gouré

CHAPTER NINE   Naval Power for a New American
Century   193
by Roger W. Barnett

NAVAL TRANSFORMATION

CHAPTER TEN   Transforming the U.S. Armed Forces:
                       Rhetoric or Reality?   215
                       by Thomas G. Mahnken

CHAPTER ELEVEN   Network-centric Warfare:
                       What's the Point?   229
                       by Edward A. Smith, Jr.

CHAPTER TWELVE   Transforming the Navy:
                       Punching a Feather Bed?   247
                       by Peter J. Dombrowski and Andrew L. Ross

CHAPTER THIRTEEN   Building the Future Fleet:
                       Show Us the Analysis!   273
                       by Eric J. Labs

CHAPTER FOURTEEN   Transformation and the Navy's Tough
                       Choices Ahead: What Are the Options
                       for Policy Makers?   281
                       by Ronald O'Rourke

Conclusion, *by Peter Dombrowski*   299

About the Authors   303

The Newport Papers   309

Foreword

Two ideas motivated this anthology of articles published in our quarterly, the *Naval War College Review*. First, the U.S. Navy is today at a critical point in its history. At a time when the nation is at war—with campaigns in two countries and engagements across the globe as part of the war on terror—the roles and missions traditionally assigned to the Navy have been called into question. Budget pressures have forced the service to reevaluate shipbuilding plans for several ships, including the DD(X) family. Second, it has been nearly ten years since selections from the *Review* have been compiled in a single, easily accessible volume; in that time there have appeared a number of articles that particularly deserve a second or third look by those who study and practice national security and naval affairs.

The articles in this volume speak directly to the Navy's evolving role in the national and military strategies. The collection should serve as a handy reference for scholars, analysts, practitioners, and general readers interested in naval issues, and also that it will be useful for adoption as a reading by national security courses both in the United States and abroad. While the articles here certainly do not exhaust the range of views and important issues involving naval operations, strategy, or tactics, they do form a foundation for those interested in learning more. Moreover, they have enduring value; the perspectives and analyses they offer will not go out of fashion.

The articles are reprinted exactly as they originally appeared, except that: proofreading errors noticed since original publication have been silently corrected; biographical notes have been updated; copyrighted art has been omitted; citation format (which evolved over the years) has been standardized in certain respects; and one author has appended a brief commentary.

The volume is divided into three sections. The first introduces the changing security environment facing the United States and, by extension, the U.S. Navy. The articles examine both the external position of the nation and the emerging internal political and institutional contexts that constrain military and naval policies and decision making. The second part looks specifically at the roles and missions of the Navy at the beginning of the twenty-first century. Its articles cover both long-standing issues, such as forward presence, and the new missions the Navy has assumed in recent years—from projecting power far inland to providing theater and national missile defense, especially against opponents armed with nuclear, biological, or chemical weapons. The last part of the volume concentrates on military and naval transformation. The articles in this section provide some perspective on, perhaps even ballast for, the claims of proponents of the revolution in military affairs. Finally, I supply a conclusion reviewing the main themes of the articles and the avenues to which they point.

The *Naval War College Review* remains one of the premier journals dedicated to publishing articles and essays with a naval and maritime focus. The chapters in the volume provide many of the intellectual building blocks for a maritime strategy designed to maintain American primacy and, if mandated by political leaderships, support a liberal empire that helps protect and spread the ideals of democracy and markets. The Navy's role will be arduous, and the need for continuous adjustments to the prevailing international security environment great. By reading or rereading the chapters that follow, specialists and nonspecialists alike can gain greater insights into the challenges ahead.

I would like to end with thanks to my predecessors as editor of the Naval War College Press—Dr. Catherine McArdle Kelleher, Dr. Thomas B. Grassey, and Professor Frank Uhlig, Jr.—under whose tutelage these and so many other excellent articles were published. It is a fine legacy to bequeath to my successor in this position, Dr. Carnes Lord.

PETER DOMBROWSKI
Editor, Naval War College Press
Newport, Rhode Island

U.S. Naval Strategy in the Twenty-first Century
A Brief Introduction

In this volume, Congressional Budget Office analyst Eric Labs issues a provocative challenge to the U.S Navy—he argues that while the Navy has done a fine job justifying the existence of a navy, it has been much less successful in defining just what type of navy the American taxpayer deserves.[1] Deciding what roles and missions the U.S. Navy should be responsible for within the overall context of the national security strategy is essential to determining what equipment the Navy buys, how many officers and sailors it requires, what types of skills, education, and training they need, where naval forces should be based, and, not the least, what doctrine and tactics it needs to develop for the coming decades. After all, rationalist approaches to defense planning usually attempt to determine the roles and missions of a nation's military services by means of top-down reviews, starting from the nation's interests and the grand strategy that is used to pursue them.[2] Military strategy, doctrine, tactics, force structure, weapons systems, and basing, among other essentials, are then organized around the ends of grand strategy. This is exactly what the formal planning processes of the Defense Department and the U.S. Navy are supposed to accomplish.

The perceived absence of a clear definition of the Navy's role in U.S. military strategy is unsurprising, however. The global threat of the Soviet Union disappeared nearly fifteen years ago, but the American military has adjusted only fitfully to the subsequent international security environment. The Navy in particular has changed only gradually. Most ships, aircraft, and other major weapons systems last decades or more; the procurement decisions and even purchases of the Ronald Reagan–era buildup in the 1980s remain with the fleet today. This will remain true far into the future. The V-22, for example, was conceived in the 1970s but is not yet operational, even though it promises to expand the ability of the U.S. Marines to project power ashore. Most general officers today had their formative professional experiences during the Cold War. More to the point, at the strategic level the Navy has gone through a number of, for the absence of a better term, "vision statements," including " . . . From the Sea"; Forward . . . from the

Sea";[3] network-centric warfare;[4] and now, Sea Power 21.[5] Yet to date, none has retained lasting hold on the Navy or the U.S. national security community in general.

Few efforts to redirect Navy strategy have endured beyond a particular set of naval leaders or their political masters in the Defense Department and the White House. Chief of Naval Operation Vernon Clarke's contribution, Sea Power 21, had the twin virtues of the apparent blessing of the civilian defense leadership and CNO's strong personal support, but it remains to be seen whether that view will prevail.[6] Critics have charged that it does not provide adequate justification for maintaining the current fleet and existing acquisition programs, let alone the most prominent programs, such as the DD(X), LPD-17, and future submarine programs in economically justifiable numbers. Recent cuts to naval programs appear to validate these concerns. Further, viewed as a window on the Navy's future, Sea Power 21 does not offer sufficient specifics to guide to transformation, at least by the model held by Secretary of Defense Donald Rumsfeld and the most strenuous proponents of transformation.[7] While Sea Power 21 may be another rethinking of the Navy's role in promoting national security, it does less well as advertisement for supporting the wider joint military strategy guiding the other services (e.g., the rhetorical approach of adding the word "sea" to standard missions—thus "Sea Strike," "Sea Shield," "Sea Warrior" and so forth—appears parochial to some). Finally, at this point in time, in the second term of George W. Bush, the administration's approach to national security beginning with the 2001 Quadrennial Defense Review and the National Security Strategy of 2002 may be undergoing a substantial reorientation.

Grand Strategy and Naval Power

Outsiders trying to influence the internal debates about the United States often look to history to determine either what choices were made at similar points in a nation's history or what other nations have done in similar strategic environments. So, for example, proponents of American military innovation have studied the interwar period, the years between World Wars I and II, to help understand how the United States should seek to preserve its current military superiority in the lull, or strategic pause, between the collapse of the Soviet Union and the emergence of another peer or near-peer competitor. Over the last decade, innovation studies have examined the origins of a number of interwar innovations that influenced the course of World War II, including carrier operations and amphibious warfare. Unfortunately, there is no period in American history comparable to the position in which the country finds itself at the beginning of the twenty-first century; Michael Ignatieff argues that "we live in a world that has no precedents since the age of the later Roman emperors."[8]

Ignatieff aside, the search for historical parallels has led to reexamining the British empire in search of lessons for the United States.[9] It has also become almost commonplace to laud the role of the Royal Navy in creating and maintaining the British overseas empire over more than three centuries.[10] Although some have claimed the British acquired its empire by accident, it is clear that over time the pursuit of global maritime superiority and an overseas empire became a conscious strategy, pursued by many generations of British political leaders.[11] It was not until the failure of Winston Churchill's late efforts to maintain the remnants of empire that the conscious policy waned; of course, Margaret Thatcher reminded us how potent the symbol of the overseas territories remain when she roused the British military and public to defend the Falkland Islands against Argentina in 1981. Interestingly, as Jeremy Black points out, the imperial leftovers controlled by London today are larger than the territories controlled in 1500, at the very beginning of Great Britain's global shopping spree.[12]

What is less often recognized, at least by nonspecialists, is that the British navy's role in supporting the imperial strategy changed more than a few times in the course of those several hundred years. In the early years of Britain's nascent empire the Royal Navy was hardly a navy at all. It was a motley collection of gifted pirates, privateers, and one-of-a-kind Crown-sponsored expeditions intended largely to harass Britain's more successful imperial rivals and earn profits for those courageous or foolhardy enough to sally forth. Later the Royal Navy qua navy emerged, growing to provide a bulwark of defense against efforts, like the Spanish Armada, to invade the home islands or, later, major colonies like India. British naval forces were deployed and redeployed across the globe to meet, contain, and combat various geopolitical challengers and maintain Britain's commercial trade routes and lifelines to its colonies. In the final European conflicts that sealed Great Britain's fate as a world power, the Royal Navy largely returned to its home waters to deter a German invasion.

The expense of maintaining its imperial commitments and in particular its global navy may ultimately have weakened Great Britain's ability to resist the imperial challenges from Germany to Japan in the first half of the twentieth century.[13] This happened despite the widespread discussion and acknowledgement of the resourcing problem at the highest levels of the British government and political class. Caught between the rock of imperial commitments and the hard place of an economy in relative decline, Great Britain tried for as long as possible to have it both ways.

Great Britain itself was a liberal empire that practiced both the "imperialism of free trade" and the acquisition of a more traditional territorial empire, given its relentless accrual of colonies, protectorates, and spheres of influence during and throughout the nineteenth and early twentieth centuries.[14] In Great Britain's version of liberal empire, the Royal Navy's lasting role was to protect commercial lines of communication, open up new markets (by force if necessary), and maintain the military infrastructure and network of bases necessary for the first two objectives.

The lessons of all this for the United States vis-à-vis the roles and missions of the U.S. Navy, military expenditures in general, and the Navy's budget in particular are highly contested. The two most recent American administrations, but most prominently the presidency of George W. Bush, have self-consciously chosen a path toward primacy, if not empire. In President Bush's first term many pundits and neoconservatives on both sides of the Atlantic clearly became increasingly comfortable with the notion that the United States already had and should strive to maintain, and perhaps expand, its liberal empire. The later stages of the president's first term and now the second term suggest that critics may have been correct in observing that primacy and running an empire, liberal or not, is harder than it looks.[15]

The implications of primacy, or perhaps a liberal empire, for the U.S. Navy are only now being explored. The issues of nonterritorial empire in the early stages of the twenty-first century facing the American navy are similar to those faced by the British navy in many ways but in the last analysis are decidedly different. The U.S. Navy, like the Royal Navy, pledges to maintain sea-lanes and protect freedom of navigation for all commercial vessels using the high seas. It has not, generally speaking, however, been asked to use force to impose its economic will on other countries and regions (although critics of U.S. foreign and national security policies claim, with some truth, that most American interventions and even wars have had a key commercial element). More recently, the Bush administration has argued its right to impose on the world American political values, including democracy and free markets. The invasion of Iraq has helped make the case; once the various rationales initially used to justify the war fell to pieces, what was left was the self-interest of the United States in controlling the second largest oil-producing state and offering the Iraqi people an opportunity to practice democracy and capitalism.

On the economic implications of maintaining a military and, specifically, a global navy capable of maintaining American primacy, the jury remains out. After several years of discussion of the Paul Kennedy's concept of "imperial overstretch" in the early 1990s, the consensus seems to be that the United States is not currently in danger of such overextension. U.S. military expenditures remain quite low, given its global missions and relative to the health and size of the American economy. Moreover, the nation manages to maintain its potent military with expenditures larger than those of any conceivable combination of potential competitors and allies, while spending roughly 4 percent of its gross domestic product in doing so.[16] The growing unpopularity of the

Iraq war and its growing cost, though, may now be demonstrating that absolute spending measures are less relevant than public perceptions.

The U.S. Navy and Primacy

The centrality of navies to the lives of great nations has long been proclaimed by navalists, culminating in the United States with Alfred Thayer Mahan and Theodore Roosevelt. Indeed there, in Germany, and other nations as well, "navalism" represented "the dedication to the creation of an imperial navy—among people in position of power."[17] American navalists won the day in the 1890s, thereby helping bring the United States to international prominence and power, though it was to take the First World War to demonstrate truly America's not-so-latent military strength. After a brief lull in the post–World War II period, when some theorists argued that the advent of the atomic age might mean the end of navies, the U.S. Navy found its métier in the Cold War. The Navy's emergence as the keeper of the third, sea-based leg of the nuclear triad ensured that later, as the strategists and politicians gradually decided that a conventional defense of Europe was possible and even desirable, if only to postpone a nuclear confrontation, the Navy's role would expand to fighting the growing Soviet fleet, which was thought to endanger the water bridge across the Atlantic that would be necessary to fight a war in the European theaters. Then as the Soviet Navy expanded its blue-water reach to include most of the world's seas and oceans, the impetus for a large and capable U.S. Navy was assured. It may be that an emerging power like China that becomes a near-peer competitor will play a similar role in the future.

As a global economic, political, and cultural power, the United States should choose to play a critical role in maintaining the global commons—from the surface to the subsurface, to airspace over international waters, to space. As Barry Posen has articulated most clearly, U.S. command of the commons—including both the ocean surfaces and undersea—has allowed it to pursue a strategy of primacy in recent years.[18] In a benign sense the United States should pursue this option in order to facilitate the cross-border movement of goods for all commercial nations. In a more self-interested sense, it needs to ensure that its exports and imports reach their ultimate destinations, especially given that 95 percent of America's imports and exports from outside North American arrive by ship. Moreover many of the tasks of the U.S. Navy discussed in the following chapters—from sea control to the defeating anti-access efforts of adversaries—also contribute to the command of the global commons. The issue, then, is calibrating the U.S. Navy's strategic vision to the fluid international system and the dynamics of domestic politics.

Notes

1. Eric J. Labs, "Building the Future Fleet: Show Us the Analysis!" *Naval War College Review* 57, nos. 3/4 (Summer/Autumn 2004), pp. 138–46. "First, while Navy officials may be doing an excellent job explaining why the United States needs a navy, they are not doing a good job explaining why it needs the navy they say it needs" (p. 138).

2. John Hattendorf provides an especially clear description of a rationalistic approach to naval strategy and planning in John B. Hattendorf, "Recent Thinking on the Theory of Naval Strategy," in *Maritime Strategy and the Balance of Power: Britain and American in the Twentieth Century,* ed. John B. Hattendorf and Robert S. Jordan (New York: St. Martin's, 1989), pp. 136–61. For a sophisticated argument that "navy budgets, procurement, and force mix" are "idea driven" and not the product of so-called rational actors, organizational or bureaucratic models of decision making, see Edward Rhodes, "Do Bureaucratic Politics Matter? Some Disconfirming Findings from the Case of the U.S. Navy," *World Politics* 47, no. 1 (October 1994), pp. 1–41.

3. Edward Rhodes, "'. . . From the Sea' and Back Again: Naval Power in the Second American Century," *Naval War College Review* 52, no. 2 (Spring 1999), pp. 13–54.

4. E. D. Smith, Jr., "Network-centric Warfare: What's the Point?" *Naval War College Review* 54, no. 1 (Winter 2001), pp. 59–75.

5. Of course, these iterations have been blessed to various degrees by the Chief of Naval Operations and the Defense Department, but they represent distinct evolutions in naval thinking since the end of the Cold War. For specifics see Rhodes, "'. . . From the Sea' and Back Again," and Peter J. Dombrowski and Andrew Ross, "Transforming the Navy: Punching a Feather Bed?" *Naval War College Review* 56, no. 3 (Summer 2003).

6. Early reports suggested it will. See "Mullen to 'remain true' to Sea Power 21 Vision," *Aerospace Daily & Defense Report,* 25 April 2005, p. 2.

7. See Dombrowski and Ross, "Transforming the Navy."

8. Michael Ignatieff, "The Challenges of American Imperial Power," *Naval War College Review* 56, no. 2 (Spring 2003), pp. 53–63.

9. For one example, see Patrick Karl O'Brien and Armand Clesse, *Two Hegemonies: Britain 1846–1914 and the United States 1941–2002* (Aldershot, U.K.: Ashgate, 2002).

10. Arthur Herman, *To Rule the Waves: How the British Navy Shaped the Modern World* (New York: HarperCollins, 2004).

11. A phrase and sentiment originally attributed to nineteenth-century historian John Robert Seeley, in his *The Expansion of England* (Chicago: Univ. of Chicago Press, repr. 1971).

12. Jeremy Black, *The British Seaborne Empire* (New Haven, Conn.: Yale Univ. Press, 2004), pp. 355–56.

13. Aaron L. Friedberg, *The Weary Titan: Britain and the Experience of Relative Decline, 1895–1905* (Princeton, N.J.: Princeton Univ. Press 1989).

14. John Gallagher and Ronald Robinson, "The Imperialism of Free Trade," *Economic History Review* 6, second series, no. 1 (1953).

15. Stephen M. Walt, "American Primacy: Its Prospects and Pitfalls," *Naval War College Review* 55, no. 2 (Spring 2002), pp. 9–28.

16. For a well informed and reasoned analysis of U.S. defense spending with some key international comparisons see Michael O'Hanlon, "U.S. Defense Strategy after Saddam," (Carlisle, Penna.: Army War College, July 2005), available at www.Carlisle.army.mil/ssi.

17. Mark Russell Shulman, *Navalism and the Emergence of American Seapower, 1882–1893* (Annapolis, Md.: Naval Institute Press, 1995), p. 2.

18. Barry Posen, "Command of the Commons: The Military Foundation of U.S. Hegemony," *International Security* 28, no. 1 (Summer 2003), pp. 5–46.

PART ONE

The Changing National Security Environment

CHAPTER ONE

The Challenges of American Imperial Power
MICHAEL IGNATIEFF

We live in a world that has no precedents since the age of the later Roman emperors. What is so remarkable is not simply the military domination of the world by a single power. In Alfred Thayer Mahan's time, Britain dominated the seas (but had to share its domination with a number of other navies). It is not just the fact that this single power, the United States, has achieved its dominance at incredibly low cost to its economy— some 3.5 percent of gross domestic product. It is not simply the awesome reach of its military capability—the ability of an air command center in Saudi Arabia to deliver B-52 strikes on a mountaintop in Afghanistan within seventeen minutes of receiving target coordinates from special forces on the ground. Nor is it resolve; terrorists everywhere have been cured of the illusion created by the American debacle in Somalia in 1993 that America lacks the stomach for a fight. What is remarkable is the combination of all these: technological dominance at a lower cost proportional to wealth than at any other time in history, absense of peer competitors, and inflexible resolve to defend its way of life—and those of other nations as well, who, like Canada (I happen to be a Canadian citizen), are happy to shelter under American imperial protection.

Parallels to the Roman Empire become evident. The difference, however, is that the Romans were untroubled by having an empire or by the idea of an imperial destiny, while the Americans, who have had an empire, it could be argued, since Theodore Roosevelt, persist in believing that they do not. The United States, then, is a unique empire—an imperial power without consciousness of itself as such. On 11 November 2002, President George W. Bush, remembering Americans in uniform who had laid down their lives, remarked in passing that America is not an empire—it has no imperial designs, no intention of conquest.*

---

* "Over the generations, Americans have defended this nation without seeking to dominate any nation. American troops do not come as conquerors, but as liberators." "President Commemorates Veterans Day at Arlington Nat[iona]l Cemetery," *The White House,* www.whitehouse.gov/news/releases/ 2002/11/20021111-3.htm.

Naval War College Review, Spring 2003, Vol. 56, No. 2

There is no reason not to take the president at his word; I am speaking of empire in a different way. Empires need not have colonies, need not be established by conquest and aggression; the United States is an empire in the sense that it structures the global order. It does so primarily with American military power, diplomatic resources, and economic assets, and it does so primarily in the service of its own national interests. If its interests can serve those of allies as well, so be it, but the United States acts on that basis even if they do not. It is impossible to understand the global order, or the sense in which it is an order at all, without understanding the permanently structuring role of American global power projection.

The well-known maps indicating the division of the globe into the "areas of responsibility" of CentCom, NorthCom, and all the other "Coms"* convey an idea of the architecture underlying the entire global order. This is a different vision of global order than Europe's—that of a multilateral world ordered by international law. There is a great deal about international law that can be admired, but it seems to miss the fundamental point—the extent to which global order is sustained by American power. In November 2002, for instance, the United Nations Security Council passed, fifteen votes to none, a resolution on Iraq. We can be perfectly sure, however, that without the inflexible, unrelenting American pursuit, through those multilateral institutions, of the U.S. national interest, nothing would have happened in respect to Saddam Hussein's weapons of mass destruction. Multilateral institutions like the United Nations are important, but their entire momentum, force, and direction are driven by American power; literally nothing happens in these institutions unless the Americans put their shoulders to the wheel. It is in that sense that I refer to America's exercise of an imperial structuring and ordering role in the world, and in that sense that there is an analogy to Rome.

But there is a more troubling parallel—troubling for those who use military power for a living—with the Roman Empire in its later centuries. It is that overwhelming military superiority does not translate into security. Mastery of the known world does not confer peace of mind. America has now felt the dread that the ancient world must have known when Rome itself was first threatened by the Goths. In the fifth century, an imperial people awakened fully to the menace of the barbarians on the frontier when they poured over the marches and sacked the city; today the menace lies just beyond the zone of stable democratic states that see the Pentagon, and until 2001 the World Trade Center, as headquarters. In those border zones, modern-day barbarians can use technology to collapse distance, to inflict devastating damage on centers of power far away. In March 2001, I asked an audience of U.S. Naval Academy midshipmen from which country the next threat to their ships would come; they could not answer the question. I

---

* The nine unified combatant commands—including U.S. Central Command and U.S. Northern Command. See "Unified Combatant Commands," *Defense Almanac,* www.defenselink.mil/pubs/almanac/almanac/organization/Combatant_Commands.

suggested Afghanistan, to stunned silence. Even to these educated young men and women, only five months after the attack on the USS *Cole,* the strategic challenge that a tiny country on India's northwest frontier could pose to the United States was not evident.

We have now awakened to the barbarians. We have awakened to the radical collapse and distance that they have wrought. Retribution has been visited on the barbarians, and more will follow, but the U.S. military knows that it has begun a campaign without an obvious end, and that knowledge has already affected the American way of life and the way Americans think about it. The most carefree empire in history now confronts the question of whether it can escape Rome's ultimate fate. The challenge can be localized, for a moment in Afghanistan, then in Iraq, but it is global in character, and that is unsettling. There are pacification operations, overt or covert, already under way in Yemen, in Somalia, in the Sudan. According to the *Washington Post,* al-Qaʻida attempts to launder financial assets have been traced to Lebanese business circles that control the export of diamonds from Sierra Leone, Liberia, Angola, and the Congo. There are cells to be rooted out in the Philippines and in Indonesia. Now, at this writing, there is the prospect of an operation against Iraq, of which the primary purpose, self-evidently, is the elimination not only of weapons of mass destruction but of the core of Arab rejectionism. Its aim is to break the logjam that has frustrated Middle East peace for fifty-odd years and then to reorder the map of an entire area to serve the strategic interests of the United States. If that is not an imperial project, what is?

An American empire that had since the defeat in Vietnam been cautious in its designs has been roused to go on the offensive. The awakening was brutal, but there might be reason, in an ironic way, to be thankful—as a great poet once said, barbarians are a "kind of solution."* Barbarism is not new; fanaticism is not new. What is new is the connection between barbarian asymmetric methods and a global ideology, Islam, that provides a bottomless supply of recruits and allies for a global war. Also new is the way in which fanatics have exploited the values of our society—our openness and freedom, as well as our technology—to take war to the heart of the empire.

The single most dangerous thing about terrorism is the claim that terrorists are responding to grievances about which, in fact, they do not care. The 11 September attackers made no demands at all, declared no explicit political agenda. They went to their deaths in complete silence. Nonetheless, hundreds of millions of people accepted them as representatives of their own long-frustrated political desires—to drive Israel into the sea, to expel America from the holy places, and so on. The hijackers themselves were more interested in the spectacle of destruction, in violence for its own sake, than in the redemption of the downtrodden, but they have been taken as martyrs for political ends.

---

* Constantine Cavafy (Konstantinos Kavafis, 1863–1933), in *Awaiting the Barbarians:* "Now what's going to happen to us without barbarians? / Those people were a kind of solution."

Unless some of those political ends can be addressed, it is not clear that there can be an appropriate solution to the problem of terrorism; the U.S. armed forces are being asked to solve militarily a problem that probably, in the end, has only political solutions. Robust military responses are needed, but they must be part of a political strategy—in fact, a geopolitical strategy, one that recognizes that the American homeland has found itself caught in the crossfire of a civil war. The terrorists are not attacking only the United States, or even the West; they are also coming after its Arab allies. They want nothing more than to return the Arab world to A.D. 640, to the time of the Prophet. The civil war is a desperate struggle between the politics of pure reaction, represented by client Arab regimes, and the politics of the impossible—the desire to take these societies out of modernity altogether. That viewpoint brings home how exposed politically the United States is. One aspect of that vulnerability that the attacks of 11 September 2001 laid bare is the extent to which the West has treated its Arab allies as mere gas stations. These Arab states have become decayed and incompetent betrayers of their own people, and betraying and incompetent defenders of U.S. interests. The American empire is in the process of discovering that in the Middle East the pillars upon which it depends for support are built of sand; that is one element of the political challenge it faces.

Another element, and one of the unacknowledged causes of "9/11," is the juxtaposition of globalized prosperity in the "American world" with the disintegration of states and state order in places that achieved independence from the colonial empires after the Second World War. American hegemony in the post–Cold War world has coincided with a process of state disintegration. The United States has achieved global hegemony just as the global order is beginning to come apart at the seams. Not only are the colonial states that arose between 1947 and 1960 in Africa and Asia starting to unravel (Exhibit A being Pakistan), but the states, like Georgia, that achieved independence with the end of the Soviet empire are also beginning to fragment. American hegemony, then, is a position of special fragility.

America as the remaining empire has been left with the problems that the older empires could not solve—creating nation-state stability in the critical postcolonial zones. In places like Pakistan, the collapse of state institutions has been exacerbated by urbanization, by the relentless growth of shantytowns that collect unemployed or underemployed males who see the promise of globalized prosperity on television in every cafe but cannot enjoy it themselves. In such places the collapsing state fabric creates a vacuum. Who fills the vacuum? The mullahs. They fill the vacuum not simply with indoctrination and cheap hatred but by provision of real services. A poor parent in rural Pakistan near the northwest frontier who wants a child to get an education sends him to a *madraseh*. Parents with children they cannot look after send them to the mullah. However uncomfortable it is to accept, terrorist movements are creating legitimacy in this way, by providing services to fill the gap left by the absence of credible and competent states.

The political Left uses "empire" as an epithet—imperial America, it declares, can do anything, can shape the world chessboard any way it wants. The implication of the foregoing, however, is that America is not in a position to create stability on whatever terms it likes. The United States is the sole guarantor of order, yet its capacity to control and determine outcomes is often quite limited, and nowhere are the limitations of American power more evident than in the Middle East. Since Franklin D. Roosevelt embraced the Saudis and Harry Truman recognized Israel, American leadership has driven out the other potential arbiters, the Russians and Europeans, without being able to impose its own terms for permanent peace. Presidents have come and gone, but they have not been able to resolve this enduring hemorrhage of American national prestige.

For fifty years, the United States paid almost nothing for its support for Israel. This was a debt of honor, a linkage between two democratic peoples. But three or four years ago, it began to pay an ever higher strategic price for the continued Israeli occupation of the Palestinian lands—an inability to broker a settlement that would guarantee security for the Palestinian and Israeli peoples on the basis, essentially, of partition. American failure to impose such a settlement has now brought national security costs; the events of 11 September 2001 cannot be understood apart from that fatal dynamic. But it is a dynamic that indicates the limitations of U.S. power, even with close and devoted allies. American presidents may well hesitate to put even more prestige on the line in this issue; if they overreach in the Middle East, they may lose everything, while if they do not invest enough, they may lose anyway. They are always managing the chief problem of empire—balancing hubris and prudence. Today, in the face of a global challenge and the collapsing of distance, the decision "triage"—making the distinction between hubristic overreach and prudential caution—is much more complicated. It is much more difficult to dismiss any nation—say, Afghanistan—as marginal, of no importance; any such nation is likely suddenly to become a national security threat.

It is not just the Middle East that highlights simultaneously America's awesome power and vulnerability. When American naval planners look south from the Suez Canal, for instance, they see nothing good. Sudan, Somalia, Djibouti, Eritrea, Yemen—all are dangerous places, and some of them have been fatal to American service men and women. One of the traditional diplomatic and political functions of the U.S. Navy is to represent and promote American imperial power by showing presence, going ashore, showing the flag. But as the United States has realized that forward land bases for its other kinds of combat power are more and more vulnerable, the Navy's role has begun to shift to that of an offshore weapons platform. Cutting back military presence in places that are too vulnerable to terrorist attack seems to be good news—after the USS *Cole* attack, certainly. The cost, however, is that reducing base presence in these places also reduces influence and potentially increases alienation. This is the well-known downside to reducing exposure to terrorist attack. Americans come to be regarded as a mysterious offshore presence, focused on weapons and discipline, not on making friends, not on making alliances, not on making local contact.

All this makes it apparent that the United States emerged from the Cold War with very little idea of the strategic challenges that would face it afterward. It won the Cold War by virtue of a strategic act of political-military discipline carried out by administration after administration from 1947 to 1989. It was one of the most sustained displays of political and military resolution in the history of republics, and it brought triumphant success. But the nation's post-1991 performance looks much more like what used to be said of the British—the consolidation of empire in a fit of absence of mind. Successive administrations—this is not a political point—thought they could have imperial dominion on the cheap. They thought that they could rule a postcolonial, post-Soviet world with the imperial architecture, military alliances, legal institutions, and international-development organizations that Franklin Roosevelt and Winston Churchill had created to defeat Hitler. As the world order arranged by Churchill and Roosevelt comes apart, no new architectures, alliances, institutions, or organizations have been established to replace the old. What has actually been put in their place is American military power—and that is asking of it more than it can do. The Greeks taught the Romans to call this failure *hubris*. But it is also a failure of historical imagination—making the American military the preferred solution for disorder that is replicating itself around the globe in overlapping zones and posing a security threat at home. It is an imperial problem that seems to be heading for disaster.

A second fundamental imperial problem for the United States, on a par with its structural vulnerability, is the fact that it is alone. Its neighbor Canada spends 1.1 percent of its gross domestic policy on national defense, and its armed forces are incapable even of defending the Canadian homeland. In Europe, large countries with long military traditions are investing in national defense at levels of 2 percent, 2.2 percent, 2.3 percent of GDP; they are no longer credible military allies. The military consequence is obvious in combined operations, but there is also a political aspect, an irony that has received too little attention—that for Europe, spending so little on weapons is an enormous, historic achievement. The Europeans spent so much on arms for 250 years that they nearly destroyed their continent in two world wars. Today, they are trading down military strength so sharply as to affect their very national identities; the European states have become postmilitary cultures. In a sense, as Europe integrates into the European Union, these states are even becoming "postnational" cultures.

This trend is producing a widening gap with the United States, not simply in defense expenditure and military capability but in mentality. Europeans—whose ancestors invented the very idea of martial patriotism, national conscription, and national anthem—now look at American patriotism and think it an utterly alien phenomenon. The United States, then, is the West's last military nation-state. It can no longer call on allies who fully understand the centrality of military power and sacrifice in national identity. This isolation will be a long-term imperial challenge, because the decline of European defense budgets seems to be irreversible, and a particularly difficult one, because America cannot do without Europe in civilian terms. However contemptible its military capabilities become, Europe's social and economic reconstruction capacity is simply essential. The United States must cooperate with these postnational, postmartial nation-states; without them the American taxpayer will have to foot the entire bill for not only their own defense but the maintenance of global order.

Thus, on a specific issue of moment, it is possible that the most efficient solution to a postinvasion occupation of Iraq would be a U.S. military government—a Douglas McArthur in Baghdad. Putting a qualified, tough American general in charge of a military chain of command would be the most efficient, and might be the cheapest, way to coordinate effort and resources. But the Europeans would not have it. No Middle Eastern state would have it. The idea is simply not acceptable internationally; if it were pushed, no one would support the reconstruction effort; the United States would bear the entire cost.

This instance points to a very different picture of the world than that entertained by liberal international lawyers and human rights activists who hope to see American power integrated into a transnational legal and economic order organized around the United Nations, the International Criminal Court, the World Trade Organization, and human rights treaties. Theirs is a feeble vision, as we have seen; without American power, the multilateral international order is a train without an engine.

There is a third imperial problem, or at least an inevitable part of a global war on terror—nation building. Afghanistan has brought the point home. However extraterritorial, nonterritorial, or nonnational a terrorist organization may be, it needs facilities, especially to train its "foot soldiers." Terrorists cannot sustain themselves without compliant states who allow them to operate secretly or even, as in this case, actually to run their foreign and domestic policies and fence off large pieces of real estate. The United States sat and watched that happen in Afghanistan for four years; that must never, ever, happen again. The United States has learned that failed states can become direct national security risks and that accordingly, like the idea or not, it is in the nation-building, or state-reconstruction, business.

The exercise of nation building, however, raises a number of ethical difficulties. In fact, there lies at the very heart of the matter a fundamental contradiction of principle and policy. The concept of human rights, which is the semiofficial ideology of the Western world, sustains the principle of self-determination—the right of each people to rule itself, free of outside interference. It is a proposition dear to Americans, who fought a revolution to secure the right to self-determination; it is the core of their democratic culture. How can the imperial act of nation building be reconciled with it? The old imperial solution is collapsing; the problem falls ineluctably to the United States; nation building is unavoidable. But how is it to be done? Bringing order is the paradigmatic imperial task, but it is essential for reasons both of economy and principle that it be done without denying local people their right to some degree of self- determination.

The old imperialism, the nineteenth-century kind, justified itself as a mission to civilize, to inculcate in tribes and "lesser breeds" the habits of self-discipline necessary for the exercise of self-rule. This is not a minor point. We often think that imperialism and self-determination are completely contradictory—self-rule by strangers. Interestingly, however, all the nineteenth-century empires used self-determination to maintain themselves. How? By making a promise: "If you submit to us now, we will train you to be free tomorrow." Self-determination and imperialism, then, are not the polar opposites they seem to be; as paradoxical as it may sound, self-determination is a means by which to perpetuate imperial rule. Canada, for instance, was for a hundred years a self-governing dominion within the British Empire. In the old imperialism, self-rule did not have to happen any time soon. The British kept their hold on India for most of the twentieth century with assurances: "You are not quite ready yet. Just be patient, and we will hand over to you." The British mandate in Palestine took the same tack.

The new imperialism works on a much shorter time span. The contradiction between imperialism and democracy is much sharper in places like Afghanistan, Kosovo, and Bosnia. The prospect of self-rule cannot be distant, because the local elites are creations of modern nationalism, of which the primary ethical content is self-determination. In Kosovo, Bosnia, and Afghanistan, and quite probably in Iraq, the mantra is that local elites must be empowered to take over as soon as imperial forces create conditions of stability and security. Nation building thus seeks to reconcile imperial power and local self-determination through the vehicle of an "exit strategy." This is imperialism in a hurry to spend money, get results, to turn over to the locals, and get out. But it is similar to the old imperialism in the sense that the real power remains in imperial capitals. Local leaders, even if elected by their own peoples, exercise limited power and must always look over their shoulders to Washington. This new imperialism, then, is humanitarian in theory but imperial in practice; it creates "subsovereignty," in which states possess independence in name but not in fact. The reason the Americans are in Afghanistan, or the Balkans, after all, is to maintain imperial order in zones essential to the interest of the United States. They are there to maintain order against a barbarian threat.

Many people, particularly in the United States, feel that this is a terrible misuse of American combat power and resources. They consider it hubris that will suck the nation into open-ended and unmanageable commitments. But are there alternatives? There seems to be no other way in which to make the world safe for the United States. Exercises of imperial power are in themselves neither illegitimate or immoral. For U.S. forces and resources to create (in Iraq, say) stable democratic institutions, establish the rule of law, and then leave would be creditable—provided, of course, that the new democratic elite is not simply an American puppet. The caveat would be especially critical in Iraq, and reconciling imperial power and democracy would become particularly delicate there. We would have to create, or help to create, or help to repatriate a genuinely credible national leadership. The Iraqi National Congress, the Iraqi exiles in general, are "not ready for prime time," and there is no credible counter-elite in the country itself. The biggest challenge the United States would have in making Iraq work is to find that elite and sustain it—and yet allow it the independence it would need to achieve acceptance within the nation. It is not at all clear how that can be done, but if the United States expels the Saddam Hussein regime, it will have to be.

Does the United States have the right, in international law, to impose regime change? I was a member of an international commission on intervention and state sovereignty funded by the Canadian government and charged to report to the UN Secretary General in September 2001. Our report set the ethical bar very high. The commission argued that the only grounds for full-scale military intervention in a state were human rights violations on the order of genocidal massacre or massive ethnic cleansing. We believed that it is not a good idea for America or any other country to knock over more or less at will sovereign regimes, even odious ones. The United States would be, or feel, called upon to intervene everywhere, and whatever remains of the UN Charter system governing the use of force in the postwar world would be destroyed. In that view—embarrassing as it is for a human rights activist to say—intervention in Iraq is not justifiable on strict human rights grounds. However, the *combination* of the regime's human rights behavior and its possession (actual or imminent) of weapons of mass destruction constitutes that ethical justification—provided that, as required by just-war theory, the military instrument is the last resort. The exercise of securing Security Council legitimacy was a matter not of obtaining permission but of establishing good faith, to document the crucial fact that the use of American power was being contemplated only after a decade of attempts to disarm Saddam Hussein by other means.

There is another ethical issue as well—under what obligation is the United States to build a new Iraqi nation once it has knocked the door down? It is not obvious in classical just-war theory that commencing hostilities obliges a nation to clean up afterward. Whether such an obligation exists is a lacuna of just-war theory. International law lists the things that legitimize the use of military force: a nation is entitled to meet force with force; when a nation is attacked, it is entitled to reply. But must it also rebuild, rehabilitate, reconstruct? What is the ethical claim here? When the Allies had pulverized the regimes of Adolf Hitler and the Japanese—as it was entirely right and proper for them to do, with the totality of their military force—were they then under an obligation to rebuild Germany and Japan? Many people, like Secretary of the Treasury Henry Morgenthau, Jr., wanted them turned into pastureland, returned to abject agricultural feudalism forever. The decision to reconstruct the two nations did not emerge from the just-war tradition; it was made on prudential, political grounds. Today, as in 1945, there is no strict, ethical obligation, but there is a prudential, political one, if the United States wants to build stability, in its own image. The intervention and state sovereignty commission tried to develop an ethical system that made the right to intervene correlative with an obligation to rebuild; that, we believed, is the way that the emerging, customary law of nations should go. But the case to rebuild Iraq is fundamentally not ethical but prudential—it is a smart thing to do, a smart investment of American power.

Democracy is always thought of as the antithesis of empire, but one of the dramas of American power in the twenty-first century is that empire has become a precondition for democracy. Neither democracy nor anything like the rule of law can be established in Afghanistan without a sustained, determined exercise of American imperial power. There is no chance at all that Iraq will emerge from forty years of authoritarianism to democracy and the rule of law without American imperial power. The United States was a democracy before it was an empire; now, suddenly, it is involved in places where the historical relationship is reversed. The nation faces a challenge that will test its own legitimacy as a democratic society—not simply to create stability, to order matters to suit its national interest, but to create institutions that represent the desire of local populations to rule themselves. Can it use imperial power to strengthen respect for self-determination, to give states back to the abused, oppressed people who deserve to rule them for themselves?

CHAPTER TWO

American Primacy
Its Prospects and Pitfalls
STEPHEN M. WALT

The end of the Cold War left the United States in a position of power unseen since the Roman Empire. The U.S. economy produces about 25 percent of the world's goods and services; it is more than twice as big as that of Japan, the world's number-two economic power. The United States spends more on defense than the next nine countries combined, and because seven of those nine countries are its close allies, the effective advantage is even larger. The United States is the world leader in higher education and information technology, and its cultural shadow—in music, cinema, television, and other arts—is enormous. America's position in the world is not perfect, perhaps, but Americans could hardly ask for much more.[1]

This position of primacy is partly due to good fortune and especially to having been founded on a continent rich in resources yet far from other major powers. But the United States is also number one because its leaders have deliberately sought to achieve and maintain that position. During the nineteenth century the United States gradually expanded to become a continental power, encouraged immigration and foreign investment, and sought to exclude other major powers from the Western Hemisphere. As the Monroe Doctrine and the concept of Manifest Destiny symbolized, the guiding star of U.S. foreign policy was the goal of making the nation a hegemon in its own neighborhood.[2]

After becoming a great power at the beginning of the twentieth century, however, the United States also sought to prevent other states from establishing similar positions of hegemony in their own regions. The logic of this policy was straightforward—so long as neither Europe nor Asia was dominated by a single power, states in both regions would be obliged to worry primarily about each other and would be unable to focus their attention on the United States. Thus, the United States intervened in Europe in World Wars I and II in order to prevent Germany from establishing hegemony there and fought in the Pacific theater to prevent Japan from dominating that region as well. During the Cold War, of course, the United States explicitly sought to remain the world's strongest power in both the military and economic realms. As the State Department's Policy Planning Staff argued in 1947, "To seek less than preponderant power would be to opt for defeat. Preponderant power must be the object of U.S. policy."[3]

Given this long-standing ambition, it is ironic that the U.S. victory in the Cold War and the growing awareness of its remarkable global position has produced a debate on the desirability of primacy and on its implications for American foreign policy. For some writers, such as Robert Jervis, the value of "primacy" is diminished in an era where nuclear weapons limit the ability of great powers to threaten each other and when relations among the major powers are regulated by norms, institutions, and a spirit of democratic compromise.[4] For others, such as Samuel P. Huntington, primacy remains an invaluable resource, and preserving it "is central to the welfare and security of America and the future of freedom."[5] American military planners continue to craft policies designed to sustain a considerable advantage, and one would be hard pressed to find a prominent U.S. politician who would openly endorse anything less than the continuation of the nation's dominance. If the United States is now a "hyperpower," to use French foreign minister Hubert Verdrine's evocative term, its present policy seems designed to maintain that position as long as possible. Given that the United States cannot alter its current position—at least not in the short term—we need to understand both the positive ends that primacy can offer and the pitfalls that it may present.

Accordingly, the first part of this article outlines the main benefits that U.S. primacy now brings. I argue that primacy increases the nation's security, fosters a more stable and prosperous world, and gives the United States far more influence over global events than any other state possesses. Given these features, it is hardly surprising that there is a strong bipartisan consensus for maintaining America's privileged position. The second part of this article examines some of the ways that primacy complicates the making of U.S. foreign policy. Being number one is an enviable thing, but it also creates special challenges that are often overlooked or misunderstood. The conclusion describes how the United States can best use its power to advance specific foreign policy goals and avoid some of the pitfalls of its present position.

What Is Primacy Good For?

The first thing to understand about U.S. primacy is that it is not new. Although the end of the Cold War highlighted America's unprecedented concentration of economic and military power, the United States has had the world's largest economy for over a hundred years and the greatest military potential for most of that time as well.[6] Despite alarmist concerns about the Soviet military during the Cold War, U.S. strength exceeded that of the Soviet Union for most (if not all) of that period. Soviet military capabilities were a match for American forces only in Europe, and the capacity of the USSR to project power globally was always distinctly inferior to the naval, air, and amphibious capabilities of the United States.

Americans, in short, are used to being number one. Those who believe that primacy does not really matter fail to appreciate how accustomed Americans are to having it; they might miss it, as they would oxygen, if it were gone. Why? Because primacy provides at least four major benefits.

Primacy Provides Security

Perhaps the most obvious reason why states seek primacy—and why the United States benefits from its current position—is that international politics is a dangerous business. Being wealthier and stronger than other states does not guarantee that a state will survive, of course, and it cannot insulate a state from all outside pressures. But the strongest state is more likely to escape serious harm than weaker ones are, and it will be better equipped to resist the pressures that arise. Because the United States is so powerful, and because its society is so wealthy, it has ample resources to devote to whatever problems it may face in the future.

At the beginning of the Cold War, for example, its power enabled the United States to help rebuild Europe and Japan, to assist them in developing stable democratic orders, and to subsidize the emergence of an open international economic order.[7] The United States was also able to deploy powerful armed forces in Europe and Asia as effective deterrents to Soviet expansion. When the strategic importance of the Persian Gulf increased in the late 1970s, the United States created its Rapid Deployment Force in order to deter threats to the West's oil supplies; in 1990–91 it used these capabilities to liberate Kuwait. Also, when the United States was attacked by the Al-Qaeda terrorist network in September 2001, it had the wherewithal to oust the network's Taliban hosts and to compel broad international support for its campaign to eradicate Al-Qaeda itself. It would have been much harder to do any of these things if the United States had been weaker.

Today, U.S. primacy helps deter potential challenges to American interests in virtually every part of the world. Few countries or nonstate groups want to invite the "focused enmity" of the United States (to use William Wohlforth's apt phrase), and countries and groups that have done so (such as Libya, Iraq, Serbia, or the Taliban) have paid a considerable price. As discussed below, U.S. dominance does provoke opposition in a number of places, but anti-American elements are forced to rely on covert or indirect strategies (such as terrorist bombings) that do not seriously threaten America's dominant position. Were American power to decline significantly, however, groups opposed to U.S. interests would probably be emboldened and overt challenges would be more likely.

This does not mean that the United States can act with impunity, nor does it guarantee that the United States will achieve every one of its major foreign policy objectives. It does mean that the United States has a margin of security that weaker states do not possess. This margin of safety is a luxury, perhaps, but it is also a luxury that few Americans would want to live without.

Primacy Provides Tranquility

A second consequence of U.S. primacy is a decreased danger of great-power rivalry and a higher level of overall international tranquility. Ironically, those who argue that primacy is no longer important, because the danger of war is slight, overlook the fact that the extent of American primacy is one of the main reasons why the risk of great-power war is as low as it is.

For most of the past four centuries, relations among the major powers have been intensely competitive, often punctuated by major wars and occasionally by all-out struggles for hegemony. In the first half of the twentieth century, for example, great-power wars killed over eighty million people. Today, however, the dominant position of the United States places significant limits on the possibility of great-power competition, for at least two reasons.

One reason is that because the United States is currently so far ahead, other major powers are not inclined to challenge its dominant position. Not only is there no possibility of a "hegemonic war" (because there is no potential hegemon to mount a challenge), but the risk of war via miscalculation is reduced by the overwhelming gap between the United States and the other major powers. Miscalculation is more likely to lead to war when the balance of power is fairly even, because in this situation both sides can convince themselves that they might be able to win. When the balance of power is heavily skewed, however, the leading state does not need to go to war and weaker states dare not try.[8]

The second reason is that the continued deployment of roughly two hundred thousand troops in Europe and in Asia provides a further barrier to conflict in each region. So long as U.S. troops are committed abroad, regional powers know that launching a war is likely to lead to a confrontation with the United States. Thus, states within these regions do not worry as much about each other, because the U.S. presence effectively prevents regional conflicts from breaking out. What Joseph Joffe has termed the "American pacifier" is not the only barrier to conflict in Europe and Asia, but it is an important one. This tranquilizing effect is not lost on America's allies in Europe and Asia. They resent U.S. dominance and dislike playing host to American troops, but they also do not want "Uncle Sam" to leave.[9]

Thus, U.S. primacy is of benefit to the United States, and to other countries as well, because it dampens the overall level of international insecurity. World politics might be more interesting if the United States were weaker and if other states were forced to compete with each other more actively, but a more exciting world is not necessarily a better one. A comparatively boring era may provide few opportunities for genuine heroism, but it is probably a good deal more pleasant to live in than "interesting" decades like the 1930s or 1940s.

Primacy Fosters Prosperity

By facilitating the development of a more open and liberal world economy, American primacy also fosters global prosperity. Economic interdependence is often said to be a cause of world peace, but it is more accurate to say that peace encourages interdependence—by making it easier for states to accept the potential vulnerabilities of extensive international intercourse.[10] Investors are more willing to send money abroad when the danger of war is remote, and states worry less about being dependent on others when they are not concerned that these connections might be severed. When states are relatively secure, they will also be less fixated on how the gains from cooperation are distributed. In particular, they are less likely to worry that extensive cooperation will benefit others more and thereby place them at a relative disadvantage over time.[11]

By providing a tranquil international environment, in short, U.S. primacy has created political conditions that are conducive to expanding global trade and investment. Indeed, American primacy was a prerequisite for the creation and gradual expansion of the European Union, which is often touted as a triumph of economic self-interest over historical rivalries. Because the United States was there to protect the Europeans from the Soviet Union *and* from each other, they could safely ignore the balance of power within Western Europe and concentrate on expanding their overall level of economic integration. The expansion of world trade has been a major source of increased global prosperity, and U.S. primacy is one of the central pillars upon which that system rests.[12] The United States also played a leading role in establishing the various institutions that regulate and manage the world economy. As a number of commentators have noted, the current era of "globalization" is itself partly an artifact of American power. As Thomas Friedman puts it, "Without America on duty, there will be no America Online."[13]

Primacy Maximizes Influence

Finally, primacy gives the United States greater freedom of action and greater influence over the entire agenda of global issues. Because it is less dependent on other countries, the United States is to a large extent able to set the terms for its participation in many international arrangements. Although cooperating with others is often in its interest, the option to "go it alone" gives the United States greater bargaining power than most (if not all) other states.[14] The United States can also choose to stay out of trouble if it wishes; because it is objectively very secure, it can remain aloof from many of the world's problems even when it might be able to play a constructive role.[15]

Yet primacy also means that the United States can undertake tasks that no other state would even contemplate and can do so with reasonable hope of success. In the past decade, for instance, the United States played a key role in guiding the reunification of Germany; negotiated a deal to end North Korea's nuclear weapons program; and convinced Ukraine, Kazakhstan, and Belarus to give up the nuclear arsenals they had inherited from the Soviet Union. It also rescued the Mexican economy during the peso crisis in 1994, brought three new members into the Nato alliance, defeated and defanged Iraq in 1991, and kept the Iraqi regime under tight constraints thereafter. The United States also played an important role in the recovery from the Asian financial crisis of 1997, led the coalition that defeated Serbia in the 1999 war in Kosovo, and used its economic power to encourage the ouster of Slobodan Milosevic and his prosecution for alleged war crimes. U.S. power probably helped prevent any number of events that might have occurred but at this writing have not—such as a direct Chinese challenge to Taiwan or a nuclear conflict between India and Pakistan. Each of these achievements required resources, and America's capacity to shape world events would be much smaller were its relative power to decline.

In short, saying that Americans like a position of primacy is akin to saying that they like power, and they prefer to have more of it rather than less. It may not be politically correct to talk about "enjoying" the exercise of power, but most people understand that it is better to have it than to lack it. Having a great deal of power may not guarantee success or safety, but it certainly improves the odds. One imagines, for example, that Senator Tom Daschle likes being *majority* leader of the U.S. Senate more than he liked being minority leader, just as one suspects that Mikhail Gorbachev, Boris Yeltsin, and now Vladimir Putin would have acted quite differently had Russian (or Soviet) power not deteriorated so dramatically. The reason is simple—when one is stronger, one can defend one's interests more effectively and can more easily prevent others from imposing their will.[16] Power also gives people (or states) the capacity to pursue positive ends, and a position of primacy maximizes one's ability to do so.

Thus, anyone who thinks that the United States should try to discourage the spread of weapons of mass destruction, promote human rights, advance the cause of democracy, or pursue any other positive political goal should recognize that the nation's ability to do so rests primarily upon its power. The United States would accomplish far less if it were weaker, and it would discover that other states were setting the agenda of world politics if its own power were to decline. As Harry Truman put it over fifty years ago, "Peace must be built upon power, as well as upon good will and good deeds."[17]

The bottom line is clear. Even in a world with nuclear weapons, extensive economic ties, rapid communications, an increasingly vocal chorus of nongovernmental organizations, and other such novel features, power still matters, and primacy is still preferable. People running for president do not declare that their main goal as commander in chief would be to move the United States into the number-two position. They understand, as do most Americans, that being number one is a luxury they should try very hard to keep.

Why Being Number One Is Harder than It Looks

Being number one is desirable, then, but it is not an unalloyed good for the incumbent. America's current position of preponderance also creates a number of significant problems for the conduct of U.S. foreign policy, problems that make it harder to use American power and more difficult to obtain the precise outcomes that the nation seeks.[18] What are these pitfalls, and how do they affect the ability of the United States to get what it wants?

Declining Public Support

The first problem created by America's favorable global position is a loss of public support for an active and engaged foreign policy. When asked, Americans still favor "engagement" over "isolationism," but public interest in foreign issues is declining, and support for a *costly* foreign policy is especially weak. In a 1998 poll by the Chicago Council on Foreign Relations, for example, when Americans were asked to name two or three important problems facing the nation, foreign policy issues did not make the top seven; they constituted only 7.3 percent of all issues mentioned. When asked to name "two or three *foreign policy* problems facing the nation," the most common response (at 20 percent) was "Don't know." Support for traditional U.S. allies has also declined significantly.[19] Thus, the United States withdrew from Somalia after eighteen soldiers were lost, stayed out of Rwanda completely, was visibly reluctant to send ground troops to Bosnia or Kosovo, and fought the air war in Kosovo from fifteen thousand feet. Public support for key international institutions has also declined, and foreign policy issues played at most a minor role in the 2000 presidential campaign. It is also worth noting that a key element of President George W. Bush's campaign platform was the need for the United States to be more "selective" in its overseas commitments. This is a far cry from the call to "pay any price and bear any burden" that animated U.S. foreign policy during the Cold War.

To be sure, there has been a surge of public interest and support in the wake of the 11 September terrorist attacks and the subsequent war against Al-Qaeda and the Taliban. Yet even here, the United States has relied heavily on proxy forces and remains ambivalent about taking on a long-term security role in Central Asia. Unless Al-Qaeda proves more resilient than it now appears, public attention is certain to wane over time. As it does, U.S. leaders will once again find themselves having to weigh their international ambitions against a rather modest level of popular interest and backing.

These shifts are not simply a function of partisan politics or of former president William Clinton's delicate relationship with the U.S. military. Rather, they are a direct consequence of America's remarkably favorable world position. Because America is in such good shape, most Americans tend to ignore international politics and to focus their attention on other problems. The point is not that Americans are unwilling to run risks or bear costs; it is that they are reluctant to do so for the kinds of interests that are now at stake. This tendency will discourage any U.S. president from pursuing an activist foreign policy, because public support for it will be thin. Paradoxically, the very strength of America's present position reduces public support for using that power in costly or risky ways, except in those (one hopes rare) moments when the United States is attacked directly. Indeed, this policy may even make sense—when the world is already one's oyster, there is not much more to gain.[20]

Hubris Can Hurt

A second pitfall is the opposite of the first—when a nation is as strong as the United States, there is a tendency for its leaders to assume that they can do almost anything. Public support for an ambitious foreign policy may be thin, but U.S. leaders may ignore that fact if they believe they can accomplish a great deal at a relatively low cost. They may also find it difficult to avoid being dragged into various quagmires and responsibilities in many parts of the world, because America's present margin of superiority makes it harder to draw the line against further commitments. As the late Senator Richard Russell once warned, "If America has the capacity to go anywhere and do anything, we will always be going somewhere and doing something."

Consider the past decade. In addition to the various achievements discussed above, the United States tried to broker a final Arab-Israeli peace settlement, re-create a stable multiethnic democracy in Bosnia in the wake of a bloody civil war, and stabilize the entire Balkan region in the aftermath of the war in Kosovo. The United States also provided logistic support for peacekeeping efforts in East Timor, Cambodia, and Sierra Leone; attempted to cement Western influence in the Black Sea and Caspian regions; and tried to get India and Pakistan to refrain from testing nuclear weapons. At the same time, it also committed itself to building a national missile defense system in the face of foreign opposition and enormous technical obstacles. American leaders have also worked to liberalize the world economy, establish a constructive relationship with a rising China, and achieve a workable agreement to combat global warming.

Now consider what the campaign against terrorism has added to America's overloaded foreign policy agenda. To support its military operations in Afghanistan (and possibly elsewhere), the United States has taken on new security obligations in Pakistan and Uzbekistan. To keep the coalition together and rebuild relations with the Arab world, the United States is trying to convince Israel and the Palestinians to make additional concessions after more than a year of bloody violence. To stabilize the Pervez Musharraf government and encourage it to sever its ties to Islamic extremists, Washington is providing economic aid to Pakistan and trying to reduce tensions between Pakistan and India. Having toppled the Taliban, the United States must now take on the challenge of nation building in an impoverished region where it has little background or experience. To ensure that Al-Qaeda does not reemerge somewhere else, the United States is trying to root out terrorist cells in a host of other countries and attempting to cut off the covert financial flows that nurture these networks. To accomplish any one of these goals will be difficult; to achieve the entire agenda will be nearly impossible.

Given these ambitions, it is hardly surprising that the United States does not accomplish everything it tries to do. The real lesson, however, is that strong states are invariably tempted to take on extremely ambitious goals—and they often find this temptation impossible to resist. In baseball, a batter who "swings for the fences" may hit more home runs than others but will probably strike out more often, too. Weaker states cannot accomplish as much as strong ones, but they may be better at recognizing the limits of what they can realistically hope to achieve and be less likely to overextend themselves.

There is an obvious tension between the first two pitfalls, but not a complete contradiction. On the one hand, the fact that foreign policy simply is not very important to most Americans (because the United States is already in very good shape) reduces public support for ambitious foreign policies. On the other hand, fifty years of international activism and America's extraordinary capabilities can lead its leaders to believe that they can achieve almost anything at an acceptable cost. The danger, of course, is that Washington will establish commitments and pursue goals for which there is little domestic support, only to be blindsided by public opposition should the costs exceed the low initial expectations.

Asymmetry of Motivation

If the United States is so powerful, why doesn't it always get what it wants? The reason is simple—although the United States is much stronger than most other countries, other states often care more about the issues at stake than America does. American leaders worry about the spread of nuclear weapons in South Asia, for example, but their Indian and Pakistani counterparts care more about acquiring a deterrent than the Americans care about stopping them. Similarly, the United States and its Nato allies were vastly stronger than Milosevic's Serbia, but he resisted their pressure for nearly a decade, because his regime cared more about the issues at stake than they did. The same dynamic limits U.S. influence in the Middle East; although the United States would like to foster a lasting peace between Israel and the Palestinians, its influence is limited, because the antagonists care more about the final outcome than it does.

Once again, the fact that other states are usually more motivated than the United States with respect to their own regional issues does not reflect some failure of strategic vision, lack of leadership, or loss of will on the part of the United States. Rather, this is a direct result of its favorable international position. Other states care more about many issues because their fates are more intimately tied to the results. Conflict in the Middle East does affect the United States, but American survival is hardly at stake in the same way that it is for the Israelis, the Palestinians, or their neighbors. If one of the great benefits of primacy is that it allows the United States to view many international issues in a detached fashion, that relative disinterest means that weaker states may be willing to pay a large price to thwart U.S. objectives.

"It's Lonely at the Top"

A fourth pitfall follows from the familiar principle of the balance of power. In a world of independent states, the most powerful country will always appear at least somewhat threatening to others, who cannot be entirely sure it will use its power wisely and well. As a result, other states usually try to find ways to keep the power of the dominant state in check, often through formal or informal alliances. This tendency will be muted if the strongest state acts in a benevolent fashion and its goals are broadly compatible with the interests of other major powers, but it never vanishes entirely.[21]

The tendency for states to "balance" the strongest power explains why France, Russia, and China joined forces to undercut U.S. policy toward Iraq and Serbia, and it underlies the principal motivation for the recent Sino-Russian Friendship Treaty.[22] It also explains why European states want to strengthen and deepen the European Union, why

President Hugo Chávez of Venezuela advocates global resistance to U.S. hegemony, and why President Putin of Russia has expressed hope that India will become a great power and help re-create a "multipolar world."[23] The desire to check U.S. influence is also evident in the recent vote ousting the United States from the United Nations Committee on Human Rights, as well as the hostile demonstrations that routinely accompany "Group of Eight" economic summits.

Efforts to balance the United States have been modest thus far (surprisingly so, when one considers how powerful the United States is), because the United States is geographically isolated from the other major power centers and does not seek to dominate any of those regions. Indeed, America's geographic position remains an enormous asset, because the major powers in Europe and Asia tend to worry more about their neighbors. But the desire to keep a leash on "Uncle Sam" is real, and U.S. leaders should not underestimate the potential for concerted anti-American action in the future.[24]

The tendency for the strongest power to provoke widespread opposition is probably the central challenge of contemporary U.S. foreign policy. The question is, how can the United States minimize the efforts of other states to keep it in check? U.S. policy cannot eliminate that tendency entirely, but it can almost certainly make the problem worse if it is insensitive to others' concerns.

Conflicting Priorities

American primacy creates one final pitfall. As the only global superpower, the United States is engaged in virtually every corner of the globe and in almost every significant issue. Even when it tries to remain aloof—as it did in the Balkans in the 1990s and in the Middle East in the first half of 2001—long-standing commitments tend to drag it in. This condition also forces U.S. leaders to make important decisions on issues where they have little background or expertise. One need only reflect on American policy in the Balkans to realize how easy it is for the United States to become engaged in areas and disputes in which it has little experience or insight. By contrast, weaker states can focus their attention on a few key issues and ignore most of the others.

To make matters worse, U.S. objectives in one region or on some particular issue often conflict with its purposes elsewhere, which means that success in one endeavor may make things worse somewhere else. For example, expanding Nato may help defuse tensions in Europe and promote democratic development there, but it inevitably undermines relations with Russia and complicates decision making within the alliance itself. Similarly, the United States wants to support Israel, wants to promote peace in the Middle East, and wants good relations throughout the Arab world; these are all worthy goals, but they are difficult to achieve simultaneously. This same problem is even more acute in the American relationship with China. The United States wants to promote a close economic relationship with China (both for strictly economic reasons and to encourage Chinese moderation), but it also wants to deter China from using force against Taiwan and to encourage Beijing to adopt more liberal human rights policies. Moreover, Washington wants to pursue these goals without alarming its other Asian allies, and to encourage democratic forces in China without destabilizing the Chinese government. The problem, of course, is that pushing hard for any of these objectives will inevitably make it more difficult to achieve others.

Once again, this conundrum is directly related to America's position of primacy. All states face trade-offs in the conduct of foreign policy, but the choices are more numerous and more complicated for the United States, because it has its fingers in many different problems. Lesser powers generally face fewer conflicts between different objectives, simply because they are not committed in as many places and are not trying to accomplish as much.

Taken together, these pitfalls explain why even a country as powerful as the United States cannot achieve all of its foreign policy objectives. They also identify some of the obstacles that U.S. leaders must overcome when engaging with other countries. Thus the final question to consider is how the United States can best exploit its remarkable advantages and minimize the constraints that its preponderant position necessarily imposes.

How to Conduct a "Humble" Foreign Policy

In the second debate of the 2000 presidential campaign, George W. Bush declared that other states would be attracted to the United States if it were strong but "humble"; they would be repulsed, he warned, if the nation were to use its power in an "arrogant" fashion. His instincts were correct, although his subsequent behavior as president suggests he has not fully embraced his own advice.

The problem is simple. Because the United States is so strong and its influence is so pervasive, it inevitably provokes suspicion by other states and finds it more difficult to gain their cooperation. As discussed above, it also tends to face awkward trade-offs in conducting foreign policy, and often its leaders can expect only thin support for major initiatives. Given such constraints, how can the United States maximize the advantages that primacy provides and avoid its pitfalls? The analysis thus far points to several recommendations.

Maintain U.S. Capabilities

U.S. power is the main source of American international influence and the ultimate guarantor of the nation's sovereignty. It is the main reason why the support of the

United States is valued and why its opposition is feared. Increasing the U.S. lead still further might not be worth the effort (given that the United States is already far ahead), but allowing others to catch up would squander most of the advantages that primacy now provides.

This means that the United States should continue to worry about the overall distribution of world power. In addition to devoting an adequate share of national wealth to the creation of politically meaningful capabilities (including military power, technological expertise, etc.), Washington must project how global trends will affect the nation's position over time. In particular, U.S. leaders will eventually have to decide whether it makes sense to try to slow the growth of certain powers and take steps to discourage the formation of even tacit anti-American coalitions. In particular, encouraging the emergence of a strong and wealthy China may not be in America's long-term interest, even if China were eventually to become more democratic.

Mailed Fist, Velvet Glove

U.S. preponderance makes other states more sensitive to the ways in which American power is used. As a result, the United States should take care to use its power judiciously, especially where military force is involved.

From this general point, two specific recommendations follow. The United States should use force with forbearance. Although it will occasionally be tempting to use force preemptively so as to minimize casualties or convey resolve, America's preponderance allows it to take a more relaxed and deliberate view of many international developments. States whose existence might be endangered should they fail to act quickly have to be ready to preempt threats and may be forced to respond vigorously to ambiguous warnings. Because the United States is objectively so secure, however, it can rely primarily on policies of deterrence and retaliation rather than preemption. For example, although American officials did have genuine grounds for launching cruise-missile strikes on Afghanistan and Sudan in 1998, the decision to do so on the basis of the inconclusive information then available ignored the larger geopolitical effects of appearing overeager to use force.[25] In general, Washington should follow a prescription of Woodrow Wilson—that the United States "can afford to exercise the self-restraint of a truly great nation, which realizes its own strength and scorns to misuse it."[26]

Second, the United States can reduce the threat perceived by other states in its overawing power by giving them a degree of influence over the circumstances in which it will use force. Confining the use of force to multilateral contexts would be an effective way to assuage potential fears about unilateral exercise of American power. This point has been lost on conservative opponents of the United Nations and other international institutions, who fail to recognize that multilateral institutions help the United States exercise its power in a way that is less threatening (and therefore more acceptable) to other states. Although exceptions will arise from time to time, the United States should for the most part rely upon a "buddy system" to regulate the large-scale use of its military power. Specifically, if it cannot persuade one or more other major powers to join in, it should refrain from using force.[27] This policy might also increase other states' incentives to maintain good relations with Washington, because close ties with the United States will give them a greater influence over how Washington chooses to use its power.

It might be asked, does not the recent war in Afghanistan teach the opposite lesson—that other states will respect U.S. power and rush to support the United States provided it acts firmly and makes clear that other states have a clear choice, either to be "with us or against us"? From this perspective, the United States should rarely, if ever, allow allies to interfere with its decision making and should for the most part chart its own course, confident that weaker states will fall into line.

Such a view is obviously appealing to Americans—because it suggests they can do pretty much what they please—and there is probably a grain of truth to it. But it would be a mistake to interpret the degree of international support that the U.S. received after 11 September as evidence that the United States can use force whenever it wants to without jeopardizing its international position. First, the United States enjoyed enormous international sympathy after 11 September because it was responding to an unprovoked attack on innocent civilians. If the United States came to be seen as the aggressor rather than the victim, however, international support would evaporate quickly. Second, other states have supported the war on terrorism either because they see it as a common danger that threatens all states or because they want to seize this opportunity to advance interests of their own. Third, it remains to be seen how long this high level of international support will last. The United States led an equally impressive coalition in the 1990–91 Persian Gulf War, but allied support faded once Kuwait was liberated; the loss of backing eventually doomed U.S. efforts to enforce the UN sanctions regime.

The central lesson underlying these suggestions is that the United States needs to think of "reassurance" as a continuous policy problem. Throughout the Cold War, the United States did a variety of things to remind its allies that its commitment to them remained solid—military exercises, visits by important officials, oral pledges, and other signals of commitment—and it did them constantly. Now that the Cold War is over and the United States is essentially unchecked, its leaders have to make a similar effort to convince other states of its good will, good judgment, and sense of restraint. American leaders cannot simply declare those values once and then act as they please; reassuring gestures have to be repeated, and reassuring statements have to be reiterated frequently. The more consistent the nation's words and deeds, the more effective such pledges will be.

Do Not Treat Potential Adversaries as Monolithic

During the Cold War, the United States sometimes viewed all leftist or Marxist regimes as indistinguishable parts of a communist "monolith." Although some U.S. officials held more subtle views (and developed strategies that reflected them), the general tendency to regard any leftist or socialist regime as a potential tool of the Kremlin often led to self-fulfilling spirals of hostility with these regimes.[28]

Because the United States has an important interest in discouraging other states from joining forces against it, it should not assume that its various opponents are part of some well-organized anti-American movement. To take the most obvious example, referring to North Korea, Iraq, Iran, and Libya collectively as anti-American "rogue states" ignores the important differences between these states, blinds the nation to the possibility of improving relations with some of them, and encourages them to cooperate with one another even more.[29] Even worse, to label Iraq, Iran, and North Korea an "axis of evil," as President Bush did in his February 2002 State of the Union speech, made it less likely that these regimes would moderate their anti-U.S. policies; it also made key allies question America's judgment. Similarly, if U.S. leaders assume that cultural differences will lead to an inevitable "clash of civilizations" between the West and various non-Western states, they are likely to act in ways that will aggravate these differences, thereby making the prophecy self-fulfilling. Equally important, they are more likely to miss opportunities to keep potentially hostile blocs divided. As it is, there are significant obstacles to the formation of a strong anti-American coalition; does the United States really want to encourage one?[30]

Rethink the Commitment to National Missile Defense

Despite widespread international misgivings, the Bush administration remains strongly committed to developing missile defenses. In particular, it has announced its intention to withdraw from the 1972 ABM treaty and is accelerating efforts to develop and deploy several forms of missile defense.

Although the Bush administration is unlikely to reverse course at this stage, it would do well to slow down and rethink the merits of rapid development, let alone deployment. Nuclear weapons are still the "trump cards" of international politics, and the acquisition of a genuine "first-strike" capability could give its possessor an extraordinary capacity to coerce or destroy other powers. The combination of large offensive nuclear forces and an effective missile defense could give the United States the capacity to strike other states with impunity. At the very least, it would make it more difficult for them to deter U.S. conventional actions by threatening to escalate. Thus, it is hardly surprising that Russia, China, and several American allies view this initiative with misgivings. It does little good to try to assure them that the system will be limited to a defense against accidental launches or "rogue states" because they cannot be sure that the United States would not try to expand it later.[31] For all these reasons, other states are likely to regard a U.S. effort to build even a "limited" national missile defense system with alarm. Although such a policy is unlikely to trigger an anti-U.S. alliance all by itself, it would certainly make such a development more likely.

Perhaps most importantly, supporters of national missile defense have yet to advance a compelling strategic rationale for such a radical departure. The most plausible justification for developing national missile defense is the desire to ensure that weaker states (such as Iraq) are not able to negate U.S. conventional military superiority by threatening to use a weapon of mass destruction. A small missile-defense system might be sufficient for this purpose, because these states are unlikely to acquire large arsenals. This means that the United States should be able to negotiate an agreement that permits a limited deployment (sufficient to protect against accidental launches or very small arsenals) while ensuring that Russia, China, and other nuclear powers remain confident that their own deterrents are not at risk. If the United States wants to reduce other states' incentives to balance against it, it should move slowly on missile defense and remain open to a mutually agreeable bargain on the size of both offensive and defensive strategic forces.

Defend the Legitimacy of U.S. Primacy

Other states will be more likely to support American initiatives (and less likely to join forces to thwart them) if they believe American primacy is broadly beneficial. If they think that U.S. power serves the interests of others as well as its own, they may occasionally grumble but will not take active measures to weaken the United States or to hinder its efforts. By contrast, if they think that the United States is insensitive, overweening, selfish, or simply misguided, then it will make sense for them to do less to help the United States and to look for ways to limit U.S. power and defeat American initiatives.

Unfortunately, there is considerable evidence to suggest that foreign elites do not see the U.S. role in the world as favorably as most Americans do. According to one recent survey, for example, only 18 percent of Americans thought that the 11 September attacks were caused by U.S. policies, but 58 percent of the foreigners polled did. Similarly, 52 percent of all Americans believe that foreigners like the United States because "it does a lot of good," but only 21 percent of the foreigners polled share this view.[32] Chinese officials habitually warn about the dangers of U.S. "hegemonism"; countries like

Iraq seek to portray the United States as a heartless great power that is indifferent to the sufferings of others; and even long-standing U.S. allies worry about the concentration of power in U.S. hands and the unilateralist tendencies that it fosters.[33]

This means that the United States has a strong incentive for genuine multilateral engagement, largely to convince others that it is not a selfish power bent on exploiting its strength solely for its own benefit. From this perspective, the Bush administration's undiplomatic rejection of the Kyoto Protocol, of the verification protocol for the biological weapons convention, of the Comprehensive Test Ban Treaty, of the international convention on land mines, and of the International Criminal Court were all steps in the wrong direction. Whatever the substantive merits of these various agreements, the United States pays a political price in consistently standing apart from the prevailing global consensus. Unless it is willing to abdicate an active leadership role in world affairs, the Bush team is going to have to convince other states it is willing to compromise and to cooperate on some important issues even when it does not get everything it wants. At the very least, U.S. leaders must go beyond the mere appearance of listening and demonstrate a genuine commitment to give-and-take with its principal allies. Failure to do so will underscore the latent belief that the United States is a "rogue superpower" that does not deserve the mantle of global leadership, making it more difficult to rally international support for initiatives that Washington wants to pursue.[34]

Does this really matter? According to some commentators, the United States does not need to compromise with others, either because it is strong enough to "go it alone" or because it can always compel their cooperation if it has to. It might be pleasant for the United States if the world worked this way, but it doesn't. The United States needed help from other countries to go after Al-Qaeda and the Taliban (and the job is not yet finished); it needs support from other states to manage the world economy; and key U.S. efforts in the Middle East, Latin America, Asia, and elsewhere will depend on intelligence collaboration and diplomatic assistance. To put it bluntly, if the United States wants to exercise global leadership, it cannot simply compel; it must also *persuade*— and sometimes it will also need to *compromise*. Other states will be easier to convince if they see U.S. leadership as serving their interests—at least some of the time—rather than just its own.

Thus, the United States faces a clear choice. It can adopt a unilateral approach to foreign policy and eschew multilateral cooperation except strictly on its own terms. Such a policy may be tempting, because U.S. power allows it to bear the short-term costs of a unilateralist policy. But an independent course would make it nearly impossible for the United States to exercise the kind of influence and leadership it has enjoyed for the past fifty years. Alternatively, the United States can maintain a principled commitment to multilateralism, using its power to ensure that most agreements are in the American interest. In other words, it can be unilateralist and disengaged, or it can be multilateralist and fully engaged. But trying to wield global leadership unilaterally is not going to work. No country—not even the United States—is strong enough for that.

Notes

1. The best recent analysis of America's global position is William C. Wohlforth's "The Stability of a Unipolar World," *International Security*, Summer 1999, pp. 5–41. Also useful is Joseph S. Nye, *Bound to Lead: The Changing Nature of American Power* (New York: Basic Books, 1990).

2. See John J. Mearsheimer, *The Tragedy of Great Power Politics* (New York: W. W. Norton, 2001), chap. 7.

3. Quoted in Melvyn J. Leffler, *A Preponderance of Power: National Security, the Truman Administration, and the Cold War* (Stanford, Calif.: Stanford Univ. Press, 1992), pp. 18–9.

4. Robert Jervis, "International Primacy: Is the Game Worth the Candle?" *International Security*, Spring 1993, p. 52.

5. Samuel P. Huntington, "Why International Primacy Matters," *International Security*, Spring 1993, p. 83.

6. The United States had the largest combined military forces at the end of World War II, and its wartime production dwarfed those of all the other participants. For evocative statistics on this point, see Paul M. Kennedy, *The Rise and Fall of British Naval Mastery* (London: Macmillan, 1983), pp. 309–10, and his *The Rise and Fall of the Great Powers: Economic Change and Military Conflict from 1500 to 2000* (New York: Random House, 1987), pp. 353–7.

7. See Joanne Gowa, *Allies, Adversaries, and International Trade* (Princeton, N.J.: Princeton Univ. Press, 1994).

8. This point is emphasized by Wohlforth, "Stability of a Unipolar World."

9. Josef Joffe, "Europe's American Pacifier," *Foreign Policy*, Spring 1984, pp. 64–82, and his "'Bismarck' or 'Britain'? Toward an American Grand Strategy after Bipolarity,"

International Security, Spring 1995, p. 94; also Christopher Bertram, *Europe in the Balance: Securing the Peace Won in the Cold War* (Washington, D.C.: Carnegie Endowment for International Peace, 1995).

10. See Dale C. Copeland, "Economic Interdependence and War: A Theory of Trade Expectations," *International Security*, Spring 1996, pp. 5–41; and Barry Buzan, "Economic Structure and International Security: The Limits of the Liberal Case," *International Organization*, Autumn 1984, pp. 597–624.

11. The seminal analysis of this issue is Joseph M. Grieco, "Anarchy and the Limits of Cooperation: A Realist Critique of the Newest Liberal Institutionalism," *International Organization*, Summer 1988, pp. 485–507. For further discussion, see David Baldwin, ed., *Neorealism and Neoliberalism: The Contemporary Debate* (New York: Columbia Univ. Press, 1993).

12. Since 1945, trade has grown from 7 percent to 21 percent of total world income. See Robert Gilpin, *The Challenge of Global Capitalism: The World Economy in the 21st Century* (Princeton, N.J.: Princeton Univ. Press, 2000), p. 20.

13. See Thomas Friedman, *The Lexus and the Olive Tree: Understanding Globalization* (New York: Farrar, Straus and Giroux, 1998), p. 376; and also Gilpin, *Challenge of Global Capitalism*, chap. 2 and pp. 347–57.

14. See Lloyd Gruber, *Ruling the World: Power Politics and the Rise of Supranational Institutions* (Princeton, N.J.: Princeton Univ. Press, 2000).

15. This capacity has been demonstrated repeatedly by the current U.S. administration, which rejected the Kyoto Protocol on global warming, the verification protocol of the Biological Weapons Convention, the land-mines convention, the agreement establishing an

international criminal court, the Comprehensive Test Ban Treaty, and a number of other prominent international conventions. Reasonable people can disagree about the merits of each of these decisions, but they do reveal America's capacity to "go it alone" in the face of nearly unanimous international opposition.

16. An anecdote from the end of the Cold War illustrates the problem nicely. When Mikhail Gorbachev complained to Secretary of State George Shultz that U.S. policy toward the Soviet Union was "one of 'extorting more and more concessions,'" Shultz smiled and replied, "I'm weeping for you.'" Quoted in Wohlforth, "Realism and the End of the Cold War," p. 121.

17. Quoted in Leffler, *Preponderance of Power*, p. 16.

18. For further discussion, see Stephen M. Walt, "Musclebound: The Limits of U.S. Power," *Bulletin of the Atomic Scientists*, March–April 1999, pp. 44–8.

19. Among other things, fewer than half of all Americans believe that "defending our allies' security" is a "very important" goal for the United States. See John E. Rielly, ed., *American Public Opinion and U.S. Foreign Policy 1999* (Chicago: Chicago Council on Foreign Relations, 1999), pp. 7–9, 16 [Emphasis supplied].

20. See James M. Lindsay, "The New Apathy: How an Uninterested Public Is Reshaping Foreign Policy," *Foreign Affairs*, September–October 2000, p. 2.

21. See Walt, *Origins of Alliances* (Ithaca, N.Y.: Cornell Univ. Press, 1987), chaps. 2, 5, and 8.

22. As one Russian commentator put it, the treaty was "an act of friendship against America." See "Russia and China Sign 'Friendship Treaty,'" *New York Times*, 17 July 2001, p. A1.

23. See Larry Rohter, "A Man with Big Ideas, a Small Country . . . and Oil," *New York Times*, 24 September 2000, p. D3; and "India a Great Power: Putin," *Times of India Online*, 2 October 2000, available at www.timesofindia/com/today/02worl3.htm.

24. I discuss these tendencies in, "Keeping the World 'Off-Balance': Self-Restraint and U.S. Foreign Policy," in *America Unrivaled: The Future of the Balance of Power*, ed. G. John Ikenberry (Ithaca, N.Y.: Cornell Univ. Press, 2002).

25. Although critics were quick to suggest that these strikes were intended to distract U.S. opinion from President Clinton's domestic troubles, the raids do raise the legitimate question of how a great power should respond to ambiguous evidence that avowed enemies are preparing a potentially lethal attack.

26. Quoted in P. Edward Haley, *Revolution and Intervention: The Diplomacy of Taft and Wilson with Mexico, 1910–1917* (Cambridge, Mass.: MIT Press, 1970), p. 100. Or as Teddy Roosevelt famously said, "Speak softly and carry a big stick."

27. Support from Great Britain alone will normally not suffice to legitimate the use of force by the United States.

28. See Robert Pastor, *Condemned to Repetition: The United States and Nicaragua* (Princeton, N.J.: Princeton Univ. Press, 1987); Walter LaFeber, *Inevitable Revolutions: The United States in Central America* (New York: W. W. Norton, 1984); and W. Anthony Lake, "Wrestling with Third World Radical Regimes: Theory and Practice," in *U.S. Foreign Policy: Agenda 1985–86*, ed. John W. Sewell, Richard E. Feinberg, and Valeriana Kallab (New Brunswick, N.J.: Transaction Books, 1985).

29. See Robert S. Litwak, *Rogue States and U.S. Foreign Policy: Containment after the Cold War* (Washington, D.C.: Woodrow Wilson Center Press, 2000).

30. See Samuel P. Huntington, *The Clash of Civilizations and the Remaking of World Order* (New York: Basic Books, 1997); see also Stephen M. Walt, "Building up New Bogeymen," *Foreign Policy*, Spring 1997, pp. 177–89.

31. Chinese and Russian officials have warned that U.S. development of NMD would force them to build additional weapons or develop countermeasures. The director-general for arms control at the Chinese Ministry of Foreign Affairs, Sha Zukang, summarized China's position by admitting that "to defeat your defenses we'll have to spend a lot of money[,] . . . but otherwise the United States will feel it can attack anyone at any time, and that isn't tolerable." U.S. assurances that the system was limited to attacks by rogue states have been unpersuasive; in Sha's words, "How can we base our own national security on your assurances of good will?" See Eric Eckholm, "China Says U.S. Missile Shield

Could Force a Nuclear Buildup," *New York
Times,* 11 May 2000, pp. A1, A6.

32. See *Little Support for Expanding War on Ter-
rorism,* Pew Global Attitudes Project, Pew
Research Center for People and the Press
(Washington, D.C.: December 19, 2001).

33. See Martin Walker, "What Europeans Think
of America," *World Policy Journal,* Summer
2000, pp. 26–38; Francois Heisbourg, "American Hegemony? Perceptions of the U.S.
Abroad," *Survival,* Winter 1999–2000, pp. 5–
19; and Peter W. Rodman, *Uneasy Giant: The*

Challenges to American Predominance
(Washington, D.C.: Nixon Center, 2000).

34. According to Richard Haass, director of policy planning at the U.S. Department of State,
the administration is committed to "multilateralism a la carte." In other words, it is
willing to cooperate on some issues but not
on others. If most states believe that the
United States is not interested in any of the
items on the global menu, however, this
seemingly sensible approach will not solve
the problem.

CHAPTER THREE

Has It Worked?
The Goldwater-Nichols Reorganization Act
JAMES R. LOCHER III

Organization has traditionally been a weak element of the American system of national defense. For the nation's first 150 years, the public actually favored a fractured military; so inattention to organizational issues has historical roots. The United States entered World War II with Departments of War and the Navy that were organizationally backward and "virtually autonomous."[1] Observing American inexperience and lack of multiservice coordination at the war's start, a British general wrote to London, "The whole organization belongs to the days of George Washington."[2] Army-Navy disputes complicated finding more appropriate wartime arrangements. The Navy entered the war embracing its cherished concepts of independent command at sea and decentralized organizations relying on cooperation and coordination. The Army's shortcomings in the Spanish-American War and its mobilization challenges during World War I had pushed that service in the direction of centralized authority and control.

The Army and the Navy were not able to solve their differences during World War II. Afterward, Congress settled the dispute in terms broadly favorable to the Navy's concepts—ones that preserved Navy and Marine Corps independence more than they met the requirements of modern warfare. Despite repeated operational setbacks over the next forty years, subsequent reorganization efforts offered only slight improvements. Such was the setting for the mid-1980s battle that produced the Goldwater-Nichols Department of Defense Reorganization Act of 1986. That bitter battle lasted for four years and 241 days—a period longer than U.S. involvement in World War II—and it pitted two former allies, Congress and the services, against each other.

In this article we will examine the changes mandated by the Goldwater-Nichols Act and assess whether they have worked. We will begin by reviewing briefly the history of defense organization and then, with that as background, outline the organization

© 2001 by James R. Locher III

Naval War College Review, Autumn 2001, Vol. 54, No. 4

problems of the mid-1980s. Then we will turn our attention to Goldwater-Nichols it-self—first outlining its key objectives and various provisions, and then assessing its ef-fectiveness and results. Finally—as if the first four headings will not be controversial enough—we will address the unfinished business of Goldwater-Nichols and organiza-tional steps for the future.

Defense Organization

Many of the problems of defense organization the United States experienced in 1986 had their origins early in the nation's history, at the beginning of the republic. It would be possible, however, to begin an analysis at the Spanish-American War, when Ameri-cans first realized that they needed centralized authority in both the War and Navy De-partments and also some mechanism for cooperation between those two departments. But for our purposes, we need go back only to World War II.

The United States entered the Second World War with an archaic organization that was incapable of coordinating land, sea, and air activities across the two military depart-ments, or even of harmonizing business (procurement, logistics, construction, trans-portation, etc.) efforts within the departments themselves. In February 1942, President

General Douglas MacArthur, President Franklin D. Roosevelt, and Admiral Chester W. Nimitz aboard the heavy cruiser USS *Baltimore* (CA 68), June 1944 (U.S. Navy photo)

Franklin D. Roosevelt created by executive direction the Joint Chiefs of Staff (or JCS), primarily to work with the British, who had a combined chiefs of staff organi-zation. The Joint Chiefs of Staff assumed an enormous role. Next to the president, they were the most powerful Americans in the war effort. They not only had major military responsibilities but also collectively played crucial roles in political, intelligence, and even economic decisions. The American public's outcry over Pearl Harbor prompted the cre-ation of unified theater commanders, like General Dwight D. Eisenhower in Europe. Service politics and jealousies prevented unifying the Pacific theater; it was divided into two commands—one led by General Douglas MacArthur, the other by Admiral Chester Nimitz. This joint centralization was paralleled by the creation of effective central authority within the War and Navy Departments, necessitated by the war effort, especially the enormous logistical tasks involved.

However, the contributions of the JCS were lessened by its adoption on its own of the principle of reaching unanimous agreement before speaking *ex cathedra*. Accordingly, the wartime Joint Chiefs—General Hap Arnold, the commanding general of the Army Air Forces; General George Marshall, the chief of staff of the Army; Admiral William

Admiral William D. Leahy (seated at head of table) presides at a meeting of the Joint Chiefs of Staff in 1944. Generals George C. Marshall and Henry H. Arnold are to Leahy's right, and Admiral Ernest J. King is to his left.

Leahy, the chief of staff to the commander in chief (that is, President Roosevelt); and Admiral Ernest King, the Chief of Naval Operations—had essentially to operate by cooperation.

A vivid example of the limitations on the ability of the Joint Chiefs of Staff to do their work arose in connection with matériel allocations. The British had recommended that steel be diverted from the construction of battleships and heavy cruisers to convoy escorts and landing craft. Admiral Leahy, who had just joined the JCS, "remarked that it looked to him as though 'the vote is three to one.' [Admiral] King replied coldly that as far as he was concerned, the Joint Chiefs was not a voting organization on any matter in which the interests of the Navy were involved."[3] Essentially, he demanded veto power. For the most part, the Joint Chiefs operated upon that principle throughout the war (and in fact until 1986). Things would proceed when the chiefs could come to unanimous agreement—which often required watering down their collective advice.

Often, however, they could not agree. There was a fair amount of interservice rivalry during World War II, both in Washington and in the field. A British air marshal once said, "The violence of interservice rivalry in the United States had to be seen to be believed and was an appreciable handicap to their war effort."[4] In fact, in 1943 the Army attempted to create a single military department, in place of the War (that is, the Army and Army Air Forces) and Navy Departments, because it had become convinced that the current arrangement was too inefficient. However, disputes between the Army and the Navy were so severe that the idea of unifying the two military departments had to be put off until after the war, when President Harry Truman supported the War Department proposals for a single department, with a single chief of staff and assistant secretaries for land, sea, and air. Truman, who had been an artillery captain during World War I and had stayed in the National Guard until 1940, rising to the rank of colonel, was very sympathetic to the Army's ideas on organization.

The Navy and the Marine Corps opposed unification, initially on organizational principles. The way the Army wanted to organize things was completely alien to the way the Navy was used to operating, rooted in the traditional ideal of independent command at sea. Eventually, however, the Navy and the Marine Corps were fundamentally driven by fear of losing aviation and land missions; the Marine Corps, in fact, saw unification as a threat to its survival. The U.S. Army Air Forces had emerged from World War II as a giant; the Navy was not certain that it could compete in a unified department with the powerful Army Air Forces, with its atomic mission, and its large parent service, the Army.

Congress was also divided on the unification issue; each service's view had strong supporters. But Congress ended up opposing Truman's proposals, for two main reasons. One was its own constitutional competition with the executive branch. Members of Congress feared that the executive branch might be able to organize its military affairs so effectively that Congress would be at a disadvantage. The second reason had to do with constituencies—where ships were to be built, where battalions would be posted, where jobs would be created; Congress would have more bargaining leverage vis-à-vis a military establishment in which authority was diffused. Congress came down, then, on the side of the Navy and the Marine Corps, forcing President Truman and the War Department to modify their approach; the National Security Act of 1947 was the ultimate result.

As Mrs. Eisenhower looks on, President Harry S. Truman shakes hands with General Dwight D. Eisenhower during an award ceremony in the White House Rose Garden on 18 June 1945 (U.S. Army photo).

Many people believe that the National Security Act of 1947 created the Department of Defense. It did not. Instead, it created something that was called, strangely, the "National Military Establishment," to be placed on top of the War and Navy Departments. The act prescribed a weak secretary of defense, with very limited powers and a small staff, and retained the World War II boards to govern the new organization. It gave legal standing to the Joint Chiefs of Staff but gave the group no chairman. The act not only continued the powerful secretaries of the military departments as cabinet members but also made them members of a new National Security Council. The services soon used their power to erect a service-dominated system. They emasculated the unified commands, despite the value they had shown in wartime. When the services were finished, the commands were unified in name only.

In 1958, President Dwight D. Eisenhower, assessing the compromises the original act reflected between Truman and Congress and between the Army and the Navy, said: "In that battle the lessons were lost, tradition won. The three services were but loosely joined. The entire structure . . . was little more than a weak confederation of sovereign military units."[5] It has been charitably said (by the Office of the Secretary of Defense Historical Office) that the National Security Act of 1947 "confirmed the principle of unification by cooperation and mutual consent."[6]

Truman and Eisenhower spent much of their energies trying to strengthen the National Security Act. There were revisions in 1949, 1953, and 1958—the latter two under Eisenhower. The 1949 legislation created the Department of Defense. All three sought to strengthen the secretary of defense. The 1949 revision established the position of chairman of the Joint Chiefs of Staff. (In the beginning, however, the chairman was not given a vote. Interestingly, some of Truman's early correspondence on the subject spoke of creating a chairman as principal military adviser, specifically to get away from the idea of JCS operation by consensus.) The military departments were downgraded in the various revisions; the secretaries were removed from the cabinet and from the National Security Council. The 1958 legislation removed the service secretaries and chiefs from the operational chain of command, in order to strengthen civilian control, as Eisenhower wished. It also gave the unified commanders full operational command of assigned forces. However, those provisions were not effectively implemented. The military departments retained a de facto role in the operational chain of command and never complied with the provision strengthening the unified commanders.

The Eighties

From 1958 to 1983, there were no major changes to defense organization; the alliance between Congress and the services was too powerful. Even Eisenhower, a war hero, was unable to overcome this alliance, and that was a salient lesson for subsequent presidents and secretaries of defense. There were continuing calls for reform—the Symington report for John F. Kennedy, Richard Nixon's Blue Ribbon Defense Panel, and the Defense Organization Studies for Jimmy Carter in the late 1970s.

During this period, the military suffered several operational setbacks: the Vietnam War, the seizure of the USS *Pueblo,* the seizure of the *Mayaguez,* the failed Iranian rescue mission, the Marine barracks bombing in Beirut, and the Grenada incursion. These failures had a number of common denominators—poor military advice to political leaders, lack of unity of command, and inability to operate jointly. The failed Iranian rescue mission exemplified these shortcomings.

Desert One

In April 1980, the United States conducted a raid to rescue fifty-three Americans held hostage in Tehran. The military had six months to organize, plan, and train, as well as fairly recent experience in conducting such a mission—the Son Tay raid about ten years before. Nonetheless, only six of the eight helicopters involved arrived at the rendez-vous point, known as "Desert One," in the middle of Iran; one of the six that got that far suffered mechanical problems and could not proceed. That did not leave enough heli-copter capacity to carry out the mission, and it was aborted. As the rescue force was departing, a helicopter collided with one of the C-130s that were car-rying commandos and helicopter fuel; eight servicemen died. The helicopters, with valu-able secret documents, weapons, and communications gear on board, were hastily abandoned.

Desert One

What were the underlying problems? No existing joint organization was capable of conducting such a raid. There was no useful contingency plan, no planning staff with the required expertise, no joint doctrine or procedures, and no relevant cross-service experience. The joint task force commander, Major General James Vaught, an Army Ranger, was a distinguished combat veteran, but he had no experience in operations with other services. The participating service units trained separately; they met for the first time in the desert in Iran, at Desert One. Even there, they did not establish com-mand and control procedures or clear lines of authority. Colonel James Kyle, U.S. Air

Force, who was the senior commander at Desert One, would recall that there were "four commanders at the scene without visible identification, incompatible radios, and no agreed-upon plan, not even a designated location for the commander."[7] How could this state of affairs have possibly arisen? It happened because the services were so separate and so determined to remain separate.

The Department of Defense—which in this period made no effort to reorganize itself fundamentally—was also suffering all manner of administrative problems. The nation was formulating security strategy unconstrained by realistic estimates of available fiscal resources, because the services could never agree on a fiscally constrained strategy and the allocation of resources to support it. Communications, refueling, and other vital systems and devices were not interoperable across the services. There were modernization/readiness imbalances, because the all-powerful services were pushing for more modernization, while the readiness needs of the weak unified commanders were underrepresented.

There were numerous procurement and spare-parts horror stories during this period. A memorable one involved the coffeepots the Air Force bought for its C-5A Galaxy aircraft at a price of seven thousand dollars each. The pots were so advanced that they could keep brewing in conditions that would kill the crews.

"The System Is Broken"

The process that led to Goldwater-Nichols began when General David Jones, the chairman of the Joint Chiefs of Staff, went before the House Armed Services Committee in a closed session on 3 February 1982, about five months before he was to retire, and said, essentially, "The system is broken. I have tried to reform it from inside, but I cannot. Congress is going to have to mandate necessary reforms." General Jones was the catalyst, the most important factor in ultimately bringing about the Goldwater-Nichols Act; the four-year, 241-day battle had begun.

Shortly after General Jones's call for reform, General Edward "Shy" Meyer, the Army chief of staff, urged fundamental reorganization of the Joint Chiefs. During congressional testimony, a third sitting JCS member, General Lew Allen, the Air Force chief of staff, also voiced support for reorganization. The naval service's JCS members—Admiral Thomas Hayward, Chief of Naval Operations, and General Robert Barrow, Commandant of the Marine Corps—vigorously opposed reform efforts. The 1982 debate—bitterly pitting the Army and Air Force against the Navy and Marine Corps—reenacted the postwar disputes over unification.

In the summer of 1982, three Joint Chiefs—Generals Jones and Allen and Admiral Hayward—reached the end of their tenures. General John Vessey, of the Army, became the new chairman and adopted an antireform stance. The new Air Force chief of staff, General Charles Gabriel, also showed no interest in JCS reform. Admiral James Watkins, the new Chief of Naval Operations, shared Admiral Hayward's strong antireform sentiments. Suddenly, General Meyer was the only Joint Chief in favor of reorganization. In late 1982, the Joint Chiefs of Staff, responding to a study request by Secretary of Defense Caspar Weinberger, recommended against major JCS reorganization. Secretary Weinberger and President Ronald Reagan supported this recommendation, and the administration took for the first time an official position in opposition to JCS reform. This stance set the stage for a fierce fight between Congress and the Pentagon.

In the meantime, the House Armed Services Committee—spurred to action by General Jones's reform plea—held extensive hearings and formulated a bill on JCS reorganization, which the House of Representatives passed on 16 August 1982. Congressman Richard White (D-Texas), chairman of the Investigations Subcommittee, led the 1982 effort. In 1983, Congressman William Nichols (D-Alabama) assumed the chair of the Investigations Subcommittee and responsibility for pushing the reform legislation.

Senators Barry Goldwater and Sam Nunn, chairman and ranking minority member of the Senate Armed Services Committee (U.S. Senate photo)

The Senate did not enter the fray until June 1983, when Senator John Tower (R-Texas), chairman of the Senate Armed Services Committee, launched a major inquiry on organization of the entire Department of Defense. At the same time, the last JCS reform supporter—General Meyer—retired. His replacement, General John Wickham, joined the antireform ranks. A new Marine commandant, General P. X. Kelley, was also appointed that summer. Like his predecessor, General Kelley was a determined opponent of reorganization. All five Joint Chiefs were now united in opposition to reorganization. When Senator Tower maneuvered to keep his committee in the antireform camp, the 1983–84 battle lines had the Pentagon and Senate squaring off against the House of Representatives. This division also reflected party politics. A Republican administration and Republican-controlled Senate were united in battling a Democratic-controlled House.

In 1985, four events began to shift the balance in favor of reform. Senator Barry Goldwater (R-Arizona) became chairman of the Senate Armed Services Committee and made defense reorganization his top priority. He formed a partnership with the committee's top Democrat, Senator Sam Nunn (D-Georgia). The bipartisan partnership of these two defense giants became the second most important factor leading to passage of the Goldwater-Nichols Act. The second event in 1985 was the elevation of Congressman Les Aspin (D-Wisconsin) to the chairmanship of the House Armed Services Committee. He was strongly proreform and provided important political and intellectual support to Congressman Nichols's efforts.

The other two events occurred in the administration. Robert McFarlane, the national security advisor, convinced President Reagan to establish a commission—the Packard Commission—to examine defense reorganization. The commission eventually endorsed reforms being considered by the Senate and House Armed Services Committees. On 1 October 1985, Admiral William Crowe, a supporter of defense reorganization, became the chairman of the Joint Chiefs. The Pentagon's official position in opposition constrained his public efforts, but behind the scenes Admiral Crowe pushed for reorganization. In 1986, these factors led the Senate and House to enact sweeping reforms despite the continued opposition of the Pentagon.

Purposes and Provisions

The organizational problems addressed by Goldwater-Nichols had existed for more than four decades. When Congress went to work on the bill, there were studies on hand by the Joint Staff and by various commissions for presidents and secretaries of defense dating back to the 1940s; there was a tremendous amount of evidence to make use of. We should note, however, that by 1996, the tenth anniversary of the act, the JCS chairman, General John Shalikashvili, could say: "The effects of Goldwater-Nichols have been so imbedded in the military that many members of the Armed Forces no longer remember the organizational problems that brought about this law."[8] That is certainly even truer today. In fact, there were really ten fundamental problems in the Defense Department to which the Congress turned its attention. Their seriousness is evidenced by the fact that Congress—which, as we have seen, had reason to like things the way they were—now collectively acknowledged that it would have to give up prerogatives in the defense area. Many in uniform also recognized problems, although the Department of Defense and the four services, as institutions, were dead set against addressing them.

The Congressional Perspective

The number-one problem plaguing the Department of Defense was an imbalance between service and joint interests. The services absolutely dominated: they had de facto vetoes in the Joint Chiefs of Staff, and they had weakened the unified commanders. On issues of major interest to them, the services aligned in opposition to the secretary of defense. General Jones had assembled a group of retired officers, the Chairman's Special Study Group, to study reform of the joint system; it agreed, "The problem is one of balance. A certain amount of service independence is healthy and desirable, but the balance now favors the parochial interests of the services too much, and the larger needs of the nation's defense too little."[9]

Second, military advice to the political leadership was inadequate. As before, it was being watered down to the lowest common denominator, so that all of the services could agree. General Jones said, "The corporate advice provided by the Joint Chiefs of Staff is not crisp, timely, very useful, or very influential."[10] James Schlesinger, secretary of defense from 1973 to 1975, was even harsher: "The proffered advice is generally irrelevant, normally unread, and almost always disregarded."[11]

General David C. Jones, chairman of the Joint Chiefs of Staff (U.S. Air Force photo)

Third, military officers serving in joint-duty assignments were insufficiently qualified, by either education or experience. As Congress found, officers did not want to serve in joint assignments; they knew that in such billets they would be monitored for loyalty by their parent services. In the Navy in the mid-1980s, joint duty was considered the "kiss of death"; it meant that one's career was over. General George Crist of the Marine Corps, as commander in chief of Central Command, testified to Congress that there had not been a single volunteer for any of the thousand billets on his headquarters staff—all of them joint billets. Everyone on his staff had been forced to serve there. Officers unlucky enough to be assigned to joint duty got orders out of it as soon as they could; their tours of duty became dysfunctionally short.

A fourth point, already mentioned, was the imbalance between the responsibility and authority of each unified commander: his responsibilities were vast, his authority weak. A fifth, related problem was that operational chains of command were confused and cumbersome. The services challenged the operational role of the secretary of defense. The Joint Chiefs collectively and the service chiefs individually were not in the operational chain of command; nonetheless, the JCS often acted as if it were part of the chain, and individual chiefs played operational roles when the unified commanders involved were from their respective services. Chains of command within a unified command were obstructed by what came to be called "the wall of the component."[12] Unified four-star commanders had difficulty penetrating the "walls" of their service component commands; three-star or four-star commanders whom the service chiefs tended to protect led these components. Accordingly, joint commanders were unable really to pull their commands together to carry out their missions. In 1970, the Blue Ribbon Defense Panel had declared: "'Unification' of either command or of the forces is more cosmetic than substantive."[13] Samuel Huntington in 1984 observed, "Each service continues to exercise great autonomy. . . . Unified commands are not really commands, and they certainly aren't unified."[14]

Sixth, strategic planning was ineffective. The entire Pentagon was devoting its attention to programming and budgeting, and neglecting the formulation of long-range plans. Seventh, large agencies had been created—the Defense Logistics Agency, the Defense Intelligence Agency—to provide common supply and service functions for all components, but mechanisms for supervising or controlling them were ineffective. An eighth issue was confusion as to the roles of the service secretaries; the National Security Act of 1947 had not defined them. The secretary of defense had been placed on top, but his relationships with the service secretaries had been left unspecified, because addressing them would have been too controversial. Ninth, unnecessary duplication existed in the military department headquarters. Each military department had (as they still do) two headquarters staffs—that of the secretary, and that of the service chief. The Department of the Navy—comprising two service chiefs—actually has three headquarters staffs.

Tenth and last was the major problem of congressional micromanagement—even as seen from Capitol Hill. Congress was finding itself too often "in the weeds," immersed in details, not doing its job as the "board of directors," providing clear, but broad, strategic direction. Senator Nunn spoke of Congress's preoccupation with trivia: "Last year [1984], Congress changed the number of smoke grenade launchers and muzzle boresights the Army requested. We directed the Navy to pare back its request for parachute flares, practice bombs, and passenger vehicles. Congress specified that the Air

Force should cut its request for garbage trucks, street cleaners, and scoop loaders. This is a bit ridiculous."[15]

Striking the Balance

The overarching objective of Goldwater-Nichols as it was ultimately formulated was to balance joint and service interests. It was not to thwart service prerogatives; the services were and would remain the most important elements of the Department of Defense. They were, and are, the foundations on which everything else had to be constructed. To strike that balance, the drafters of the Goldwater-Nichols Act adopted nine objectives:

- Strengthen civilian authority

- Improve military advice to the president (in his constitutionally specified capacity as commander in chief of the armed forces), secretary of defense, and National Security Council

- Place clear responsibilities on the unified commanders in chief for mission accomplishment

- Ensure that a unified commander's authority is commensurate with his responsibilities

- Increase attention to strategy formulation and contingency planning

- Provide for the more efficient use of resources

- Improve joint officer management

- Enhance the effectiveness of military operations

- Improve Defense Department management and administration.

In the past, Congress had tried to limit the authority of the secretary of defense, because, as has been noted, its direct links with the services, and to the industries that served them, worked to the benefit of members of Congress in local politics. But in the report accompanying the Goldwater-Nichols Act, Congress finally declared: "The secretary of defense has sole and ultimate power within the Department of Defense on any matter on which the secretary chooses to act."[16] That is, no one in the Defense Department, civilian or military, possessed authority that was independent of the secretary. Eisenhower had decreed effectively the same thing in 1953, through an executive directive; only in 1986 was Congress prepared to legislate the point.

To strengthen further civilian authority, Goldwater-Nichols gave the secretary a powerful military ally in the JCS chairman. The chairman was freed from the necessity of negotiating with the service chiefs, and his institutional perspective was to be similar to that of the secretary. The 1986 legislation also specified the responsibilities of each service secretary to the defense secretary. Addressing civilian authority at the military department level, it clarified and strengthened the roles of each service secretary.

To improve military advice, the act transferred all corporate functions of the JCS to the chairman (in which he was to be assisted by a newly created vice chairman). Specifically, it designated the chairman of the Joints Chief of Staff as the principal military adviser, with a mandate to provide that advice on the basis of the broadest military perspective. Further, it made the Joint Staff (which supports the Joint Chiefs) responsible exclusively to the chairman, and it made elaborate provisions to improve the quality of officers assigned to the Joint Staff, as well as to the staffs of the unified commanders in chief.

It did so by ordering fundamental improvements in joint officer management generally—an arena that became the last battleground in the drafting, passage, and ultimate enactment of the Goldwater-Nichols legislation. The services saw that if they retained absolute control of promotions and assignments, Congress could pass all the laws it wanted—not much was going to change in the Department of Defense. Congress was equally determined to reward officers who accepted and performed well in billets that were outside of their services; to that end it created through Goldwater-Nichols a joint officer management system. Specifically, a joint career specialty was established, and joint education was much more closely regulated—the services, for example, had been sending officers to joint schools but had assigned only a few graduates to joint billets.

```
              National        President
              Command        Secretary of Defense
              Authority

          Office of the Secretary of Defense

   Military Departments              Chairman of the JCS
      Train & equip                     Plan & coordinate

                    Unified Commands
                   Conduct operations
```

Components of the Department of Defense (DoD chart)

As for the unified commanders in chief, the act made them clearly responsible to the president and the secretary of defense—constituted collectively as the "national command authority"—for the performance of missions and the preparedness of their commands. Goldwater-Nichols required the assignment of all combat forces to the unified commanders and removed the JCS from the operational chain of command. No longer could the services move forces in and out of regional commands without the approval, or even the knowledge, of the commanders in chief. (An investigation after the 1983 bombing of the Marine barracks in Beirut found that thirty-one units in Beirut had been sent there unbeknownst to Commander in Chief, U.S. European Command.)

To ensure sufficient authority for the unified commanders, the law essentially gave them all the authority that is traditionally given to a military commander. Unified commanders were empowered to issue authoritative direction on all aspects of operations, joint training, and logistics, to prescribe internal chains of command, to organize commands and forces, and to employ forces. A unified commander in chief could now assign command functions to subordinate commanders and approve certain aspects of administration and support. In addition, unified commanders could now exercise personnel authority: they could select their headquarters staffs and subordinate commanders (matters in which they had had almost no say in the past); they could suspend subordinates; and they could convene courts-martial. As might be imagined, all of this caused heartburn among the services. But Congress had decided that unified commanders had to have these kinds of authority if they were to be effective.

Goldwater-Nichols addressed the lack of emphasis on high-level planning by requiring the president to submit annually a national security strategy, on the basis of which the chairman was to prepare fiscally constrained strategic plans. (The Pentagon at first had major objections here, but a year's experience with the new process put them to rest.) The secretary of defense was to provide—with the assistance of the under secretary of defense for policy—guidance to the chairman of the Joint Chiefs of Staff and unified commanders for the preparation and review of contingency plans. Goldwater-Nichols also prescribed a role for the under secretary in assisting the secretary's review of the plans. (These were major advances. Lacking policy and political guidance, the military drafters of contingency plans had been forced to formulate their own assumptions. Also, until then the JCS had jealously guarded contingency plans, permitting only the secretary—and no other civilian—to see them in completed form.)

In the resource area, the act called upon the secretary to provide policy guidance for the effective use of resources. He was to address objectives and policies, mission priorities, and resource constraints. Interestingly, Goldwater-Nichols told the military departments, in effect, that their collective role, their entire raison d'être, was now to fulfill as far as practicable the current and future requirements of unified commanders in chief. To the same end, the act strengthened the supervision, budget review, and combat readiness of the growing defense agencies. Congress also assigned ten new resource-related duties to the chairman of the Joint Chiefs of Staff, in the search for the independent joint budget perspective that had been missing.

Many of the above initiatives, taken together, constituted Congress's effort to improve the effectiveness of military operations. That left a final goal, improved management and administration—and here Congress's concerns included excessive spans of control. The Office of the Secretary of Defense and the service headquarters staffs had grown very large, and organizationally "excessively flat" —forty-two people reported directly to the secretary of defense, and some service chiefs directly supervised more than fifty. The Goldwater-Nichols drafters moved to reduce these spans of control. Believing that Pentagon headquarters were too large, they mandated personnel reductions in them. Addressing unnecessary duplication between service secretariats and military head-quarters staffs, Goldwater-Nichols consolidated seven functions in the secretariats. Last, the act sought to promote a mission orientation in the Pentagon and overcome the excessive focus on functional activities—manpower, research and development, health affairs, and so on.

Results

How well have the objectives that Goldwater-Nichols set been achieved? Have those objectives been met in terms of the Defense Department's performance?

Some commentators believe they have. Congressman (later secretary of defense) Les Aspin immediately called Goldwater-Nichols "one of the landmark laws of American history . . . probably the greatest sea change in the history of the American military since the Continental Congress created the Continental Army in 1775."[17] Admiral William Owens believes it was "the watershed event for the military since the Second World War."[18] William J. Perry, secretary of defense from 1994 to 1997, considers Goldwater-Nichols "perhaps the most important defense legislation since World War II."[19]

A few have been more critical. John Lehman, Secretary of the Navy in the Ronald Reagan years, charged in 1995 that the new Joint Staff reflected a gradual edging toward the old German general-staff system.[20] Richard Kohn has expressed concern about erosion of civilian control of the military.[21] The drafters of Goldwater-Nichols hoped for a Joint Staff that was as capable as the Office of the Secretary of Defense. Now, unfortunately, the Joint Staff is much *more* capable than the staff of the secretary of defense, and only partly due to improved quality of the work of the former—the performance of the Office of the Secretary of Defense has been weaker. Others have had similar unease regarding the current viability of civilian control. Professor Mackubin Owens of the Naval War College has argued, "The contributions of the Goldwater-Nichols Act . . . are marginal at best, and . . . the unintended consequences of the act may well create problems in the future that outweigh any current benefits."[22] Let us review the objectives again, this time in light of the experience of a decade and a half.

Admiral William J. Crowe, Jr., chairman of the Joint Chiefs of Staff (DoD photo by Seaman Oscar Sosa)

There is no dispute about the stature of the secretary of defense. He clearly is the ultimate authority in the Department of Defense, and his role in the chain of command is clear. He enjoys the independent military advice of the chairman of the Joint Chiefs of Staff, to such an extent that policy disputes are now generally between the secretary and chairman on one side, and the services on the other; such debates are no longer civil/military in nature, and that is fortunate. The secretary of defense now has well-understood relationships with the service secretaries, and their internal authority, in turn, has been clarified. There does appear to have been a reluctance on the part of secretaries of defense to exercise fully their newly won authority. The weaker performance of the Office of the Secretary of Defense—leading to an imbalance between the influence of that office and the Joint Staff—has diminished the civilian voice in decision making. The Goldwater-Nichols objective of strengthening civilian authority has produced results of a "B-minus," middling quality; there are problems here. Still, they are manageable ones; the problems that once crippled the secretary's authority have been overcome.

As for the quality of military advice to the national command authority, recent advisers and advisees have described it as greatly improved. Richard Cheney, as the secretary of defense under President George H. W. Bush, thought it represented "a significant improvement" over the "lowest common denominator."[23] General Shalikashvili said, "We have been able to provide far better, more focused advice."[24] Previously, initiatives in the Joint Staff went through five levels of review, in which each service had, effectively, a veto. Papers tended to be reduced to the lowest common denominator, inoffensive to any service, even before they reached the chiefs themselves, where the necessity for unanimous agreement caused them to be denatured even further. In the end, the secretary of defense would turn to his own civilian staff for the substantial advice that he could not get from military officers. Goldwater-Nichols freed the JCS from these staffing procedures. The Joint Staff now works for the chairman, and the chairman— though he may consult the service chiefs and unified commanders—need "coordinate" his advice with no one. Not all observers are impressed; Secretary Lehman believes that making the chairman principal military adviser has "limited not only the scope of military advice available to the political leadership, but also the policy- and priority-setting roles of the service chiefs and civilian service secretaries."[25] Nonetheless, the overwhelming opinion believes that progress in this part of Goldwater-Nichols merits a grade of A, for tremendous improvement.

It is universally agreed that the same is true regarding clarifying the mission responsibility of the unified commanders in chief. Military officers and defense officials have repeatedly cited the benefits of a clear, short operational chain of command. General Norman Schwarzkopf, commander in chief of Central Command during DESERT STORM, found that the clarification of his responsibilities made a tremendous difference: "Goldwater-Nichols established very, very clear lines of command authority and responsibilities for subordinate commanders, and that meant a much more effective fighting force."[26] I would give this an A as well.

Goldwater-Nichols has also effectively made the authority of the unified commanders commensurate with their responsibilities. Overwhelming successes in military operations and peacetime activities have provided visible evidence of the positive results. The act's provisions have worked out very well because the Goldwater-Nichols drafters had a great model—the authority that the military has traditionally given to a unit commander—to use in assigning command authority to unified commanders. General Shalikashvili has characterized the improvement here in very positive terms: "This act, by providing both the responsibility and the authority needed by the CINCs [commanders in chief], had made the combatant commanders vastly more capable of fulfilling their warfighting role."[27] Observers are divided as to whether the unified commanders have too much, or too little, influence in resource issues. Nonetheless, the current state of affairs is probably about right—another grade of A.

World events and regional trends have thrust the unified commanders with geographic responsibilities into broader roles, in which they are seen as representing the U.S. government. Of all government agencies, only the Department of Defense has officials in the field with regionwide responsibilities. The unified commanders have performed well in this role, but to have U.S. security interests represented so powerfully around the world by military officers may in the long term become unacceptable, because the military dimension of national-security interests overseas is decreasing.

Of course, the most conspicuous success for Goldwater-Nichols has been in the realm of military effectiveness; there have been overwhelming operational successes since the law was passed. General Colin Powell observed, "Performance of the Armed Forces in joint operations has improved significantly and Goldwater-Nichols deserves a great

General Colin L. Powell, chairman of the Joint Chiefs of Staff, and General H. Norman Schwarzkopf, commander in chief, U.S. Central Command, at the Pentagon on 15 August 1990 (DoD photo by R. D. Ward)

deal of the credit."[28] Of U.S. joint warfighting capabilities, General Shalikashvili said, "No other nation can match our ability to combine forces on the battlefield and fight jointly."[29] Areas of concern might be slow progress on joint doctrine and resistance to the missions of the Joint Forces Command (formerly Atlantic Command) in the training, integration, and provision of joint forces and experimentation with new concepts. Nonetheless, the Department of Defense has clearly been doing "A" work in the Goldwater-Nichols structure to improve operational effectiveness.

In the remaining objective areas, the Goldwater-Nichols experience has been less pleasant. Strategy formulation has improved, but the results are not yet very strong; published strategic documents still betray strong attachment to the past. Contingency plans have been improved tremendously, but there are still barriers between the civilian policy makers and operational staffs in crisis-action contingency planning. Strategy making and contingency planning under Goldwater-Nichols collectively merits a grade of C—unimpressive.

The effect of Goldwater-Nichols with respect to more efficient use of resources has been barely acceptable, if that—a grade of D. There have been some positives—the Base Force, recommended after the Cold War by General Colin Powell, then chairman of the Joint Chiefs of Staff, to reduce the military by 25 percent; and the Joint Warfighting Capability Assessments developed in the Joint Staff, largely at the initiative of Admiral Owens. But the services continue to fund Cold War systems, cannot seem to break their attachment to them, and the Joint Requirements Oversight Council has rubber-stamped the services' choices. As Admiral Owens has argued, the inability of the defense establishment to make some fundamental decisions has squandered the post–Cold War period.[30]

The qualifications of joint officers have improved dramatically—thanks not to the Department of Defense, which has been until recently indifferent in its implementation of the act's joint officer provisions, but to the initiative of the officers themselves. These officers have come to see joint experience as something that can promote their careers or provide useful skill sets for the future. The department itself, however, still has no concept of its needs for joint officers or of how to prepare and reward them. The officer corps is much smaller now than it was when Goldwater-Nichols was passed; this is no area in which to be adrift. It requires, again, a balance between joint and service emphasis. Joint officer education can be pushed too far; service capabilities and perspectives are very important, for instance, and they can be taught only at command-and-staff and war colleges. The bottom-line grade for Goldwater-Nichols's objective of improving joint officer management is a C+.

Finally, the remedies applied by Goldwater-Nichols to defense management and administration have largely been ineffective. They were never a priority for the act's drafters, and troubling trends remain. Management of the large defense agencies is still weak. The Pentagon, with its large staffs including two (or three) headquarters staffs in each military department, is choking on bureaucracy. The division of work among the major components is blurred. The orientation to mission in business activities is still weak, and management doctrine, so to speak, is a relic of the 1960s. The Defense Department under Goldwater-Nichols gets a D here—barely getting by.

The overall report card, then, is mixed. In the areas that the original sponsors of the Goldwater-Nichols Act considered most pressing—military advice, the unified commanders, contingency planning, joint officer management, and military operations—the Department of Defense has made gratifying, sometimes striking, progress. That is, the act has been very successful in improving the operational dimension of the Department of Defense. The "business" reforms of Goldwater-Nichols, however, have not worked. These concerns, which may have been secondary fifteen years ago, are urgent now.

Yesterday's Winning Formula

The unfinished business of Goldwater-Nichols cannot be resolved from the bottom up; the Department of Defense is too large, and the rate of change it confronts is too rapid. The process will have to be driven from the top, by leadership with vision and communication skills. In 1997, Secretary of Defense William S. Cohen sought to stimulate a "revolution in business affairs" in the Defense Department—the office of the secretary, the military departments, "business activities," and the defense agencies. He wanted to "bring to the department management techniques and business practices that have restored American corporations to leadership in the marketplace."[31] The effort needs to be accelerated tremendously—in a Defense Department with a culture that is markedly change resistant.

Resistance to change is a natural tendency of both humans and large organizations, but in a world characterized by accelerating change, it is a strategic liability. As two business scholars observed, "Yesterday's winning formula ossifies into today's conventional wisdom before petrifying into tomorrow's tablets of stone."[32] The world is moving very rapidly—and the U.S. Department of Defense is too attached to the past.

The dual headquarters at the top of each of the military departments must be combined into one; the current arrangement is far too inefficient for a fast-paced world, and it consumes far too much manpower. The defense agencies—which now expend more money than the Department of the Army—should be collected into a "fourth department," for support of the entire Defense Department—under an executive, a director of defense support, who can impose high-quality management techniques in this vital area. In the operational area, standing joint task force headquarters should be established in each regional unified command, despite the personnel and resource commitment that will involve; as it is, the military assembles forces for operations as if it were picking teams in a neighborhood basketball game. Joint Forces Command needs—in fact, all joint activities should have—a budget and authority to buy systems unique to joint operations. The present dependence on service executive agents gives the services too much control over progress in joint activities.

The Goldwater-Nichols story offers, in my view, two key lessons. First, defense organization is important; it deserves continuous and innovative attention. Congress came to the department's rescue in 1986, but today the Pentagon's organizational problems are again stacking up, and at an ever faster pace. Second, Goldwater-Nichols brings to the fore the struggle of each officer to find that balance between loyalty to service and devotion to the larger needs of the nation. All who work in elements of large organizations face a similar challenge. The natural impulse is to defend that element—to protect it against marauders, to be sure it gets its fair share, to demonstrate that its contributions are more vital than those of others, and, when necessary, to fight against its evil foes. Such impulses have their time and place, but increasingly, America will need officers who can resist them when the nation's security demands something more.

Notes

1. Vernon E. Davis, *The History of the Joint Chiefs of Staff in World War II: Organizational Development,* vol. 1, *Origin of the Joint and Combined Chiefs of Staff* (Washington, D.C.: Joint Chiefs of Staff, 1972), p. xi.

2. Eric Larrabee, *Commander in Chief: Franklin Delano Roosevelt, His Lieutenants, and Their War* (New York: Harper and Row, 1987), p. 17.

3. William Frye, *Marshall: Citizen Soldier* (Indianapolis: Bobbs-Merrill, 1947), p. 325.

4. Larrabee, *Commander in Chief,* p. 105.

5. Quoted in Alice C. Cole et al., eds., *The Department of Defense: Documents on Establishment and Organization, 1944–1978* (Washington,

D.C.: Office of the Secretary of Defense, 1978), p. 177.

6. Roger R. Trask and Alfred Goldberg, *The Department of Defense, 1947–1997: Organization and Leaders* (Washington, D.C.: Office of the Secretary of Defense, 1997), p. 11.

7. James H. Kyle, *The Guts to Try: The Untold Story of the Iran Hostage Rescue Mission by the On-Scene Desert Commander* (New York: Orion Books, 1990), p. 283.

8. John M. Shalikashvili [Gen., USA], "A Word from the Chairman," *Joint Force Quarterly,* Autumn 1996, p. 1.

9. Chairman's Special Study Group, *The Organization and Functions of the JCS: Report for the Chairman, Joint Chiefs of Staff* (Arlington, Va.: Systems Research and Applications Corp., 1982), p. 54.

10. Congress, House, Committee on Armed Services [HASC], Investigations Subcommittee, *Reorganization Proposals for the Joint Chiefs of Staff: Hearings before the Investigations Subcommittee,* 97th Cong., 2d sess., 1982, HASC no. 97-47, p. 54.

11. Congress, Senate, Committee on Armed Services, *Organization, Structure, and Decisionmaking Procedures of the Department of Defense: Hearings before the Committee on Armed Services,* 98th Cong., 1st sess., S. Hrg. 98-375, pt. 5, 2 November 1983, p. 187.

12. John H. Cushman, *Command and Control of Theater Forces: The Korea Command and Other Cases* (Cambridge, Mass.: Harvard Univ. Press, 1986), pp. 5–23.

13. Blue Ribbon Defense Panel, *Report to the President and the Secretary of Defense on the Department of Defense* (Washington, D.C.: U.S. Govt. Print. Off., 1970), p. 50.

14. Samuel P. Huntington, "Defense Organization and Military Strategy," *Public Interest,* Spring 1984, p. 24.

15. Congress, Senate, Senator Nunn of Georgia speaking on congressional oversight of national defense, 99th Cong., 1st sess., *Congressional Record,* 1 October 1985, pp. 25350–4.

16. Congress, House, *Goldwater-Nichols Department of Defense Reorganization Act of 1986: Conference Report* [to accompany H.R. 3622], 99th Cong., 2d sess., Report 99-824, p. 101.

17. Aspin quoted in House Armed Services Committee, "House-Senate Conference Wraps Up Defense Reorganization Bill," news release, 11 September 1986.

18. William A. Owens, "'Jointness' Is His Job," *Government Executive,* April 1995, p. 61.

19. William J. Perry, speech honoring Senator Sam Nunn, Pentagon, 12 July 1996.

20. John F. Lehman, "Is the Joint Staff a General Staff?" *Armed Forces Journal International,* August 1995, p. 16.

21. Richard H. Kohn, "The Crisis in Military-Civilian Relations," *National Interest,* Spring 1994, pp. 3–17.

22. Mackubin T. Owens, Jr., "Goldwater-Nichols: A Ten-Year Retrospective," *Marine Corps Gazette,* December 1996, pp. 48–53.

23. "About Fighting and Winning Wars: An Interview with Dick Cheney," U.S. Naval Institute *Proceedings,* May 1996, p. 33.

24. John M. Shalikashvili [Gen. USA], "Goldwater-Nichols: Ten Years from Now," remarks, National Defense University Symposium, Washington, D.C., 3 December 1996.

25. John F. Lehman and Harvey Sicherman, "America's Military Problems and How to Fix Them," *Foreign Policy Research Institute WIRE: A Catalyst for Ideas,* 9 February 2001, available at www.fpri.org.

26. Congress, Senate, Committee on Armed Services, *Operation Desert Shield/Desert Storm: Hearings before the Committee on Armed Services,* 102d Cong., 1st sess., 24 April; 8, 9, 16, 21 May; and 4, 12, 20 June 1991, p. 318.

27. Shalikashvili, "Goldwater-Nichols."

28. "The Chairman as Principal Military Adviser: An Interview with Colin L. Powell," *Joint Force Quarterly,* Autumn 1996, p. 30.

29. Shalikashvili, "A Word from the Chairman."

30. Bill Owens with Ed Offley, *Lifting the Fog of War* (New York: Farrar, Straus, and Giroux, 2000), p. 207.

31. William S. Cohen, "Message from the Secretary," in *Defense Reform Initiative: The Business Strategy for Defense in the 21st Century* (Washington, D.C.: Department of Defense, 1997), p. i.

32. Sumantra Ghoshal and Christopher A. Bartlett, "Changing the Role of Top Management: Beyond Structure to Processes," *Harvard Business Review,* January–February 1995, p. 94.

CHAPTER FOUR

The Erosion of Civilian Control of the Military in the United States Today

RICHARD H. KOHN

In over thirty-five years as a military historian, I have come to have great respect for and trust in American military officers. The United States is truly blessed to have men and women of the highest character leading its youth and safeguarding its security. That fact makes the present subject all the more troubling and unpleasant, whether to write or read about it. However, the subject is crucial to the nation's security and to its survival as a republic. I am speaking of a tear in the nation's civil and political fabric; my hope is that by bringing it to the attention of a wide military and defense readership I can prompt a frank, open discussion that could, by raising the awareness of the American public and alerting the armed forces, set in motion a process of healing.

My subject is the civil-military relationship at the pinnacle of the government, and my fear, baldly stated, is that in recent years civilian control of the military has weakened in the United States and is threatened today. The issue is not the nightmare of a coup d'état but rather the evidence that the American military has grown in influence to the point of being able to impose its own perspective on many policies and decisions. What I have detected is no conspiracy but repeated efforts on the part of the armed forces to frustrate or evade civilian authority when that opposition seems likely to preclude outcomes the military dislikes.

While I do not see any crisis, I am convinced that civilian control has diminished to the point where it could alter the character of American government and undermine national defense. My views result from nearly four decades of reading and reflection about civilian control in this country; from personal observation from inside the Pentagon during the 1980s; and since then, from watching the Clinton and two Bush administrations struggle to balance national security with domestic political realities.

© 2002 by Richard H. Kohn

Naval War College Review, Summer 2002, Vol. 55, No. 3

Understanding the problem begins with a review of the state of civil-military relations during the last nine years, a state of affairs that in my judgment has been extraordinarily poor, in many respects as low as in any period of American peacetime history. No president was ever as reviled by the professional military—treated with such disrespect, or viewed with such contempt—as Bill Clinton. Conversely, no administration ever treated the military with more fear and deference on the one hand, and indifference and neglect on the other, as the Clinton administration.

The relationship began on a sour note during the 1992 campaign. As a youth, Clinton had avoided the draft, written a letter expressing "loathing" for the military, and demonstrated against the Vietnam War while in Britain on a Rhodes scholarship. Relations turned venomous with the awful controversy over gays in the military, when the administration—in ignorance and arrogance—announced its intention to abolish the ban on open homosexual service immediately, without study or consultation. The Joint Chiefs of Staff responded by resisting, floating rumors of their own and dozens of other resignations, encouraging their retired brethren to arouse congressional and public opposition, and then more or less openly negotiating a compromise with their commander in chief.[1]

The newly elected president was publicly insulted by service people (including a two-star general) in person, in print, and in speeches. So ugly was the behavior that commanders had to remind their subordinates of their constitutional and legal obligations not to speak derogatorily of the civilian leadership; the Air Force chief of staff felt obliged to remind his senior commanders "about core values, including the principle of a chain of command that runs from the president right down to our newest airman."[2]

Nothing like this had ever occurred in American history. This was the most open manifestation of defiance and resistance by the American military since the publication of the Newburgh addresses over two centuries earlier, at the close of the American war for independence. Then the officers of the Army openly contemplated revolt or resignation en masse over the failure of Congress to pay them or to fund the pensions they had been promised during a long and debilitating war. All of this led me, as a student of American civil-military relations, to ask why so loyal, subordinate, and successful a military, as professional as any in the world, suddenly violated one of its most sacred traditions.

While open conflict soon dropped from public sight, bitterness hardened into a visceral hatred that became part of the culture of many parts of the military establishment, kept alive by a continuous stream of incidents and controversies.[3] These included, to cite but a few: the undermining and driving from office of Secretary of Defense Les Aspin in 1993, followed by the humiliating withdrawal of his nominated replacement; controversies over the retirements of at least six four-star flag officers, including the early retirement of an Air

Force chief of staff (an unprecedented occurrence); and the tragic suicide of a Chief of Naval Operations (also unprecedented). There were ceaseless arguments over gender, the most continuous source of conflict between the Clinton administration and its national security critics.[4] The specific episodes ranged from the botched investigations of the 1991 Tailhook scandal to the 1997 uproar over Air Force first lieutenant Kelly Flinn, the first female B-52 line pilot, who (despite admitting to adultery, lying to an investigating officer, and disobeying orders) was allowed to leave the service without court-martial. Other related incidents included the outrages at Aberdeen Proving Ground,

William J. Clinton
(White House)

where Army sergeants had sex with recruits under their command, and the 1999 retirement of the highest-ranking female Army general in history amid accusations that she had been sexually harassed by a fellow general officer some years previously. In addition, there were bitter arguments over readiness; over budgets; over whether and how to intervene with American forces abroad, from Somalia to Haiti to Bosnia to Kosovo; and over national strategy generally.[5]

So poisonous became the relationship that two Marine officers in 1998 had to be reprimanded for violating article 88 of the Uniform Code of Military Justice, the provision about contemptuous words against the highest civilian officials. The assistant commandant of the Marine Corps felt constrained to warn all Marine generals about officers publicly criticizing or disparaging the commander in chief.[6] The next year, at a military ball at the Plaza Hotel in New York City, a local television news anchor, playing on the evening's theme, "A Return to Integrity," remarked that he "didn't recognize any dearth of integrity here" until he "realized that President Clinton was in town" and the crowd, "which included 20 generals" and was made up largely of officers, went wild.[7] During the election of 2000, the chief legal officers of two of the largest commands in the Army and Air Force issued warnings lest resentment over Gore campaign challenges to absentee ballots in Florida boil over into open contempt.[8]

These illustrations emphasize the negatives. In contrast, by all accounts people in uniform respected and worked well with Secretary of Defense William Perry. Certainly Generals John Shalikashvili and Hugh Shelton, successive chairmen of the Joint Chiefs of Staff after 1993, appeared to have been liked and respected by civilians in the Clinton administration. But these men, and other senior officers and officials who bridged the two cultures at the top levels of government, seemed to understand that theirs was a delicate role—to mediate between two hostile relatives who feared and distrusted each other but realized that they had to work together if both were to survive.

Now, to discount the Clinton difficulties as atmospherics and thus essentially insignificant would be mistaken, for the toxicity of the civil-military relationship damaged national security in at least three ways: first, by paralyzing national security policy; second, by obstructing and in some cases sabotaging American ability to intervene in foreign crises or to exercise leadership internationally; and third, by undermining the confidence of the armed forces in their own uniformed leadership.

In response to that first, searing controversy over open homosexual service, the administration concluded that this president—with his Democratic affiliation, liberal leanings, history of draft evasion and opposition to the Vietnam War, and admitted marital infidelity and experimentation with marijuana—would never be acceptable to the military.[9] One knowledgeable insider characterized the White House of those years as reflecting the demography of the post-Vietnam Democratic Party—people who had never served in uniform and who had a "tin ear" for things military. Knowing little or nothing about military affairs or national security and not caring to develop a deep or sympathetic understanding of either, the administration decided that for this president, military matters constituted a "third rail."[10] No issue with the military was worth exposing this vulnerability; nothing was worth the cost. All controversy with the military was therefore to be avoided. In fact, the Clintonites from the beginning tried to "give away" the military establishment: first to the congressional Democrats, by making Les Aspin secretary of defense; then, when Aspin was driven from office, to the military itself, by nominating Admiral Bobby Inman; then, when he withdrew, to the military-industrial complex (with William Perry as secretary and John Deutsch and John White as deputies), an arrangement that lasted until 1997; and finally to the Republicans, in the person of Senator William Cohen of Maine. From the outset, the focus of the administration in foreign affairs was almost wholly economic in nature, and while that may have been genius, one result of the Clintonites' inattention and inconstancy was the disgust and disrespect of the national security community, particularly those in uniform.[11] By the time Clinton left office, some officials were admitting that he had been "unwilling to exercise full authority over military commanders."[12] "Those who monitored Clinton closely during his eight years as president believed . . . that he was intimidated more by the military than by any other political force he dealt with," reported David Halberstam. Said "a former senior N[ational] S[ecurity] C[ouncil] official who studied [Clinton] closely, . . . 'he was out-and-out afraid of them.'"[13]

Forging a reasonable and economical national security policy was crucial to the health and well-being of the country, particularly at a time of epochal transition brought on by the end of the Cold War. But both the first Bush and then Clinton's administration studiously avoided any public discussion of what role the United States should play in the world, unless asserting the existence of a "new world order" or labeling the United States "the indispensable nation" constitutes discussion.[14] As for the Clinton administration, indifference to military affairs and the decision to take no risks and expend no political capital in that area produced paralysis. Any rethinking of strategy, force structure, roles and missions of the armed services, organization, personnel, weapons, or other choices indispensable for the near and long term was rendered futile. As a result, today, over a decade after the end of the Cold War, there is still no common understanding about the fundamental purposes of the American military establishment or the principles by which the United States will decide whether to use military power in pursuit of the national interest.

The Clinton administration held itself hostage to the organization and force structure of the Cold War.[15] At the beginning of Clinton's first term, Secretary Aspin attempted to modify the basis of American strategy—an ability to fight two "major regional contingencies" (changed later to "major theater wars") almost simultaneously. But Aspin caved in to charges that such a change would embolden America's adversaries and weaken security arrangements with allies in the Middle East and Asia.[16] The result was a defense budget known to be inadequate for the size and configuration of the military establishment even without the need to fund peacetime intervention contingencies, which constantly threw military accounts into deficit.[17] Budgets became prisoners of readiness. Forces could not be reduced, because of the many military commitments around the world, but if readiness to wage high-intensity combat fell or seemed to diminish, Republican critics would rise up in outrage. Thus the uniformed leadership—each service chief, regional or functional commander, sometimes even division, task force, or wing commanders—possessed the political weight to veto any significant change in the nation's fundamental security structure.

As a result, the Clinton administration never could match resources with commitments, balance readiness with modernization, or consider organizational changes that would relieve the stresses on personnel and equipment.[18] All of this occurred when the services were on the brink of, or were actually undergoing, what many believed to be changes in weaponry and tactics so major as to constitute a "revolution in military affairs."[19] One consequence of the insufficiency of resources in people and money to meet frequent operational commitments and growing maintenance costs was the loss of many of the best officers and noncommissioned officers, just as economic prosperity and other factors were reducing the numbers of men and women willing to sign up for military service in the first place.

The paralysis in military policy in the 1990s provoked the Congress to attempt by legislation at least four different times to force the Pentagon to reevaluate national security policy, strategy, and force structure, with as yet no significant result.[20] Perhaps the last of these efforts, the U.S. Commission on National Security/21st Century (also called the Hart-Rudman Commission), which undertook a comprehensive review of national security and the military establishment, will have some effect. If so, it will be because the Bush administration possessed the political courage to brave the civil-military friction required to reorganize an essentially Cold War military establishment into a force capable of meeting the security challenges of the twenty-first century.[21] But the prospects are not encouraging when one considers Secretary of Defense Donald Rumsfeld's secrecy and lack of consultation with the uniformed military and Congress; the forces gathering to resist change; the priority of the Bush tax cut and national missile defense, which threaten to limit severely the money available and to force excruciating choices; and Rumsfeld's fudging of the very concept of "transformation." Even the 11 September 2001 terrorist attacks have not broken the logjam, except perhaps monetarily. The administration has committed itself to slow, incremental change so as not to confront the inherent conservatism of the armed services or imperil the weapons purchases pushed so powerfully by defense contractors and their congressional champions.[22] The White House has done so despite its belief that the failure to exert civilian control in the 1990s left a military establishment declining in quality and effectiveness.

Donald Rumsfeld
(Defenselink)

Second, the Clinton administration—despite far more frequent occasions for foreign armed intervention (which was ironic, considering its aversion to military matters)—was often immobilized over when, where, how, and under what circumstances to use military force in the world. The long, agonizing debates and vacillation over intervention in Africa, Haiti, and the former Yugoslavia reflected in part the weakness of the administration compared to the political power of the uniformed military.[23] The between the two sides distorted decision making to an extreme. Sometimes the military exercised a veto over the use of American force, or at least an ability so to shape the character of American intervention that means determined ends—a roundabout way of exercising a veto. At other times, civilians ignored or even avoided receiving advice from the military. By the 1999 Kosovo air campaign, the consultative relationship had so broken down that the president was virtually divorced from his theater commander, and that commander's communications with the secretary of defense and chairman of the Joint Chiefs were corrupted by misunderstanding and distrust. The result was a campaign misconceived at the outset and badly coordinated not only between civilian and military but between the various levels of command. The consequences could have undone the Nato alliance, and they certainly stiffened Serbian will, exacerbated divisions within Nato councils, increased criticism in the United States, and prolonged the campaign beyond what almost everyone involved had predicted.[24]

Last, the incessant acrimony—the venomous atmosphere in Washington—shook the confidence of the armed forces in their own leadership. Different groups accused the generals and admirals, at one extreme, of caving in to political correctness, and at the other, of being rigid and hidebound with respect to gender integration, war-fighting strategy, and organizational change. The impact on morale contributed to the hemorrhage from the profession of arms of able young and middle-rank officers. The loss of so many fine officers, combined with declines in recruiting (which probably brought, in turn, a diminution in the quality of new officers and enlisted recruits), may weaken the nation's military leadership in the next generation and beyond, posing greater danger to national security than would any policy blunder. Certainly many complex factors have driven people out of uniform and impaired recruiting, but the loss of confidence in the senior uniformed leadership has been cited by many as a reason to leave the service.[25]

Now, to attribute all of these difficulties to the idiosyncrasies of the Clinton administration alone would be a mistake. In fact, the recent friction in civil-military relations and unwillingness to exert civilian control have roots all the way back to World War II. Unquestionably Mr. Clinton and his appointees bungled civil-military relations badly, from the beginning. But other administrations have done so also, and others will in the future.

If one measures civilian control not by the superficial standard of who signs the papers and passes the laws but by the relative influence of the uniformed military and civilian policy makers in the two great areas of concern in military affairs—national security policy, and the use of force to protect the country and project power abroad—then civilian control has deteriorated significantly in the last generation. In theory, civilians have the authority to issue virtually any order and organize the military in any fashion they choose. But in practice, the relationship is far more complex. Both sides frequently disagree among themselves. Further, the military can evade or circumscribe civilian authority by framing the alternatives or tailoring their advice or predicting nasty consequences; by leaking information or appealing to public opinion (through various indirect channels, like lobbying groups or retired generals and admirals); or by approaching friends in the Congress for support. They can even fail to implement decisions, or carry them out in such a way as to stymie their intent. The reality is that civilian control is not a fact but a process, measured across a spectrum—something *situational*, dependent on the people, issues, and the political and military forces involved. We are not talking about a coup here, or anything else demonstrably illegal; we are talking about who calls the tune in military affairs in the United States today.[26]

Contrast the weakness of the civilian side with the strength of the military, not only in the policy process but in clarity of definition of American purpose, consistency of voice, and willingness to exert influence both in public and behind the scenes.

The power of the military within the policy process has been growing steadily since a low point under Secretary of Defense Robert McNamara in the 1960s. Under the 1986 Goldwater-Nichols Defense Reorganization Act, the chairman of the Joint Chiefs of Staff (JCS) has influence that surpasses that of everyone else within the Pentagon except the secretary of defense, and the chairman possesses a more competent, focused, and effective staff than the secretary does, as well as, often, a clearer set of goals, fewer political constraints, and under some circumstances greater credibility with the public.[27] In the glow of success in the Gulf War, efforts to exorcise Vietnam, the high public esteem now enjoyed by the armed forces, and the disgust Americans have felt for politics in general and for partisanship in particular, the stature of the chairman has grown to a magnitude out of proportion to his legal or institutional position.

The Joint Staff is the most powerful organization in the Department of Defense; frequently, by dint of its speed, agility, knowledge, and expertise, the Joint Staff frames the choices.[28] The Joint Requirements Oversight Council (the vice chiefs, convening under the vice chairman to prioritize joint programs in terms of need and cost) has gathered influence and authority over the most basic issues of weapons and force structure.[29] Within the bureaucracy, JCS has a representative in the interagency decision process, giving the uniformed military a voice separate from that of the Department of Defense. Similarly, the armed services maintain their own congressional liaison and public affairs offices, bureaucracies so large that they are impossible to monitor fully. (One officer admitted to me privately that his duty on Capitol Hill was to encourage Congress to restore a billion dollars that the Pentagon's civilian leadership had cut out of his service's budget request.)[30] Moreover, the regional commanders have come to assume such importance in their areas—particularly in the Pacific, the Middle East, and Central Asia—that they have effectively displaced American ambassadors and the State Department as the primary instruments of American foreign policy.[31] In recent reorganizations, these commanders have so increased in stature and influence within the defense establishment that their testimony can sway Congress and embarrass or impede the administration, especially when the civilians in the executive branch are weak and the Congress is dominated by an aggressively led opposition political party.

One knowledgeable commentator put it this way in early 1999: "The dirty little secret of American civil-military relations, by no means unique to this [the Clinton] administration, is that the commander in chief does not command the military establishment; he cajoles it, negotiates with it, and, as necessary, appeases it."[32] A high Pentagon civilian privately substantiates the interpretation: what "weighs heavily . . . every day" is "the reluctance, indeed refusal, of the political appointees to disagree with the military on any matter, not just operational matters." In fact, so powerful have such institutional forces become, and so intractable the problem of altering the military establishment, that the new Rumsfeld regime in the Pentagon decided to conduct its comprehensive review of national defense in strict secrecy, effectively cutting the regional commanders, the service chiefs, and the Congress out of the process so that resistance could not organize in advance of the intended effort at transformation.[33]

Furthermore, senior military leaders have been able to use their personal leverage for a variety of purposes, sometimes because of civilian indifference, or deference, or ignorance, sometimes because they have felt it necessary to fill voids of policy and decision making. But sometimes the influence is exercised intentionally and purposefully, even aggressively. After fifty years of cold war, the "leak," the bureaucratic maneuver, the alliance with partisans in Congress—the *ménage à trois* between the administration, Congress, and the military—have become a way of life, in which services and groups employ their knowledge, contacts, and positions to promote personal or institutional agendas.[34] In the 1970s, responding to the view widely held among military officers that a reserve callup would have galvanized public support for Vietnam, allowed intensified prosecution of the war, and prevented divorce between the Army and the American people, the Army chief of staff deliberately redesigned divisions to contain "round-out" units of reserve or National Guard troops, making it impossible for the president to commit the Army to battle on a large scale without mobilizing the reserves and Guard.[35] In the 1980s, the chairman of the Joint Chiefs, Admiral William J. Crowe, worked "behind the scenes" to encourage Congress to strengthen his own office even though the secretary of defense opposed such a move. During the Iran-Iraq War Crowe pushed for American escort of Kuwaiti tankers in the Persian Gulf, because he believed it important for American foreign policy. He and the chiefs strove to slow the Reagan administration's strategic missile defense program. Crowe even went so far as to create a personal communications channel with his Soviet military counterpart, apparently unknown to his civilian superiors, to avert any possibility of a misunderstanding leading to war. "It was in the nature of the Chairman's job," Crowe remembered, "that I occasionally found myself fighting against Defense Department positions as well as for them."[36]

In the 1990s, press leaks from military sources led directly to the weakening and ultimate dismissal of the Clinton administration's first secretary of defense.[37] In 1994 the Chief of Naval Operations (CNO) openly discussed with senior commanders his plans to manipulate the Navy budget and operations tempo to force his preferred priorities on the Office of the Secretary of Defense and Congress. When a memo recounting the conversation surfaced in the press, no civilian in authority called the CNO to account.[38] The 1995 Commission on the Roles and Missions of the Armed Forces recommended consolidating the staffs of the service chiefs and the service secretaries; no one mentioned the diminution of civilian control that would have taken place as a result.[39]

Even during the 1990s, a period when the administration appeared to be forceful, insisting upon the use of American forces over military objections or resistance, the uniformed leadership often arbitrated events. The 1995 Bosnia intervention was something of a paradigm. American priorities seem to have been, first, deploying in overwhelming strength, in order to suffer few if any casualties; second, establishing a deadline for exit; third, issuing "robust" rules of engagement, again to forestall casualties; fourth, narrowing the definition of the mission to ensure that it was incontrovertibly "doable"; and fifth—*fifth*—reconstructing Bosnia as a viable independent country.[40]

In recent years senior uniformed leaders have spoken out on issues of policy— undoubtedly often with the encouragement or at least the acquiescence of civilian officials, but not always so. Sometimes these pronouncements endeavor to sell policies and decisions to the public or within the government before a presidential decision, even though such advocacy politicizes the chairman, a chief, or a regional commander and inflates their influence in discussions of policy. A four-star general, a scant ten days after retiring, publishes a long article in our most respected foreign affairs journal, preceded by a *New York Times* op-ed piece. In them, he criticizes the administration's most sensitive (and vulnerable) policy—and virtually no one in the press or elsewhere questions whether his action was professionally appropriate.[41] The chairman of the Joint Chiefs of Staff gives "an impassioned interview" to the *New York Times* "on the folly of intervention" in Bosnia as "the first Bush administration" is pondering "the question of whether to intervene."[42] Another chairman coins the "Dover Principle," cautioning the civilian leadership about the human and political costs of casualties when American forces are sent into some crisis or conflict (and service members' bodies return through the joint mortuary at Dover Air Force Base). This lecture clearly aimed to establish boundaries in the public's mind and to constrain civilian freedom of action in intervening overseas.

Certainly Generals Shalikashvili and Shelton have been fairly circumspect about speaking out on issues of policy, and the current chairman, Air Force general Richard B. Myers, even more. However, their predecessor, Colin Powell, possessed and used extraordinary power throughout his tenure as chairman of the JCS. He conceived and then sold to a skeptical secretary of defense and a divided Congress the "Base Force" reorganization and reduction in 1990–91. He shaped the U.S. prosecution of the Gulf War to ensure limited objectives, the use of overwhelming force, a speedy end to combat, and the immediate exit of American forces. He spoke frequently on matters of policy during and after the election of 1992—an op-ed in the *New York Times* and a more comprehensive statement of foreign policy in the quarterly *Foreign Affairs*. Powell essentially vetoed intervention in Somalia and Bosnia, ignored or circumvented the chiefs on a regular basis, and managed the advisory process so as to present only single alternatives to civilian policy makers. All of this antedated his forcing President Clinton in 1993 to back down on allowing homosexuals to serve openly.[43] In fact, General Powell became so powerful and so adept in the bureaucratic manipulations that often decide crucial questions before the final decision maker affixes a signature that in 2001 the Bush administration installed an experienced, powerful, highly respected figure at the Defense Department specifically lest Powell control the entire foreign and national security apparatus in the new administration.[44]

All of these are examples—and only public manifestations—of a policy and decision-making process that has tilted far more toward the military than ever before in American history in peacetime.

Now an essential question arises: do these developments differ from previous practice or experience in American history? At first glance, the answer might seem to be no. Military and civilian have often differed, and the military has for many years acted on occasion beyond what might be thought proper in a republican system of government, a system that defines civilian control, or military subordination to civil authority, as obligatory.

Historical examples abound. Leading generals and chiefs of staff of the Army from James Wilkinson in the 1790s through Maxwell Taylor in the 1950s have fought with presidents and secretaries of war or defense in the open and in private over all sorts of issues—including key military policies in times of crisis. Officers openly disparaged

Abraham Lincoln during the Civil War; that president's problems with his generals became legendary.[45] Two commanding generals of the Army were so antagonistic toward
the War Department that they moved their headquarters out of Washington: Winfield
Scott to New York in the 1850s, and William Tecumseh Sherman to St. Louis in the
1870s.[46] In the 1880s, reform-minded naval officers connived to modernize the Navy
from wood and sail to steel and steam. To do so they drew the civilian leadership into
the process, forged an alliance with the steel industry, and (for the first time in American history, and in coordination with political and economic elites) sold naval reform
and a peacetime buildup of standing forces to the public through publications, presentations, displays, reviews, and other precursors of the promotional public relations that
would be used so frequently—and effectively—in the twentieth century.[47] In the 1920s
and 1930s, the youthful Army Air Corps became so adept at public relations and at generating controversy over airpower that three different presidential administrations were
forced to appoint high-level boards of outsiders to study how the Army could (or could
not) properly incorporate aviation.[48]

Both Presidents Roosevelt complained bitterly about the resistance of the armed services to change. "You should go through the experience of trying to get any changes in
the thinking . . . and action of the career diplomats and then you'd know what a real
problem was," FDR complained in 1940. "But the Treasury and the State Department
put together are nothing as compared with the Na-a-vy. . . . To change anything in the
Na-a-vy is like punching a feather bed. You punch it with your right and you punch it
with your left until you are finally exhausted, and then you find the damn bed just as it
was before you started punching."[49]

The interservice battles of the 1940s and 1950s were so fierce that neither Congress nor
the president could contain them. Internecine warfare blocked President Harry Truman's
effort to unify the armed forces in the 1940s ("unification" finally produced only loose
confederation) and angered President Dwight D. Eisenhower through the 1950s. Neither administration fully controlled strategy, force structure, or weapons procurement;
both had to fight service parochialism and interests; and both ruled largely by imposing
top-line budget limits and forcing the services to struggle over a limited funding "pie."
Eisenhower replaced or threatened to fire several of his chiefs. Only through Byzantine
maneuvers, managerial wizardry, and draconian measures did Robert McNamara bring
a modicum of coherence and integration to the overall administration of the Defense
Department in the 1960s. The price, however, was a ruthless, relentless bureaucratic
struggle that not only contributed to the disaster of Vietnam but left a legacy of suspicion
and deceit that infects American civil-military relations to this day.[50] (Even today, embit-
tered officers identify their nemesis by his full name—Robert Strange McNamara—to
express their loathing.) The point of this history is that civil-military relations *are* messy

and frequently antagonistic; military people *do* on occasion defy civilians; civilian control *is* situational.[51]

But the present differs from the past in four crucial ways.

First, the military has now largely *united* to shape, oppose, evade, or thwart civilian choices, whereas in the past the armed services were usually divided internally or among themselves. Indeed, most civil-military conflict during the Cold War arose from rivalry between the services, and over roles, missions, budgets, or new weapons systems—not whether and how to use American armed forces, or general military policy.

Second, many of the *issues* in play today reach far beyond the narrowly military, not only to the wider realm of national security but often to foreign relations more broadly. In certain cases military affairs even affect the character and values of American society itself.

Third, the role of military leaders has drifted over the last generation from that primarily of advisers and advocates within the private confines of the executive branch to a much more *public* function. As we have noted, they champion not just their services but policies and decisions in and beyond the military realm, and sometimes they mobilize public or congressional opinion either directly or indirectly (whether in Congress or the executive branch) prior to decision by civilian officials. To give but three examples: senior officers spoke out publicly on whether the United States should sign a treaty banning the use of land mines; on whether American forces should be put into the Balkans to stop ethnic cleansing; and on whether the nation should support the establishment of the International Criminal Court. Again, such actions are not unprecedented, but they have occurred recently with increasing frequency, and collectively they represent a significant encroachment on civilian control of the military.[52]

Fourth, senior officers now lead a *permanent* peacetime military establishment that differs fundamentally from any of its predecessors. Unlike the large citizen forces raised in wartime and during the Cold War, today's armed services are professional and increasingly disconnected, even in some ways estranged, from civilian society. Yet in comparison to previous peacetime professional forces, which were also isolated from civilian culture, today's are far larger, far more involved worldwide, far more capable, and often indispensable (even on a daily basis) to American foreign policy and world politics. Five decades of warfare and struggle against communism, moreover, have created something entirely new in American history—a separate military community, led by the regular forces but including also the National Guard and reserves, veterans organizations, and the communities, labor sectors, industries, and pressure groups active in military affairs. More diverse than the "military-industrial complex" of President Eisenhower's farewell address forty years ago, this "military" has become a recognizable interest group. Also, it is larger, more bureaucratically active, more political, more partisan, more purposeful, and more influential than anything similar in American history.[53]

One might argue that this is all temporary, the unique residue of sixty years of world and cold war, and that it will dissipate and balance will return now that the Clinton administration is history. Perhaps—but civil-military conflict is not very likely to diminish. In "Rumsfeld's Rules," Donald Rumsfeld states that his primary function is "to exercise civilian control over the Department for the Commander-in-Chief and the country." He understands that he possesses "the right to get into anything and exercise it [i.e., civilian control]." He recognizes as a rule, "When cutting staff at the Pentagon, don't eliminate the thin layer that assures civilian control."[54] Nonetheless, his effort to recast the military establishment for the post–Cold War era—as promised during the 2000 presidential campaign—provoked such immediate and powerful resistance (and not just by the armed forces) that he abandoned any plans to force reorganization or cut "legacy" weapons systems.[55] In the Afghanistan campaign, Rumsfeld and other civilian leaders have reportedly been frustrated by an apparent lack of imagination on the part of the military; in return, at least one four-star has accused Rumsfeld of "micromanagement."[56] There is also other evidence of conflict to come; traditional conceptions of military professionalism—particularly the ethical and professional norms of the officer corps—have been evolving away from concepts and behaviors that facilitate civil-military cooperation.

If the manifestations of diminished civilian control were simply a sine curve—that is, a low period in a recurring pattern—or the coincidence of a strong Joint Chiefs and a weak president during a critical transitional period in American history and national defense (the end of the Cold War), there would be little cause for concern. Civilian control, as we have seen, is situational and indeed to a degree cyclical. But the present decline extends back before the Clinton administration. There are indications that the current trend began before the Vietnam War and has since been aggravated by a weakening of the nation's social, political, and institutional structures that had, over the course of American history, assured civilian control.

For more than two centuries, civilian control has rested on four foundations that individually and in combination not only prevented any direct military threat to civilian government but kept military influence, even in wartime, largely contained within the boundaries of professional expertise and concerns. First has been the rule of law, and with it reverence for a constitution that provided explicitly for civilian control of the military. Any violation of the Constitution or its process has been sure to bring retribution from one or all three of the branches of government, with public support. Second,

Americans once kept their regular forces small. The United States relied in peacetime on ocean boundaries to provide sufficient warning of attack and depended on a policy of mobilization to repel invasion or to wage war. Thus the regular military could never endanger civilian government—in peacetime because of its size, and in wartime because the ranks were filled with citizens unlikely to cooperate or acquiesce in anything illegal or unconstitutional. The very reliance on citizen soldiers—militia, volunteers, and conscripts pressed temporarily into service to meet an emergency—was a third safeguard of civilian control. Finally, the armed forces themselves internalized military subordination to civil authority. They accepted it willingly as an axiom of American government and the foundation of military professionalism. "You must remember that when we enter the army we do so with the full knowledge that our first duty is toward the government, entirely regardless of our own views under any given circumstances," Major General John J. Pershing instructed First Lieutenant George S. Patton, Jr., in 1916. "We are at liberty to express our personal views only when called upon to do so or else confidentially to our friends, but always confidentially and with the complete understanding that they are in no sense to govern our actions."[57] As Omar Bradley, the first chairman of the Joint Chiefs of Staff, put it, "Thirty-two years in the peacetime army had taught me to do my job, hold my tongue, and keep my name out of the papers."[58]

Much has changed. More than sixty years of hot and cold war, a large military establishment, world responsibilities, a searing failure in Vietnam, and changes in American society, among other factors, have weakened these four foundations upon which civilian control has rested in the United States.

The first, and most troubling, development is the skepticism, even cynicism, now expressed about government, lawyers, and justice, part of a broad and generation-long diminution of respect for people and institutions that has eroded American civic culture and faith in law. Polling data show that Americans today have the most confidence in their least democratic institutions: the military, small business, the police, and the Supreme Court. Americans express the least confidence in the most democratic: Congress.[59] So dangerous is this trend that Harvard's Kennedy School of Government established a "Visions of Governance for the Twenty-first Century" project to explore the phenomenon, study its implications, and attempt to counteract some of its more deleterious effects.[60] Americans cannot continue to vilify government, the U.S. government in particular, and expect patriotism to prosper or even survive as a fundamental civic value.

Second, the media, traditionally the herald of liberty in this society, has become less substantial, more superficial, less knowledgeable, more focused on profit, less professional, and more trivial. About the only liberty the media seems to champion vocally is the freedom of the press. Issues of civilian control seem to escape the press; time after time, events or issues that in past years would have been framed or interpreted as touching upon civilian control now go unnoticed and unreported, at least in those terms.[61]

Third, the nation's core civic culture has deteriorated. Such basic social institutions as marriage and the family, and such indicators of society's health as crime rates and out-of-wedlock births, while stabilizing or improving in the 1990s, clearly have weakened over time. Our communities, neighborhoods, civic organizations, fraternal groups, and social gatherings have diminished in favor of individual entertainment; people are staying at home with cable television, the videocassette recorder, and the Internet, thereby avoiding crime, crowds, traffic, and the crumbling physical and social infrastructure of our society. American society has become more splintered and people more isolated into small groups, "clustered" geographically and demographically around similar values, culture, and lifestyles. With this deterioration of civic cohesion—gated communities being perhaps emblematic—has come a weakening of shared values: less truthfulness, less generosity, less sacrifice, less social consciousness, less faith, less common agreement on ethical behavior, and more advocacy, acrimony, individualism, relativism, materialism, cynicism, and self-gratification. The 11 September attacks and the war on terrorism are unlikely to reverse these trends as long as the national leadership exhorts the American people to go back to "normal."[62]

Civilian control is one common understanding that seems to have faded in American civic consciousness. The American people—whose study and understanding of civics and government generally have declined—have lost their traditional skepticism about the professional military that made civilian control a core political assumption, one that was widely understood and periodically voiced. Simply put, the public no longer thinks about civilian control—does not understand it, does not discuss it, and does not grasp how it can and should operate.[63] An occasional popular movie like *The Siege* and *Thirteen Days* raises the issue, but most recent films caricature the military or, like *GI Jane* and *Rules of Engagement*, lionize an honest, brave, faithful military and demonize lying, avaricious politicians.[64]

Fourth, in the last generation the United States has abandoned the first principle of civilian control, the bedrock practice extending back into premodern England—reliance on the citizen soldier for national defense.[65] National security policy no longer seriously envisions mobilizing industry and the population for large-scale war. Americans in uniform, whether they serve for one hitch or an entire career, are taught to (and do) view themselves as professionals. In the National Guard and reserves, whose members are thought to be the apotheosis of citizen soldiers, some hold civilian government jobs in their units or elsewhere in the government national security community, and others serve on active duty considerably more than the traditional one weekend a month and two weeks a year.[66]

Furthermore, while Guardsmen and reservists both voice and believe the traditional rhetoric about citizen-soldiering, the views of their up-and-coming officers mirror almost exactly those of their regular counterparts.[67] Reserve forces are spending more and more time on active duty, not simply for temporary duty for the present crisis of homeland defense. Increasingly, the National Guard and reserves are being used interchangeably with the regulars, even in overseas deployments on constabulary missions, something wholly unprecedented.[68] Even if they call themselves citizen soldiers, the fundamental distinction between citizens and soldiers has so blurred that in 1998, at two of the most respected U.S. institutions of professional military education, Marine majors who had spent their adult lives in uniform and National Guard adjutant generals who had done the same could both insist that they were "citizen soldiers."[69] Americans have lost the high regard they once possessed for temporary military service as an obligation of citizenship, along with their former understanding of its underlying contribution to civic cohesion and civilian control of the military.[70]

Today, fewer Americans serve or know people who do, and the numbers will decline as smaller percentages of the population serve in uniform.[71] Their sense of ownership of or interest in the military, and their understanding of the distinctiveness of military culture—its ethos and needs—have declined. In recent years the number of veterans serving in the U.S. Congress has fallen 50 percent, and the remaining veterans constitute a smaller percentage of the members of Congress than veterans do of the population as a whole, reversing (in 1995) a pattern that had endured since the turn of the century.[72] The effect is dramatic; less than ten years ago, 62 percent of the Senate and 41 percent of the House were veterans. Today in the 107th Congress, the figure for the Senate is 38 percent, and for the House, 29 percent.[73]

Finally, at the same time that civilian control has weakened in the awareness of the public, so too has the principle declined in the consciousness and professional understanding of the American armed forces. Historically, one of the chief bulwarks of civilian control has been the American military establishment itself. Its small size in peacetime, the professionalism of the officers, their political neutrality, their willing subordination, and their acceptance of a set of unwritten but largely understood rules of behavior in the civil-military relationship—all had made civilian control succeed, messy as it sometimes was and situational as it must always be. In the last half-century, however, while everyone in the armed forces has continued to support the concept, the ethos and *mentalité* of the officer corps have changed in ways that damage civil-military cooperation and undermine civilian control.

Reversing a century and a half of practice, the American officer corps has become partisan in political affiliation, and overwhelmingly Republican. Beginning with President Richard Nixon's politics of polarization—the "southern strategy" and reaching out to the "hard-hats"—Republicans embraced traditional patriotism and strong national defense as central parts of their national agenda. During the late 1970s—years of lean defense budgets and the "hollow force"—and in the 1980s, when Ronald Reagan made rebuilding the armed forces and taking the offensive in the Cold War centerpieces of his presidency, Republicans reached out to the military as a core constituency. They succeeded in part because, in the wake of Vietnam, the Democratic Party virtually abandoned the military, offering antimilitary rhetoric and espousing reduced defense spending. During the same period, voting in elections began to become a habit in the officer corps. In the 1950s, the Federal Voting Assistance Program came into existence in order to help enlisted men, most of whom were draftees or draft-induced volunteers, to vote. In every unit an officer was designated to connect the program to the men, and undoubtedly the task began to break down slowly what had been something of a taboo against officers exercising their franchise. How (the logic must have been) could officers encourage their soldiers to vote if they themselves abstained?[74]

Today the vast majority of officers not only vote but identify with a political philosophy and party. Comparison of a sample by the Triangle Institute of Security Studies of active-duty officers (see endnote 25) with earlier data shows a shift from over 54 percent independent, "no preference," or "other" in a 1976 survey to 28 percent in 1998–99, and from 33 percent to 64 percent Republican today.[75] In the presidential election of 2000, Republicans targeted military voters by organizing endorsements from retired flag officers, advertising in military publications, using Gulf War heroes Colin Powell and H. Norman Schwarzkopf on the campaign trail, urging service members to register and vote, and focusing special effort on absentee military voters—a group that proved critical, perhaps the margin of victory, in Florida, where thousands of armed forces personnel maintain their legal residency.[76]

Before the present generation, American military officers (since before the Civil War) had abstained as a group from party politics, studiously avoiding any partisanship of word or deed, activity, or affiliation. By George C. Marshall's time, the practice was not even to vote.[77] A handful of the most senior officers pursued political ambitions, usually trying to parlay wartime success into the presidency. A very few even ran for office while on active duty. But these were exceptions. The belief was that the military, as the neutral servant of the state, stood above the dirty business of politics. Professional norms dictated faith and loyalty not just in deed but in spirit to whoever held the reins of power under the constitutional system. For Marshall's generation, partisan affiliation and voting conflicted with military professionalism.[78]

Marshall and his fellow officers must have sensed that the habit of voting leads to partisan thinking, inclining officers to become invested in particular policy choices or decisions that relate directly to their professional responsibilities.[79] Officers at every level have to bring difficult and sometimes unpopular duties to their troops and motivate the latter to carry them out. Likewise, senior officers must represent the needs and perspectives of the troops to political leaders even when they are unsolicited or unwanted. How effective can that advice be if the civilians know the officers are opposed to a policy in question? What are the effects on morale when the troops know their officers dislike, disrespect, or disagree with the politicians, or think a mission is unwise, ill conceived, or unnecessary?

The consequences of partisanship can also be more subtle and indirect but equally far-reaching, even to the point of contempt for civilian policy and politicians or of unprofessional, disruptive behavior, as in 1993. The belief is current today among officers that the core of the Democratic Party is "hostile to military culture" and engaged in a "culture war" against the armed forces, mostly because of pressure for further gender integration and open homosexual service.[80] During the 2000 election campaign, when Al Gore stumbled briefly by supporting a "litmus test" on gays in the military for selecting members of the Joint Chiefs, he confirmed for many in uniform the idea that Democrats do not understand the military profession or care about its effectiveness. His campaign's effort to minimize the effect of absentee votes in Florida and elsewhere through technical challenges outraged the armed forces, raising worries that a Gore victory might spark an exodus from the ranks or that a Gore administration would have relations with the military even more troubled than Clinton's.[81]

Partisan politicization loosens the connection of the military to the American people. If the public begins to perceive the military as an interest group driven by its own needs and agenda, support—and trust—will diminish. Already there are hints. When a random survey asked a thousand Americans in the fall of 1998 how often military leaders would try to avoid carrying out orders they opposed, over two-thirds answered at least "some of the time."[82]

Partisanship also poisons the relationship between the president and the uniformed leadership. When a group of retired flag officers, including former regional commanders and members of the Joint Chiefs, endorsed presidential candidates in 1992 and again in 2000, they broadcast their politicization to the public and further legitimated partisanship in the ranks—for everyone knows that four-stars never really retire. Like princes of the church, they represent the culture and the profession just as authoritatively as their counterparts on active duty. If senior retired officers make a practice of endorsing presidential contenders, will the politicians trust the generals and admirals on active duty, in particular those who serve at the top, to have the loyalty and discretion not to retire and use their inside knowledge to try to overturn policies or elect opponents? Will not presidents begin to vet candidates for the top jobs for their pliability or (equally deleteriously) their party or political views, rather than for excellence, achievement, character, and candor? Over time, the result will be weak military advice, declining military effectiveness, and accelerating politicization.

The investment of officers in one policy or another will lead civilians to question whether military recommendations are the best professional advice of the nation's military experts. Perhaps one reason Bill Clinton and his people dealt with the military at arm's length was that he and they knew that officers were the most solidly Republican group in the government.[83] One need only read Richard Holbrooke's memoir about negotiating the Dayton accords in 1995 to plumb the depth of suspicion between military and civilian at the highest levels. Convinced that the military opposed the limited bombing campaign against the Bosnian Serbs, Holbrooke and Secretary of State Warren Christopher believed that the vice chairman of the Joint Chiefs was lying to them when he asserted that the Air Force was running out of targets.[84]

Certainly officers have the right to vote and to participate privately in the nation's political life. No one questions the legal entitlement of retired officers to run for office or endorse candidates. But these officers must recognize the corrosive effects on military professionalism and the threat to the military establishment's relationship with Congress, the executive branch, and the American people that such partisan behavior has. Possessing a right and exercising it are two very different things.

A second example of changing military professionalism has been the widespread attitude among officers that civilian society has become corrupt, even degenerate, while the military has remained a repository for virtue, perhaps its one remaining bastion, in an increasingly unraveling social fabric, of the traditional values that make the country strong. Historically, officers have often decried the selfishness, commercialism, and disorder that seems to characterize much of American society.[85] But that opinion today has taken on a harder, more critical, more moralistic edge; it is less leavened by that sense of acceptance that enabled officers in the past to tolerate the clash between their values and those of a democratic, individualistic civilian culture and to reconcile the conflict with their own continued service.

Nearly 90 percent of the elite military officers (regular and reserves) surveyed in 1998–99 by the Triangle Institute for Security Studies agreed that "the decline of traditional values is contributing to the breakdown of our society." Some 70 percent thought that "through leading by example, the military could help American society become more moral," and 75 percent believed that "civilian society would be better off if it adopted more of the military's values and customs."[86] Is it healthy for civilian control when the members of the American armed forces believe that they are morally, organizationally, institutionally, and personally superior to the rest of society—and are contemptuous of that society? Do we wish civic society in a democratic country to adopt military norms, values, outlooks, and behaviors? In my judgment that is an utter misreading of the role and function of our armed forces. Their purpose is to defend society, not to define it. The latter is militarism, in the classic definition—the same thinking that in part inclined the French and German armies to intervene in the politics of their nations in the twentieth century.

A third, and most disturbing, change in military sentiment is the belief that officers should confront and resist civilians whose policies or decisions they believe threaten to weaken national defense or lead the country into disaster. Many hold that officers should speak out publicly, or work behind the scenes, to stop or modify a policy, or resign in protest. Some senior leaders have been willing to speak publicly on issues of national security, foreign relations, and military policy before it is formulated, and afterward as spokespersons for what are often highly controversial and partisan initiatives or programs. In 1998 and 1999, the respected retired Army colonel and political scientist Sam Sarkesian, and the much-decorated Marine veteran, novelist, and former secretary of the Navy James Webb, called publicly for military leaders to participate in national security policy debates, not merely as advisers to the civilian leadership but as public advocates, an idea that seems to resonate with many in the armed forces today.[87] "Military subservience to political control applies to existing policy, not to policy debates," admonished Webb—as if officers can subscribe to policy and debate it honestly at the same time.[88] Such behavior politicizes military issues and professional officers directly, for rare is the military issue that remains insulated from politics and broader national life.

This willingness—indeed, in some cases eagerness—to strive to shape public opinion and thereby affect decisions and policy outcomes is a dangerous development for the U.S. military and is extraordinarily corrosive of civilian control. Is it proper for military officers to leak information to the press "to discredit specific policies—procurement decisions, prioritization plans, operations that the leaker opposes," as Admiral Crowe in his memoirs admits happens "sometimes," even "copiously"?[89] Is it proper for the four services, the regional commanders, or the Joint Chiefs every year to advocate to the public directly their needs for ships, airplanes, divisions, troops, and other resources, or their views on what percentage of the nation's economy should go to defense as opposed to other priorities?[90] This advocacy reached such a cacophony in the fall of 2000 that the secretary of defense warned the military leadership not "to beat the drum with a tin cup" for their budgets during the presidential campaign and the transition to a new administration.[91]

Do we wish the military leadership to argue the merits of intervention in the Balkans or elsewhere, of whether to sign treaties on land-mine use or war crimes, in order to mobilize public opinion one way or the other, before the president decides? Imagine that we are back in 1941. Should the Army and the Navy pronounce publicly on the merits or demerits of Lend-Lease, or convoy escort, or the occupation of Iceland, or the Europe-first strategy? Or imagine it is 1861—should the nation's military leaders publicly discuss whether to reinforce Fort Sumter? Would it be advisable for senior officers to proclaim openly their varied opinions of whether the South's secession ought to (or can) be opposed by plunging the country into civil war? Should senior military officers question the president's strategy in the midst of a military operation, as was done in 1999 through media leaks in the first week of the bombing campaign over Kosovo?[92] In such instances, what happens to the president's, and Congress's, authority and credibility with the public, and to their ability to lead the nation? How does such advocacy affect the trust and confidence between the president, his cabinet officers, and the most senior generals and admirals, trust and confidence that is so necessary for effective national defense?[93]

The way in which military officers have interpreted a study of the role of the Joint Chiefs of Staff in the decision on intervention and in the formulation of strategy for Southeast Asia in 1963–65 exemplifies the erosion of professional norms and values. H. R. McMaster's *Dereliction of Duty: Lyndon Johnson, Robert McNamara, the Joint Chiefs of Staff and the Lies That Led to Vietnam* is by all accounts the history book most widely read and discussed in the military in the last several years.[94] Officers believe that McMaster validates long-standing military convictions about Vietnam—that the Joint Chiefs, lacking a proper understanding of their role and not having the courage to oppose the Johnson administration's strategy of gradualism that they knew would fail, should have voiced their opposition, publicly if necessary, and resigned rather than carry out that strategy. Had they done so, goes this credo, they would have saved the country a tragic, costly, humiliating, and above all, unnecessary, defeat.[95]

McMaster's book neither says nor implies that the chiefs should have obstructed U.S. policy in Vietnam in any other way than by presenting their views frankly and forcefully to their civilian superiors, and speaking honestly to the Congress when asked for their views. It neither states nor suggests that the chiefs should have opposed President Lyndon Johnson's orders and policies by leaks, public statements, or by resignations, unless an officer personally and professionally could not stand, morally and ethically, to carry out the chosen policy. There is in fact no tradition of resignation in the

American military. In 1783, at Newburgh, New York, as the war for independence was ending, the American officer corps rejected individual or mass resignation—which can be indistinguishable from mutiny. George Washington persuaded them not to march on Congress or refuse orders in response to congressional unwillingness to pay them or guarantee their hard-earned pensions. The precedent has survived for more than two centuries. No American army ever again considered open insubordination.

Proper professional behavior cannot include simply walking away from a policy, an operation, or a war an officer believes is wrong or will fail. That is what the Left advocated during the Vietnam War, and the American military rightly rejected it. Imagine the consequences if the Union army had decided in late 1862 that it had signed on to save the Union but not to free the slaves and had resigned en masse because of disagreement (which was extensive) with the Emancipation Proclamation. More recently, Air Force chief of staff Ronald Fogleman did not resign in protest in 1997, as many officers wish to believe; he requested early retirement and left in such a manner—quietly, without a full explanation—precisely so as *not* to confront his civilian superior over a decision with which he deeply disagreed.[96] All McMaster says (and believes), and all that is proper in the American system, is that military officers should advise honestly and forthrightly, or advocate in a confidential capacity, a course of action. Whether their advice is heeded or not, if the policy or decision is legal, they are to carry it out.

Resignation in protest directly assails civilian control. Issuing a public explanation for resignation, however diplomatically couched, amounts to marshaling all of an officer's military knowledge, expertise, and experience—as well as the profession's standing with the public and reputation for disinterested patriotism—to undercut some undertaking or concept that the officer opposes. The fact that officers today either ignore or are oblivious to this basic aspect of their professional ethics and would countenance, even admire, such truculent behavior illustrates both a fundamental misunderstanding of civilian control and its weakening as a primary professional value.[97]

Our military leaders have already traveled far in the direction of self-interested bureaucratic behavior in the last half-century, to become advocates for policy outcomes as opposed to advisers—presenting not only the military perspective on a problem, or the needs of the military establishment and national defense, or the interests of their services or branches, but their own views of foreign and military policy—even, as we have seen, pressing these efforts outside the normal advisory channels. Some of this is unthinking, some the product of civilian abrogation of responsibility, and some is the unintended consequence of the Goldwater-Nichols Act, which so strengthened the chairman and the regional commanders. But let us be clear: some is quite conscious. In his memoirs, Colin Powell, the most celebrated soldier of the era, wrote that he learned as a White House Fellow, from his most important mentor, that in the government "you never know what you can get away with until you try."[98] Is that a proper standard of professional behavior for a uniformed officer? He also declared that his generation of officers "vowed that when our turn came to call the shots, we would not quietly acquiesce in halfhearted warfare for half-baked reasons that the American people could not understand or support."[99] Is that a proper view of military subordination to civilian authority?

Unfortunately, General Powell's views mirror attitudes that have become widespread over the last generation. The survey of officer and civilian attitudes and opinions undertaken by the Triangle Institute in 1998–99 discovered that many officers believe that they have the duty to force their own views on civilian decision makers when the United States is contemplating committing American forces abroad. When "asked whether . . . military leaders should be neutral, advise, advocate, or insist on having their way in . . . the decision process" to use military force, 50 percent or more of the up-and-coming active-duty officers answered "insist," on the following issues: "setting rules of engagement, ensuring that clear political and military goals exist . . . , developing an 'exit strategy,'" and "deciding what kinds of military units . . . will be used to accomplish all tasks."[100] In the context of the questionnaire, "insist" definitely implied that officers should try to compel acceptance of the military's recommendations.

In 2000, a three-star general casually referred to a uniformed culture in the Pentagon that labels the Office of the Secretary of Defense as "the enemy"—because it exercises civilian control.[101] In 1999, staff officers of the National Security Council deliberately attempted to promulgate a new version of the national security strategy quickly enough to prevent the president from enunciating his own principles first.[102] In 1997 the chairman of the Joint Chiefs urged the chiefs to block Congress's effort to reform the military establishment through the Quadrennial Defense Review.[103] In the early 1990s, senior officers presented alternatives for the use of American forces abroad specifically designed to discourage the civilian leadership from intervening in the first place.[104] Twice in the past five years members of the Joint Chiefs have threatened to resign as a means of blocking a policy or decision.[105]

Thus, in the last generation, the American military has slipped from conceiving of its primary role as advice to civilians followed by execution of their orders, to trying—as something proper, even essential in some situations—to impose its viewpoint on policies or decisions. In other words, American officers have, over the course of the Cold War and in reaction to certain aspects of it, forgotten or abandoned their historical stewardship of civilian control, their awareness of the requirement to maintain it, and their understanding of the proper boundaries and behaviors that made it work properly and effectively. That so many voices applaud this behavior or sanction it by their silence suggests that a new definition of military professionalism may be forming, at least in civil-military relations. If so, the consequences are not likely to benefit national security; they could alter the character of American government itself.

Even military readers who accept my presentation of facts may find my concerns overblown. Certainly, there is no crisis. The American military conceives of itself as loyal and patriotic; it universally expresses support for civilian control as a fundamental principle of government and of military professionalism. Yet at the same time, the evidence is overwhelming that civil-military relationships have deteriorated in the U.S. government. The underlying structures of civilian society and the military profession that traditionally supported the system of civilian control have weakened. Over the course of the last generation, much influence and actual power has migrated to the military, which has either been allowed to define, or has itself claimed, an expanded role in foreign policy and national security decision making.[106] The reasons are complex—partly circumstance, partly civilian inattention or politically motivated timidity. But a further reason is that military leaders have either forgotten or chosen to ignore the basic behaviors by which civil-military relations support military effectiveness and civilian control at the same time. Whatever the causes, the consequences are dangerous. Increased military influence, combined with the American people's ignorance of or indifference to civilian control and the misreading of the bounds of professional behavior on the part of senior military officers, could in the future produce a civil-military clash that damages American government or compromises the nation's defense.

That civilians in the executive and legislative branches of government over the last generation bear ultimate responsibility for these developments is beyond doubt. Some on both sides seem to sense it. Secretaries of defense came into office in 1989, 1993, and 2001 concerned about military subordination and determined to exert their authority. Civilian officials have the obligation to make the system work, not to abdicate for any reason. But to rely on the politicians to restore the proper balance is to ignore the conditions and processes that can frustrate civilian control. The historical record is not encouraging. Over two centuries, the officials elected and appointed to rule the military have varied enormously in knowledge, experience, understanding, and motivation. Their propensity to exercise civilian control and to provide sound, forceful leadership has been variable, largely situational, and unpredictable.[107]

Nor can the changes in American society and political understanding that have weakened civilian control be easily reversed. National defense will capture at best superficial public attention even during a war on terrorism, unless military operations are ongoing or the government asks for special sacrifice. In wartime, Americans want to rely more on military advice and authority, not less. Over time, a smaller and smaller percentage of Americans are likely to perform military service; without a conscious effort by the media to avoid caricaturing military culture, and by colleges and universities to expand programs in military history and security studies, future generations of civilian leaders will lack not only the experience of military affairs but the comprehension of the subject needed to make civilian control work effectively.

A better way to alter the equation is for officers to recall the attitudes and rejuvenate the behaviors that civilian control requires. Certainly every officer supports the concept; every officer swears at commissioning "to support and defend the Constitution of the United States" and to "bear true faith and allegiance" to the same.[108] Because civilian control pervades the Constitution, the oath is a personal promise to preserve, protect, defend, and support civilian control, in actual practice as well as in words. The requirement for such an oath was written into the Constitution for precisely that purpose.[109] Officers do not swear to strive to maximize their services' budgets, or to try to achieve certain policy outcomes, or to attempt to reshape civilian life toward a military vision of the good society.

Individual officers at every level would do well to examine their personal views of civilians, particularly of their clients: the American people, elected officials, and those appointed to exercise responsibility in national security affairs. A certain amount of caution, skepticism, and perhaps even mistrust is healthy. But contempt for clients destroys the professional relationship. Lawyers cannot provide sound counsel, doctors effective treatment, ministers worthwhile support, teachers significant education—when they do not understand and respect their clients. Military officers who feel contempt for their elected or appointed supervisors, or the voters who placed them in office, are unlikely to advise them wisely or carry out their policies effectively.

Officers should investigate their own professional views of civilian control. On what do you base your thinking? Much of the problem I have discussed may stem from the Cold War, or from one particular campaign of it, Vietnam, which continues to cast a long, if sometimes unnoticed, shadow. Are you positive that your thinking about civil-military relations does not rest on the mistaken beliefs—and they *are* mistaken—that the war was lost because of too much civilian control, or that we succeeded so magnificently in the Persian Gulf in 1991 because the civilians "[got] out of the way and let the military fight and win the war"?[110] Neither of those interpretations fit the facts of what happened in either war.[111]

Ponder whether you are prepared to accept, as a principle of civilian control, that it includes the right of civilians to be wrong, to make mistakes—indeed, to insist on making mistakes.[112] This may be very hard to accept, given that people's lives, or the security of the nation, hang in the balance. But remember that the military can be wrong, dead wrong, about military affairs—for after all, you are not politicians, and as Carl von Clausewitz wrote long ago, war is an extension of politics.[113] Were you prepared to work for and with, and to accept, a Gore administration had the Democratic candidate won the 2000 election? If there is doubt on your part, ponder the implications for civil-military relations and civilian control. It is likely that within the next dozen years, there will be another Democratic administration. If the trend toward increasing friction and hostility in civil-military relations during the last three—those of Johnson, Carter, and Clinton—continues into the future, the national security of the United States will not be well served.

Last of all, consider that if civilian control is to function effectively, the uniformed military will have not only to forswear or abstain from certain behavior but actively encourage civilians to exercise their authority and perform their legal and constitutional duty to make policy and decisions. You cannot and will not solve those problems yourselves, nor is it your responsibility alone. Civilian behavior and historical circumstances are just as much the causes of the present problems in civil-military relations as any diminution of military professionalism. But you can help educate and develop civilian leaders in their roles and on the processes of policy making, just as your predecessors did, by working with them and helping them—without taking advantage of them, even when the opportunity arises. Proper professional behavior calls for a certain amount of abstinence. What is being asked of you is no more or less than is asked of other professionals who must subordinate their self-interest when serving their clients and customers: lawyers to act against their self-interest and advise clients not to press frivolous claims; doctors not to prescribe treatments that are unnecessary; accountants to audit their clients' financial statements fully and honestly; clergymen to refrain from exploiting the trust of parishioners or congregants.[114] It will be up to you to shape the relationship with your particular client, just as others do. At its heart, the relationship involves civilian control in fact as well as form.

Civilian control ultimately must be considered in broad context. In the long history of human civilization, there have been military establishments that have focused on external defense—on protecting their societies—and those that have preyed upon their own populations.[115] The American military has never preyed on this society. Yet democracy, as a widespread form of governance, is rather a recent phenomenon, and our country has been fortunate to be perhaps the leading example for the rest of the world. For us, civilian control has been more a matter of making certain the civilians control military affairs than of keeping the military out of civilian politics. But if the United States is to teach civilian control—professional military behavior—to countries overseas, its officers must look hard at their own system and their own behavior at the same time.[116] Our government must champion civilian control in all circumstances, without hesitation. In April 2002 the United States acted with stupefying and self-defeating hypocrisy when the White House initially expressed pleasure at the apparent overthrow of President Hugo Chavez in Venezuela by that country's military, condoning an attempted coup while other nations in the hemisphere shunned the violation of democratic and constitutional process.[117] "No one pretends that democracy is perfect or all-wise," Winston Churchill shrewdly observed in 1947. "Indeed, it has been said that democracy is the worst form of Government except all those other forms that have been tried."[118] Churchill certainly knew the tensions involved in civil-military relations as well as any democratic head of government in modern history. Both sides—civilian and military—need to be conscious of these problems and to work to ameliorate them.

Notes

1. Defenders of the chiefs' behavior in the 1992–93 firestorm over gays in the military often assert that the Clinton administration's intention to lift the ban on homosexual service was blocked not by the military but by Congress. However, military leaders very clearly encouraged their retired predecessors to lobby the Congress against Clinton's intentions. "The word went out to the senior retirees," recalls a knowledgeable, well-connected retired Army brigadier general; "'We've lost unless you can generate enough pressure on Congress to block this.'" Theodore Metaxis to the author, 24 October 1999. See also Theo. C. Metaxis, "Discipline, Morale Require Ban on Homosexuals," *Fayetteville (North Carolina) Observer-Times*, 28 January 1993, p. 15A, especially the closing two paragraphs, in which Metaxis calls on the public to "let the president and Congress know how you feel" and on the military to "put on your 'civilian hat,' the one you wear when you vote. Write your friends and relatives and let them know how you feel, and ask them to write to Washington. Then sit down and write to the president and Congress—let them know how you personally feel. For the officers and NCOs, tell them how your responsibility to command will be eroded. For the soldiers living in barracks, since the Clinton administration just doesn't 'get it,' call or write to them, explaining what the effect would be on you. If you don't take action, the torrent of PR publicity from the homosexual lobby may carry the day." See also Eric Schmitt, "The Top Soldier Is Torn between 2 Loyalties," *New York Times*, 6 February 1993, p. 1; "Aspin Seeks a Deal on Gays That the Brass Will Bless," *Congressional Quarterly*, 26 June 1993, p. 1670; Eric Schmitt and Thomas L. Friedman, "Clinton and Powell Forge Bond for Mutual Survival," *New York Times*, 4 June 1993, p. 1; Richard Lacayo, "The Rebellious Soldier," *Time*, 15 February 1993, p. 32; Janet E. Halley, *Don't: A Reader's Guide to the Military's Anti-Gay Policy* (Durham, N.C.: Duke Univ. Press, 1999), pp. 20–5. The extent of the president's defeat is revealed in George Stephanopoulos, *All Too Human: A Political Education* (Boston: Little, Brown, 1999), pp. 155–63; Elizabeth Drew, *On the Edge: The Clinton Presidency* (New York: Simon and Schuster, 1994), pp. 42–8, 248–51.

2. Quoted in John Lancaster, "Air Force General Demands Tight Formation for Commander in Chief," *Washington Post*, 22 April 1993, p. 1, and "Accused of Ridiculing Clinton, General Faces Air Force Probe," *Washington Post*, 8 June 1993, p. 21. See also "The President and the General," 11 June 1993, p. 20, and "Transcript of President Clinton's News Conference," 16 June 1993, p. 14, both *Washington Post;* "A Military Breach?" *Seattle Post-Intelligencer*, 11 June 1993, p. 10; David H. Hackworth, "Rancor in the Ranks: The Troops vs. the President," *Newsweek*, 28 June 1993, p. 24; and Associated Press, "General's Lampoon of Clinton Not His First," *Washington Times*, 8 July 1993, p. 5.

3. The events described below were covered extensively in the daily press, journals of opinion, and other local and national media, 1993–2001.

4. The vitriol on gender and sexual orientation is revealed by Stephanie Gutman, *The Kinder, Gentler Military: Can America's Gender-Neutral Fighting Force Still Win Wars?* (New York: Scribner's, 2000).

5. The arguments over readiness became so ugly by 1998 that the Joint Chiefs and U.S. senators engaged in public accusations of dishonest testimony and lack of support. See Eric Schmitt, "Joint Chiefs Accuse Congress of Weakening U.S. Defense," *New York Times*, 30 September 1998, p. 1. The military opposition to Clinton's interventions was almost immediate; see Richard A. Serrano and Art Pine, "Many in Military Angry over Clinton's Policies," *Los Angeles Times* (Washington ed.), 19 October 1993, p. 1. The arguments over readiness continued. See Elaine M. Grossman, "Congressional Aide Finds Spending on 'Core Readiness' in Decline," *Inside the Pentagon*, 28 June 2001, p. 1.

6. Rowan Scarborough, "Marine Officer Probed for Blasting Clinton," *Washington Times*, 11 November 1998, p. 1, and "Major Gets Punished for Criticizing President," *Washington Times*, 7 December 1998, p. 1; C. J. Chivers, "Troops Obey Clinton despite Disdain," *USA Today*, 18 November 1998, p. 27A; Pat Towell, "Keeping a Civil Tongue," *CQ Weekly*, 2 January 1999, p. 26. Article 88, "Contempt toward officials," reads: "Any commissioned officer who uses contemptuous words against the President, the Vice President, Congress, the Secretary of Defense, the Secretary of a military department,

the Secretary of Transportation, or the Governor or the legislature of any State, Territory, Commonwealth, or possession in which he is on active duty or present shall be punished as a court-martial may direct." U.S. Defense Dept., *Manual for Courts-Martial United States (1995 Edition)* (Washington, D.C.: Joint Service Committee on Military Justice, 1995), pp. A2–A23. The history of this provision and its enforcement is covered in John G. Kester, "Soldiers Who Insult the President: An Uneasy Look at Article 88 of the Uniform Code of Military Justice," *Harvard Law Review*, vol. 81, 1967–68, pp. 1697–769; Daniel Blumenthal, "A Brief Overview of Article 88 of the Uniform Code of Military Justice," Strategy and Policy Seminar, Johns Hopkins School of Advanced International Studies, Washington, D.C., 4 December 1998.

7. "Wicked Wit," *New York Post*, 11 October 1999, p. 6.

8. Thomas E. Ricks, "Military Personnel Warned on Politics," *Washington Post*, 30 November 2000, p. 35. An Army officer, receiving the reminder by mass distribution in his command, recalled that "this was perhaps the fourth or fifth time in the past 8 years [i.e., the Clinton administration] that I have received some official reminder of Article 88." E-mail to the author, 27 November 2000. See also Robert G. Bracknell [Capt., USMC], "The Marine Officer's Moral and Legal Imperative of Political Abstinence," *Marine Corps Gazette*, September 2000, pp. 102–7.

9. Another major embarrassment singed the new administration when a female civilian staffer insulted Army lieutenant general Barry McCaffrey, a much-decorated and thrice-wounded veteran of Vietnam and commander of the 24th Infantry Division in the Gulf War. McCaffrey was then serving as assistant to the chairman of the Joint Chiefs of Staff. In response to a casual "good morning" in the White House, the staffer replied something to the effect of "We [or I] don't talk to people in uniform." Within hours the incident ricocheted all over Washington and into the press, to the mortification of the administration. The impact of this insult was felt most acutely inside the Washington Beltway, and especially in the officer corps. Kenneth T. Walsh, Bruce B. Auster, and Tim Zimmermann, "Clinton's Warrior Woes,"

U.S. News and World Report, 15 March 1993, pp. 22ff.; Carl M. Cannon, "Military Feeling Resentful toward the White House," *Buffalo (New York) News,* 23 March 1993, p. 5. McCaffrey was one of the officers featured in James Kitfield, *Prodigal Soldiers* (New York: Simon and Schuster, 1995); see also Jay Nordlinger, "Clinton's Good Soldier," *National Review,* 3 May 1999, pp. 20–3.

10. Conversation with a senior official, Office of the Secretary of Defense, April 1993.

11. President Clinton undertook from the beginning to woo the military, in an attempt to overcome the hostility. Walsh et al., "Clinton's Warrior Woes," p. 22; Carl M. Cannon, "Clinton Reaches for Military Trust," *Baltimore Sun,* 30 May 1992, p. 22. But five years later, the relationship was hardly better than "a wary truce." "I can't think of any one thing the president has put more personal attention and caring into than his relationship with the military at all levels," White House press secretary Michael McCurry was quoted as saying. "He did it because he understood that he began with a significant deficit. He has tried to make a personal and human connection with his commanders and all the way down the chain." Brian McGrory, "U.S. Military, Clinton Achieve a Wary Truce," *Boston Globe,* 22 February 1998, p. 1. Indeed, two four-star officers having professional relationships with Clinton praised his discharge of his duties as commander in chief. See Richard H. Kohn, ed., "The Early Retirement of General Ronald R. Fogleman, Chief of Staff, United States Air Force," *Aerospace Power Journal,* Spring 2001, p. 16; Wesley K. Clark [Gen., USA], *Waging Modern War: Bosnia, Kosovo, and the Future of Combat* (New York: PublicAffairs, 2001), p. 290. However, the "personal and human connection" apparently never altered the Clinton-hating in the officer corps generally, which lasted for both his terms. See David Halberstam, *War in a Time of Peace: Bush, Clinton, and the Generals* (New York: Scribner's, 2001), pp. 415–9; Joseph Curl, "Military Finds Refreshing Change with New Commander in Chief," *Washington Times,* 13 February 2001, p. 1. For the economic trade emphasis of the administration's foreign policy, see Halberstam, *War in a Time of Peace,* p. 242; David E. Sanger, "Economic Engine for Foreign Policy," *New York Times,* 28 December 2000, p. A1. Scholarly analyses

of the Clinton foreign policy are William C. Berman, *From the Center to the Edge: The Politics and Policies of the Clinton Presidency* (Lanham, Md.: Rowman and Littlefield, 2001), pp. 35–8; Andrew J. Bacevich, *American Empire: The Realities and Consequences of U.S. Diplomacy* (Cambridge, Mass.: Harvard Univ. Press, in press [due fall 2002]).

12. Jane Perlez, "For 8 Years, a Strained Relationship with the Military," *New York Times,* 28 December 2000, p. A13.

13. "Clinton and the Generals," *Vanity Fair,* September 2001, p. 230.

14. In 1996, former congressman and secretary of defense (and now vice president) Dick Cheney observed: "If you look at the '92 election, the '94 congressional election, and I think even the 1996 presidential election, there has been almost no discussion—this will be the third election cycle without it—of the U.S. role in the world from a security standpoint, or strategic requirements, what our military ought to be doing, or how big the defense budget ought to be." Quoted in Stephen M. Duncan, *Citizen Warriors: America's National Guard and Reserve Forces and the Politics of National Security* (Novato, Calif.: Presidio, 1997), p. 225.

15. The most insightful brief analysis of the overall character of the military establishment is Eliot A. Cohen, "Defending America in the Twenty-first Century," *Foreign Affairs,* November/December 2000, pp. 40–56. For another persuasive argument for continuity with the Cold War establishment, see William Greider, *Fortress America: The American Military and the Consequences of Peace* (New York: PublicAffairs, 1998).

16. Michael R. Gordon, "Cuts Force Review of War Strategies," *New York Times,* 30 May 1993, p. 16. Barton Gellman, "Rumblings of Discord Heard in Pentagon; Aspin's Civilian Leadership, Management Style and Agenda Irk Some Officers," *Washington Post,* 20 June 1993, p. 1; John Lancaster, "Aspin Opts for Winning 2 Wars—Not 1½—at Once; Practical Effect of Notion Is Uncertain amid Huge Military Budget Cuts," *Washington Post,* 25 June 1993, p. A6. For a broad analysis of the Bottom-Up Review, see Donald Kagan and Frederick W. Kagan, *While America Sleeps: Self-Delusion, Military Weakness, and the Threat to Peace Today* (New York: St. Martin's, 2000), chap. 14.

17. The disjunction between resources and requirements, which became the subject of much debate and recrimination in the late 1990s, was clear by 1995. See Daniel Gouré and Jeffrey M. Ranney, *Averting the Defense Train Wreck in the New Millennium* (Washington, D.C.: Center for Strategic and International Studies, 1999), p. 1; Don M. Snider, "The Coming Defense Train Wreck," *Washington Quarterly*, Winter 1996, 89–101, with commentary on "what to do about it," pp. 103–24. Wesley Clark recalls that when he was a lieutenant general and head of plans (J-5) on the Joint Staff, beginning in 1994, "We had constructed a closed cycle bureaucratic instrument that would focus the U.S. Armed Forces' thinking on only two primary conflicts and then drive marginal investments of scarce resources to enhance these capabilities at the expense of other possible employments." This "wasn't intended to be a strategy for employing the forces—it was meant to defend the size of the military." Clark, *Waging Modern War*, pp. 47, 36.

18. A brief analysis of these dilemmas is John F. Lehman and Harvey Sicherman, "Demilitarizing the Military," Foreign Policy Research Institute *Wire*, July 1997. More extended analyses are Gouré and Ranney, *Averting the Defense Train Wreck*, chaps. 1–2; and Greider, *Fortress America*, esp. pp. 28–9, 36–9, 42–5.

19. For recent indications of how electronics and miniaturization, leading to greater accuracy of weapons, faster acquisition of targets, and more comprehensive networking of computer systems, and the like, might be affecting warfare and the armed services, see James Kitfield, "The Permanent Frontier," *National Journal*, 17 March 2001, p. 780; Joseph Fitchett, "Spying from Space: U.S. to Sharpen the Focus," *International Herald Tribune*, 10 April 2001, p. 1; Glenn W. Goodman, Jr., "Futuristic Army Vision: The Service's Future Combat System Is a True Leap-Ahead Program," *Armed Forces Journal International*, May 2001, p. 26; James Ware, "Virtual Defense," *Foreign Affairs*, May/June 2001, pp. 98–112; Nicholas Lemann, "Dreaming about War," *The New Yorker*, 16 July 2001, pp. 32–8; Bill Owens [Adm., USN, Ret.] with Ed Offley, *Lifting the Fog of War* (New York: Farrar, Straus, Giroux, 2000). An argument for continuity, at least for ground warfare, is Stephen Biddle, "Assessing Theories of Future Warfare," in *The Use of Force after the Cold War*, ed. H. W. Brands (College Station: Texas A&M Univ. Press, 2001), pp. 217–88. For an overview, see Lawrence Freedman, *The Revolution in Strategic Affairs*, International Institute for Strategic Studies, Adelphi Paper 318 (Oxford, U.K.: Oxford Univ. Press, 1998).

20. Congress began pressing the Joint Chiefs of Staff and Department of Defense to consider the problem of overlapping roles and missions among the armed services as early as 1992. Congress formed a commission to address those issues in 1995, pressed for a broader Quadrennial Defense Review (QDR) in 1997 (with a National Defense Panel to review and critique the effort immediately after), another QDR in 2001, and in 1998 urged the U.S. Commission on National Security/21st Century, to take an "end to end," or more comprehensive, look at national security and report in 2001. See Les Aspin, *Report on the Bottom-Up Review* (Washington, D.C.: Office of the Secretary of Defense, October 1993), available at www.fas.org/man/docs/bur/index.html; *Directions for Defense, Roles and Missions Commission of the Armed Forces: Report to Congress, the Secretary of Defense, and the Chairman of the Joint Chiefs of Staff*, 24 May 1995, executive summary, available at www.fas.org/man/docs/corm95/di1062.html; William S. Cohen, *Report of the Quadrennial Defense Review*, May 1997, available at www.defenselink.mil/pubs/qdr/index.html; Report of the National Defense Panel, December 1997, *Transforming Defense: National Security in the 21st Century*, available at www.fas.org/man/docs/ndp/toc.htm (links from this table of contents); *Road Map for National Security: Imperative for Change: The Phase III Report of the U.S. Commission on National Security/21st Century, March 15, 2001* (n.p. [Washington]: n.p. [U.S. Commission on National Security/21st Century], 2001); Background on the Quadrennial Defense Review May 1997, H.R. 3230, *National Defense Authorization Act for Fiscal Year 1997*, Title IX, Subtitle B, Sec. 923, *Quadrennial Defense Review—Force Structure Review*, available at www.comw.org/qdr/backgrd.html. For background, see Lorna S. Jaffe, *The Development of the Base Force* (Washington, D.C.: Joint History Office, Office of the Chairman of the Joint Chiefs of Staff, July 1993); *National Security Strategy of the United States* (Washington, D.C.: White House, August

1991); Colin Powell, Les Aspin, "DOD Bottom-Up Review, September 1, 1993," Defense Department briefing, Federal Information Systems Corporation, Federal News Service, accessed through Academic Universe, s.v. "Bottom Up Review" (13 December 2000). For an insider's admission of paralysis on change within the Pentagon and the failure of outside reform efforts, see Owens, *Lifting the Fog of War*, pp. 32–42, 166–77, 207–19. Revealing reportage about the 1997 QDR is in George Wilson, *This War Really Matters: Inside the Fight for Defense Dollars* (Washington, D.C.: Congressional Quarterly Press, 2000), chaps. 1–3.

21. As of 26 June 2001, some two-thirds of the fifty major recommendations of the U.S. Commission on National Security/21st Century "were being acted upon in some fashion by the Administration or Congress." Memorandum, "Recommendations' Status," 26 June 2001, enclosed in Charles G. Boyd to the author, 27 June 2001. The author was a member of the national security study group supporting the commission. The G. W. Bush administration is at least rhetorically committed to change; see James Gerstenzang, "Bush Offers New Vision of Military," *Los Angeles Times*, 12 December 2001, p. 1.

22. The battle over transforming defense policy during the first months of the Bush administration in 2001 was covered extensively in the press. See, for example, reports by Thomas E. Ricks, *Washington Post*, 20, 25 May; 22 June; 14, 19, 25 July; 3, 7, 18, 31 August; 9 December 2001; by Al Kamen, *Washington Post*, 16 May 2001. Also reports by Elaine Grossman, *Inside the Pentagon*, 31 May; 14 June; 5, 19, 26 July; 17 August 2001; Stan Crock, *Business Week*, 2 July, 6 August 2001; James Dao, Thom Shanker, Thomas L. Friedman, *New York Times*, 3 June; 11, 13, 14, 19, 26, 30 July; 18 August; 2 September 2001; James Kitfield, Sydney J. Freedberg, Jr., and George C. Wilson, *National Journal*, 3 March, 9 June, 14 July, 3 November 2001; Bill Gertz, Rowan Scarborough, *Washington Times*, 24 April; 25 May; 11, 29 June; 13 July; 30 August 2001; Robert Holzer, *Defense News*, 4–10 June, 23–29 July 2001; Morton M. Kondracke, *Roll Call*, 26 July 2001; Andrea Stone, *USA Today*, 27 July 2001; by William M. Arkin, washingtonpost .com, 4 June, 16 July 2001; by Pat Towell, *Congressional Quarterly Weekly*, 12 May, 21 July 2001; by Eun-Kyung Kim, Lisa Burgess,

European Stars and Stripes, 24 May, 2 June 2001; by Vago Muradian, Hunter Keeter, *Defense Daily International*, 4 May 2001, and *Defense Daily*, 11, 25 May 2001; and by Michael Duffy, *Time*, 27 August 2001. Also, editorials and opinion pieces in the *Washington Post*, 7 February, 27 August 2001; *Weekly Standard*, 14 May, 23 July 2001; *Los Angeles Times*, 24 May 2001; *New York Times*, 25 May, 13 July, 20 August 2001; *Washington Times*, 25 May, 10 June 2001; *London Financial Times*, 27 June, 31 July 2001; *Wall Street Journal*, 13 July; 1, 27 August 2001; *USA Today*, 18 July 2001; *Boston Globe*, 22 July 2001; *U.S. News and World Report*, 13 August 2001; *Milwaukee Journal Sentinel*, 27, 28 August 2001; and *Newsweek*, 3 September 2001. The first public attacks on Rumsfeld's efforts by the services came in a widely disseminated e-mail from former Army chief of staff Gordon Sullivan, head of the Association of the U.S. Army, on 5 May and from active-duty and retired naval officers defending aircraft carriers (Captain William Toti in the *Washington Times*, 23 April 2001; the Chief of Naval Operations, Admiral Vernon Clark, quoted in *Inside the Navy*, 4 June 2001; retired admiral Leighton W. Smith, Jr., in *National Defense*, June 2001). For an analysis of the institutional barriers to change, see Thomas Mahnken, "Transforming the U.S. Armed Forces: Rhetoric or Reality?" *Naval War College Review* 54, no. 3 (Summer 2001), pp. 81–9. "If we could achieve a 15 percent transformation in 10 years, I would consider that reasonable," Deputy Secretary of Defense Paul Wolfowitz admitted in August 2001; "I do not think there is going to be a single decision that will not be opposed by someone." Tom Canahuate, "Total U.S. Military Transformation in 10 Years Not Realistic, Says Wolfowitz," DefenseNews.com, 16 August 2001. For the current direction of "transformation," see Wolfowitz, keynote address, Fletcher Conference on "Focusing National Power," Washington, D.C., 14 November 2001, available at www.defenselink.mil/speeches/2001/ s20011114 -depsecdef.html.

23. See, for example, Paul Quinn-Judge, "Doubts of Top Brass on the Use of Power Carry Great Weight," *Boston Globe*, 20 April 1994, p. 12; Donald H. Rumsfeld, "Transforming the Military," *Foreign Affairs*, May/June 2002, pp. 20–32; Eliot A. Cohen, "A Tale of Two Secretaries," *Foreign Affairs*, May/June 2002,

pp. 33–46; and Elaine M. Grossman, "Reformers Unimpressed by Rumsfeld Plan to Overhaul Military Brass," *Inside the Pentagon,* 18 April 2002, p. 1.

24. My understanding of the Kosovo air campaign comes from Clark, *Waging Modern War;* Andrew J. Bacevich and Eliot A. Cohen, eds., *War over Kosovo: Politics and Strategy in a Global Age* (New York: Columbia Univ. Press, 2001); Halberstam, *War in a Time of Peace*, pp. 364ff.; Benjamin S. Lambeth, *NATO's Air War for Kosovo: A Strategic and Operational Assessment* (Santa Monica, Calif.: RAND Corporation, 2001); Michael Mandelbaum, "A Perfect Failure," *Foreign Affairs*, October 1999, pp. 2–8; and Daniel L. Byman and Matthew C. Waxman, "Kosovo and the Great Air Power Debate," and Barry R. Posen, "The War for Kosovo," both *International Security,* Spring 2000, pp. 5–84.

25. In 1998–99, the Triangle Institute for Security Studies "Project on the Gap between the Military and Civilian Society" compared the attitudes, opinions, values, and perspectives of elite officers on active duty and in the reserves with a sample of elite civilians in the United States, and with the mass public. The officer sample came from senior-year cadets and midshipmen at the service academies and in the Reserve Officers Training Corps, and from officers selected for in-residence attendance at staff and war colleges and for the Capstone Course (for new flag officers) at National Defense University, in Washington, D.C. Comparable samples of reserve and National Guard officers were also surveyed. The elite civilian sample was a random selection from *Who's Who in America* and similar biographical compilations. The general-public sample came from a telephone poll, using a portion of the survey's questions, conducted by Princeton Survey Research Associates. Information on the project and its methods can be found at www.poli.duke.civmil and in the introduction and conclusion in Peter D. Feaver and Richard H. Kohn, eds., *Soldiers and Civilians: The Civil-Military Gap and American National Security* (Cambridge, Mass.: MIT Press, 2001). The figures for military officers cited in this essay do not include students in precommissioning programs. In the survey, 49 percent of the active-duty military officers said they would leave military service "if the senior uniformed leadership does not

stand up for what is right in military policy." This was the second most-listed choice of nine offered, exceeded only by "if the challenge and sense of fulfillment I derive from my service were less" (68 percent). (All percentages are rounded to the nearest whole number.) For a sense of the bitterness in the officer corps, particularly toward the senior uniformed leadership, see "Chief of Staff of the Army's Leadership Survey: Command and General Staff College Survey of 760 Mid-Career Students (Majors with a Few LTCs)," n.d. [Spring 2000], available at www.d-n-i.net/FCS_Folder/leadership_ comments.htm; Ed Offley, "Young Officers' Anger, Frustration Stun Navy's Top Brass," *Seattle Post-Intelligencer*, 29 January 2000, available at seattlep-i.nwsource.com/local/navy29.shtml; Rowan Scarborough, "Army Colonels Reject Choice Assignments," *Washington Times*, 1 November 2000, p. A1; Paul Richter, "Glamour of America's Military Schools Fading for Youth," *Los Angeles Times*, 15 August 2000, p. 16; Justin P. D. Wilcox [Cpt., USA], "Military Experience Exposes 'Readiness Lie,'" *USA Today*, 5 September 2000, p. 26. Wilcox, a West Pointer, was leaving the service after five years because of underfunding, "more attention placed on landscaping and details . . . than on training," because "pursuit of mediocrity has become the norm," and for other reasons. "When," he asked, "will a general officer finally lay his stars on the table and stand up to the current administration for his soldiers?" One of the earlier attacks on the senior leadership was David H. Hackworth, "Too Much Brass, Too Little Brash," *Atlanta Constitution*, 2 March 1994, p. 11. For survey data and analysis, see *American Military Culture in the Twenty-first Century: A Report of the CSIS International Security Program* (Washington, D.C.: Center for Strategic and International Studies, 2000), pp. xxii, xxv, 17–8, 23–4, 45, 71–2. For an indication of a slippage in quality, see David S. C. Chu and John Brown, "Ensuring Quality People in Defense," in *Keeping the Edge: Managing Defense for the Future*, ed. Ashton B. Carter and John P. White (Cambridge, Mass.: MIT Press, 2001), p. 206. These events followed the downsizing of the armed services, which in the Army officer corps damaged morale, loosened organizational commitment, and undermined professionalism. See David McCormick, *The Downsized Warrior: America's Army in Transition*

(New York: New York Univ. Press, 1998), chap. 4, esp. pp. 127–9.

26. I am indebted to Alfred Goldberg, historian in the Office of the Secretary of Defense since 1973, for the insight about civilian control being situational. I used this definition first in "Out of Control: The Crisis in Civil-Military Relations," *National Interest*, Spring 1994, pp. 16–7. A similar definition, emphasizing the relative weight of military and civilian in decisions and decision making, is found in Michael Desch, *Civilian Control of the Military: The Changing Security Environment* (Baltimore: Johns Hopkins Univ. Press, 1999), esp. chaps. 1–3 and appendix. See also the discussion in Yehuda Ben Meir, *Civil-Military Relations in Israel* (New York: Columbia Univ. Press, 1995), chap. 2 ("Civilian Control"). In an important forthcoming work on civil-military relations, Peter Feaver distinguishes between trying to overthrow civilian authority (as in a coup) and simply shirking in carrying out the orders or wishes of the civilians. He explores the latter in depth, interpreting military subordination to civil authority as a variable rather than a given. See his *Armed Servants: Agency, Oversight, and Civilian Control* (Cambridge, Mass.: Harvard Univ. Press, in press).

27. See James R. Locher III, "Has It Worked? The Goldwater-Nichols Reorganization Act," *Naval War College Review* 54, no. 4 (Autumn 2001), pp. 108–9.

28. Pentagon reporter David Martin, in his "Landing the Eagle," *Vanity Fair*, November 1993, p. 153, described the Joint Staff this way: "Made up of 1,400 men and women, mostly in uniform, the Joint Staff analyzes the military consequences of the various options proposed by the administration. The answers they come up with can stop a fledgling policy dead in its tracks. You want to stop the bloodshed in Bosnia? Sure, we can do it. But it will take 500,000 troops and the second you pull them out the fighting will resume." For an indication of the Joint Staff's analytical (and political) advantages over the Office of the Secretary of Defense in the 2001 QDR, see Elaine Grossman, "Shelton Mulls Holding Key Civilian-Led Review to Exacting Standards," *Inside the Pentagon*, 2 August 2001, p. 1. See also James Kitfield, "Pentagon Power Shift," *Government Executive*, April 1994, p. 72.

29. Owens, *Lifting the Fog of War*, pp. 172–4; John M. Shalikashvili et al., "Keeping the Edge in Joint Operations," in *Keeping the Edge*, ed. Carter and White, pp. 39–42, 44–5; Robert Holzer and Stephen C. LeSueur, "JCS Quietly Gathers Up Reins of Power," *Defense News*, 13–19 June 1994.

30. Conversation with an officer at a war college, June 1999. In late 2001, Secretary of Defense Donald Rumsfeld asked Congress's permission to reduce the various legislative liaison staffs in the Pentagon by almost half, to 250, because, as he reportedly believed, "some congressional liaison officers may be working at cross purposes with the Bush administration's plan by pushing their own agency or command instead of the Pentagon's top priorities." Rick Maze, "Senate Wants to Reduce Number of Military Liaisons," ArmyTimes.com, 4 December 2001.

31. Dana Priest, "The Proconsuls: Patrolling the World," in three front-page installments: "A Four-Star Foreign Policy?" "An Engagement in 10 Time Zones," and "CINCs Don't Swim with State," *Washington Post*, 28, 29, and 30 September 2000, respectively. See also the remarks of Dana Priest and Robert B. Oakley in the State Department Open Forum, 23 March 2001, and U.S. Secretary of State, "Civil Military Affairs and U.S. Diplomacy: The Changing Roles of the Regional Commanders-in-Chief," cable message to all diplomatic and consular posts, 1 July 2001. Writing from Paris, the journalist William Pfaff had highlighted the change a year earlier. "It is not too much to say that there is a distinct foreign policy of military inspiration, conducted from the Pentagon," he wrote, citing the conflicting messages sent by the American military to its Indonesian counterparts during the East Timor crisis. See "Beware of a Military Penchant for a Parallel Foreign Policy," *International Herald Tribune*, 22 September 1999, available at www.iht.com/IHT/WP99/wp092299.html. For an indication of how one regional commander actively sought to determine policy and influence diplomacy, in this case intervention to prevent ethnic cleansing in Kosovo, see Clark, *Waging War*, chaps. 5–6. Another regional commander, Marine Corps general Anthony Zinni of U.S. Central Command, described himself as a "proconsul," hinting an analogy with a post in the ancient Roman republic and empire that mixed enormous political, military, and judicial powers over the population of a

province. This author may have been the first to suggest that label to General Zinni, in an exchange at U.S. Central Command headquarters, Tampa, Florida, April 1998.

32. Andrew J. Bacevich, "Discord Still: Clinton and the Military," *Washington Post*, 3 January 1999, p. C01.

33. See the sources in note 22 above. An insightful summation is Michael Duffy, "Rumsfeld: Older but Wiser?" *Time*, 27 August 2001, pp. 22–7.

34. Wilson, *This War Really Matters*, takes a detailed, and particularly revealing, look at the "decision-making process for national defense" (p. 3) for the 1997–99 period, especially the interactions between the civilians in the executive branch, the Congress, and the Joint Chiefs. To understand the extent to which the armed services are expected to press their own institutional interests with Congress, see Stephen K. Scroggs, *Army Relations with Congress: Thick Armor, Dull Sword, Slow Horse* (Westport, Conn.: Praeger, 2000).

35. Lewis Sorley, *Thunderbolt: General Creighton Abrams and the Army of His Times* (New York: Simon and Schuster, 1992), pp. 361–4; Herbert Y. Schandler, *The Unmaking of a President: Lyndon Johnson and Vietnam* (Princeton, N.J.: Princeton Univ. Press, 1977), pp. 39, 56, 103, 305; and Eric Q. Winograd, "Officials: Homeland Defense Mission Will Mean Changes for the Guard," *Inside the Army*, 19 November 2001, p. 1. James Schlesinger, the secretary of defense who must have approved this change in force structure, confirmed this interpretation in the very process of questioning it: "This would not really be like Abe [Abrams]. He had the view that the military must defer to the civilians, even to an extraordinary degree. I speculate that the military sought to fix the incentives so that the civilians would act appropriately." Quoted in Duncan, *Citizen Warriors*, pp. 271–2.

36. William J. Crowe, Jr. [Adm., USN], *The Line of Fire: From Washington to the Gulf, the Politics and Battles of the New Military* (New York: Simon and Schuster, 1993), pp. 41, 127, 152–9, 161, 177, 180–5, 189–90, 212–41, 304–5, 309, 312–9, 341–5; Bob Woodward, *The Commanders* (New York: Simon and Schuster, 1991), p. 40.

37. See, for example, Barton Gellman, "Rumblings of Discord Heard in Pentagon," *Washington Post*, 20 June 1993, p. A1.

38. J. G. Prout III, memorandum for the Commander in Chief, U.S. Pacific Fleet, "Subj: CNO Comments at Surface Warfare Flag Officer Conference (SWFOC)," 23 September 1994, copy in possession of the author.

39. *Directions for Defense;* Robert Holzer, "Experts: Streamlined Staff at OSD Could Save Billions," *Defense News*, 2–8 December 1996, p. 28.

40. For insight into the military's influence over the character of the intervention in Bosnia, see Ivo H. Daalder, *Getting to Dayton: The Making of America's Bosnia Policy* (Washington, D.C.: Brookings Institution Press, 2000), pp. 140–53, 173–8; Dan Blumenthal, "Clinton, the Military, and Bosnia, 1993–1995: A Study in Dysfunctional Civil Military Relations," Soldiers, Statesmen, and the Use of Force Seminar, Johns Hopkins School of Advanced International Studies, Washington, D.C., 7 June 1999; and Clark, *Waging War*, pp. 55–66, 73, 79–80. Clark, who was the senior U.S. military adviser at the Dayton negotiations, put it this way (p. 59): "Under our agreement, we were seeking to limit the obligations of the military . . . but to give the commander unlimited authority to accomplish these limited obligations." A background analysis is Susan L. Woodward, "Upside-Down Policy: The U.S. Debate on the Use of Force and the Case of Bosnia," in *Use of Force*, ed. Brands, pp. 111–34. In an analysis of civil-military conflicts between 1938 and 1997, Michael C. Desch argues that civilian control weakened in the United States during the 1990s. He finds that civilians prevailed in fifty-nine of sixty-two instances of civil-military conflict before the 1990s but in only five of twelve in that decade. See his *Civilian Control of the Military*, chap. 3 and appendix.

41. Charles G. Boyd, "America Prolongs the War in Bosnia," *New York Times*, 9 August 1995, p. 19, and "Making Peace with the Guilty: The Truth about Bosnia," *Foreign Affairs*, October 1995, pp. 22–38. The op-ed began, "Having spent the last two years as deputy commander of the U.S. European Command, I have found that my views on the frustrating events in Bosnia differ from much of the conventional wisdom in Washington."

42. Bill Keller, "The World according to Powell," *New York Times Magazine*, 25 November 2001, p. 65.

43. For a fuller discussion of General Powell's efforts to circumvent civilian control, see Kohn, "Out of Control," pp. 8–13, and with Powell's reply, comments by John Lehman, William Odom, and Samuel P. Huntington, and my response in *National Interest*, Summer 1994, pp. 23–31. Other profiles and supporting material are in Jon Meacham, "How Colin Powell Plays the Game," *Washington Monthly*, December 1994, pp. 33–42; Charles Lane, "The Legend of Colin Powell," *New Republic*, 17 April 1995, pp. 20–32; Michael R. Gordon and Bernard E. Trainor, "Beltway Warrior," *New York Times Magazine*, 27 August 1995, pp. 40–3; Keller, "World according to Powell," pp. 61ff.; Michael C. Desch and Sharon K. Weiner, eds., *Colin Powell as JCS Chairman: A Panel Discussion on American Civil-Military Relations, October 23, 1995*, Project on U.S. Post–Cold War Civil-Military Relations, Working Paper 1 (Cambridge, Mass.: Harvard University, John M. Olin Institute for Strategic Studies, December 1995); Lawrence F. Kaplan, "Yesterday's Man: Colin Powell's Out-of-Date Foreign Policy," *New Republic*, 1 January 2001, pp. 17–21.

44. Eric Schmitt and Elaine Sciolino, "To Run Pentagon, Bush Sought Proven Manager with Muscle," *New York Times*, 1 January 2001, p. 1; Bill Gertz and Rowan Scarborough, "Inside the Ring," *Washington Times*, 26 January 2001, p. A9. Significantly, Powell's close friend Richard Armitage, who had been mentioned frequently for the position of deputy secretary of defense, was not offered that position and instead became deputy secretary of state.

45. T. Harry Williams, *Lincoln and His Generals* (New York: Random House, 1952), remains indispensable. See also Richard N. Current, *The Lincoln Nobody Knows* (New York: McGraw-Hill, 1958), p. 169; David Herbert Donald, *Lincoln* (New York: Simon and Schuster, 1995), pp. 386–8; and Bruce Tap, *Over Lincoln's Shoulder: The Committee on the Conduct of the War* (Lawrence: Univ. Press of Kansas, 1998), pp. 151–4.

46. Timothy D. Johnson, *Winfield Scott: The Quest for Military Glory* (Lawrence: Univ. Press of Kansas, 1998), pp. 217–9; John E. Marszalek, *Sherman: A Soldier's Passion for Order* (New York: Free Press, 1993), pp. 386–9.

47. Mark Russell Shulman, *Navalism and the Emergence of American Sea Power, 1882–1893* (Annapolis, Md.: Naval Institute Press, 1995), pp. 46–57, 152–3; Paul A. C. Koistinen, *Mobilizing for Modern War: The Political Economy of American Warfare, 1865–1919* (Lawrence: Univ. Press of Kansas, 1997), pp. 48–57; Benjamin Franklin Cooling, *Gray Steel and Blue Water Navy: The Formative Years of America's Military-Industrial Complex, 1881–1917* (Hamden, Conn.: Archon Books, 1979), chaps. 3–4, postscript. See also Kurt Hackemer, *The U.S. Navy and the Origins of the Military-Industrial Complex, 1847–1883* (Annapolis, Md.: Naval Institute Press, 2001), and his "Building the Military-Industrial Relationship: The U.S. Navy and American Business, 1854–1883," *Naval War College Review* 52, no. 2 (Spring 1999), pp. 89–111.

48. DeWitt S. Copp, *A Few Great Captains: The Men and Events That Shaped the Development of U.S. Air Power* (Garden City, N.Y.: Doubleday, 1980); David E. Johnson, *Fast Tanks and Heavy Bombers: Innovation in the U.S. Army, 1917–1945* (Ithaca, N.Y.: Cornell Univ. Press, 1998), pp. 66–9, 81–4, 86–90, 102–3, 158–60, 220–2, 227–8; Randall R. Rice, "The Politics of Air Power: From Confrontation to Cooperation in Army Aviation Civil-Military Relations, 1919–1940" (dissertation, University of North Carolina at Chapel Hill, 2002).

49. Quoted in Marriner Eccles, *Beckoning Frontiers: Public and Personal Recollections*, ed. Sidney Hyman (New York: Knopf, 1951), p. 336. For a sense of Theodore Roosevelt's troubles with the services, see his letters to Elihu Root, 7 March 1902; to Oswald Garrison Villard, 22 March 1902; to Leonard Wood, 4 June 1904; and to Truman H. Newberry, 28 August 1908, quoted in Elting E. Morison, ed., *The Letters of Theodore Roosevelt*, 8 vols. (Cambridge, Mass.: Harvard Univ. Press, 1951–54), vol. 3, pp. 241, 247; vol. 4, p. 820; vol. 6, p. 1199. See also the forthcoming study of Roosevelt as commander in chief by Matthew M. Oyos, who supplied excerpts from the above documents; and Oyos, "Theodore Roosevelt, Congress, and the Military: U.S. Civil-Military Relations in the Early Twentieth Century,"

Presidential Studies Quarterly, vol. 30, 2000, pp. 312–30.

50. The civil-military battles of the 1940s, 1950s, and 1960s are covered in a number of works, among them: Demetrios Caraley, *The Politics of Military Unification: A Study of Conflict and the Policy Process* (New York: Columbia Univ. Press, 1966); Herman S. Wolk, *The Struggle for Air Force Independence, 1943–1947* (Washington, D.C.: Air Force History and Museums Program, 1997); Jeffrey G. Barlow, *Revolt of the Admirals: The Fight for Naval Aviation, 1945–1950* (Washington, D.C.: Naval Historical Center, 1994); Steven L. Rearden, *The Formative Years, 1947–1950,* vol. 1 of *History of the Office of the Secretary of Defense* (Washington, D.C.: Historical Office, Office of the Secretary of Defense, 1984); Robert L. Watson, *Into the Missile Age, 1956–1960,* vol. 4 of *History of the Office of the Secretary of Defense* (Washington, D.C.: Historical Office, Office of the Secretary of Defense, 1997); Andrew J. Bacevich, "Generals versus the President: Eisenhower and the Army, 1953–1955," in *Security in a Changing World: Case Studies in U.S. National Security Management,* ed. Volker C. Franke (Westport, Conn.: Praeger, 2002), pp. 83–99; and Deborah Shapley, *Promise and Power: The Life and Times of Robert McNamara* (Boston: Little, Brown, 1993).

51. For a brief history of civilian control, see Richard H. Kohn, "Civil-Military Relations: Civilian Control of the Military," in *The Oxford Companion to American Military History,* ed. John Whiteclay Chambers II (New York: Oxford Univ. Press, 1999), pp. 122–5. Similar interpretations of the conflict inherent in the relationship are Russell F. Weigley, "The American Military and the Principle of Civilian Control from McClellan to Powell," *Journal of Military History,* special issue, vol. 57, 1993, pp. 27–59; Russell F. Weigley, "The American Civil-Military Cultural Gap: A Historical Perspective, Colonial Times to the Present," in *Soldiers and Civilians,* ed. Feaver and Kohn, chap. 5; Ronald H. Spector, "Operation Who Says: Tension between Civilian and Military Leaders Is Inevitable," *Washington Post,* 22 August 1999, p. B1; and Peter D. Feaver, "Discord and Divisions of Labor: The Evolution of Civil-Military Conflict in the United States," paper presented at the annual meeting of the American Political Science Association, Washington, D.C., 1993. A particularly cogent analysis from a generation ago, by a scholar who both studied the issues and participated as a senior civilian official in the Pentagon, is Adam Yarmolinsky, "Civilian Control: New Perspectives for New Problems," *Indiana Law Journal,* vol. 49, 1974, pp. 654–71.

52. See, for example, Dana Priest, "Mine Decision Boosts Clinton-Military Relations," *Washington Post,* 21 September 1997, p. A22; Ernest Blazar, "Inside the Ring," *Washington Times,* 8 June 1998, p. 11; Jonathan S. Landay, "U.S. Losing Handle on Its Diplomacy in a Kosovo 'at War,'" *Christian Science Monitor,* 5 June 1998, p. 7; Daniel Rearick, "An Unfortunate Opposition: U.S. Policy toward the Establishment of the International Criminal Court" (honors thesis, University of North Carolina at Chapel Hill, 2000).

53. In *The Clustered World: How We Live, What We Buy, and What It All Means about Who We Are* (Boston: Little, Brown, 2000), a study of consumerism and lifestyles, Michael J. Weiss identifies the military as one of "sixty-two distinct population groups each with its own set of values, culture and means of coping with today's problems" (p. 11). His thesis is that the country has become splintered and fragmented (see pp. 258–9 and chap. 1). For the military's "presence" in American society, see the late Adam Yarmolinsky's comprehensive *The Military Establishment: Its Impacts on American Society* (New York: Harper and Row, 1971), and James Burk, "The Military's Presence in American Society," in *Soldiers and Civilians,* ed. Feaver and Kohn, chap. 6. In 1985, "a group of 31 military and veterans organizations that lobby for the uniformed services on personnel and pay issues" representing some "6 million veterans and their families" banded together to form the "Military Coalition," a force that in the opinion of one thoughtful retired general is "potentially far more numerous and powerful than the NRA!!!" Stephen Barr, "Military Pay Expert Retires," *Washington Post,* 12 March 2001, p. B2; Ted Metaxis e-mail to the author, 24 October 1999.

54. Donald Rumsfeld, "Rumsfeld's Rules," rev. ed., January 17, 2001, available at www.defenselink .mil/news/jan2001/rumsfeldsrules.pdf.

55. Department of Defense, *Quadrennial Defense Review Report,* 30 September 2001, available at www.defenselink.mil/pubs/ qdr2001.pdf; Anne Plummer, "Pentagon

Launches Some 50 Reviews in Major Defense Planning Effort," *Inside the Pentagon*, 15 November 2001, p. 1; John Liang, "Rumsfeld Supports Switching Future QDRs to Administration's Second Year," InsideDefense.com, 6 December 2001.

56. Thomas E. Ricks, "Target Approval Delays Cost Air Force Key Hits," *Washington Post*, 18 November 2001, p. 1, and "Rumsfeld's Hands-On War: Afghan Campaign Shaped by Secretary's Views, Personality," *Washington Post*, 19 December 2001, p. 1; Esther Schrader, "Action Role a Better Fit for Rumsfeld," *Los Angeles Times*, 11 November 2001, p. 22; Lawrence F. Kaplan, "Ours to Lose: Why Is Bush Repeating Clinton's Mistakes?" *New Republic*, 12 November 2001, pp. 25–6; Robert Kagan and William Kristol, "Getting Serious," *Weekly Standard*, 19 November 2001, pp. 7–8; J. Michael Waller, "Rumsfeld: Plagues of Biblical Job," *Insight Magazine*, 10 December 2001; Damian Whitworth and Roland Watson, "Rumsfeld at Odds with His Generals," *London Times*, 16 October 2001, p. 5; Toby Harnden, "Rumsfeld Calls for End to Old Tactics of War," *London Daily Telegraph*, 16 October 2001, p. 8.

57. Quoted in Donald Smythe, *Guerrilla Warrior: The Early Life of John J. Pershing* (New York: Scribner's, 1973), p. 278.

58. Omar N. Bradley, *A Soldier's Story* (New York: Henry Holt, 1951), p. 147. For an outline of the four factors underlying civilian control in the United States historically, see my "Civilian Control of the Military," pp. 122–5.

59. The Gallup polling organization has surveyed Americans annually on their confidence in major institutions since the early 1970s, and the military has topped the list since 1987, with over 60 percent expressing a "great deal" or "quite a lot" of confidence. See Frank Newport, "Military Retains Top Position in Americans' Confidence Ratings," 25 June 2001, available at www.gallup.com/poll/releases/pr010625.asp and "Small Business and Military Generate Most Confidence in Americans," 15 August 1997, available at www.gallup.com/poll/releases/pr970815.asp; "Gallup Poll Topics: A-Z: Confidence in Institutions," 8–10 June 2001, available at www.gallup.com/poll/indicators/indconfidence.asp. For excellent analyses of the change in public attitudes toward the military since the

late 1960s, see David C. King and Zachary Karabell, "The Generation of Trust: Public Confidence in the U.S. Military since Vietnam," revision of a paper presented to the Duke University political science department, 29 January 1999, to be published in 2002 by the American Enterprise Institute; and Richard Sobel, "The Authoritarian Reflex and Public Support for the U.S. Military: An Anomaly?" paper presented at the annual meeting of the Midwest Political Science Association, 16 April 1999. Respect for lawyers is low and has been declining in recent years. See Darren K. Carlson, "Nurses Remain at Top of Honest and Ethics Poll," 27 November 2000, available at www.gallup.com/poll/releases/Pr001127.asp.

60. Joseph S. Nye, Jr., Philip D. Zelikow, and David C. King, eds., *Why People Don't Trust Government* (Cambridge, Mass.: Harvard Univ. Press, 1997); Albert H. Cantril and Susan Davis Cantril, *Reading Mixed Signals: Ambivalence in American Public Opinion about Government* (Washington, D.C.: Woodrow Wilson Center Press, 1999). The decline in trust of government and confidence in public institutions has not been limited to the United States. See Susan J. Pharr and Robert D. Putnam, eds., *Disaffected Democracies: What's Troubling the Trilateral Countries?* (Princeton, N.J.: Princeton Univ. Press, 2000). Trust in government in the United States after the 11 September attacks jumped dramatically to the highest level since 1968. Frank Newport, "Trust in Government Increases Sharply in Wake of Terrorist Attacks," 12 October 2001, available at www.gallup.com/poll/releases/pr011012.asp; Alexander Stille, "Suddenly, Americans Trust Uncle Sam," *New York Times*, 3 November, p. A11; and John D. Donahue, "Is Government the Good Guy?" *New York Times*, 13 December 2001, p. A31. Whether the attacks will reverse the long-term trend remains to be seen.

61. For critiques of journalism in general and coverage of the military in particular, see Bill Kovach and Tom Rosenstiel, *Warp Speed: America in the Age of Mixed Media* (New York: Century Foundation Press, 1999); Scott Shuger, "First, the Bad News: The Big Daily Newspapers Get Some Things Right. National Defense Isn't One of Them," *Mother Jones*, September/October 1998, pp. 72–6. My views come from a decade of close reading of reporting on national security

issues. An example of lack of interest in civil-military relations is the absence in the media of reaction to and interpretation of the detailed and persuasive reports of Dana Priest (see note 31 above) about the growth in power of the regional commanders, discussed previously. Typical of press misunderstanding is the editorial "Unifying Armed Forces Requires Radical Change" in the 18 June 2001 *Honolulu Star-Bulletin,* calling for abolition of the separate military departments, replacement of the JCS by a "single Chief of Military Staff who would command the armed forces," and further empowerment of the regional commanders. The editorial purports to "make the Secretary of Defense a genuine master of the Pentagon rather than a referee among warring factions," but the recommendations would destroy a secretary's ability to monitor and supervise one of the world's largest, and most complex, bureaucratic structures.

62. See William J. Bennett, *The Index of Leading Cultural Indicators: American Society at the End of the Twentieth Century,* updated and expanded ed. (New York: Broadway Books, 1999); Marc Miringoff and Marque-Luisa Miringoff, *The Social Health of the Nation: How America Is Really Doing* (New York: Oxford Univ. Press, 1999); James H. Billington, "The Human Consequences of the Information Revolution," Ditchley Foundation Lecture 37 (Chipping Norton, U.K.: Ditchley Foundation, 2000); Robert D. Putnam, *Bowling Alone: The Collapse and Revival of American Community* (New York: Simon and Schuster, 2000); Everett Carl Ladd, *The Ladd Report* (New York: Free Press, 1999); Weiss, *The Clustered World,* pp. 10–1, 14–5, 19–25, 43–4; Theda Skocpol and Morris P. Fiorina, eds., *Civic Engagement in American Democracy* (Washington, D.C.: Brookings Institution Press, 1999), essays 1, 12, 13; Derek Bok, *The Trouble with Government* (Cambridge, Mass.: Harvard Univ. Press, 2001), pp. 386–98; William Chaloupka, *Everybody Knows: Cynicism in America* (Minneapolis: Univ. of Minnesota Press, 1999); Robert D. Kaplan, *An Empire Wilderness: Travels into America's Future* (New York: Random House, 1998); and Adam B. Seligman, *The Problem of Trust* (Princeton, N.J.: Princeton Univ. Press, 1997). More hopeful though still cautious pictures are Robert William Fogel, *The Fourth Great Awakening & the Future of Egalitarianism* (Chicago: Univ. of Chicago Press,

2000); and Francis Fukuyama, *The Great Disruption: Human Nature and the Reconstitution of Social Order* (New York: Free Press, 1999).

63. In the TISS survey, a number of the 250-some questions examined attitudes about the proper role of the military in society. For example, 49 percent of elite civilians and 68 percent of the mass public agreed ("strongly" or "somewhat") that "in wartime, civilian government leaders should let the military take over running the war," a position echoed by even as distinguished a scholar as Amitai Etzioni ("How Not to Win the War," *USA Today,* 7 November 2001, p. 15). To the question, "Members of the military should be allowed to publicly express their political views just like any other citizen," 59 percent of the civilian elite and 84 percent of the general public agreed. Civilians were much more likely than the military to condone leaking documents to the press in various situations. The distinguished sociologist James A. Davis felt the results "make one's hair stand on end" but suggested as a "simple explanation" that they are accounted for by "cynicism about civilian politics," Americans' high regard for "their military," and by the ideas that civilian control is "a fairly sophisticated doctrine, while common sense suggests that important decisions should be made by people who are best informed." See his "Attitudes and Opinions among Senior Military Officers and a U.S. Cross-Section, 1998–1999," in *Soldiers and Civilians,* ed. Feaver and Kohn, p. 120 and esp. table 2.10. My point is that whatever the explanation, the very positive image of the military held by Americans in the last dozen or so years diverges considerably from what seems to have been the historical norm. See C. Robert Kemble, *The Image of the Army Officer in America: Background for Current Views* (Westport, Conn.: Greenwood, 1973); Samuel P. Huntington, *The Soldier and the State: The Theory and Politics of Civil-Military Relations* (Cambridge, Mass.: Harvard Univ. Press, 1957), particularly part 2. At the same time, 47 percent of the general public did *not* think "civilian control of the military is absolutely safe and secure in the United States," and 68 percent thought that "if civilian leaders order the military to do something that it opposes, military leaders will seek ways to avoid carrying out the order" at least "some of the time" (30 percent thought "all" or

"most of the time"). For the decline in civics education and understanding, see Chris Hedges, "35% of High School Seniors Fail National Civics Test," *New York Times*, 21 November 1999, p. 17; Bok, *Trouble with Government*, pp. 403–6.

64. For the caricatures in popular literature and films, see Howard Harper, "The Military and Society: Reaching and Reflecting Audiences in Fiction and Film," *Armed Forces & Society*, vol. 27, 2001, pp. 231–48. Charles C. Moskos, "Toward a Postmodern Military: The United States as a Paradigm," in *The Postmodern Military: Armed Forces after the Cold War*, ed. Charles C. Moskos, John Allen Williams, and David R. Segal (New York: Oxford Univ. Press, 2000), p. 20; Moskos, "What Ails the All-Volunteer Force: An Institutional Perspective," *Parameters*, Summer 2001, pp. 34–5; and "Interview: James Webb," U.S. Naval Institute *Proceedings*, April 2000, pp. 78–9, all argue that the military is pictured negatively in film. But King and Karabell, "Generation of Trust," pp. 6–7, judge that current portrayals are the most "positive . . . since World War II."

65. Gary Hart, *The Minuteman: Restoring an Army of the People* (New York: Free Press, 1998), particularly chaps. 1, 3.

66. In the TISS survey of "elite" officers, some 40 percent of the National Guard and 25 percent of the reserve respondents listed their occupation as "military," which suggests that they are in uniform full-time or work somewhere in national defense, either for government or industry. See David Paul Filer, "Military Reserves: Bridging the Culture Gap between Civilian Society and the United States Military" (M.A. thesis, Duke University, Durham, North Carolina, 2001), pp. 46–7. In the fiscal year 2001 defense authorization act, 6.6 percent of the Army National Guard and 20.6 percent of the Air National Guard were authorized to be "dual status" civilian technicians and uniformed members. Charlie Price (National Guard Bureau of Public Affairs) e-mail to author, 12 February 2001.

67. The similarity "attitudinally" between active-duty officers and the National Guard and reserves on some of the questions in the TISS survey is addressed in Filer, "Military Reserves." Other congruence is evident in the data.

68. See, for example, Jack Kelly, "U.S. Reliance on Guards, Reservists Escalating," *Pittsburgh Post-Gazette*, 28 October 2000, p. 9; Steven Lee Myers, "Army Will Give National Guard the Entire U.S. Role in Bosnia," *New York Times*, 5 December 2000, p. A8; Winograd, "Officials: Homeland Defense Mission Will Mean Changes for the Guard," p. 1; David T. Fautua, "Army Citizen-Soldiers: Active, Guard, and Reserve Leaders Remain Silent about Overuse of Reserve Components," *Armed Forces Journal International*, September 2000, pp. 72–4; John J. Miller, "Unreserved: The Misuse of America's Reserve Forces," *National Review*, 23 July 2001, pp. 26ff.; and Duncan, *Citizen Warriors*, pp. 214–7 and n. 25. Duncan calls the 1995 deployment of Guardsmen and reserves to the Sinai for six months of peacekeeping duty "unprecedented." See also Peter Bacqué, "Guard Troops Will Head for Sinai in '95," *Richmond Times-Dispatch*, 28 January 1994, p. B6. The reserve-component contribution to active-duty missions has risen from about one million man-days in 1986 to approximately thirteen million in each of the years 1996, 1997, and 1998. CSIS, *American Military Culture*, p. 19. See also Conrad C. Crane, *Landpower and Crises: Army Roles and Missions in Smaller-Scale Contingencies during the 1990s* (Carlisle, Penna.: U.S. Army Strategic Studies Institute, January 2001), pp. 29–30.

69. Personal exchange, panel discussion on civil-military relations, Marine Corps Staff College, Quantico, Virginia, September 1998; personal exchange, lecture/discussion with twenty-six state adjutant generals, U.S. Army War College, Carlisle, Pennsylvania, October 1998.

70. The decline in citizen-soldiering and some of its implications are addressed in Andrew J. Bacevich, "Losing Private Ryan: Why the Citizen-Soldier Is MIA," *National Review*, 9 August 1999, pp. 32–4. Also Elliott Abrams and Andrew J. Bacevich, "A Symposium on Citizenship and Military Service"; Eliot A. Cohen, "Twilight of the Citizen-Soldier"; and James Burk, "The Military Obligation of Citizens since Vietnam"; all *Parameters*, Summer 2001, pp. 18–20, 23–8, 48–60, respectively. Also Hart, *Minuteman*, esp. pp. 16–7, 21–5. For a recent review of the end of conscription, see David R. Sands, "Military Draft Now Part of Past: Spain and Italy are the Latest European Nations to Abandon Compulsory Service," and "U.S. Talk of a Draft Probably Hot Air," *Washington Times*, 31 December 2000, pp. 1, 4, respectively.

71. In the TISS survey, well over 90 percent of the civilian elite said that the people they came into contact with "in the social or community groups to which [they] belong" were either "all civilians" or "mostly civilians with some military." The same was true (over 90 percent of respondents) in the workplace. Americans (both elite and general public) who have not served in the military also have fewer close friends who now serve or are veterans. The prospects for diminished civilian contact with, understanding of, and support for the military are analyzed in Paul Gronke and Peter D. Feaver, "Uncertain Confidence: Civilian and Military Attitudes about Civil-Military Relations," in *Soldiers and Civilians*, ed. Feaver and Kohn, chap. 3. Congressman Ike Skelton, ranking Democrat on the House Armed Services Committee, had already discerned the trend and its implications for support of the military; see Rasheeda Crayton, "Skelton Calls for More Military Support," *Kansas City Star*, 12 November 1997, p. 15. A more general comment comes from Brent Scowcroft, national security adviser to Presidents Gerald Ford and George H. W. Bush: "With the lessened contact between the American people and the military, . . . the results will not be healthy." Scowcroft, "Judgment and Experience: George Bush's Foreign Policy," in *Presidential Judgment: Foreign Policy Decision Making in the White House,* ed. Aaron Lobel (Hollis, N.H.: Hollis, 2001), 115. The declining propensity of youth to serve is noted in Thomas W. Lippman, "With a Draft Cut Off, Nation's Society Climate Changed Sharply," *Washington Post*, 8 September 1998, p. 13. Lippman cites Pentagon "Youth Attitude Tracking Survey" figures indicating that some 32 percent of youth "expressed some desire to join the military" in 1973, the last year of the Cold War draft, but that by 1993 the figure had dropped to 25 percent and by 1997 to 12 percent. See also Moskos, "What Ails the All-Volunteer Force," pp. 39–41.

72. William T. Bianco and Jamie Markham, "Vanishing Veterans: The Decline of Military Experience in the U.S. Congress," in *Soldiers and Civilians*, ed. Feaver and Kohn, chap. 7.

73. Norman Ornstein, "The Legacy of Campaign 2000," *Washington Quarterly*, Spring 2001, p. 102; William M. Welch, "Most U.S. Lawmakers Lack Combat Experience," *USA Today*, 12 November 2001, p. 12. Writing before 11 September, Ornstein calls the present "

Congress . . . clearly and irrevocably a post–Cold War Congress. Eighty-three percent, or 363 members, of the House were first elected in the 1990s, since the Berlin Wall fell, along with 57 members of the Senate. Few of these lawmakers, in either party, have an abiding interest in the U.S. role in the world. International issues are simply not high on their priority list." He notes also that in a typical post–World War II Congress, some three-quarters of the senators and more than half the representatives were veterans. Importantly, the newer veterans in Congress are quite likely to be Republicans, whereas in the past veterans were more or less evenly split. Donald N. Zillman, "Maintaining the Political Neutrality of the Military," *IUS* [Inter-University Seminar on Armed Forces and Society] *Newsletter*, Spring 2001, p. 17. In 2000, a retired rear admiral "started a 'National Defense P[olitical]A[ction]C[ommittee]' to support congressional candidates who have served in the armed forces." "Inside Washington, D.C.: G.I. Joes and G.I. Janes Ready Their PAC," *National Journal*, 9 September 2000, p. 2759.

74. According to the newsletter of the Federal Voting Assistance Program, the military began voting in greater percentages than the public in 1984, and in 1996 "at an overall rate of 64%, compared to the 49% rate generated by the general public. The Uniformed Services' high participation rate can be directly attributed to the active voter assistance programs conducted by Service Commanders and to assistance from the state and local election officials in simplifying the absentee voting process and accommodating the special needs of the Uniformed Services." See "Military Retains High Participation Rates," *Voting Information News*, July 1997, p. 1. In the 1980 election, military voting was below civilian (49.7 to 52.6 percent). In the 1992 election, the Defense Department expanded the program, according to a reporter, "to register and turn out military voters," changing the "emphasis . . . from ensuring availability of voting forms to mustering ballots at the polls." Setting "for the first time . . . a target rate for participation," this "new focus on voter turnout . . . has led some Democratic and some independent analysts to suspect the Bush administration is trying to energize a predictably sympathetic voter base." Barton Gellman, "Pentagon Intensifies Effort to Muster Military Voters," *Washington Post*, 17 September 1992, p. A1. See also Daniel A. Gibran,

Absentee Voting: A Brief History of Suffrage Expansion in the United States (Washington, D.C.: Federal Voting Assistance Program, August 2001).

75. Ole R. Holsti, "A Widening Gap between the U.S. Military and Civilian Society? Some Evidence, 1976–1996," *International Security*, Winter 1998/1999, p. 11; TISS survey data. Some observers think the actual Republican figure is much higher, many officers being reluctant to reveal a preference, "knowing full and well what the reaction would be if the percentage of Republicans in the elite military ranks was seen to approach 85 to 90 per cent, which I am told is a reasonable figure." This well-connected West Point graduate continued, "We're in danger of developing our own in-house Soviet-style military, one in which if you're not in 'the party,' you don't get ahead. I have spoken with several . . . who were run out of the Army near the beginning of their careers when commanders became aware that they had voted for Clinton in 1992. I have no doubt they are telling me the truth, and . . . I've spoken with some . . . who confirm their stories." Enclosure in Tom Ricks to the author, 20 November 2000. Generals and admirals—who, as older, more senior, and more experienced officers could be expected to be imbued with the more traditional ethic of nonaffiliation—have a slightly higher independent or nonpartisan self-identification. In 1984, *Newsweek* (9 July, p. 37) surveyed 257 flag officers, about a quarter of those on active duty; the results were Republican 52 percent, Democrat 4 percent, independent 43 percent, "don't know" 1 percent. Holsti's 1984 officer sample contained 29 percent independents. The TISS survey included seventy-four one and two-star officers: Republican 57 percent; Democrat 9 percent; independent, no preference, and other 34 percent. The TISS active-duty sample was 28 percent independent/no preference/other.

76. Pat Towell, "GOP Advertises Differences with Commander in Chief in Military-Oriented Papers," *Congressional Quarterly Weekly*, 11 December 1999, p. 2984; Republican National Committee advertisement, "Keeping the Commitment: Republicans Reverse Years of Military Neglect," *Air Force Times*, 13 December 1999, p. 57; Republican National Committee postcard to University of North Carolina Army ROTC cadre members, n.d. [fall 2000], in possession of author; Frank Abbott to author, 11 October 2000; David Wood, "Military Breaks Ranks with Non-Partisan Tradition," *Cleveland Plain Dealer*, 22 October 2000, p. 16. Just prior to the election, the Republican National Committee paid for e-mail messages from Colin Powell urging recipients to vote for "our Republican team"; Powell to Alvin Bernstein, subject "A Message from Colin L. Powell," 6 November 2000, in possession of author. In the 2000 election, about 72 percent of *overseas* military personnel, targeted particularly by Republicans, voted. The overall voting rate for the civilian population was 50 percent. Robert Suro, "Pentagon Will Revise Military Voting Procedures," *Washington Post*, 23 June 2001, p. 2. The Bush campaign pushed to count overseas military ballots, even questionable ones, in counties where Bush was strong and to disqualify those in counties where Gore was strong, nearly resulting in a large enough net gain to swing the outcome by itself. David Barstow and Don Van Natta, Jr., "How Bush Took Florida: Mining the Overseas Absentee Vote," *New York Times*, 15 July 2001, p. 1.

77. Christopher McKee, *A Gentlemanly and Honorable Profession: The Creation of the U.S. Naval Officer Corps, 1794–1815* (Annapolis, Md.: Naval Institute Press, 1991), pp. 107–8; William B. Skelton, *An American Profession of Arms: The Army Officer Corps, 1784–1861* (Lawrence: Univ. Press of Kansas, 1992), chap. 15; Edward M. Coffman, *The Old Army: A Portrait of the American Army in Peacetime, 1784–1898* (New York: Oxford Univ. Press, 1986), pp. 87–96, 242–3, 266–9; Peter Karsten, *The Naval Aristocracy: The Golden Age of Annapolis and the Emergence of Modern American Navalism* (New York: Free Press, 1972), pp. 203–13.

78. General Lucian K. Truscott, Jr., in *The Twilight of the U.S. Cavalry: Life in the Old Army, 1917–1942* (Lawrence: Univ. Press of Kansas, 1989), remembers that "there was never much partisan political feeling on military posts, even during years of presidential elections. . . . [T]he military were isolated from the political rivalries. . . . Then too, Regular Army officers were sworn to uphold and defend the Constitution . . . and . . . carried out orders regardless of the political party in power. . . . Further, few officers maintained voting residence, and absentee voting was

relatively rare at this time" (p. 130). Edward M. Coffman, who has spent over two decades studying the peacetime Army (his volume covering the social history of the Army, 1898–1941, to follow his *The Old Army*, is near completion), found that regular officers in the nineteenth century "generally stayed out of politics with rare exceptions" and during "the 20th century" had "virtually no participation in voting. For one thing, the absentee ballot was not in vogue—and then there was the problem of establishing residency but, as I picked up in interviews [Coffman has done several hundred with veterans of the 1900–40 era], they didn't think it was their place to vote. Again and again, both officers and their wives told me that they didn't vote until after retirement." Coffman e-mail to the author, 23 July 1999. Nonpartisanship and lack of voting in the 1930s is confirmed by Daniel Blumenthal in "Legal Prescriptions, Customary Restrictions, Institutional Traditions: The Political Attitudes of American Officers Leading Up to World War II," seminar paper, National Security Law Course, Duke University Law School, 4 April 1998.

79. I agree with Lance Betros, "Political Partisanship and the Military Ethic in America," *Armed Forces & Society*, vol. 27, 2001, pp. 501–23, that the mere act of voting is not partisan, but I think that continual voting over time for the same party can lead to partisanship that *does* harm military professionalism. In a March 1999 discussion at the Naval War College, Admiral Stanley Arthur felt that officers who are sincere about their votes "take ownership" of them, a commitment that could undermine their ability to be neutral, apolitical instruments of the state. I do not find that promoting one's armed service, writing about national defense issues to affect policy, and making alliances with politicians to advance one's own personal and service interests are the same as the partisanship of identifying personally with the ideology and political and cultural agendas of a political party, which is the kind of partisanship that has emerged in the last two decades. For a different view, see Betros, "Officer Professionalism in the Late Progressive Era," in *The Future of Army Professionalism,* ed. Don Snider and Gayle Watkins (New York: McGraw-Hill, 2002).

80. Mackubin Thomas Owens, "The Democratic Party's War on the Military," *Wall Street*

Journal, 22 November 2000, p. 22. See also Tom Donnelly, "Why Soldiers Dislike Democrats," *Weekly Standard*, 4 December 2000, p. 14.

81. Ed Offley, "Rejected Military Votes Spark New Furor in Florida Election Count," *Stars and Stripes Omnimedia*, 20 November 2000; Thomas E. Ricks, "Democratic Ballot Challenges Anger Military," *Washington Post*, 21 November 2000, p. A18; Kenneth Allard, "Military Ballot Mischief," *Washington Times*, 27 November 2000; Elaine M. Grossman, "Rift over Florida Military Ballots Might Affect a Gore Administration," *Inside the Pentagon*, 30 November 2000, p. 1.

82. Triangle Institute for Security Studies, "Survey on the Military in the Post Cold War Era," 1999. The question read: "If civilian leaders order the military to do something that it opposes, military leaders will seek ways to avoid carrying out the order: all of the time [9 percent chose this answer]; most of the time [21 percent]; some of the time [38 percent]; rarely [20 percent]; never [8 percent]; no opinion [4 percent]." The telephone survey of over a thousand people was administered by Princeton Survey Research Associates in September 1998.

83. I made this argument more fully in "The Political Trap for the Military," *Raleigh (North Carolina) News & Observer*, 22 September 2000, p. A19, orig. pub. *Washington Post* 19 September 2000, p. A23. See also Charles A. Stevenson, "Bridging the Gap between Warriors and Politicians," paper presented at the annual meeting of the American Political Science Association, Atlanta, Georgia, 2–5 September 1999.

84. Richard Holbrooke, *To End a War* (New York: Random House, 1998), pp. 144–6, 361–2. An indication of the bitterness that developed between Holbrooke and Admiral Leighton W. Smith, Commander in Chief, Allied Forces Southern Europe, who carried out the bombing on behalf of Nato's governing body, is in "Frontline: Give War a Chance," WGBH Educational Foundation, 2000, aired 11 May 1999, Public Broadcasting System. For a dispassionate view of the misunderstanding between political and military officials, see "Summary," in *Deliberate Force: A Case Study in Effective Bombing*, ed. Robert C. Owen [Col., USAF] (Maxwell Air Force Base [hereafter AFB], Ala.: Air Univ. Press, 2000), pp. 500–5.

85. Huntington, *Soldier and the State*, chaps. 2, 8–11, pp. 361–7; James L. Abrahamson, *America Arms for a New Century: The Making of a Great Military Power* (New York: Free Press, 1981), pp. 138–47; Karsten, *Naval Aristocracy*, 187–93.

86. In the TISS survey, the answers "agree strongly" or "agree somewhat" were given to the assertion, "The decline of traditional values is contributing to the breakdown of our society," according to the following distribution ("military" being defined as active-duty, reserve on active duty, and National Guard up-and-coming officers): military, 89 percent; civilian elite, 70 percent; mass public, 82 percent. For the statement "Through leading by example, the military could help American society become more moral" the figures were military 70 percent and civilian elite 42 percent (the mass public was not surveyed on this question). For "Civilian society would be better off if it adopted more of the military's values and customs," the distribution was: military, 75 percent; civilian elite, 29 percent; and mass public, 37 percent. See also Davis, "Attitudes and Opinions," in *Soldiers and Civilians*, ed. Feaver and Kohn, pp. 116–9. For more analysis of the military view of civilian society, see Gronke and Feaver, "Uncertain Confidence," pp. 147ff. On p. 149 they write, "Elite military officers evaluate civilian society far more negatively than do elite civilians." The use of the military as a role model for society has a long history in American thinking; in the 1980s, the Chief of Naval Operations, James D. Watkins, was a leading proponent of that view. Peter Grier, "Navy as National Role Model?" *Christian Science Monitor*, 4 June 1986, p. 1.

87. Sam C. Sarkesian, "The U.S. Military Must Find Its Voice," *Orbis*, Summer 1998, pp. 423–37; James H. Webb, Jr., "The Silence of the Admirals," U.S. Naval Institute *Proceedings*, January 1999, pp. 29–34. Sarkesian expanded the argument in Sam C. Sarkesian and Robert E. Connor, Jr., *The U.S. Military Profession into the Twenty-first Century: War, Peace and Politics* (London: Frank Cass, 1999), esp. chaps. 11, 12. Even as respected and experienced a defense reporter as George C. Wilson has implied that the senior military leadership should speak out publicly in disagreement with their civilian superiors. This sentiment became something of a mantra in the middle and late 1990s as senior officers were accused of caving in to political correctness. See Wilson, "Joint Chiefs Need to Be More Gutsy," *National Journal*, 20 November 1999, p. 3418.

88. Webb, "Silence of the Admirals," p. 34.

89. Crowe, *Line of Fire*, p. 214. The 1998–99 TISS survey asked under what circumstances "it is acceptable for a military member to leak unclassified information or documents to the press." The figures for active-duty officers were (rounded up):

Reserve and National Guard officers were slightly more willing to agree to leak, but a higher percentage of them (46 percent) answered "never."

90. Peter J. Skibitski, "New Commandant Intends to Push for More Resources for Pentagon," *Inside the Navy*, 15 November 1999, p. 1; Hunter Keeter, "Marine Commandant Calls for Defense Spending Increase," *Defense Daily*, 16 August 2000, p. 6; John Robinson, "Outgoing 6th Fleet Commander Warns Fleet Size Is Too Small," *Defense Daily*, 22

OPINION	AGREE (%)	DISAGREE (%)	NO OPINION (%)
"A crime has been committed and the chain of command is not acting on it."	26	70	4
"Doing so may prevent a policy that will lead to unnecessary casualties."	30	65	6
"Doing so discloses a course of action that is morally or ethically wrong."	28	65	7
"He or she is ordered to by a superior."	17	76	7
"Doing so brings to light a military policy or course of action that may lead to a disaster for the country."	39	55	6
"Never"	41	49	10

September 2000, p. 1; Elaine M. Grossman, "Defense Budget Boost to 4 Percent of GDP Would Pose Dramatic Shift," *Inside the Pentagon*, 31 August 2000, p. 3; Steven Lee Myers, "A Call to Put the Budget Surplus to Use for the Military," *New York Times*, 28 September 2000, p. A24; Cindy Rupert, "Admiral: Navy Pales to Past One," *Tampa Tribune*, 21 October 2000, p. 2; Linda de France, "Senior Navy Officers: 'We Need More Ships, Planes, Subs,'" *Aerospace Daily*, 30 October 2000, and "In Next QDR, 'Budgets Need to Support Our Tasking,' General Says," *Aerospace Daily*, 4 December 2000; Vickii Howell, "Admiral Tells Civic Clubs Navy Needs More Ships, Subs," *Birmingham (Alabama) News*, 16 November 2000, p. 6B; Robert I. Natter, "Help Keep This the Greatest Navy," U.S. Naval Institute *Proceedings*, December 2000, p. 2; Rowan Scarborough, "Military Expects Bush to Perform," *Washington Times*, 26 December 2000, p. 1.

91. Rowan Scarborough, "Cohen Tells Military Leaders 'Not to Beat Drum with Tin Cup,'" *Washington Times*, 8 September 2000, p. 4. Secretary Cohen told them, according to his spokesman, "to be honest but. . . ." According to Thomas E. Ricks and Robert Suro, "Military Budget Maneuvers Target Next President," *Washington Post*, 5 June 2000, p. 1, the armed services began ignoring civilian orders on the budget as early as June 2000, in order to "target" the next administration. "'We're going for the big money,' an officer on the Joint Staff was quoted as saying. . . . Pentagon insiders say the Clinton administration, which long has felt vulnerable on military issues, doesn't believe it can afford a public feud with the chiefs—especially in the midst of Gore's campaign. So, these officials say, aides to defense Secretary William S. Cohen are seeking only to avoid confrontation and to tamp down the controversy. . . . One career bureaucrat in the Office of the Secretary of Defense said privately that he was offended by the arrogant tone service officials have used in recent discussions. . . . By contrast, a senior military official said the chiefs' budget demands represent a 'repudiation of bankrupt thinking' in both the White House and Congress, which have asked the military to conduct a growing number of missions around the world in recent years without paying the full bill."

92. Bradley Graham, "Joint Chiefs Doubted Air Strategy," *Washington Post*, 5 April 1999, p. A1. See also Kenneth R. Rizer [Maj., USAF], *Military Resistance to Humanitarian War in Kosovo and Beyond: An Ideological Explanation*, Air University Library, Fairchild Paper (Maxwell AFB, Ala.: Air Univ. Press, 2000), pp. 1–2, 7, 41–2.

93. The regular public promotion of service interests by officers began when the Navy and Army in the late nineteenth and early twentieth centuries formed coherent understandings of their own roles in national defense and formal doctrines for war-fighting in their respective domains of sea and land (and later air). The institutionalization of service advice on military subjects and public pronouncements on national security affairs has circumscribed civilian control to a degree. Efforts to limit the military's public voice, beginning perhaps in the first Wilson administration (1913–17), have been episodic and often ineffective. See Allan R. Millett, *The American Political System and Civilian Control of the Military: A Historical Perspective* (Columbus: Mershon Center of the Ohio State University, 1979), pp. 19, 27–30; Karsten, *Naval Aristocracy*, pp. 301–13, 362–71; Abrahamson, *America Arms for a New Century*, pp. 147–50; Betros, "Officer Professionalism," in press; Johnson, *Fast Tanks and Heavy Bombers*, pp. 68–9.

94. Published in New York by HarperCollins, 1997. The author was McMaster's adviser at the University of North Carolina at Chapel Hill, 1992–96, for the seminar papers, master's thesis, and Ph.D. dissertation that resulted in the book.

95. McMaster hints at such an interpretation only by implying that the Army chief of staff, Harold K. Johnson, might have been justified in resigning (p. 318); by implying that the chiefs should have "confront[ed] the president with their objections to McNamara's approach to the war" (p. 328); by stating that "the president . . . expected the Chiefs to lie" and "the flag officers should not have tolerated it" (p. 331); and by blaming the chiefs for going along with a strategy they believed would fail, and thus sharing the culpability with their deceitful civilian superiors for losing the war "in Washington, D.C., even before Americans assumed sole responsibility for the fighting in 1965 and before they realized the country was at war; indeed, even before the first American units were deployed" (pp. 333–4). The interpretation of long standing in

military thinking since the Vietnam War is that the war lacked clear objectives; that it was lost because a fallacious strategy was imposed by deceitful politicians who limited American power and micromanaged military operations; and because the American people, with no stake in the war (in part because elites avoided service), were biased against the American effort by a hostile press. Rosemary Mariner, a retired naval captain and pioneer naval aviator, remembers "a certain litany to the Vietnam War story" in "every ready room" and at every "happy hour" from "flight training and throughout subsequent tactical aviation assignments" (she was commissioned in 1973), a "tribal lore that Robert S. McNamara was the devil incarnate whom the Joint Chiefs obviously didn't have the balls to stand up to. . . . Had the generals and admirals resigned in protest or conducted some kind of a second 'admiral's revolt,' the war would have either been won or stopped." Thus Mariner's "initial reaction to McMaster's book was that it simply affirmed what had been viewed as common wisdom." Conversation with the author, 13 April 2000, Durham, N.C.; e-mail to the author, 14 May 2001. Indications of the impact of Vietnam on officer thinking are in George C. Herring, "Preparing Not to Fight the Last War: The Impact of the Vietnam War on the U.S. Military," in *After Vietnam: Legacies of a Lost War,* ed. Charles Neu (Baltimore: Johns Hopkins Univ. Press, 2000), pp. 73–7; David Howell Petraeus, "The American Military and the Lessons of Vietnam: A Study of Military Influence and the Use of Force in the Post-Vietnam Era" (Ph.D. dissertation, Princeton University, Princeton, New Jersey, 1987); and Frank Hoffman, *Decisive Force: The New American Way of War* (Westport, Conn.: Praeger, 1996).

96. Fogleman explained his motives in a 1997 interview and specifically rejected the notion that he resigned in protest. Kohn, ed., "Early Retirement of Fogleman," pp. 6–23, esp. p. 20.

97. While there is no tradition of resignation in the American armed forces, it has happened, and occasionally senior officers have considered or threatened it. In 1907, "Admiral Willard H. Brownson resigned as chief of the Bureau of Navigation after the president [Theodore Roosevelt], over Brownson's protests, appointed a surgeon rather than a line officer to command a

hospital ship." Oyos, "Roosevelt, Congress, and the Military," p. 325. George C. Marshall offered or intimated resignation, or was reported to have done so, at least a half-dozen times when chief of staff, but he claimed later to have actually threatened it only once—and in retrospect characterized his action as "reprehensible." Forrest C. Pogue, *George C. Marshall: Ordeal and Hope* (New York: Viking, 1966), pp. 461 n. 33, 97–103, 285–7, and *George C. Marshall: Organizer of Victory, 1943–1945* (New York: Viking, 1973), pp. 246–7, 492–3, 510–1. General Harold K. Johnson considered resigning several times, and in August 1967 the Joint Chiefs (absent one member) considered resigning as a group over the Vietnam War. See Lewis Sorley, *Honorable Warrior: General Harold K. Johnson and the Ethics of Command* (Lawrence: Univ. Press of Kansas, 1998), pp. 181–2, 223–4, 263, 268–70, 285–7, 303–4. In 1977, on a flight to Omaha from Washington, General F. Michael Rogers suggested to four of his colleagues that all of the Air Force's four-stars should resign over President Jimmy Carter's cancelation of the B-1 bomber, but nothing came of the discussion. See Erik Riker-Coleman, "Political Pressures on the Joint Chiefs of Staff: The Case of General David C. Jones," paper presented at the annual meeting of the Society for Military History, Calgary, Alberta, 27 May 2001. The source for the discussion of mass resignation is Bruce Holloway [Gen., USAF], oral history interview by Vaughn H. Gallacher [Lt. Col., USAF], 16–18 August 1977, pp. 424–6, U.S. Air Force Historical Research Agency, Maxwell AFB, Alabama. In a discussion about pressure to resign over the cancelation of the B-1, General David C. Jones (oral history interview by Lt. Col. Maurice N. Marynow, USAF, and Richard H. Kohn, August–October 1985 and January–March 1986, pp. 178–9, 181) commented, "I think there are cases where people should perhaps resign: first, if they are ever pressured to do something immoral, illegal, or unethical; second, if you possibly felt you hadn't had your day in court—if you hadn't been able to express your views; or if we had been inhibited in the conversation to the Congress. . . . It seems to me that it is very presumptuous that somebody in the military can set themselves up on a pedestal, that they have the answer to the country, that the President who has just been elected on a platform of cutting the defense budget, is somehow so wrong that we are in this pedestal position, that we know the answers in this country. . . . It is up to the military to make its case, and then salute smartly once that case is made. . . . The only thing I have seen while I was in the military that really would be . . . a condition of resignation would be somehow during the Vietnam War. But probably . . . it would have been for the wrong reasons[—] . . . the White House . . . determining the targets . . . or whatever. The more fundamental reason is how in the world did we get ourselves involved in a land war in Southeast Asia[?]. . . [W]e are really servants of the people. The people make their decisions on the President. We are not elected; the President is elected. It's only in that regard if number one, they are trying to corrupt you by ignoring you and by muzzling you and all that sort of stuff. . . . Or if something is of such national importance, and I'm not sure anybody can predict it." In 1980, General Edward N. Meyer, chief of staff of the Army, was asked by the secretary of the Army to rescind a statement he had made to Congress about "a hollow army." Meyer refused and offered his resignation, but it was not accepted. Kitfield, *Prodigal Soldiers*, pp. 201–3. Retired Marine Corps commandant Charles C. Krulak (question and answer session, Joint Services Conference on Professional Ethics, Springfield, Virginia, 27–28 January 2000, enclosed in an e-mail from a colleague to the author, 1 February 2000) claimed that "it had become known within the Pentagon that 56 Marine General Officers would 'turn in their suits' if mixed gender training were imposed on the Marine Corps. . . . The Marines drew a line in the sand, and the opposition folded."

98. Colin L. Powell with Joseph E. Persico, *My American Journey* (New York: Random House, 1995), p. 167.

99. Ibid., p. 149. In May 1983, then Lieutenant Colonel Wesley Clark "suggested a line of argument" to then Brigadier General Powell for introducing a transition plan to the incoming Army chief of staff: "Isn't the most important thing never to commit U.S. troops again unless we're going in to win? No more gradualism and holding back like in Vietnam, but go in with overwhelming force?" According to Clark, "Powell agreed. . . . This argument captured what so many of us felt after Vietnam." Clark, *Waging*

Modern War, p. 7. Clark remembered that "in the Army, it had long been an article of resolve that there would be 'no more Vietnams,' wars in which soldiers carried the weight of the nation's war despite the lack of public support at home" (p. 17).

100. Ole R. Holsti, "Of Chasms and Convergences: Attitudes and Beliefs of Civilians and Military Elites at the Start of a New Millennium," in *Soldiers and Civilians*, ed. Feaver and Kohn, pp. 84, 489, and tables 1.27, 1.28.

101. Ronald T. Kadish [Lt. Gen., USAF], Director, Ballistic Missile Defense Organization, "Remarks," 6 December 2000, Space and Missile Defense Symposium and Exhibition, Association of the United States Army, El Paso, Texas, available at www.ausa.org/kadish.html.

102. Frank Hoffman e-mail to the author, 14 March 2000. Hoffman, a member of the national security study group assisting the U.S. Commission on National Security/21st Century, reported his conversation with a "Joint Staff Officer that the Joint Staff and the military officers in the NSC were coordinating a rapid schedule to preclude the president from announcing a Clinton Doctrine on the use of force in late October. It was expressed in the conversation that it was hoped that publishing a strategy with narrow use of force criteria would cut out the president from contradicting himself late in the month in a speech that would contravene the military's idea of how to use military force."

103. Kohn, ed., "Early Retirement of Fogleman," p. 12.

104. "Why is it . . . that whatever the question is—enforcing a peace agreement in Bosnia, evacuating the U.N. from Bosnia, or invading Haiti, the answer is always 25,000 Army troops?" asked one Marine officer of a reporter. By mid-1995, the uniformed leadership was more divided on opposing interventions. See Thomas E. Ricks, "Colin Powell's Doctrine on Use of Military Force Is Now Being Questioned by Senior U.S. Officers," *Wall Street Journal*, 30 August 1995, p. A12; Quinn-Judge, "Doubts of Top Brass," p. 12.

105. Kohn, ed., "Early Retirement of Fogleman," p. 18. Another possible resignation was voiced privately in 2000. Conversation with a senior military officer, January 2001.

106. In "The Pentagon, Not Congress or the President, Calls the Shots," *International*

Herald Tribune, 6 August 2001, available at www.iht.com/articles/28442.htm, journalist William Pfaff calls the military "the most powerful institution in American government, in practice largely unaccountable to the executive branch." He considers the Pentagon's "power in Congress" to be "unassailable." In "The Praetorian Guard," *National Interest*, Winter 2000/2001, pp. 57–64, Pfaff asserts (p. 63) that American "military forces play a larger role in national life than their counterparts in any state outside the Third World." See also Desch, *Civilian Control*, chap. 3 and appendix; Charles Lane, "TRB from Washington," *New Republic*, 15 November 1999, p. 8; Melvin Goodman, "Shotgun Diplomacy: The Dangers of Letting the Military Control Foreign Policy," *Washington Monthly*, December 2000, pp. 46–51; Gore Vidal, "Washington, We Have a Problem," *Vanity Fair*, December 2000, pp. 136ff.

107. For the long-term congressional forfeiture of authority in national security, see Louis Fisher, *Congressional Abdication on War & Spending* (College Station: Texas A&M Univ. Press, 2000), chaps. 1–4.

108. The oath every American military officer takes upon commissioning reads: "I, [name], do solemnly swear (or affirm) that I will support and defend the Constitution of the United States against all enemies, foreign and domestic; that I will bear true faith and allegiance to the same; that I take this obligation freely, without any mental reservation or purpose of evasion; and that I will well and faithfully discharge the duties of the office on which I am about to enter. So help me God." The requirement and wording is in 5 U.S.C. §3331 (1966). An oath to support the Constitution is required of "all executive and judicial officers" as well as senators and representatives, of the national and state governments, by Article VI, para. 3.

109. For civilian control in the Constitution, see Richard H. Kohn, "The Constitution and National Security: The Intent of the Framers," in *The United States Military under the Constitution of the United States, 1789-1989*, ed. Richard H. Kohn (New York: New York Univ. Press, 1991), pp. 61–94.

110. This is George Bush's characterization, in "A Nation Blessed," *Naval War College Review* 54, no. 4 (Autumn 2001), p. 138. The actual civil-military relationship and the extent of

civilian oversight are revealed in the works cited in endnote 111, below.

111. A good bibliography of the literature on the Vietnam War is George C. Herring, *America's Longest War: The United States and Vietnam, 1950–1975*, 3d ed. (New York: McGraw-Hill, 1996). The most convincing explanations of the American defeat explore the inability of the United States and South Vietnam to prevent communist forces from contesting the countryside and thereby continuing combat, and the failure to establish an indigenous government that could command the loyalty or obedience of the population, in the crucial period 1965–68, before the American people lost patience with the cost and inconclusiveness of the struggle and forced American disengagement. The best discussion to date of civil-military relations in the Persian Gulf War is Michael R. Gordon and General Bernard E. Trainor, *The Generals' War: The Inside Story of the Conflict in the Gulf* (Boston: Little, Brown, 1995). The memoirs of Generals Powell and Schwarzkopf confirm the very strong oversight and occasional intervention by the Bush administration in strategy and operations during the fighting. The senior British commander in the Gulf, General Sir Peter de la Billiere, *Storm Command: A Personal Account* (London: HarperCollins, 1992), remembers (p. 103) that "Schwarzkopf was under intense pressure from Washington . . . to consider other plans being dreamt up by amateur strategists in the Pentagon," but (pp. 139–40) that as late as early December 1990 he "had no written directive as to how he should proceed[,] . . . no precise instructions as to whether he was to attack Iraq as a whole, march on Baghdad, capture Saddam, or what." See also George Bush and Brent Scowcroft, *A World Transformed* (New York: Random House, 1998), pp. 302ff.

112. That civilian control includes the right of the civilians to be "wrong" is the insight of Peter D. Feaver. See his "The Civil-Military Problematique: Huntington, Janowitz and the Question of Civilian Control," *Armed Forces & Society*, vol. 23, 1996, p. 154.

113. The importance of firm civilian control, even to the point of interference in technical military matters, in order to assure a strong connection between ends and means, is the argument of Eliot A. Cohen, "The Unequal

Dialogue," in *Soldiers and Civilians*, ed. Feaver and Kohn, chap. 12.

114. S. L. A. Marshall, the famous journalist and reserve officer who from the 1930s through the 1970s studied and wrote so influentially about soldiers, soldiering, battle, and war, was not contrasting the military from other professions but people in uniform from all others when he wrote: "The placing of the line of duty above the line of self interest . . . is all that distinguishes the soldier from the civilian. And if that aspect of military education is slighted for any reason, the nation has lost its main hold on security." *The Soldier's Load and the Mobility of a Nation* (1947; repr. Quantico, Va.: Marine Corps Association, 1980), p. 104.

115. I am indebted to University of North Carolina at Chapel Hill emeritus professor of political science Raymond Dawson for this distinction.

116. Since the end of the Cold War, the Department of Defense has created at least three new institutes for security studies to teach democratic defense practices, particularly civilian control of the military, to other nations. Presently there are at least four, meant to serve uniformed officers, defense officials, and political leaders from formerly communist countries in Europe and Central Asia, Latin America, Africa, and the Asia-Pacific region.

117. Larry Rohter, "Fear of Loss of Democracy Led Neighbors to Aid Return," *New York Times,* 15 April 2002, p. A6; Christopher Marquis, "Bush Officials Met with Venezuelans Who Ousted Leader," *New York Times,* 16 April 2002, pp. A1, A8; and Peter Hakim, "Democracy and U.S. Credibility," *New York Times,* 21 April 2002, p. 4 wk.

118. Speech to the House of Commons, 11 November 1947, quoted in Robert Rhodes James, ed., *Winston S. Churchill: His Complete Speeches,* 8 vols. (New York: Chelsea House, 1974), vol. 7, p. 7566.

CHAPTER FIVE

"9/11" and After
A British View
SIR MICHAEL HOWARD

It may seem rather unnecessary to call any assertion by an Englishman "a British view." The views that I am going to express are probably shared by many Americans, continental Europeans, and Russians, to say nothing of Chinese, Indians, Brazilians, and the rest of the human race. I also suspect that quite a large number of my fellow countrymen may not share them—mine is certainly not *the* British view. But my views have inevitably been shaped, and probably prejudiced, by my national background and personal experience.

The British experience of terrorism on our own soil—mainly, though not entirely, at the hands of the Irish—goes back for well over a hundred years. I myself lived for two decades in London when it was a target of terrorist attacks. The loss of life was mercifully light, but those attacks did kill people, caused untold damage to property, and inflicted immense inconvenience to millions of London commuters. To take only one small but telling example: even today you will not find, in any main-line railway station, either a trash can or a left-luggage locker. They are far too convenient for the placement of Irish Republican Army bombs. In Belfast, of course, the situation was far worse. Many more people were killed, and much property was destroyed. There were times, I admit, seeing collectors for NORAID (the Irish Northern Aid Committee) rattling their boxes in the bars of Boston, when some of us thought that the United States might do just a little more to help us with our own war against terrorism. I make this point not just to have a dig at the Yanks (though this never does any harm) but to remind them that terrorism, in one form or another, has been going on for quite a long time and that the ethics involved are not always straightforward.

But the IRA attacks, of course, were pinpricks compared to the atrocities of 11 September 2001. This was an escalation of terrorist activity as great, and as threatening to

© 2002 by Sir Michael Howard
Naval War College Review, Autumn 2002, Vol. 55, No. 4

mankind, as was the explosion of the first nuclear weapon in comparison to the "conventional" campaigns that had preceded it. We understood very well that "9/11" posed a threat to ourselves, not just to the United States. By "ourselves" I mean not simply the British or even "the West" but every country—irrespective of location, race, or creed—that was attempting to create or maintain civil societies based on democratic consensus, human rights, and the rule of law—all the principles for which we had fought two terrible world wars. The attack on the Pentagon in Washington may have been aimed specifically at the United States, but those on the World Trade Center in New York, a supranational institution housing a multinational population in the greatest polyglot city in the world, was directed against the nerve centre of an international community of which the United States is certainly the heart but that embraces the whole developed world. That was why the whole of that world—in fact, the whole world, with the exception only of a few predictable rogue states—immediately declared its support to the United States in its hour of need.

That is why I must admit to a twinge of annoyance whenever I hear the phrase "America's War against Terror." It is not just "America's War." We are all in it. Of course, Americans were the major victims, or at least have been up till now. Of course, the Americans are able, with their immense military resources, to make the major contribution in any military campaign that has to be fought. But American citizens were not the only people who suffered on 11 September. The United States is not the only nation with troops in Afghanistan—and if there are not larger contributions from allies, it is because the U.S. high command made it clear from the very beginning, for understandable reasons, that it did not want them.

In any case, armed forces are not the only, or perhaps even the most important, instruments in dealing with terrorism. Intelligence services, police forces, immigration officials, financial managers, diplomats, even theologians, can play, and indeed are playing, an equally important role in the struggle. So to call it "America's War," and even more to wage it as if it were just "America's War," is to miss its full significance. It is a profound and global confrontation between, on the one hand, those who believe in all the civilized and civilizing values inherited from the Enlightenment, and on the other those who detest those values and fear them as a threat to their own core beliefs and traditional ways of life. In this confrontation armed force must inevitably play a part, but the struggle can never be won by armed forces alone—not even those of the United States.

So is "war" the right word to describe the conflict? I do not think that it is pedantic to ask this question. Journalists and politicians may have to reduce complex issues to headlines or sound bites; professional students of war and of international relations have to be more precise. The word "war" is dangerously misleading. It suggests a conflict waged against a clearly defined political adversary by armed forces to whose activities everything else is subsidiary; more important, it connotes a conflict that can end in a clear victory. This mind-set is revealed whenever the press speculates about "the next phase" in "the war against terror." For the media it is a conflict conducted in a series of military campaigns. After Afghanistan, where? Iraq? Somalia? Yemen?

But in fact there need be no "next phase." The campaign is being waged the whole time, twenty-four hours a day, seven days a week, all over the world. So long as there are no further outrages, we can be said to be winning it—winning through international police work, diplomacy, financial pressure, and propaganda. Whether another military campaign will be needed remains an open question. If we play our cards properly, we may succeed in rooting out al-Qa'ida and its associates without any further military action at all.

Still, it is perhaps inevitable that the word "war" should be used as an analogy, in the same way that we speak of a war against disease, or against drugs, or against crime—the mobilisation of all national resources to deal with a great social evil. But these are campaigns that cannot be "won" in any military sense. Crime and disease as such cannot be "defeated." We have to live with them. They can, however, be reduced to acceptable levels. It is the same with terrorism. Terrorism is a strategy, a means of making war, the classic instrument of the weak against the strong. It is used by desperate and ruthless people who are determined to bring down apparently immoveable forces of authority by any methods that lie to hand. It was used long before al-Qa'ida was ever thought of, and it will continue to be used long after al-Qa'ida has been forgotten. But if we are to deal with terrorism effectively, we need to know precisely who our adversaries are, how they are motivated, and where they come from.

First, even if a "war" against "terrorism" in general can no more be "won" than a war against disease, particular diseases can nonetheless be controlled or even eliminated. So can particular terrorist groups. Today we are dealing with an exceptionally dangerous network of transnational conspirators using all the traditional instruments of terrorism. They strike at soft targets. Their object is to gain publicity for their cause, to demoralise and discredit established authorities, and to gain popular support by provoking them into overreaction. Governments should regard them as criminals—criminals of a particularly dangerous kind. The appropriate instruments for dealing with them will be intelligence services and police, backed where necessary by special warfare units. The use of regular armed forces should be seen as a last resort, especially if one is dealing with urban terrorists. It is one thing to conduct a campaign in the sparsely inhabited mountains of Afghanistan or the jungles of Malaya. It is quite another to do so in the streets of a modern city, whether Londonderry or Jenin. In such an environment, armies, however hard they may try to exercise restraint, are bound to cause collateral damage that plays into the hands of terrorist propaganda. In plain English, a great many innocent people—small children, pregnant women, the elderly, the helpless—will be killed. The British learned all about this in Northern Ireland. The Israeli defence forces are experiencing this in dealing with Palestinian terrorists today. Such a campaign gives the terrorists exactly the kind of publicity, and belligerent status, that they need.

If terrorists can provoke the government to using regular armed forces against them, they have already taken a very important trick. They have been promoted to the status of "freedom fighters," a "liberation army," and may win popular support from sympathisers all over the world. Even if they are defeated, their glorious memory will inspire their successors. Pictures of Che Guevara adorned the walls of student dormitories for a generation, and I am afraid that images of Osama bin Laden will occupy the same place of honour in Islamic equivalents for quite as long.

Nonetheless, there are times when one cannot avoid the use of military force. It has to be used when the terrorists are able to operate on too large a scale to be dealt with by normal policing methods, as was the case in Ireland and is now in Israel. It has to be used when enemies establish themselves in territory that is virtually "no-man's-land." Finally, it has to be used when they enjoy the protection of another sovereign state.

For the flushing of terrorists or their equivalents out of no-man's-land we have plenty of historical precedent. The Caribbean was a nest of pirates until cleaned up in the eighteenth century. The coasts of the Mediterranean were terrorised by Barbary pirates until the U.S. Marine Corps landed on the shores of Tripoli. Today "failed states" like Yemen and Somalia cannot prevent their territory being used as terrorist bases, and armed force must be used to flush such foes out. Even states that in other respects may be achieving limited success in establishing the rule of law, such as Colombia, Indonesia, and the Philippines, may need help in eliminating terrorist elements on their own territory. When a terrorist organization enjoys the open protection and support of another sovereign state, as was the case with al-Qaʿida and the ruling government of Afghanistan, there is a serious casus belli, and a regular war may be the only way to bring the criminals to justice. (Whether it is always wise to do so is another matter. In 1914 the Austrian government took advantage of that excuse to declare war on Serbia and thereby caused a world war. Also, it is not at all obvious that the best way of dealing with IRA supporters in the United States would have been for the British to burn down the White House again.)

The struggle against a global terrorist network, then, though it may be misleading to call it a war, may involve specific wars. When it does involve such a war, if we are to retain our self-respect and the regard of the international community as a whole, we should conduct it in accordance with the obligations and constraints that the civilized world has developed for armed conflicts over the past three hundred years. The war should not be undertaken unless legitimized by general international support. In conducting it, care should be taken to avoid collateral damage. Enemy forces should be given the protection of the Geneva Conventions that we expect for our own. The status of members of terrorist organizations that do not belong to the armed forces of the enemy should be defined, and individuals suspected of criminal acts should be tried and judged accordingly. Not least important, we should have a clear vision of the long-term objective of the war; victory in the field must be converted into a stable peace. War, in short, is a serious matter, not just a manhunt on a rather larger scale.

That is why there was so much hesitation in the international community as a whole, not least in the United Kingdom, when the president of the United States linked the campaign against the terrorist network responsible for the atrocities of 11 September with a broader "axis of evil,"* consisting primarily of countries hostile to the United States that are developing "weapons of mass destruction"—Iraq, Iran, and North Korea. These are all very different cases, and each of them needs to be considered on its merits. There is some evidence linking Saddam Hussein with al-Qaʻida, but no more than points to Libya, or Syria, or even Saudi Arabia. The real charge against Saddam is that he is continuing to develop weapons of mass destruction in defiance of United Nations prohibition, and he should certainly be stopped—but that is rather a different matter. In the case of Iran there is a stronger connection with al-Qaʻida, which enjoys the open support of the mullahs; however, in that country modernising and Western-leaning elements have made huge headway since the days of the Ayatollah Ruholla Khomeini, and to condemn their entire nation as "evil" does little to help them. As for North Korea, though it is a very rogue state indeed, linking it with the Islamic fundamentalism that inspired the perpetrators of "9/11" has caused general bewilderment.

Certainly, all three are problem states that pose dangers to global stability, but opinions quite justifiably differ as to how urgent are the threats they respectively pose and how they can best be dealt with. Their connection with the "9/11" atrocity is at best remote, and "regime changes" in them could not prevent a new such outrage. There is a real danger that in enlarging the objective of its campaign from a war against a specific terrorist organization to a general and almost indefinable "War against Terror," the United States is not only losing the support of many of its friends and necessary allies but becoming distracted from the real long-term threat that emerged in Manhattan, the Pentagon, and rural Pennsylvania on 11 September. That horrific event was like the sudden

---

* State of the Union address, Washington, D.C., 29 January 2002.

eruption of a flame from a fire that had long been smouldering underground. It will continue to smoulder whatever happens to Saddam Hussein.

Although terrorism, like war itself, is probably as old as mankind, there are two particularly alarming features of the present situation. The first is the new vulnerability to terrorist attack of our fragile and interdependent societies. The destruction of the twin towers and the gouging of the Pentagon were horrific and spectacular, but the actual damage caused was finite. The massacre of some three thousand people was horrific and spectacular enough, but if nuclear or chemical weapons had been used the death toll would have been at least ten times as great. The disruption of world trade was traumatic, but it was temporary and minimal; skilful infestation of global computer networks could have magnified and prolonged that disruption indefinitely. The terrorist attacks of 11 September constituted a single if terrible act; a linked series of such catastrophes could have caused widespread panic, economic crisis, and political turbulence on a scale that could make democratic government almost impossible.

Dystopian scenarios of a kind hitherto confined to Hollywood have now become real possibilities, if not yet probabilities. They could all be caused, like the destruction of the twin towers, by conspiratorial networks that need no state sponsorship to provide them with weapons, expertise, finance, or motivation. These "nonstate actors" (to use political-science jargon) are nourished and supported by the very societies they are attempting to destroy. Their members have been educated in Western universities, trained in Western laboratories and flying schools, and financed, however unwittingly, by global consortiums. They are not tools of Saddam Hussein or anyone else. We have bred and educated them ourselves. One can buy box-cutters and airway schedules nearer home than Baghdad, Tehran, or Pyongyang.

The second feature of this breed of terrorists is even more disquieting—their motivation. Normally, terrorism has been a method used to achieve a specific political objective. In nineteenth-century Russia, where the technique was invented, the goal was the overthrow of the tsarist regime. In the Ireland of Sinn Fein it was liberation from British rule. In British-ruled Palestine in the 1940s, the terrorist tactics of Irgun and the Stern Gang were highly effective in securing the establishment of a Jewish state. Once their objective is achieved, such terrorists—now transformed into "freedom fighters"—are welcomed into the community of nations and their leaders become respected heads of state, chatting affably with American presidents on the lawn of the White House. The terrorist activities of contemporary Islamic fundamentalists are certainly linked to one particular political struggle—what they see as the attempt of the Palestinians to achieve independent statehood and recognition, which is a struggle that, in spite of the methods they use, enjoys a wide measure of support throughout the Islamic world. But even if that attempt were successful and President Arafat were once again received in the White House, this time as head of a fully fledged Palestinian state, the campaign of the fundamentalists would not come to an end. The roots of the campaign go far deeper, and the objectives of the terrorists are far more ambitious. The fundamentalist campaign is rooted in a visceral hatred and contempt for Western civilization as such and resentment at its global ascendancy. The object of the extremists is to destroy it altogether.

Here this analysis becomes influenced not so much by a British as a European background—or rather, by European history. This teaches that there is nothing new about such hatred and that it is not peculiar to Islam. It originated in Europe two centuries ago in reaction to the whole process of what is loosely known as the Enlightenment. It was a protest against the erosion of traditional values and authorities by the rationalism, the secularism, and the freethinking that both underlay and were empowered by the American and French Revolutions. It gained further strength in the nineteenth century as industrialisation and modernisation transformed European society, creating general disorientation and alienation that was to be exploited by extreme forces on both the Left and the Right. By the beginning of the twentieth century it was reinforced by mounting alarm at the development of a global economy that, in spite of the growth of democracy, seemed to place the destinies of millions in the hands of impersonal and irresponsible forces beyond the control of national governments. It was, in short, a cry of rage against the whole seemingly irresistible process that has resulted from the dissolution of traditional constraints on thought and enterprise and the release of the dynamic forces of industrial development collectively known as "capitalism." It was to provide the driving force behind both fascism and communism, and it was to be one of the underlying causes of the Second, if not indeed the First, World War.

The experience of Europe in the nineteenth century was to be repeated in the twentieth and continues today throughout what is still, for want of a better label, described as the "third world." There also industrialisation has led to urbanisation, with the resulting breakdown of traditional authority and the destruction of cultures rooted in tribal rule and land tenure. There also medical advances, by reducing the death rate, have led to unprecedented increases in the population. There also a surplus population has fled from the countryside to overcrowded cities, and from the cities to, where possible, overseas. But there the similarity ends. In the nineteenth century there was a New World prepared to accept immigrants on an unlimited scale. Today there is not. The third world has to absorb its own surplus population, as best it can.

In nineteenth-century Europe the immiseration of the Industrial Revolution was certainly eased by emigration, but it was eventually conquered by the very economic development that had originally caused it. Market economies overcame their teething troubles and converted their hungry masses into consumers with money in their pockets. State activities expanded to curb the excesses of the market and to care for its casualties. Today the general assumption in the West is that the problems of the third world, with the help of Western capital and technology, will ultimately be solved by the same process—the creation of thriving national economies that will absorb surplus labour and transform the unemployed masses into prosperous consumers, within a stable infrastructure provided by an efficient and uncorrupt state.

The trouble is that this very goal—that of a prosperous materialist society with religion as an optional extra—appalls Islamic fundamentalists, as well as many Muslims who are not fundamentalists. They regard Western society not as a model to be imitated but as an awful warning, a Sodom and Gomorrah, an example of how mankind should *not* live. Instead they embrace a heroic anticulture, one that has much in common with the European ideologues who protested against the decadence of Western materialism and preached redemption of mankind through war; they hold it, however, with a fanaticism possible only to those who believe that they will receive their reward in an afterlife. Like fascism and communism, their creed appeals to the idealistic young, especially those who feel rejected by the society around them, as do all too many immigrants in the cities of Europe. Like fascism and communism, it attracts all who are disillusioned with the promises of liberal capitalism or are suffering from its defects.

It is only natural that this appeal should be most effective among peoples for whom the world of Western capitalism is not only profoundly alien and offensive in itself—with its godlessness, its shamelessness, its materialism, and its blatant vulgarity—but worse, seems to be winning, bulldozing away the world of their ancestors and the values that held their societies together for aeons. For them the enemy is not just Western capitalism as such but its powerhouse, the United States, the Great Satan. More specifically, it is those elements within Islamic societies that appear to be cooperating with it.

Nevertheless—and this cannot be too often or too strongly stressed—there is as little sympathy in the Islamic world for the methods and objectives of the terrorists as there is in the West. Whatever their self-appointed spokesmen may say, the rising expectations of the Islamic peoples are almost certainly focused on achieving the kind of material well-being that the West ultimately promises (and the terrorists reject), so long as that goal remains compatible with their core cultural beliefs. Al-Qa'ida and its associates are exactly the kind of puritanical iconoclasts who emerge in all revolutionary situations and try to remould humanity to fit their own ideal worlds. In unstable societies the ruthlessness and fanaticism of such people bring them to the fore and enable them, however briefly, to seize power and do an untold amount of harm.

So the global reach of contemporary terrorists should not blind us to the fact that their strength derives from the general instability of contemporary Islamic societies and that therefore the problem, ultimately, is one for Islam itself. If there is indeed "a war against terrorism," it has to be fought and won within the Islamic world. The role of the West must be to support and encourage those who are fighting that war, and we must take care that we do nothing to make their task more difficult.

This will not be easy. How can we support our friends in the Islamic world, those who are seeking their own path to modernisation, without making them look like Western stooges, betraying their own cultures? How should we treat their leaders who are as hostile to—and as threatened by—Islamic fundamentalism as we are but who use what we regard as unacceptable methods to suppress it? How can we avoid being associated with the wealthy elements in Islamic countries that are most resistant to the social changes that alone can make possible the spread and acceptance of Western ideas?

These are all problems for the long run. What about the short?

There are two paradigms for dealing with "international terrorism," both equally mis-leading. One is the liberal ideal, held by well-meaning Europeans and perhaps a good many well-meaning Americans as well. According to this, international terrorists should be dealt with by police action under the auspices of the United Nations. Any military action should be conducted by UN forces, and suspected terrorists should be brought to trial before an international court. The other is rather more popular in the United States—"America's War," a private fight conducted by the armed forces of the United States against almost cosmic forces of evil. In this conflict no holds are barred; America must do "whatever it takes" to destroy those forces. The support of the outside world is welcomed, indeed expected—as President Bush put it, "Either you are with us, or you are with the terrorists"*—but the war will be waged and won by Americans without any interference by well-intentioned but wimpish allies, condemnation by woolly-minded do-gooders, or constraints imposed by outmoded concepts of interna-tional law.

The first of these paradigms, the liberal ideal, may be desirable, but is quite unrealistic. Apart from anything else, in their present mood the American people are simply not prepared to subject themselves to any international authority or to hand over the

---

* "Address to a Joint Session of Congress and the American People," U.S. Capitol, Washington, D.C., 20 September 2001.

perpetrators of the "9/11" massacre to any foreign jurisdiction. In any case, the record shows that "the international community" as such is quite unable to organize any serious military intervention unless the United States not only supports it but plays a leading role. Whether the other nations involved like it or not, the campaign against international terrorism must be conducted on terms acceptable to, though not necessarily dictated by, the United States, and in waging it American resources will be indispensable.

The other view, "America's War," may be realistic, but it is both undesirable and likely to be counterproductive. By nationalising the war in this manner, there is a real danger that the United States will antagonise the entire Moslem world, lose the support of its natural allies in the West, and play into the hands of its former opponents, at present quiescent but by no means eliminated, in Russia and the People's Republic of China. This would be a profound tragedy. In 1945 the United States was able to convert a wartime alliance into a framework for world governance capable of embracing its former enemies and surviving the tensions and trials of the Cold War. In 1990 its rapid liquidation of the Cold War and generosity to its former adversaries held out genuine promise of a New World Order. The impact of "9/11" seemed to provide just such another catalytic moment. America's traditional rivals and adversaries fell over one another in offering support, which was eagerly accepted. It looked as if a genuine world community was being forged, one of entirely new range and strength. Out of the evil done on 11 September, it seemed, unprecedented good might come. It still might, and it still should.

But it will only come if the United States abandons its unilateral approach to the handling of international terrorism and recognises that the problem can effectively be dealt with only by the international community that America has done so much to create—a community embracing the bulk of the Islamic world—and that still needs American leadership if it is to function effectively.

There is considerable risk that otherwise, however effective America's armed forces may prove in the field and however many "regime changes" they may precipitate, the United States may end up not only alienating its traditional allies but indefinitely facing a sullen and hostile Islamic world where terrorists continue to breed prolifically and the supporters of the West live in a state of permanent siege. It would be a world in which, to my own perhaps parochial perspective, countries like Britain with large Islamic minorities will live under a perpetual shadow of race war. Is it too much to hope that I shall live to see a world where it is safe to have trash cans in our railway stations?

PART TWO

Naval Strategy

CHAPTER SIX

Fighting at and from the Sea
A Second Opinion

FRANK UHLIG, JR.

In our concentration on the excellent sensors, weapons, computers, and communications systems now or soon to be in our hands, strategic and operational naval theory has faded from our minds—in some cases, it may never even have entered. Hence, the great effects imposed on the Navy and, indeed, on the world at large by Captain Alfred Thayer Mahan seemingly have passed forever. Since Mahan, who died nearly ninety years ago, few have ventured into this still ill-explored field of endeavor, and the names of those who have done so do not easily come to the minds of others.

However, naval theory beyond the management of arms, sensors, and communications is alive, if not perfectly well.[1] Those writing today in this field invite thought on several matters, but here I will comment on only one—the methods for the use of naval forces in war.

One well informed and thoughtful scholar lists six such methods.[2] These, in the order discussed below, are coastal defense, maritime power projection, commerce raiding, the fleet-in-being, fleet battle, and blockade. Over the centuries navies have used, or tried, all of them, and others, too. In the last half-century they have added two new methods. Perhaps a third is in the offing.

The defense of coasts, and especially of harbors, against superior forces coming from the sea has most often and most powerfully been undertaken from ashore by armies and air forces. The usual result of a strong harbor defense is that the potential invader either chooses a less desirable place through which to begin his campaign ashore, or he does not try at all. Cases in point are Manila in World War II and, also in World War II, some of the French Atlantic ports, all of them well defended. The Japanese, impressed by the harbor defenses at Manila, began their drive upon that city in December 1941 at

© 2002 by Frank Uhlig, Jr.

Lingayen Gulf, 120 miles to the north. At the time of the Allied amphibious attack at
Normandy in 1944, British and American respect for the German defenses of the
French Atlantic ports led them to land near none of them. Through the use of small
craft, including submarines, and minefields, local naval forces can contribute, in an ad-
junctive manner, to the defense of a coast or port, but they have seldom had the principal role and seem unlikely to do so often in the foreseeable future.

Maritime power projection consists of bombardments by aircraft, missiles, and guns,
small-unit raids ashore, and invasions, all coming from across the sea. Whatever the
form, this is what coastal defenses are supposed to thwart. These offensive actions from
the sea are an option for strong navies when the enemy's navy is weak and even more
so when his coastal defenses, too, are thin. When the defending enemy is strong the attacking fleet, and the landing force as well, must be very strong.

Nowadays, it might be argued, a large amphibious force would surely be detected well
ahead of time, the defenders alerted, and the amphibious assault crushed. Still, in most
such assaults of the last century, even though the defender usually did not know exactly
when the attack was coming, he hardly ever was unprepared to oppose it vigorously. Yet,
almost without exception, the amphibious assault carried the day. Thus, one should not refrain from using the amphibious weapon simply because it may no longer be hidden. In effect, it seldom ever was.

In 2001–2002, Osama bin Laden and his Taliban hosts probably imagined that in the
absence of an Afghan coastline to be assaulted, they were safe from American reprisals
mounted from the sea for bin Laden's murderous attacks on the United States of 11
September. No doubt to the consternation of bin Laden and the others, American diplomacy opened the Pakistani gates between Afghanistan and the Indian Ocean, as well
as other gates well inland, and the American reprisals on the Taliban and their admir-
ing guest came anyway. First the reprisals came from aircraft flying off carriers in the
Arabian Sea and, not long after, from Air Force aircraft too. Some of the latter flew from
Diego Garcia in the Indian Ocean, others from countries bordering on Afghanistan, and
some directly from the United States. All American aircraft en route to Afghanistan
needed the help of not only diplomacy but also, because of the long distances they had
to fly in order to reach their objectives, that of tanker aircraft. The carrier planes were,
for instance, "heavily dependent on shore-based tanking, much of which was provided
by the RAF."[3] Altogether the aircraft, assisted by several dozen Tomahawk land-attack
cruise missiles fired from ships at sea, achieved a great deal. In cooperation with a few
hundred Special Forces troops and a number of Afghan tribal armies, within a short
time they chased the Taliban and its guests out of the lowlands and the cities into the
mountains, where the survivors still lurk. The outcome of the struggle in Afghanistan is

unclear and may remain so for some time. But the aviators flying from afloat and ashore were essential to the improvements so far achieved.

In whatever form it comes, maritime power projection works best when at least the immediate objectives are at, or near, the coast, or at most within the normal combat radius of the fleet's aircraft, including those of the landing force. It need not involve any combat afloat, though if such combat is among the possibilities, a navy had best be prepared to engage in it successfully. In 1917–18 this country advanced an army of two million soldiers across three thousand miles of the contested Atlantic to friendly French ports. To protect the forward-moving battalions, regiments, brigades, and divisions in their transports from German U-boats, the Navy provided each convoy with a substantial escort of destroyers. Once the troops were disembarked, authorities ashore took over and moved them to where they would be needed, eventually to the fighting front three or four hundred miles inland. Though not an invasion, that enormous achievement, right up to disembarkation, certainly was "maritime power projection."

On a much smaller scale but mounted much more swiftly and over a much greater distance—eight thousand miles—the Royal Navy also projected power ashore in 1982, in response to the Argentine invasion of the Falkland Islands. The British navy landed the rescuing troops not in a friendly port but across a hostile, though undefended, beach fifty miles from the objective, which was the garrisoned village of Port Stanley. The Argentines chose to oppose the British amphibious assault—that is, they engaged in coastal defense—not with the troops they had on the islands, nor with missile-armed surface combatants, but with naval and air force aircraft flying from bases four hundred miles distant. It was only by a slight margin that the Argentine aviators failed. But they did, and in a few days the British landing force had recaptured the archipelago.

Whether the objective is near to, or far from, the beach, maritime power projection has so far had the most influence when the power projected from the ships consisted chiefly of troops in sufficient numbers to meet the need, and when the fleet supported them, during the landing and thereafter, with fire and logistics. A new form of fire support for forces ashore or about to go ashore is that of defending them, and the ships in which they are embarked, against attack by ballistic missiles. This may prove to be a heavy burden, to be borne by only a small number of ships. In our recent small wars, the primary forces projected, whether from ashore or afloat, have consisted of bomber and attack aircraft, with troops and surface-to-surface missiles in a supporting role.[4] Be that as it may, a successfully landed army soon enough will provide its own fire, including that against ballistic missiles, but while the fighting lasts, its need for logistical support will be unending.

A few small, short-distance airborne assaults were carried out during World War II, notably by the Germans at Crete in 1941. But as a rule, the projection of an army across the water has been successful only when either there was little danger to shipping at sea or the side that wished to project force ashore had gained at least momentary command of those parts of the sea that were of interest to it. It had to continue to maintain such command for as long as it wished to sustain its forces on the other shore. After their air-landed assault forces had defeated the British defenders on Crete, the Germans achieved adequate local sea command, chiefly through the use of shore-based aviation.

Sometimes the weaker side at sea will engage in *commerce raiding*—that is, attacks on enemy shipping where no core issues are at stake, where distances are great, and where, while enemy merchant ships may be scarce, enemy warships are scarcer yet. The objective is, as inexpensively as possible, to annoy and inconvenience the enemy as much as possible without attracting too much of the enemy's strength to the defense of its distant merchantmen. This mode is exemplified by the nineteenth-century Confederate raider *Alabama* and by Germany's newly armed former merchant ships roaming the lonely southern ocean in the last century's world wars. This might still work, but probably not for long.

It was the weaker side too, and it alone, that would engage in the practice of a *fleet-in-being*. This required little more than a substantial naval presence with which to inhibit useful activities on the part of the more powerful opponent. The mere presence of the large German High Seas Fleet in the southeastern corner of the North Sea through the entire First World War is an example. It prevented the British from shifting important elements of the more powerful Grand Fleet (based at Scapa Flow, in that sea's northwestern corner) to other waters where they would have been most welcome. As the example suggests, the effect of a fleet-in-being was likely to be marginal. After 1918 this passive and largely ineffective form of warfare had just about died. Current means of intelligence and communications have buried the corpse.[5]

Fleet battle is aimed, through the defeat and even destruction of the enemy's main force at sea, at gaining command of that sea. Why does one seek such command? What can one do with it? One seeks such command so that friendly shipping, filled with cargoes or people necessary for the survival of a nation and the success of its forces in battle, can sail to where it is needed when it is needed, and so that hostile shipping cannot do those things.

Once the enemy's main force at sea is defeated or destroyed, one's own combatant ships can then be dispersed in ways that will help ensure the destruction of the enemy's weaker warships and the capture, blockade, or destruction of his military and commercial shipping. Moreover, concentrated anew, they can protect and support forces engaged in the projection of power ashore.

What do we mean by "shipping"? Commercial shipping, normally privately owned but in wartime usually under government control, consists of ships carrying fuel (gas, coal, oil, refined products), dry bulk cargoes (grains and ores), food and manufactured goods (now almost always in containers), autos and trucks, and heavy and bulky structures (sometimes including damaged ships). Commercial shipping also includes ships and boats engaged in fishing, in support of those extracting oil and gas from the sea, and in the swift or clandestine transport of such illegal cargoes as drugs and unsought immigrants. Though they are not ships, oil and gas rigs in the ocean, and transoceanic cables too, are as worthy of naval attack and defense as any ship might be.

Military shipping, often commissioned naval vessels, includes all those ships that do not take part in the struggle for command of the sea—such as those intended for amphibious warfare and for the logistical support of forces engaged in combat afloat, aloft, or ashore. Ballistic missile submarines come under this heading too.

Though there have been many actions between small and medium-sized naval forces—such as at Manila Bay (1898), Dogger Bank (1915), and the bloody night actions in Ironbottom Sound (1942)—there have never been many fleet battles. In the First World War there was only Jutland (1916). On that occasion the German admirals had neither sought nor expected their encounter with the Grand Fleet; thereafter they made sure it would not be repeated. The battle's most important effect was that the German navy shifted the bulk of its effort to direct attack on hostile shipping by means of submarines. In the Second World War there were no fleet battles at all in either the Atlantic or the Mediterranean, and very few in the Pacific. It seems likely that no one now, or soon to be, in any navy will ever experience such an action.

Blockades attempt in another way to achieve what successful fleet battles theoretically do. The military blockade is an attempt by the stronger fleet to keep the weaker fleet locked in port where it can do its own side no good, its enemy no harm. Even in the old days blockades were more common than big battles, because while the stronger fleet longed for a fleet action, the weaker one dreaded such a thing. Since the coming of the aircraft and now of the long-range missile as well, ships in port are not likely to be any safer than those at sea. The difference is that ships at sea can do things, and they often are hard for an enemy to find, while those in port can do nothing and are easy for an enemy to find.

Just before the First World War, with the submarine an established part of every fleet, the aircraft not far behind, and the effectiveness of minefields upon incautious ships beyond doubt, the British decided that next time they would establish a "distant" blockade (hundreds of miles from the ports of interest) rather than a "close" one.

When war broke out in 1914, traffic across the once commercially lively North Sea ended, as a result of the British blockade; that sea became, in the words of a German admiral, Edward Wegener, a "dead sea."[6] So it remained as long as the war lasted. Mainly in its commercial form, the distant blockade was a great success. Almost no ships, civil or naval, tried to sail from outside into German ports or from German ports to destinations outside. Only U-boats tried that. They made such voyages routinely, but they alone.

In the role of counterblockaders the U-boats proved highly successful. In the English Channel, the Western Approaches to Britain, and the Mediterranean too, they could not capture British and other Allied shipping, but they could sink it. Soon an old truth reasserted itself—that Britain and its allies, much more than a wholly continental alliance, were dependent for their very lives on the flow of merchant shipping in and out. The defeat of Allied shipping by the U-boats would have meant the defeat of the entire Allied war effort. In the nick of time, the British, both naval officers and merchant mariners, reluctantly recognized that the way to overcome the deadly threat was to form merchantmen into convoys guarded by small warships suitable to the task. This they did; as a result, the threat to shipping was cut to a bearable size. The Allies recovered their strength, and before the end of 1918 they had defeated Germany on the western front.

In the second war, that of 1939–45, as soon as possible the struggle at sea between submarines and convoys took the form of submarine "wolf packs" deployed operationally against convoys by headquarters ashore on the strength of communications intelligence. The convoys, this time protected not only by small warships but also by large, land-based aircraft, came to depend as well on advice, commands, and communications intelligence from their own headquarters ashore. In keeping with the Allied objective at sea—the safe and timely arrival of the convoys—the most important use of such intelligence was to route the convoys away from where it was expected that U-boats would be. The next most important use of it was to direct Allied aircraft and warships not needed for escort of convoys to where U-boats would most likely be found. It took the Allies three and a half years to win this struggle. Once they had the upper hand they never loosened their grip, for victory in the Atlantic was the prerequisite for victory on and over the continent of Europe.

What we have seen here—sustained heavy assault on, and defense of, shipping far at sea—is something not often found in lists of naval functions. However, since the world wars we have not seen, nor are we likely soon to see again, anything like it. Rather, the assault on, and defense of, shipping has abandoned the open oceans and moved into coastal waters and the narrow seas. Aircraft and surface combatants large and small have engaged in such warfare during the last half-century in the Sea of Japan, Yellow

Sea, Taiwan Strait, South China Sea, Persian Gulf, Red Sea, eastern Mediterranean, and Falkland Sound. Some of their actions have had much greater influence, or impact, on the course of the war than the small size of the craft often engaged would lead one to expect.

By the middle of the twentieth century we had seen the end, so it appears, of commerce raiding, the fleet battle, and the fleet-in-being. What remained for navies was, by whatever means were both possible technically and acceptable politically, to ensure that friendly shipping could reach its destination in a safe and timely fashion and that hostile shipping could not. Should friendly shipping be able to do as desired, then and only then would it also be possible, if necessary, to engage in maritime projection of power—that is, to assault the enemy ashore, in whatever ways seemed most suitable.

Since then, two methods of using naval forces have been added and two strategic conditions have changed. The first new method to be added was the deterrence of nuclear attack—the forestalling of any such attack upon one country by means of the threat of an equal or greater nuclear blow upon the country that had launched the attack. The necessity for this arose shortly after the Soviet Union demonstrated its ability to manufacture and use nuclear weapons. In the United States, at first nuclear deterrence was entirely the responsibility of the Air Force, but over time it shifted toward the sea, and now, through its ballistic-missile submarines, the Navy has a large, perhaps the largest, part to play. For the same reason as the United States, the Soviets, British, and French also supplied themselves with such submarines. With Russia having reasserted its own existence in place of the sinister Soviet Union and the good relations now enjoyed among all four powers possessing such submarines, the deterrence task has lost the salience it once had. Moreover, it has no part in our current struggle against a stateless enemy, Osama bin Laden and his criminal gang of religious zealots. But against a small power potentially possessing some "weapons of mass destruction," the deterrent effect of our ready nuclear forces should be as dependable at least as it was in the days of an immensely powerful, aggressive, and overtly hostile Soviet Union. As the years go by it will be important to replace old ships, weapons, and all else necessary to the success of the force dedicated to the role of nuclear deterrence.

The other new method of employing naval forces is that of making sure friendly air traffic can pass over the sea and hostile military air traffic cannot. Let us quickly review an example. In the fall of 1973 the United States responded to an Israeli demand for help during the war that had broken out between that country and Egypt (to the southwest) and Syria (to the northeast). U.S. combat aircraft were flown from this country to Israel; to ensure their safe and timely arrival, the Sixth Fleet strung itself out almost from one end of the Mediterranean to the other. Its immediate tasks were navigational assistance to transiting aircraft, protection against air interdiction originating in North Africa, and help in the event of a mishap. Two carriers of the three available in that theater provided tanker support to aircraft that needed it, while the third made room for some of those same aircraft on its flight deck. Shortly, it appeared that the other great power actively engaged in the area, the Soviet Union, might be preparing to airlift some of its own troops to Egypt. In response, the Sixth Fleet concentrated south of Crete, where, should the situation arise, it could both protect Israeli-bound shipping and aircraft, and destroy Soviet shipping and aircraft bound for Egypt. Meanwhile Soviet warships, which had been stationed where they could protect supply ships and air transports bound for Syria, moved south so they could provide similar protection to air transports bound for Egypt. They might have performed that task either by means of surface-to-air missiles with which to engage U.S. fighter planes headed toward the transport aircraft, or by means of surface-to-surface missiles with which to engage the carriers from which the aircraft would fly. By that time, however, a truce respected by both sides had taken hold ashore. The Soviets did not try to fly their troops to Egypt. Slowly the ships dispersed, and the crisis wound down.[7]

At the top of the preceding paragraph is an inequality: a fleet must ensure the passage of "friendly *air traffic*" and prevent the passage of "hostile *military air traffic*." The reason for protecting all friendly air traffic is plain. But attack on hostile civil aircraft, at least at the beginning of a war, could result in the destruction of an airplane filled with hundreds of civilian passengers trying merely to go about their private lives. In 1988 a U.S. warship did shoot down an Iranian civil airliner (having mistaken it for an attacking combat plane), and nearly three hundred people perished unnecessarily. Nothing much came of this, for the United States expressed its regrets immediately and did what little it could to make amends. A more ominous analog was the sinking by a U-boat in 1915 of the British passenger liner *Lusitania,* an attack that cost over a thousand lives, including those of many Americans. Most people in this country had been indifferent to the outcome of the European war, but the sinking turned many of them into opponents of Germany and helped bring about the American decision two years later to enter the war against that country. So, although passage of hostile military aircraft over the sea, or even inland within reach of the fleet's weapons, should be prevented, passage of an enemy's civil aircraft is a different matter.

The potential third new method of employing naval forces in war or near-war is that of forward defense of countries friendly to us from attack by ballistic missiles. If this task, which is likely to be separate from that of defending our own forces, were undertaken by the U.S. Navy, it would require the services of perhaps a large portion of the nation's not very numerous modern surface combatants, at some measurable cost to the accomplishment of other assigned, or assumed, missions.

In order to destroy a hostile ballistic missile before it has gained too much speed or advanced too far into space for a forward-deployed ship to counter, our ship might have to be very close to the launching site. However, its being there would mark it as a clear and present danger to one of the potential enemy's most highly prized possessions. Thus, before launching a missile (not necessarily only one missile), the enemy might reasonably seek to disable, sink, or capture our forward-located ballistic missile–defense ship. Because the hair-trigger nature of our ship's duty will demand the full attention of all on board, to assure that it can carry out its assigned task, we might find it advisable to deploy additional forces for its protection. This is one of those old naval issues that, when ignored, bring great difficulty. Consider the catastrophes that enveloped those lonely far-forward ships, the USS *Liberty* in 1967 and the USS *Pueblo* in 1968.[8]

Perhaps the threat to a hostile ruler of being annihilated himself, along with all he values, posed by our, and other countries' nuclear deterrent forces, so successful for so long, will still prove to be the least provocative, most effective defense we will have against hostile missiles.[9]

The ability and willingness to counter-attack is inherent in deterrence. So it will be necessary for the government to make clear to everyone that no matter what its nature or means of delivery, any "weapon of mass destruction" fired at this country, at our forces, or at one of our allies who does not itself possess nuclear deterrent forces, will yield in return more than one nuclear explosion in the land of the perpetrator.

The first of the two strategic conditions that changed in the second half of the last century is that most of the countries that had maintained large navies and used them vigorously in the wars of the first half of that century have lost interest in engaging in wars against their neighbors and thus also lost the resources needed to do so, let alone to engage in warfare against countries at a significant distance. Thus, except for the United States, they now see no further need to have large navies. Moreover, though powerful militarily ashore, neither China nor India seems ready to match its strength there with similar strength afloat. For its part, with 337 ships in commission at the end of 2001, the U.S. Navy, currently the biggest in the world by far, has about the same number of ships in commission as it did during the years of pacifism and economic depression between the two world wars. This number is far smaller than at any time since those days.[10] It is a number not soon likely to grow.

The second changed strategic condition is that few major countries—China is the great exception—nowadays man or maintain substantial merchant fleets under their own flags. Indeed, in Europe and North America, once the world's main sources and users of seagoing ships of all kinds, not many people even know how to build a merchant ship. What has not changed is that almost all those countries are as dependent as ever on the safe and timely flow of merchant ships into their ports, each ship filled with necessary or at least desirable imports. In general, they are equally dependent on the safe and timely flow of such ships *out* of their ports, many of them filled with important exports. Few people today know that oceangoing merchant ships are not only much larger than their predecessors but also more numerous than they have been for a long time.[11] The coming into common use of the highly efficient cargo container, which can swiftly be moved from ship to truck or train, has led to the economical commercial practice of "just in time" resupply of goods or products from source to store. No one wishes disruption of this efficient flow—that is, no one except those at war with important exporters or importers.

During their long war of 1980–88, Iran and Iraq came to attack each other's oil exports. Iraq did so by means of missiles launched from aircraft at what mainly were neutral tankers attempting to fill themselves at Iranian terminals. Iran did so primarily by laying mines in the channel between Kuwait (which was Iraq's seaport proxy) and the exit from the Persian Gulf.

The Iraqi pilots hit many ships with their missiles. But despite the almost complete absence of naval or air protection, the flow of neutral tankers willing to risk attack never ended—the Iraqi attack on shipping failed. In contrast, the United States, which favored Iraq as the lesser of evils and feared what the Iranian mines and other naval instruments might do to Iraq's ability to continue the war, arranged to have a number of foreign-flag tankers placed under American colors. This justified the employment of U.S. warships to protect the tankers from any form of Iranian attack. A series of skirmishes followed that led, among other results, to the destruction of several Iranian warships and oil drilling platforms at sea, as well as serious mine damage to an American frigate. The most important effect of these activities, albeit one little noticed, was that all merchant ships under the protection of the U.S. fleet arrived where they were needed when they were needed. After a year Iran called a halt to the war, not only that against the United States but also that against Iraq.[12]

It is to the advantage of most countries that neither tankers nor container ships be sunk at sea and that tankers, at least, not be sunk in port either. If a tanker were to be sunk at sea, someone's fishing grounds could be ruined, or a coast fouled, for years—if in port, the result would be even worse. Should a container ship be fatally damaged at sea, not only would the ship's entire cargo be lost but hundreds, or even thousands, of buoyant or semibuoyant containers could break loose from the sinking ship and form a giant floating minefield, albeit a nonexplosive one, endangering all ships and craft nearby, perhaps for months. A new task for navies, or for the U.S. Coast Guard if the problem is in American waters, will be to round up all those floating containers in such a contingency, either placing them aboard some self-submerging ship—such as a dock landing ship (LSD) or a heavy-lift ship—or sinking them so they will be no more a source of danger to others. This task will be tedious, dangerous, and important. Hence, it is a good thing that the U.S. and other navies have revived the old practice from sailing ship days of organizing boarding parties in order to examine, and perhaps seize, merchant ships of interest—as well as, for intelligence purposes, the people on board. Thus, in this old way twenty-first-century navies can conduct blockades (or embargoes, quarantines, or other terms suitable to non-war confrontations) in a highly effective fashion.[13]

However, that does not mean belligerents opposed to the safe passage of the enemy's ships, or enemy-supporting neutral ships, across the seas and oceans will not resort to whatever means they have to sink them. If the ships in question are ours or supporting us, the U.S. fleet must protect them. If they are the enemy's or supporting the enemy, that same fleet must blockade, capture, or sink them.

For an important reason, it will not be enough for navies just to be able to board, examine, and perhaps seize merchant ships of interest. They must retain the ability to sink them, for without that, the people in those ships might choose to brush off the attentions of would-be boarding parties. When one considers in particular the current need to keep dangerous ships out of our ports and those of our neighbors, the importance of retaining the capability to sink them looms large.

For that reason the U.S. fleets should consider establishing on each coast, or other areas of concern, "flying squadrons" of suitable forces able to concentrate on ships of interest as far at sea as intelligence will permit. If such a ship resists seizure, it should be sunk, and sunk as quickly as possible. No resource of ours is better suited to that task than a submarine, for no other ships, and few aircraft, have weapons so effective for that purpose as a submarine's full-sized torpedo—or two, or three, as needed. Other resources will be needed to rescue survivors from the sea and, should any such survivors still be filled with murderous hate, to control them until they are delivered to the authorities ashore.

How does this play out in a world dominated by information?

Commanders in the time of George Washington and Horatio Nelson had to fight their battles, campaigns, and wars in an era of information poverty. Commanders now must fight in an era of information wealth, or even of information excess.

We celebrate today the enormous volume, variety, and accuracy of information we gather and the speed with which we move it over great distances. We seek, send, receive, store, and delete information. Sometimes between receiving information and deleting it we examine and act upon it well. Information now not only comes from, but also goes to, great numbers of devices that we have conceived, created, and deployed. One example is the direct coupling of sensors and navigators to weapons.[14] Hitherto, forces were accustomed to firing, launching, or dropping many weapons in the hope of gaining at most a few hits. With the current coupling, the likelihood of a hit is so high that only one weapon, or a few, need be directed at any target. The influence of this change on the requirements for ships, aircraft, launchers, weapons, fuel, parts, and crews has been enormous. Now only a few (or a little) of each of these can achieve as much as once required many (and much). This both eases a navy's problem of protecting logistical ships and aircraft and magnifies the effect of the loss of even one. In time the enemy, whoever it may be, will be operating under the same influences.

All the foregoing—people, ships, weapons, and the rest—must be harnessed by the commander in order to carry out his (or her, not yet its) intent. Nowadays that commander is more likely than ever before to be at a great distance from the scene of action; yet he possesses the ability to make tactical decisions in a timely fashion. This ability is something far beyond the reach of Admiral Chester Nimitz in Hawaii during World War II, or even in the thick of battle, as Vice Admiral Nelson was at Trafalgar in 1805. Current and future very senior officers and civilian officials having such power likely will see it as a good thing. Among the others, at least some will see it otherwise.

Whether information comes from near or far, or reaches the recipient through his eyes or ears, the great efforts we make now (and made in the past, too) to gain and transmit it are all intended to influence, affect, and direct in a timely way their recipients' thoughts and actions. The same purposes lie behind efforts to deny the enemy timely access to accurate information and, in the same fashion, to provide him instead with believable misinformation.[15]

Hence, both sender and receiver must be able to trust that the signal received is identical to the signal sent. They must also be able to understand accurately what has come in and, if a message is just wrong, or fraudulent, to sense that. (Recent experiences in Eastern Europe and Central Asia suggest we have room for improvement here.) Finally, those to whom information is sent must be able to decide swiftly what to do about it—sometimes to do nothing is best—and send out to their subordinates orders that are coherent, practical, and suitable to the occasion.

It is in this context that naval forces now and in the foreseeable future must carry out their missions. How will they do that?

Mainly, it appears, they will make sure that friendly ships, and aircraft flying over the sea, can go where they are needed when they are needed, and that enemy ships and military aircraft flying over the sea cannot do those things. Furthermore, if necessary or desirable, they will land forces ashore, supporting them then, and thereafter, with fire and logistics. (If sufficient ground forces are already in place, the provision by the fleet of fire and logistics will be enough.) For those who like labels, this can be called "objective-centered warfare."

Little of the foregoing is new. Less is dramatic. Often those engaged in a navy's work must demonstrate high skill and courage. As they do so, they must understand that the world will most likely have focused its attention elsewhere and will never notice how well they perform. But those are everlasting characteristics of war at sea, and from the sea.

Addendum

Professor Uhlig offers this later commentary on the concept of the "fleet-in-being," supplied to him by Captain Wayne Hughes (USN, Ret.), of the Naval Postgraduate School:

You could without missing a beat strengthen the case, because there was a middle ground between (1) the evidence you offer of the beginning of the end of a fleet-in-being with the Grand Fleet's distant blockade, and (2) the present circumstances when satellites and other advanced systems will pinpoint a fleet in a harbor and make it vulnerable. . . . The middle ground occurred in World War II when carrier aircraft surprised supposedly safe fleets and did so much harm that [the fleets] were driven back or reduced to impotence. Examples: Taranto 1940, resulting in the Italians' withdrawing to La Spezia; Pearl Harbor 1941, which eliminated the U.S. battleships' viability for over a year; Rabaul in 1943, when a U.S. carrier attack did so much harm to the Japanese cruisers that the Imperial Japanese Navy recognized the base was useless; and Truk 1944, when in the expectation of a U.S. carrier air attack the Japanese fleet fled from its strongest bastion east of the Philippines. There are other examples in the Pacific, on the Atlantic face of Europe, and in the Mediterranean—and with instruments other than carriers, such as full-sized and mini-submarines, as well as land-based aircraft.

Technically, in none of these instances did the suffering fleet think of itself as a fleet-in-being, in port merely to forestall or tie down the attacker's fleet. It is interesting that in each case the fleet was the target, and command of the seas the objective. In no case was the attack connected with an invasion somewhere nearby.

By 1945 all naval officers saw that what had been a sanctuary was now more likely to be a death trap. What was bad enough with conventional bombs was going to be much worse with the coming of atomic (fission) bombs.

Notes

1. The point is made with particular clarity by Roger Barnett—Captain, U.S. Navy (Ret.), and professor emeritus of the Naval War College—in his "Naval Power for a New American Century," *Naval War College Review* 55, no. 1 (Winter 2002), pp. 43–62. Because it invites new thought from others, its publication was particularly welcome.

2. Ibid., p. 46.

3. David C. Isby, "Carrier Battle Group and Its Alternatives," *Air Forces Monthly,* September 2002.

4. David R. Mets, *The Long Search for a Surgical Strike: Precision Munitions and the Revolution in Military Affairs* (Maxwell Air Force Base, Ala.: Air University Press, 2001), pp. 34–50. In the preface to his small book Dr. Mets says (p. xii) that even if airpower "cannot carry the day alone, we would be derelict to our duty as citizens not to consider the possibility of increasing use of airpower as the supported force and ground and sea power as the supporting forces."

5. Wayne P. Hughes [Capt., USN, Ret.], of the Naval Postgraduate School, Monterey, California, conversation and notes in Newport, Rhode Island, 3 October 2002.

6. Edward Wegener [Rear Adm., Federal German Navy, Ret.], "Theory of Naval Strategy in the Nuclear Age," in *Naval Review 1972,* ed. Frank Uhlig, Jr. (Annapolis, Md.: Naval Institute Press, 1972), p. 195. (This annual also served as the May 1972 issue of the Naval Institute *Proceedings.*) On the same page Admiral Wegener states that "sea traffic is the object of naval war."

7. This is a shortened version of my account of those events on pages 360–61 and 362 of *How Navies Fight* (Naval Institute Press, 1994). Sources for that account are Robert G. Weinland, *Superpower Naval Diplomacy in the October 1973 Arab-Israeli War* (Arlington, Va.: Center for Naval Analyses, 1978); and Stephen S. Roberts, "The October 1973 Arab-Israeli War," in *Soviet Naval Diplomacy,* ed. Bradford Dismukes and James M. McConnell (New York: Pergamon, 1979).

8. On the swiftly emerging issue of the defense of both our forces and nearby allies from theater-range and area-range ballistic missiles see Charles C. Swicker [Cdr., USN], *Theater Ballistic Missile Defense from the Sea: Issues for the Maritime Component Commander* (Newport, R.I., Naval War College Press, 1998). Commander Swicker's is a remarkably clear and concise discussion of a subject that lends itself to long-winded murkiness.

9. For an interesting account of an earlier naval effort to help defend the nation against a land-to-land attack from over the ocean, see Joseph F. Bouchard [Capt., USN], "Guarding the Cold War Ramparts: The U.S. Navy's Role in Continental Air Defense," *Naval War College Review* 52, no. 3 (Summer 1999), pp. 111–31.

10. Naval Historical Center, *U.S. Navy Active Ship Force Levels, 1917–* (Washington, D.C.: Ships Histories Branch, 23 January 2002).

11. According to a table of shipping statistics compiled by the Maritime Administration in 1992 and sent me two years later by Mike Blouin, then of that organization, in 1940 (before the sinkings and building programs of war had had much time in which to distort peacetime figures) there were in the world 12,798 seagoing merchant ships of 80,600,000 deadweight tons. Half a century later, in 1990, the number of ships had nearly doubled, to 22,983, and their deadweight tonnage, or carrying capacity, had multiplied more than seven times, to 609,479,000. Since 1990 these numbers have risen.

12. For an excellent contemporary account of how this task is handled in one area, the upper reaches of the Persian Gulf, see James Goldrick [Commodore, Royal Australian Navy], "In Command in the Gulf," U.S. Naval Institute *Proceedings,* December 2002, pp. 38–41.

13. In *Tanker Wars: The Assault on Merchant Shipping during the Iran-Iraq Crisis, 1980–1988* (London: I. B. Taurus, 1996), Martin S. Navias and E. R. Hooton provide a thorough account of that subject. Other sources are: Anthony S. Cordesman and Abraham R. Wagner, *The Lessons of Modern War,* vol. 2, *The Iran-Iraq War* (Boulder, Colo.: Westview, 1990), pp. 135, 271–73, 338; Michael A. Palmer, *Guardians of the Gulf: A History of America's Expanding Role in the Persian Gulf, 1833–1992* (New York: Free Press, 1992), pp. 119–49; and Uhlig, *How Navies Fight,* pp. 378–83.

14. This combination of sensors, navigating devices, and weapons has taken unto itself much of the work formerly carried out by the tactician, who usually has concerned himself, at least up to now, first with finding the enemy and then with placing his own command where it can deliver its fire upon that enemy with greatest effect, keeping in mind the desirability of minimizing the enemy's ability to return fire effectively.

15. Commander G. Guy Thomas, U.S. Navy (Ret.), pointed out recently that "one seeks command of the electro-magnetic spectrum for reasons analogous to the reasons a navy seeks command of the sea: so that friendly information necessary for the survival of a nation and the success of its forces in battle can get where it is needed when it is needed, and that hostile information cannot do these things" (conversation, 3 September 2002). Commander Thomas is the liaison officer between the Johns Hopkins University Applied Physics Laboratory in Baltimore and the Navy Warfare Development Command in Newport, R.I.

CHAPTER SEVEN

"... From the Sea" and Back Again
Naval Power in the Second American Century
EDWARD RHODES

> *The necessity of a navy ... springs ... from the existence of peaceful
> shipping, and disappears with it, except in the case of a nation which
> has aggressive tendencies, and keeps up a navy merely as a branch of the
> military establishment.*
>
> Captain A. T. Mahan,
> *The Influence of Sea Power on History, 1660–1783*, 1890

> *The primary purpose of forward-deployed naval forces is to project
> American power from the sea to influence events ashore in the littoral
> regions of the world across the operational spectrum of peace, crisis and
> war. This is what we do.*
>
> Admiral Jay L. Johnson,
> "Forward ... from the Sea: The Navy Operational Concept," March 1997

Why does a liberal democratic republic of nearly continental size require a navy? How does naval power contribute to national security and the achievement of national objectives? What does this imply about the kinds of naval forces that a liberal democratic republic requires and about the peacetime and wartime naval strategies it must pursue?

In the 1990s, as at critical junctures in the past, long-standing answers to these questions about what necessitates the maintenance of naval power and what it is that a navy does that justifies the expenditure of national wealth on it have been called into question. This essay explores the efforts of the U.S. Navy to design a naval force posture and strategy consistent with the images of national purpose and international conflict that dominate fin de siècle American political discussion. Central to the Navy's efforts to link naval power to national security in the new century has been the rejection of

Naval War College Review, Spring 1999, Vol. 52, No. 2

Mahanian notions of naval power, with their emphasis on the control of the international commons, and the embrace of the assumption that to be relevant to American security objectives, naval power must be applied "from the sea" against sovereign transoceanic actors. Understanding the forces that led the Navy to this conclusion offers insight both into the difficulties the Navy is presently encountering in operationalizing its vision of naval power and into the range of alternatives available to the service as the nation moves into its second century of global politico-military preeminence.

Naval Power in National Strategy

Postwar military planning is notoriously difficult, and the synchronization of Navy strategy with national grand strategy has historically been problematic for the U.S. Navy. How to make naval power relevant to the concerns of national decision makers, given their particular conception of world politics, American national interest, and international violence has resurfaced as a critical issue with remarkable regularity: in the early 1890s, the early 1920s, the late 1940s, the late 1960s, and again today.

In the aftermath of World War I, for example, Navy and national leadership operated from sufficiently different assumptions that for roughly a decade the liberal isolationist Republicans who controlled the White House found it expedient essentially to exclude the Navy from the nation's naval planning. The "new order of sea power" that emerged from the Washington Treaties of 1922 was negotiated without significant input from the Navy; the resulting American fleet lacked capabilities that Navy leaders, operating within a very different intellectual framework for understanding national security, regarded as necessary for the effective protection of American national interests. After World War II, the disjuncture between Navy planning and national strategy reached such a magnitude that in 1949 the Navy's top leadership lined up to testify in Congress against the administration's policies, in the so-called "revolt of the admirals," and paid the predictable price. Two decades later, as the nation wrestled with the lessons of Vietnam, the Navy's force-posture and strategic accommodation to the national political currents was perhaps more successful, but the costs to the Navy as an institution, measured in morale and a protracted period of "hollow" forces, were enormously high.

By comparison, adaptation to post–Cold War structural and political realities appears to have proceeded remarkably smoothly: the Navy's difficulties in remaking its strategic concepts and force structure to adjust to post–Cold War foreign and national security strategy appear to have been remarkably modest. Virtually overnight, the Navy redefined how it proposed to contribute to the national weal, shifting its justification for American naval power from a "Maritime Strategy" that emphasized the value of destroying the enemy's fleet and controlling the high seas to a littoral strategy that stressed employing Navy forces to project military power ashore. This shift was not simply rhetorical: it involved a substantial refocusing of naval capabilities and efforts, from forces designed and trained to seek out aggressively and give battle to an advanced and highly capable opponent, to forces designed and trained to exercise gunboat diplomacy across a spectrum of violence from peace to major war. Within the naval family, it also involved a redefinition of the always-sensitive relationship between the Navy and Marine Corps.

The apparent ease with which the Navy achieved internal consensus about the direction in which it needed to move and the dispatch with which it has proceeded should not obscure the magnitude of this achievement. Redefining the meaning of naval power and the Navy's central tasks was an enormous undertaking, both intellectually and bureaucratically. Intellectually, the new littoral strategy required writing off the substantial human investment that had gone into developing, elaborating, and institutionalizing the Maritime Strategy in the early and mid 1980s. The emotional, cognitive, and organizational costs associated with abandoning the monumental edifice of the Maritime Strategy and adopting a vision of naval warfare that had never, in the Navy's two-hundred-year history, dominated thinking or shaped actions should not be underestimated simply because they were paid. Nor were the bureaucratic obstacles small or painless: abandoning the high-seas focus of the post-Vietnam Navy and adopting a littoral one necessitated a significant shift in resources within the Navy itself, from the submariners (who had increasingly come to dominate the Navy in the 1980s) to aviators and surface sailors. This was a strategic shift with real human consequences, demanding that individuals make and endorse decisions that would put their own futures in the Navy, and the futures of their junior officers, in jeopardy.

For scholars who have speculated that absent intervention by political authorities, military services are extremely limited in their capacity to engage in nonevolutionary strategic adjustment, the Navy's development of its littoral strategy offers extraordinarily interesting disconfirming evidence.[1] Avoiding the errors of 1922 and 1949, the Navy recognized that new postwar conditions (domestic as well as international) would mean not only a change in the nation's grand strategy but a wider, more sweeping transformation of the national leadership's underlying assumptions about the nature of American foreign policy and international conflict—and that the Navy would have to adapt its vision of national security and war to match that of the political leadership if it was to remain relevant. Simultaneously avoiding the errors of 1968–1974, the Navy recognized that a broad reeducation process within the service, designed to create an institutionalized consensus on the purpose of naval power, was necessary if strategic adjustment was to occur without destroying the Navy as a functioning institution. Tailoring Navy force posture and strategy to new grand strategic concepts was by itself insufficient: a broadly shared understanding of the new role and missions of the Navy would be necessary if the process was to be successful. (Indeed, the Navy has actively sought not only to build an intellectual consensus within itself but to educate the other services and create a joint consensus on the meaning and uses of naval power.) The Navy's approach to developing and institutionalizing its new strategic conception was thus a deliberately self-conscious one.[2]

The problem of strategic adjustment has not simply been one of overcoming intellectual and bureaucratic inertia, however. Uncertainty made—and continues to make— the process of developing a Navy strategy consistent with national grand strategy a difficult one. The environment of the early 1990s was ambiguous in two critical regards. First, the international strategic climate was unclear. The kind of threat the Navy would face—the kind of war it would next be called upon to fight, or the kinds of peacetime policies it would be called upon to support—was, and indeed still remains, uncertain at best. Second, the internal cognitive-political environment in which the Navy found itself was equally unclear. In the early 1990s the nation's vision of national security and of the nature of international conflict was in transition, its ultimate content undetermined. Thus both what the Navy would be called upon to do and the terms or intellectual framework within which the service would have to justify itself to the nation's political establishment were indeterminate.

To be sure, that the end of the Cold War logically demanded a change in Navy strategy was abundantly clear. DESERT STORM brought this lesson home to the Navy. As Admiral William Owens observes:

> Unlike our Army, Air Force, and Marine Corps comrades in arms, we left the first of the post–Cold War conflicts without the sense that our doctrine had been vindicated. Quite the contrary. We left knowing not only that the world had changed dramatically, but that our doctrine had failed to keep pace. Little in Desert Storm supported the Maritime Strategy's assumptions and implications. No opposing naval forces challenged us. No waves of enemy aircraft ever attacked the carriers. No submarines threatened the flow of men and materiel across the oceans. The fleet was never forced to fight the open-ocean battles the Navy had been preparing for during the preceding twenty years. Instead, the deadly skirmishing of littoral warfare dominated. . . . For the Navy, more than any other service, Desert Storm was the midwife of change.[3]

But what change would prove acceptable to the nation's political leadership and would harmonize with national strategy was less clear. The end of the Cold War and the cultural tensions associated with movement to a postindustrial economy and an explicitly multicultural society meant that the elite's conception of both American national security policy and naval power was malleable at best and fluid at worst.

National Security in the National Imagination

For roughly forty-five years, Navy strategy could safely be predicated on the assumption that the dominant national vision of national security was a Realist-internationalist one. By 1946 or 1947 a consensus had developed within the American political elite that the world was an inherently conflictual place—that security could not be guaranteed by cooperative international institutions but required active military measures to guarantee some sort of favorable international balance of power—that the American state's political essence and America's national interests demanded military engagement in world affairs—and that ultimately American political life was not purely an internal matter but rather derived its meaning and purpose through its interaction with the outside world. The American republic could not, in this conception, survive indefinitely as an island of liberal democracy in a hostile world, and the hostility of that world could neither be eliminated nor held in check through international institutions. Together the Realist vision of a violent world and the internationalist vision of a globally engaged America implied a national security policy aimed at vigorous maintenance of an international balance of power or, better, at a preponderance of power that would roll back forces inherently and unalterably hostile to the continued survival of the American republic.

For the Navy, this Realist-internationalist national vision, and the national security policy consensus in favor of global containment that derived from it, justified a major national investment in forward-deployed naval power. The familiarity and "normality" of this naval posture and strategy to the two generations of Americans who matured during the Cold War should not obscure its striking oddity: a liberal, democratic republic, basically self-sufficient in economic resources, possessing a competitive industrial base, and lacking any imperial pretensions or objectives, built and trained naval forces to exercise nothing less than global naval hegemony—and paid for this capability a price roughly equal to 2 percent of gross national product. This naval strategy made sense only in the context of a vision of national security that assumed the external world was populated by forces implacably hostile to America and that even if it secured its own borders, the American republic could not survive in a world dominated by such forces.

By the late 1980s, however, both of the underlying elements of this Realist-internationalist vision were in question. On the one hand, a mellowing image of communism (followed by the collapse of communism as a viable ideological alternative), in conjunction with a domestic social transformation that underscored the potential for tolerance and cooperation among disparate groups, challenged the conflictual foundation of the Realist perspective. Increasingly, liberal ideas, stressing the potential for such institutions as the market and law to provide satisfactory mechanisms for resolving conflicts—ideas redolent with the tradition of Woodrow Wilson and Franklin Roosevelt—reentered political discourse, suggesting the possibility that American security policy ought to be based on liberal institutions, not military power. Beginning with Nixonian détente, the notion that security might be achieved through institutions like arms control and trade began to burrow its way into American political consciousness, like a liberal worm in the comfortably solid reality of the Realist apple. Though the post-Afghanistan Cold War reprise froze such heretical ideas, pushing uncommitted thinkers such as Jimmy Carter back into Realist patterns of thought (and pushing such liberal heretics as Cyrus Vance out of government circles entirely), and though the Reagan administration's view of an inherently dangerous "evil empire" led it to doubt the efficacy of even such limited security institutions as Mutual Assured Destruction, Realism's hold on the American imagination was loosening for a variety of reasons, including long-postponed generational change in leadership circles. By the early 1990s even George Bush would speak openly of the potential for a new world order.

At the same time that Realist presumptions of an inevitably disordered and conflictual international system were being challenged, the internationalist vision of America—of an America whose essence was defined, or at least proved, by its active, positive role in the world—was also being called into question, though admittedly to a lesser degree. The integration of American society and economy into the larger world and the existence of improved means of mass communication (able to convey world events to American households with a heightened immediacy) worked strongly against a return of isolationism. Nonetheless, the social dislocations associated with movement to a postindustrial economy, coupled with the absence of any clearly identifiable external adversary to blame for internal distresses, resulted in increasing cognitive tensions in maintaining the old internationalist image and in a growing presumption that the principal focus of the American state's attentions ought to be internal, not external.[4]

The end of the Cold War thus coincided with and exacerbated an emerging cultural struggle over how to visualize national security. This struggle between four competing visions—Realist-internationalist, liberal-internationalist, Realist-isolationist, and liberal-isolationist—logically has an enormous impact on the type of naval power the United States requires.

In the twenty-first century no less than during the Cold War, a Realist-internationalist vision of American security policy implies the need for a large, forward military capability backed up by substantial mobilization potential. Given the Realist-internationalist framework for conceptualizing American security requirements, the U.S. military must be able to act unilaterally to contain or defeat the hostile powers—China, Russia, an Islamic world—that inevitably will emerge to challenge the United States and the balance of power that protects its interests. Clearly, this sort of Realist-internationalist vision of security policy, which drove the American pursuit of naval power from 1890 to 1922 and from 1946 to the end of the Cold War, has deep roots in the political culture of industrial America. The continued attractiveness of this model of world politics is reflected both in the popular appeal of "clash of cultures" theses and in the strenuous intellectual efforts in the Pentagon and elsewhere to envision China as a looming and inevitable adversary, demanding vigorous balancing action.[5]

By comparison, an America with a liberal-internationalist vision of its world might require marginally smaller forces. These forces, however, would still have to be substantial and quite possibly would require increased flexibility. (Indeed, the substantial scale of military capabilities implied by this vision is suggested by an examination of the programs of Woodrow Wilson and Franklin Roosevelt.) While in the Realist-internationalist model forward engagement is necessary to maintain the balance of power and to contain aggressors bent on world domination—that is, to prevent dominos from falling—in the liberal-internationalist conception forward engagement is needed to reassure more timid members of the international community of the security provided by emerging liberal, democratic institutions; to support the nation and state building that will provide the institutional building blocks of international order; and to deter atavistic "rogue" states, like Iraq, Iran, and North Korea, from lashing out before they finally succumb to the dialectic social and economic forces of liberal democracy. Where in the Realist-internationalist view military forces can be tailored for fighting war, possibly even for fighting the general war that represents the ultimate danger, in the liberal-internationalist understanding military forces need to be capable of a wider variety of activities and need to be able to act in concert with allies or within a coalition framework, even when such cooperation is not militarily necessary.

By contrast, a Realist-isolationist vision of America and its world would dictate military forces capable of shielding fortress America from the dangers outside—missiles, terrorists, refugees, and drugs—and of punishing aggressors who attempt to interfere in American affairs. If Realist internationalism represented the worldview of Teddy Roosevelt, Harry Truman, and John Kennedy, and if liberal internationalism reflected the vision of Woodrow Wilson and Franklin Roosevelt, the American exemplars of a Realist-isolationist vision might be George Washington and John Adams. Essentially an updating and translation into modern, high-tech form of the kinds of military forces this nation possessed in its first century, a navy for a Realist-isolationist America would resemble a super–Coast Guard, enhanced with ballistic and cruise-missile defenses and an effective area-denial capacity, married to a specialized force able to conduct purely punitive operations against aggressors. While, depending on the magnitude of foreign military threats, Realist-isolationists may see the need for substantial American military efforts, they are unlikely to support efforts that would involve America overseas or provide the United States with the means of transforming other societies. Apart from immediate threats to American shores, they are unlikely to be concerned either about the maintenance of some sort of global balance of power (since developments elsewhere in the world are not viewed as matters appropriate for American intervention) or about the impact that American defense efforts might have on the behavior of others (since the hostility of others is assumed).

A liberal-isolationist vision of America, like that embraced by the Republicans of the 1920s, underscores the need to avoid military forces that would trigger security dilemmas, that would interfere with the organic growth of liberal democratic societies abroad, or that would enhance the power of militarist and antidemocratic ideologies and interest groups at home. Where Realist isolationists see the world as a dangerous place and attempt to protect American security by establishing a barrier against it, liberal isolationists see it as a potentially friendly place but find no reason to become deeply involved, at least militarily, in its affairs. International order is quite possible and highly desirable, but it develops naturally out of the interaction between liberal democratic societies. The contrast with liberal internationalism is revealing: where Wilsonians assumed that liberal democratic institutions might at least sometimes grow out of the barrel of a gun and that the emergence of liberal national polities could be helped along through timely outside intervention, and where FDR's liberal internationalism emphasized the need for policemen even in well ordered societies, the liberal-isolationist vision stresses that a peaceful international system requires that each national society focus on its own perfection, and concludes that external military interference is more likely to be a hindrance than a help.[6] While American forces might be called upon to participate in overseas humanitarian ventures, for liberal isolationists the central problem in designing forces is a negative one: how to avoid stimulating undesirable reactions abroad or a militarist culture at home. The difference between the internationalist and isolationist versions of liberalism thus hinges principally on the assumption of where the principal danger to liberal democratic polities lies: externally, from aggressive neighbors, or internally, from illiberal or undemocratic social forces.

Part of the problem facing the U.S. Navy in the early 1990s was thus to anticipate the framework within which national leadership would visualize American national security. It is unclear whether awareness of the lesson of the 1920s was widespread within the Navy, but that lesson was certainly there to be learned: in the 1920s when Navy leadership tried to justify naval power in the Realist-internationalist terms that had shaped national thinking from 1890 to 1912 to a political elite that had come to view the world in liberal-isolationist terms, the result was disastrous. Because they made no sense in the intellectual framework employed by national leaders, Navy efforts to explain the national need for naval power were dismissed as parochial special pleading. This was clearly a danger again in the 1990s.

War in the National Imagination

At the same time, however, Navy leadership also had to pay close attention to a second set of competing visions, more specifically about the nature of war and the role of naval power in war. Across the nation's history, American thinking has shifted between two fundamentally opposed views of warfare. One, with roots in the colonial experience and linked to a construction of national identity that is largely independent of the state, has seen war as a struggle between competing national societies or ways of life— English versus Indian, American versus English, American versus Mexican, Northern versus Southern, democratic versus fascist/militarist, free/democratic versus enslaved/ communist—that ultimately pits an entire people against another. The other has its roots in the European state tradition and is linked, in American history, first to Hamiltonian efforts at state building and, a century later, to the Progressive movement's efforts to transform the American state into an institution capable of dealing with such national social problems as industrialization and Reconstruction. This second vision has interpreted war as a clash between rival states and their professional military establishments.

These competing countersocietal and countermilitary visions of war obviously have very different implications with respect to the appropriate uses and targets of violence. In its extreme form, the first seeks the extirpation or transformation of an opposing society, and in its moderate form is willing to impose pain directly on an opposing society in order to gain political concessions; the second views war as a chivalrous clash between warriors, a competition between champions, to adjudicate a dispute between rival states. In the first, war is Hiroshima, the *Lusitania*, Sherman through Georgia, and the destruction of Indian villages' winter grain stocks; in the other it is Jutland, Ypres, or the charge up San Juan Hill. In one, the deliberate reduction of the Soviet Union to radioactive rubble is acceptable; in the other, the accidental death of a few hundred civilians in a Baghdad shelter is unacceptable.

In the same way that it has shifted between countersocietal and countermilitary visions of war, American political culture has also shifted between oceanic and cis- or transoceanic visions. Oceanic visions assume that the political objectives of war can be accomplished by controlling the international commons and thereby dominating participation in international society: while invasion may follow, control of the ocean is by itself determinative of outcome. The economic, military, political, and social value of using the commons or engaging in international interaction is regarded as sufficiently high to decide the fate of states and nations. Control of the oceans implies control not simply of the world economy but, through the capability to support coalitions and alliances, of the global balance of power.

Cis- and transoceanic visions, by contrast, assume that war requires the destruction or occupation of the adversary's territory to achieve its purpose. Protection of one's own homeland (the cisoceanic vision) assures political stalemate; successful assault on the adversary's sovereign domain (the transoceanic vision) is necessary for decisive political victory. In this view, actions on the international commons merely facilitate action in this decisive theater of terrestrial sovereignty.

In the period from 1949 to 1968, the Navy harmonized its strategy with national strategy by accepting the political leadership's view of war as essentially a transoceanic countersocietal exercise. That is, the dominant view in political circles, which (after the revolt of the admirals) the Navy under Admiral Forrest Sherman and his successors accepted, was that to achieve its political effect war would need to be brought to the sovereign territory of the adversary to seize control over that territory, and that the appropriate target of military action was the adversary's society, not simply his military forces. For the Navy this meant that the principal justification for naval power was its ability to bring strategic war to the adversary's homeland and to facilitate a war of occupation that would bring the adversary's society under American military control. The Navy's 1946–1949 efforts to justify its program in alternative, more traditional terms— in terms of the Navy's ability to defeat an opposing fleet and control the oceans—had met with increasing incomprehension and, in 1949, with the public rejection of the Navy program in favor of the Air Force's plans for strategic bombardment. In the post-1949 period, therefore, the Navy pursued a "balanced fleet" whose mission in general war was to seize and support forward bases for strategic bombing and, ultimately, for the invasion of the Soviet Union. In more limited conflicts, this "balanced fleet" would support force projection into the Third World. Consistent with this vision of warfare, as the Cold War progressed the Navy vigorously sought a capability to conduct carrier-based and later ballistic missile attacks on the Soviet Union, to control sea lanes of communication to critical theaters, and to project strike air and significant Marine power into the Third World.

For a variety of reasons, the American elite and attentive public abandoned this vision of war in the late 1960s, and by the early 1970s a new vision, an oceanic countermilitary one, was firmly fixed.[7] Americans would fight war by controlling the commons and by using this systemic dominance to shift the military balance of power in favor of allies and proxies. The Navy, or at least its top echelons, moved lockstep with national leadership in this transition. Between 1968 and 1974 the Navy dramatically reconfigured itself, slashing forces for amphibious warfare and for maintaining the defensive sea control needed to protect the convoys required for transoceanic operations. Initially, this transformation required no justification, since it meshed with national thinking (most clearly expressed in the Nixon Doctrine, regarding the potential for winning wars at a distance by using control of the commons to empower proxies) and with popular disillusionment with any image of war that suggested the necessity of actually occupying or transforming a hostile society. The post-1968 Navy was thus reoptimized for aggressive operations against enemy fleets aimed at seizing control of the oceanic commons. As a practical matter, this meant redesigning the fleet to take the war into Soviet home waters and destroying Soviet naval power, root and branch.

During the Carter administration, Navy policy moved too far in the direction of an oceanic countermilitary strategy for the comfort of some political leaders. Figures in the Carter administration, most notably Robert Komer, who clung to a transoceanic countersocietal image of war, were openly critical of the Navy, arguing that the key pillar of American security was protecting Western society along the central front in Europe and that the essential Navy contribution to national security was the protection of sea lanes of communication to this terrestrial front.[8] In response, the Navy began to develop and articulate its oceanic countermilitary vision and to explicate the ways in which the reoptimized Navy could be used to generate the desired political outcomes. In the 1980s, these efforts came to fruition in the Maritime Strategy.[9]

As with alternative visions of national security, alternative visions of war imply the need for different types of naval power as well as suggest different frameworks for justifying the acquisition of the tools of naval power. As noted, transoceanic countersocietal images of war imply a navy designed to launch strategic blows and to support the Marine Corps, Army, and Air Force as they bring war to the homes and workplaces of an enemy society. The enemy's military establishment represents a target only to the extent that it possesses a capacity to interpose itself between American military power and the target society; the enemy's navy needs to be neutralized if it threatens to interfere with forward operations, but its destruction has no value in itself; while sea lanes of communication must be protected, a task requiring broadly dispersed forces and sustained effort, enemy bastions need not be invaded. Unless the war can be won quickly with strategic bombardment, victory will require the occupation of the adversary's homeland and the subjugation of his society, and this implies the need for a substantial mobilization base for a protracted war. While the Navy plays a generally supporting, rather than independently decisive, role in this conception of war, the requirements for naval power may still be enormous, as Forrest Sherman and his successors as Chief of Naval Operations (CNO) in the 1950s and 1960s were able to argue. In addition to ballistic missile submarines and nuclear-armed carrier aviation, the Navy could make the case for substantial amphibious lift, extensive antisubmarine warfare capability to protect the flow of forces to the transoceanic theater and raw materials to the homeland, and sufficient battle fleet superiority to deter a concentrated sortie by enemy units.

Though on first blush a transoceanic countermilitary image of war would seem to have many of the same implications for the Navy as a transoceanic countersocietal one, this proves not to be correct. Most obviously, strategic bombardment recedes in importance. More broadly, since victory is seen as requiring the destruction of the adversary's military capacity rather than control over his society, a transoceanic countermilitary image of war keeps open the door for an independently decisive navy: by projecting precise, focused power into the littoral, destroying the military establishment of an adversary with air strikes or Marine operations, an optimally designed navy can defeat small adversaries or create conditions for victory by regional allies. In larger conflicts, the Navy would play a key role in joint efforts, taking timely actions to shape the battlespace, protect allies from politically or militarily devastating initial blows, and hold or open beachheads and lanes of communication for intervention by U.S. Army and Air Force units. More than any other vision of war, this one implies the importance of a navy designed and trained for routine forward presence and precision strike. The four obvious force elements suggested by this vision are carriers able both to strike and provide air superiority; cruise missile–armed warships; advanced air and ballistic missile defenses able, at a minimum, to protect fleet units and preferably to protect critical political and military targets ashore; and highly capable, highly mobile Marine units, able to carry out high-value precision attacks.

By contrast, oceanic countermilitary images of war like those popularized by Mahan in the 1890s and which gained currency in the post-Vietnam period imply a navy optimized to destroy an adversary's fleet. This activity is, in itself, expected to convey decisive political advantage by isolating the adversary, cutting his contact with clients and allies, and eliminating his ability to use the oceans for military purposes, such as deploying ballistic missiles. In this vision of war, a rational adversary will seek political terms when the destruction of his fleet deprives him of the ability to control or use the oceanic commons. The Navy for this kind of war would have to be prepared to go deep into harm's way to impose a Trafalgar or Copenhagen on an unwilling adversary. While such a force would need to be extraordinarily capable, it would not have to deploy forward routinely in peacetime, nor would it have to be capable of broadly dispersed, protracted sea-control activities. Nuclear-powered attack submarines, armed with strike as well as antiship and antisubmarine weapons, would play a key role in this vision of war, disrupting enemy defenses and opening an opportunity for the battle fleet to advance; the main naval force, presumably organized around carriers, would require extremely capable air-defense and missile-defense escorts.

While sharing the view of the ocean as the decisive theater, oceanic countersocietal visions of war assume that the critical target of both one's own and the enemy's action is commerce, not military forces, and that decisive pressure can be applied without destroying the adversary's naval forces. Such a vision implies the kind of naval capabilities endorsed by the French *jeune école* or embodied in the German U-boat fleets. While American political culture never fully embraced this "raider" vision of war, the countersocietal elements of this thinking were clearly present in the naval strategy of the early republic. Prior to 1890, commerce raiding by privateers and cruisers occupied an important place in American strategy: while their activities were not expected to be decisive, they were expected to make the stalemate created by the effective militia-based defense of American society ultimately unacceptable to an imperial aggressor. The implications of this image for a twenty-first-century fleet are intriguing. For offensive action, improved intelligence and reconnaissance, presumably space based, would be a high priority, as would be the ability to protect such systems. Long-range aviation and missiles might provide the means of destroying commerce once detected, reducing the need for more traditional surface and subsurface raiders. Alternatively, the Navy could seek to close down oceanic commerce at its end points, through aggressive mining of harbors or forward submarine patrols, or through the destruction of critical port facilities. To defend one's own maritime commerce, a substantial investment in convoy escorts would likely be required; aggressive action to negate the opponent's intelligence and detection systems would also be highly attractive. In any case, an American fleet prepared to engage in war thus conceived would be highly specialized.

". . . From the Sea"

Obviously, given this range of possible visions and naval forces, the question facing the Navy in the early 1990s was how to think about national security and war. What was an appropriate vision on which to base Navy post–Cold War planning? What was it that the Navy would do in the post–Cold War world?

The DESERT STORM experience provided some indication about how the nation and its leaders viewed these questions. That George Bush ultimately found it useful to justify action in terms of international norms and principles—for example, the violation of Kuwaiti sovereignty, human rights abuses, and world order—rather than in terms of national interest—the price of oil—spoke tellingly about the emerging liberal consensus in America. Similarly, that the American people concluded that their nation's obligations extended to Kuwait spoke to the continuing power of an internationalist vision of America. That, after debate, Congress and the administration failed to buy the argument in favor of a long-run, oceanic approach to dealing with the situation—to wait for sanctions and Iraq's isolation to bite—and instead concluded that satisfactory resolution of the crisis would require action on the ground provided evidence that transoceanic images of war, culturally problematic since Vietnam, were again not only conceivable but conceived. And that the American public recoiled so violently from civilian casualties suggested the strength of a countermilitary image of war: even if Americans were willing to conceive of war as an invasion of a foreign country, they were still unwilling to view that invasion as being aimed against a foreign people.

Clearly, however, the collapse of the Soviet Union, the experience of the Gulf War, and perhaps most importantly the obvious budgetary implications of a peace dividend suggested the need for more careful examination of the future. Between October 1991 and April 1992 the Navy and Marine Corps undertook what they titled the "Naval Forces Capabilities Planning Effort" (NFCPE).[10] The NFCPE was explicitly aimed at developing a new strategic concept for the Navy and Marine Corps, assessing the naval capabilities the nation required and the appropriate roles and missions for U.S. naval forces. The NFCPE concluded that the collapse of the Soviet Union meant that deterrence of regional crisis and conflict would move to the forefront of the political-military agenda and that U.S. security would increasingly be based on informal coalitions, which would require greater peacetime presence and partnership building, rather than on formal alliances. Further, expanding economic interdependence underscored, on the one hand, the need for a continuous global peacetime presence to ensure stability and, on the other hand, the potentially growing role of naval actions to enforce trade sanctions. Finally, the NFCPE worried about the accelerating pace of technological change and the impact of real-time mass media coverage of military actions. Though this analysis of the changing realities of world politics logically suggested strategic movement in potentially conflicting directions (the emphasis on trade sanctions, for example, logically suggested an oceanic vision of war), the NFCPE analysis emphasized the role of the Navy in creating stability, supporting international "law enforcement," and preventing and controlling crises. To accomplish these aims, the NFCPE concluded, it was necessary to exploit the freedom provided by American control over the international commons to project power and influence ashore—to threaten or undertake actions against the sovereign territory of adversaries to shape their behavior. More broadly, the Navy appears to have emerged from the NFCPE process convinced that it needed to think about naval strategy within the framework of a liberal-internationalist vision of national security and within the framework of a transoceanic countermilitary image of war.

The Navy's new strategic vision was spelled out in ". . . From the Sea," a white paper signed jointly by the Secretary of the Navy, the Chief of Naval Operations, and the Commandant of the Marine Corps in September 1992. ". . . From the Sea" envisioned naval power being used to help create a stable global environment, deterring dissatisfied regional powers from challenging the emerging international order. "While the prospect of global war has receded," the authors observed, "we are entering a period of enormous uncertainty in regions critical to our national interests. Our forces can help to shape the future in ways favorable to our interests by underpinning our alliances, precluding threats, and helping to preserve the strategic position we won with the end of the Cold War."[11]

Backing away from the centrality of warfighting as the justification for naval power, ". . . From the Sea" established the line that naval power was uniquely valuable in the nation's political-military tool kit for what it could contribute to peacetime stability, deterrence, and crisis control. Naval power could be used flexibly and precisely across a range of missions, "from port visits and humanitarian relief to major operations." Implicitly endorsing fully the liberal-internationalist view of world politics and the notion that American military power, forward deployed, could play an important role in the construction and maintenance of institutions of cooperation, the authors of ". . . From the Sea" argued that

> the Navy and Marine Corps operate forward to project a positive American image, build foundations for viable coalitions, enhance diplomatic contacts, reassure friends, and demonstrate U.S. power and resolve. Naval Forces will be prepared to fight promptly and effectively, but they will serve in an equally valuable way by engaging day-to-day as peacekeepers in the defense of American interests. Naval Forces are unique in offering this form of international cooperation.[12]

The shift in emphasis here is important to note. "Presence" had long been identified as a Navy mission. Admiral Elmo Zumwalt's widely cited fourfold classification of Navy duties—sea control, power projection, deterrence, and presence—for example, explicitly noted the value of presence. But in the post–World War II American navy, "presence" was always the last and least justification of naval power, the residual category. ". . . From the Sea" reversed that prioritization: "presence" was the Navy's unique contribution. This shift was not of simply rhetorical significance. It meant that while the other services, in making their cases for the minimum force size required, would base their claims on what would be required to fight and win a war, the Navy would base its claim on what was required to shape the peacetime environment and control crises—and, given the Navy's widely dispersed areas of operation and the multiplier required to keep rotational forces forward, this was significantly more than would be required to win any of the anticipated conflicts.

In addition to centering the Navy's responsibilities on presence, ". . . From the Sea" unequivocally endorsed a littoral approach:

> Our ability to command the seas in areas where we anticipate future operations allows us to resize our Naval Forces and to concentrate more on capabilities required in the complex operating environment of the "littoral" or coastlines of the earth. . . . This strategic direction, derived from the National Security Strategy, represents a fundamental shift away from open-ocean warfighting *on* the sea— toward joint operations conducted *from* the sea. The Navy and Marine Corps will now respond to crises and can provide the initial, "enabling" capability for joint operations in conflict—as well as continued participation in any sustained effort.[13]

The strategic conception of ". . . From the Sea" centered on four principles. First, naval forces would operate in an expeditionary role. "Expeditionary" was taken to mean that naval forces would be able to respond swiftly and on short notice, undertake a wide range of actions across the full spectrum of conflict while forward deployed, operate forward for protracted periods and unconstrained by foreign governments, and thus be able to act to shape the environment "in ambiguous situations before a crisis erupts."

Second, the Navy would be designed for joint operations with the Marine Corps: "The Navy and Marine Corps are full partners in joint operations." In one sense this is simply a logical corollary of the basic conception of a littoral strategy: if the point of naval power is to project force ashore, Marines are a critical element. It is, however, remarkable in two regards. In the first place, this marriage gave unprecedented prestige and power to the Marine Corps; the Navy was acknowledging the Corps as at least an equal partner, and possibly as the critical partner, in naval operations. The Marines represented the point of the Navy's spear. In the second place, this conception of "joint" operations ignored the Army and Air Force. The Navy was thus essentially making the claim that the Navy–Marine Corps team, without any involvement of the other services, was capable of undertaking the joint operations, or at least the joint operations in the world's littoral, that would be demanded by national decision makers. Thus while the Navy conceded a remarkable degree of its autonomy, it conceded it only to the Corps.

Third, ". . . From the Sea" reiterated the Navy's position that the Navy must operate *forward*. Forward operation was seen as necessary to demonstrate American commitment, to deter regional conflict, and to manage crises. Stressing the diplomatic side of naval power rather than its military character, ". . . From the Sea" underscored the importance of naval power in peacetime and crisis.[14] Ironically, however, the argument that the United States needed to operate its navy forward in peacetime represented a strong argument for increased investment in high-technology naval warfare systems. Essentially, by linking its future to the littoral the Navy was laying the groundwork for an "all-high mix" of naval combatants. While with the demise of the Soviet Navy the United States faced only limited challenges to its operations on the high seas, the coastal environment was highly threatening: "Mastery of the littoral should not be presumed."

Finally, abandoning a one-size-fits-all approach to operations, ". . . From the Sea" concluded that naval forces would have to be precisely tailored to meet national tasking. Enhanced responsiveness of the Navy to the political-military needs of national leadership during crisis was seen as critical: "Responding to crises in the future will require great flexibility and new ways to employ our forces. . . . The answer to every situation may not be a carrier battle group."

". . . From the Sea" also highlighted several qualities of naval power that it regarded as particularly valuable, given its understanding of the nation's grand strategy. First, the maneuverability of naval power meant that naval forces would be able to "mass forces rapidly and generate high-intensity, precise offensive power at the time and location of their choosing under any weather conditions, day or night." In other words, naval power would permit American leaders to gain the political and military advantage of seizing the strategic or tactical initiative. Second, naval power would permit national leaders to take forceful action without obtaining consent from friends or allies and without putting American servicemen at risk: "Our carrier and cruise missile firepower can also operate independently to provide quick, retaliatory strike capability short of putting forces ashore." Third, naval power would permit the United States to sustain its pressure and influence indefinitely: "The military options available can be extended indefinitely because sea-based forces can remain on station as long as required."[15]

"Forward . . . from the Sea"

". . . From the Sea" thus clearly outlined the Navy's new conception of itself and of its contribution to national security. The principal impact of a follow-up white paper issued in 1994, "Forward . . . from the Sea," was not to revise this conception in any significant way but to underscore and clarify certain elements of it and to edge away tactfully from one position that was controversial in joint arenas and from one that was controversial within the Navy.

Even more plainly than ". . . From the Sea," "Forward . . . from the Sea" emphasized the liberal-internationalist, transoceanic-countermilitary vision endorsed by the Navy. Far from stressing the inevitability of conflict, "Forward . . . from the Sea" argued that the essential contribution of naval power to national security was the support it provided to global regional stability, reassuring liberal-democratic friends, assisting the emergence of democratic societies, and supporting international institutions.

> Most fundamentally, our naval forces are designed to fight and win wars. Our most recent experiences, however, underscore the premise that the most important role of naval forces in situations short of war is to be engaged in forward areas, with the objectives of preventing conflicts and controlling crises.[16]

Underscoring the globality of American interests, and by implication attacking any notion of isolationism, "Forward . . . from the Sea" reiterated the position that the Navy was the handmaiden of American diplomacy:

> Naval forces are an indispensable and exceptional instrument of American foreign policy. From conducting routine port visits to nations and regions that are of special interest, to sustaining larger demonstrations of support to long-standing regional security interests, such as with UNITAS exercises in South America, U.S. naval forces underscore U.S. diplomatic initiatives overseas.[17]

Though reaffirming the partnership between the Navy and the Marine Corps, "Forward . . . from the Sea" edged back from the narrow definition of "jointness" suggested by the earlier document. While still maintaining that "the enhanced combat power produced by the integration of all supporting arms, which we seek to attain through joint operations, is inherent in naval expeditionary forces," the white paper conceded that "no single military service embodies all of the capabilities needed to respond to every situation and threat" and that "just as the complementary capabilities of Navy and Marine Corps forces add to our overall strength, combining the capabilities and resources of other services and those of our allies will yield decisive military power."[18] The new formulation, making the case that naval power was necessary though not sufficient to win transoceanic engagements, was that

> focusing on the littoral area, Navy and Marine Corps forces can seize and defend advanced bases— ports and airfields—to enable the flow of land-based air and ground forces, while providing the necessary command and control for joint and allied forces. The power-projection capabilities of specifically tailored naval expeditionary forces can contribute to blunting an initial attack and, ultimately, assuring victory. The keys to our enabling mission are effective means in place to dominate and exploit littoral battlespace during the earliest phases of hostilities.[19]

Similarly, while still arguing that naval forces could be deployed in flexible, tailored packages, "Forward . . . from the Sea" moved away from a position that might be interpreted as suggesting that something less than aircraft carriers and fully-capable Marine Expeditionary Units might be satisfactory for peacetime presence:

> Our basic presence "building blocks" remain Aircraft Carrier Battle Groups— with versatile, multi-purpose, naval tactical aviation wings—and Amphibious Ready Groups—with special operations–capable Marine Expeditionary Units. These highly flexible naval formations are valued by theater commanders precisely because they provide the necessary capabilities forward. They are ready and positioned to respond to the wide range of contingencies and are available to participate in allied exercises, which are the bedrock of interoperability.[20]

Although the Navy remains committed to the littoral strategy articulated in ". . . From the Sea" and "Forward . . . from the Sea," pressure to redefine or refine this conception of naval power has come from the joint arena as well as from within the Navy. Budgetary realities, of course, have served as the immediate stimulus for debate. But it would be wrong to dismiss the resulting discussion as mere bureaucratic politics or budgetary gamesmanship. Rather, what has emerged has been a profoundly interesting analysis of what a liberal-internationalist transoceanic-countermilitary navy looks like, whether this makes any sense in today's world, and whether the nation is likely to support this kind of force for very long.

Forward . . . into the Future?

By any measure, ". . . From the Sea," "Forward . . . from the Sea," and the littoral strategy they articulated represent a highly successful effort to adapt to the end of the Cold War and to chart a Navy course through the dangerous currents of strategic adjustment in the early 1990s. In remarkable contrast to earlier postwar experiences, the Navy successfully developed, explicated, and institutionalized a strategy that accommodated to the national leadership's liberal-internationalist vision of security and transoceanic-countermilitary image of war, linking naval power to national grand strategy and offering a convincing justification for Navy budgets and programs.

This success, however, should not obscure the problems looming for the Navy as it attempts to move into the coming century. As the 1990s draw to a close, the Navy needs to carefully consider whether a strategy of employing naval power "from the sea" represents an appropriate basis and vision for long-run policy or whether another abrupt change of course is demanded. Events of the last several years have already made clear that at least three dangers lie ahead if the Navy continues to steer by its littoral strategy.

The first and most immediate danger is from competitors to the littoral strategy: there are, as Army and Air Force voices have noted, a variety of ways besides projecting power "from the sea" to support a liberal-internationalist foreign policy and to fight a transoceanic-countermilitary war. While budgetary realities have stimulated this strategic competition between the services and are likely to continue to serve as the spur, it would be wrong to dismiss this challenge to the littoral strategy as mere interservice rivalry or budgetary gamesmanship. Rather, what has developed is a serious, if admittedly parochially grounded, intellectual debate over alternative national military strategies—over alternative ways to use America's military potential in support of "engagement and enlargement." While a littoral naval strategy is consistent with a liberal-internationalist vision of national security and a transoceanic-countermilitary image of war, it is not the only military strategy of which that can be said, and the Army and Air Force have successfully articulated alternative military strategies that call into question the need for significant naval effort in the littorals.

The second danger, linked to the first, is that the Navy may be unable to develop a workable operational concept for putting the littoral strategy into effect. Indeed, the Navy has found it remarkably difficult to script a convincing story about precisely how a littoral strategy works—that is, the Navy has had a hard time identifying what it is about naval operations in the littorals that yields political-military leverage and what forces and activities are therefore required. The failure of "Forward . . . from the Sea" to address the issue of alternative force packages is illustrative in this regard: continued insistence that carrier battle groups and amphibious ready groups are needed at all times in all theaters reflects the conceptual and bureaucratic difficulty of determining the actual requirements of a littoral strategy. Any decision to change deployment patterns, mixes, or timetables would at least implicitly require a prioritization of peacetime, crisis, and wartime duties; it would also represent a reallocation of resources within the service. But without a clear understanding of the process by which littoral operations generate the peacetime, crisis, and wartime outcomes sought, the Navy will find it impossible to make the difficult tradeoffs demanded by budgetary pressures. Indeed, as budgetary pressures, the need to moderate personnel and operational tempos, and the need to modernize become greater, the imperative for a clearer understanding of the relative value of (for example) forward peacetime presence, forward peacetime presence by carriers and amphibious forces, rapid crisis response, and massive wartime strike capacity will increase. Ultimately the danger is that a littoral strategy will become unworkable through an inability of the Navy to make the required tradeoffs, in which case it will find itself with forces that are too small, too overstretched, too poorly maintained, too poorly trained or manned, too obsolescent, or simply improperly configured to meet what prove to be the essential demands of a littoral strategy.

The third danger, more basic and more beyond the control of the Navy than the first two, is that the vision of warfare underlying the littoral strategy will be abandoned by the nation. The DESERT STORM image of war as a transoceanic countermilitary encounter is increasingly vulnerable, and as the elite and public begin to imagine war in other, more traditional terms, the attractiveness and importance of projecting power "from the sea" will become less apparent. To stay in harmony with national leadership and national strategy, the Navy will be called upon to offer a revised account of the utility of naval power.

As the Navy tries to plan for the next century, it needs to take all three of these dangers into account. At the same time, it also needs to explore the underlying question of what it is that naval power can actually accomplish given the political, economic, and military realities of the twenty-first century. Across the spectrum of violence, from peace through crisis to war, how vulnerable or sensitive are opponents and friends to the various actions that navies can undertake?

Army, Navy, Marine Corps, and Air Force Views

By the mid-1990s the other military services, like the Navy, had come to view the nation's national security problem in primarily liberal-internationalist terms and to envision war in basically transoceanic countermilitary ones. Even operating within this generally shared intellectual framework, however, the four services reached strikingly different conclusions about the necessary direction of U.S. military policies and about how to employ military force to reach American aims. Not surprisingly, each service's conclusion underscored the value of its own contribution. But this predictable parochialism does not in any way negate the fact that each service's strategic conception was highly developed, sophisticated, intellectually nuanced, clearly articulated, and in at least three of the four cases, remarkably consistent internally.

While each service produced a variety of vision statements during the 1990s, perhaps the clearest opportunity for comparison of the services' alternative conceptions of

American strategy came as part of the Joint Strategy Review process in 1996 and 1997. While the final output of the Joint Strategy Review was a consensus document, each service provided its own individual input, outlining the threat and the appropriate American response as it saw it. Comparison of these inputs offers a useful insight into the range of strategy and force posture alternatives conceivable, even given a broadly shared view of the world and war.

Fully endorsing the liberal-internationalist vision of American responsibilities ("As a responsible member of the international community and a prominent member of the world's most important intergovernmental institutions, the United States will continue to be bound to support international initiatives that establish or maintain stability in key areas of the world, to minimize human suffering, and to foster conditions that favor the growth of representative government and open economies"), the Army viewed the role of American military power in the construction of order as a broad one.[21] Like the Navy, the Army saw a critical peacetime and crisis role for American forces, stabilizing international politics and supporting peaceful solutions to or resolutions of international disagreements.

> The U.S. Armed Forces will be required to engage across the range of military operations, and increasingly in military operations other than war.... Increasingly ... conflict prevention, conflict resolution, and peacetime engagement will assume greater importance as the United States seeks to shape the future security environment.... There is a growing emphasis on the role that military force plays in facilitating diplomatic and political solutions to conflicts. The interconnectedness of the emerging security system will lend greater weight to solving conflicts rather than simply defeating enemies.[22]

Similarly, the Army fully embraced and vigorously advanced the transoceanic conception of conflict. The Army's position was that overseas presence represented the sine qua non of U.S. defense policy, necessary for deterrence of aggression and reassurance of allies and to implement the National Security Strategy of democratic "engagement and enlargement."

The Army's understanding of the transoceanic character of war, however, led it to reach two further conclusions about this overseas presence—one that placed it at odds with the Air Force and the other with the Navy and Marine Corps. First, the Army argued against the notion of a "virtual" overseas presence, claiming that

> historical example indicates that authoritarian regimes are less frequently deterred or compelled by the threat of punishment from afar; thus a physical presence will be required for the most effective deterrent.... Given anticipated trends, a physical and highly visible presence (vice some form of virtual, transient, or distant presence) will be required to deter or defeat aggression.[23]

Second, the Army reasoned that to be effective, overseas presence needed to be ashore rather than offshore: "Because deterrence is based on perception and because most potential U.S. adversaries are primarily land powers, a U.S. land power presence may be the most effective deterrent."[24]

While, consistent with the liberal transoceanic character of its vision, the Army emphasized the importance of coalitions—"coalition partners provide political legitimacy,
which is sometimes critical to facilitating access and support for U.S. operations (and
denying those to our adversaries)"—it cautioned against overreliance on partners.[25]
This caution derived from several concerns. First, U.S. interest in maintaining the system as a whole might transcend the particular interests of local partners, and the
United States might therefore see the need to act even when partners did not. Second,
partners would be unwilling to act if the United States provided only "high technology
or unique capabilities"—that is, if the United States slipped toward an oceanic vision of
conflict or relied too heavily on sea or air power. Finally, dependence on coalition partners would have political costs:

> If the United States continues to reduce its armed forces and instead relies on coalition forces to provide
> a sizable portion of fighting forces, the United States may be compelled to make substantial concessions
> to gain the cooperation of future partners. . . . This may . . . require the United States to alter its objec-
> tives to conform to the desires of its partners, and which may led [sic] to unappealing compromises.[26]

In other words, if the United States desired to retain control over the agenda for creating a liberal international order, it would have to pay the price of supporting an army.
Liberal leadership could not be had at a bargain price, in either blood or treasure. It
would require not only a transoceanic capability but that this capability be provided on
the land, not from the sea, and that it not be dependent on allied contributions.

In an attack directed principally at the Air Force, the Army also rejected the notion that
technology would offer some sort of panacea for the problems of protecting American
interests, particularly if those interests continued to be defined in liberal-internationalist
terms. On this, the Army was blunt in its appraisal:

> While the risk of a high technology peer competitor cannot be discounted, trends indicate an increasing
> frequency of U.S. involvement in lesser regional conflicts and operations other than war (e.g., peace sup-
> port operations, security assistance, humanitarian relief, combating terrorism). Retention of engagement
> and enlargement (or an evolutionary successor) as a national security strategy will increase the frequency
> of such operations. While technology can assist in the conduct of such operations, rarely can precise,
> highly lethal weapons delivered from a distance redress the strategic conditions that created the chal-
> lenges to U.S. interests. Nor may those high technology solutions apply to the increasing likelihood of ir-
> regular and nonconventional warfare or operations conducted in urban areas.[27]

In other words, the Army wanted to be on record that it doubted that more effective
means of killing people and destroying things would solve the problem of creating liberal democratic societies.

The Navy agreed with the Army on many of these issues. The Navy position, drafted by
the Strategy and Concepts Branch of the Navy Staff (N513, in Pentagon parlance—the
successor to the old OP-603, the shop that had prided itself on having provided the
critical intellectual impetus in developing the Maritime Strategy), followed the lines
suggested by ". . . From the Sea" and "Forward . . . from the Sea."

Though couching its concerns in more Realist, less liberal phraseology than the Army, the Navy too saw the United States as having a fundamental national interest in protecting and expanding international order, and it concluded that this would mean the United States would need to be involved, even militarily, in events on the farther shores of the world's oceans.

> The United States will have vital interests overseas arising from its alliance commitments and historic ties with several nations, its broad strategic interest in preventing the rise of regional hegemons, its responsibility to protect U. S. citizens abroad, and its international economic interests, including trade, investment and access to resources. U.S. security strategy will continue to be transoceanic in order to protect and promote those interests.[28]

Again like the Army, the Navy argued that overseas presence was the key to stabilizing the international order, deterring aggression, and preventing conflict. "Posturing with forces in the continental United States, such as by increasing their readiness for deployment, can be used to strengthen the message conveyed by forward deployed forces, but cannot be a substitute for on-scene combat credible forces."[29]

Where the Navy departed from the Army was on the issue of whether overseas presence ashore would be possible or necessarily desirable.

> Nationalism and ethnic politics will cause declining access to overseas bases, increasing operational restrictions on the use of remaining bases, and growing reluctance to enter in status of forces agreements that grant U.S. personnel special status in their countries. Lack of clear and present danger will lead to less willingness on the part of other nations to allow either permanent or temporary basing of U.S. forces in their countries. It will also lead to less willingness to grant over-flight rights through their airspace to U.S. military aircraft not directly supporting their immediate defensive needs.[30]

This skepticism that shared interests in liberal order would be sufficient to support continued U.S. military presence within the sovereign boundaries of other states was heightened by concern that "future adversaries will attempt to use intimidation and coercion to prevent U.S.-led coalitions from forming and to prevent potential coalition partners from granting base access to U.S. forces."[31] In the Navy's view, bases and land power were unlikely to be available for unconstrained use at the right time and in the right place. Worse yet, because of their fixed, sovereignty-challenging nature, such bases and forces would serve as vulnerable lightning rods.

> Overseas bases in unstable, trouble-prone regions will be vulnerable to a variety of threats, including terrorism, special operations forces, and WMD [weapons of mass destruction] delivered by ballistic missiles, tactical aircraft or unconventional means. Thus, in some countries routine peacetime overseas shore basing may not be desirable even when it is available.[32]

The implications of this were clear: overseas presence would have to be provided by naval forces.

> By providing a highly visible expression of U.S. resolve and capabilities, naval forces will shape the strategic environment, enhance the U.S. leadership role abroad, reassure friends and allies, enhance regional stability, and deter potential aggressors. Operating with strategic mobility on the high seas,

free of the political constraints that can deny U.S. forces direct routes through foreign airspace or access to forward bases ashore, naval forces will remain the force of choice for preventing troublesome
situations at the low end of the conflict spectrum from escalating to war. . . . Their multifaceted ability
to take decisive, early action ashore is essential to containing crises and deterring conflicts. . . . The
flexibility and mobility of naval forces make them particularly valuable for deterring the potential aggressor who might exploit U.S. involvement in a major conflict elsewhere as an opportunity for strategic advantage. Finally, the deterrent value of naval forces is greatly enhanced by their ability to extend
full-dimensional protection over allies and critical infrastructure ashore.[33]

The Marine Corps shared the Army's and Navy's belief in the importance of overseas
presence and the Navy's skepticism that land-basing would be possible: "In the future,
overseas sovereignty issues will limit our access to forward land bases and geo-
prepositioning."[34] The solution, in the Corps' view, was to maintain forward-deployed,
at-sea forces able not only "to conduct operations other than war (OOTW) and other
expeditionary operations" but most importantly, to engage in forcible entry—the
Corps' core competency.[35]

Like the Army, however, the Corps was explicitly skeptical about technology as a solution to the nation's strategic problems. The Corps' skepticism, however, was more prag-
matic than the Army's: the problem with technology was not that finding more
effective ways of killing the enemy would fail to provide effective political leverage but
that technology was unlikely to work.

While we must capitalize on technology as a force multiplier, history repeatedly teaches that technology promises more than it ultimately delivers. U.S. military strategy must retain the flexibility to ac-
commodate a failure of technology. Such failures, whether enemy induced, mechanical malfunctions,
or deficiencies in design, must not prevent accomplishment of the mission.[36]

The Corps' major contribution to the intellectual debate was its introduction of the concept of "chaos" and its skepticism that liberal democracy would take successful root in the
Third World. The Corps' embrace of liberal internationalism was thus weaker than the
Navy's and far weaker than the Army's. Thinking in the more traditional Realist-
internationalist terms of the Cold War, the Corps tended to assume the inevitability of
conflict and the improbability that international institutions would restrain humanity's
violent tendencies. Foreseeing failed economies, failed states, internal upheaval, shortages
of and competition for natural resources, surging populations, undereducation and
overurbanization, mass migration, awareness of income disparities, proliferating military
technology including weapons of mass destruction, and fertile conditions for terrorism,
the Corps painted a bleak picture.

The epicenter of instability will be in the world's littorals where 70 percent of [the] world's population
now lives. By 2010, that percentage will increase. Countering these threats will not be easy. As overseas bases close, America will rely more and more upon the most flexible and adaptable crisis response
force. These forces must be capable of loitering in close proximity, near enough to influence events,
but far enough away to avoid agitating potentially explosive situations.[37]

The Air Force, by contrast, offered a strikingly different, if not entirely internally consistent, solution. While providing a threat assessment not dissimilar from the Marine Corps' and acknowledging the continued importance of military OOTW, the Air Force concluded that engagement and environment shaping could be handled from a distance—from bases in the continental United States or in space. This move away from forward operations would be dictated by the fact that "forward deployed forces (i.e., staging areas, patrol areas, airbases, maritime task forces, etc.) will face increased risk."[38] The Air Force vision called for coupling improved information technology with longer-range strike capability to enhance American capacity to target and destroy objects and people precisely and with impunity. How exactly these improvements in military technology would translate into political influence or the capacity to shape political outcomes in a chaotic world was never specified. The Air Force did, however, assert that "nuclear weapons will continue to be relevant to U.S. national security for the foreseeable future," though it warned that "U.S. nuclear strategy must be updated. Nuclear proliferation and a decrease in U.S. conventional strength requires a coherent plan about the long-term role and utility of nuclear weapons in achieving U.S. strategic objectives."[39] In sum, the Air Force suggested, technology and not forward engagement would represent the key to stabilizing a turbulent world.

"2020 Vision" and the NOC

Outside the Navy, then, very different visions of how to accomplish the goals of U.S. national security policy were circulating, challenging the Navy's preferred strategy. Even inside the Navy, however, important questions remained.

". . . From the Sea" and "Forward . . . From the Sea" offered some explicit prescriptions for shifting resources within the Navy, away from forces for open-ocean and sea-control missions and toward forces for littoral force projection. Beyond this, however, these white papers did not offer much specific advice. Given the enormous budgetary pressures on the Navy in the late 1990s, some clearer appreciation of exactly how a littoral strategy would work was highly desirable. For example, could lesser force packages be substituted for carriers and amphibious ready groups? Could forward operating tempos be lightened? Could forces be shifted between deployment hubs to get a more optimal distribution of resources? Could modernization in some technical areas be slowed? Answers to these questions, of course, hinged on a clear and shared understanding of what it is about forward operation in the littorals that is valuable—that is, about how to "operationalize" the littoral strategy.

In the 1995–1997 time frame, two distinct answers were developed within the Navy. At one level, the struggle was a classic bureaucratic one between two competing offices—the CNO's Executive Panel (the CEP, or in Pentagon nomenclature, N00K) and the

Strategy and Concepts Branch of the Navy Staff in the Pentagon (N513). At another level, however, what emerged was a real intellectual debate, in which two clearly articulated visions of naval power were presented and carefully considered.

Because of its close ties to Admiral Jeremy Boorda, the principal action was initially in N00K's hands. Throughout 1996 N00K briefed and gamed repeated revisions of "2020 Vision," a draft white paper intended for the CNO's signature. Under the principal authorship of Captain Edward A. Smith, Jr., "2020 Vision" attempted to uncover the implicit logic of "... From the Sea" and "Forward ... from the Sea."

The essential argument of "2020 Vision" was that precision engagement, or massed precision engagement, would permit naval forces to have a decisive impact, obviating the need for a lengthy war of attrition. Drawing on superior information about the location of targets and about how the adversary's political and military authority and command was structured—what the key nodes, or "targets that mattered," were—naval forces would be able to direct precise fires of sufficient magnitude to stun an adversary, destroying his capacity to wage war effectively and potentially compelling a political settlement. Operating forward and maneuvering freely, naval forces would be able to deliver this knockout blow immediately and at will.

The heart of "2020 Vision" was its notion of three tiers, or "axes," of targeting: national political, military infrastructure, and battlefield forces. While "2020 Vision" maintained that any of these tiers might be attractive, the implicit message was that either of the first two tiers offered a critical vulnerability that the Navy would be able to exploit, avoiding the necessity of going against the adversary's probable strength, the sheer mass of his battlefield force.

There were several interesting implications in "2020 Vision." In the first place, it moved warfighting capability back to center stage. N00K reasoned that the peacetime and crisis influence of U.S. naval forces depended entirely on the meaningful wartime options at their disposal. "Presence" might be valuable, but it had an impact only to the degree that those forces could affect wartime outcomes. Peacetime and crisis-environment shaping ought therefore to be regarded as a positive externality, not a central focus for Navy planning. Deterrence—the major peacetime mission, in the view of "2020 Vision"—would hinge on a visible capacity to identify and strike swiftly, massively, and repeatedly critical targets without running significant risk of enemy counterattack. Forward operation might be necessary to remind an adversary of this capability and to ensure that such blows could be executed in a timely fashion, but it was the capability for massed precision attack that lay at the core of deterrence.

Second, "2020 Vision" put air power—both manned aircraft and cruise missiles—at the core of its account. Where "... From the Sea" and "Forward ... from the Sea" had made the Navy–Marine Corps marriage the linchpin of a littoral strategy, "2020 Vision" was principally a vision of unilateral Navy impact. To be sure, it suggested that massed precision strike would also enable ground operations ashore, both by disrupting the adversary's capacity for organized resistance and by providing supporting fires. But even in this regard, "2020 Vision" moved away from the close partnership with the Marine Corps and toward a broader conception of jointness that embraced the Army, Air Force, and coalition partners.

Third, "2020 Vision" emphasized the interaction of mass and precision in firepower. Precision alone would fail to have the desired effect. If the purpose of the blow was to induce shock and paralysis, a handful of missiles or air strikes would not be enough. Further, gradual attrition of key targets was unlikely to have the necessary impact: what was needed was the ability to take down an entire political system or an entire military infrastructure in a short period of time—with the clear capacity to do it again if the opponent attempted to reconstruct its control. "2020 Vision" assumed that with proper intelligence and careful modeling of the opponent's systems, the mass necessary to achieve these blows could be kept to achievable levels; "2020 Vision" also assumed that the cost of precision weapons would fall.

The upshot of "2020 Vision" was clear: effective presence requires concentrating on real warfighting plans. These would center on forward naval air and missile power. "2020 Vision" thus made a strong implicit case for the proposed arsenal ship—essentially a large, inexpensive floating missile magazine, with a small crew, deployed for very extended periods of time in critical theaters. The arsenal ship would be able to "pickle off" large numbers of cruise missiles in a relatively short period of time, delivering the kind of initial massed precision attack envisioned.

A secondary theme in both "2020 Vision" and in the arsenal ship design, but one that grew in importance as war games explored the concepts, was theater ballistic missile defense (TBMD). The potential importance of TBMD in both the political equation (preventing potential coalition partners or targets of coercion from being pressured into concessions early on) and in the military equation (keeping critical ports and airfields open, particularly given the danger of chemical and biological attacks) became clear. Forward naval forces and a TBMD-armed arsenal ship might be critical in this role.

Perhaps not surprisingly, "2020 Vision" faced considerable opposition. The Marine Corps was openly hostile, of course. Within the Navy, many officers viewed it as a bureaucratic misstep, for two reasons. First, by stressing air and missile strikes as the Navy's critical contribution to national security, "2020 Vision" left the Navy vulnerable to (correct or incorrect) claims from the Air Force that it could perform the Navy's functions more cheaply. Second, by tying the presence mission so closely to warfighting requirements at a time when the Navy was larger than the warfighting requirements established by the Office of the Secretary of Defense, it left the Navy vulnerable to pressures for downsizing. Sub rosa, the linkage to the arsenal ship probably also generated hostility: the arsenal ship was seen by aviators as a threat to the carrier in a capital ship role, and it was seen by surface sailors as a threat to more capable high-technology missile shooters. Finally, war gaming failed to resolve doubts among skeptics about the decisiveness of the actions envisioned by "2020 Vision."

At a deeper level, however, the problem with "2020 Vision" was its fundamentally Realist flavor. Apart from recognizing that coalition partners might be more likely to cooperate if the Navy could provide TBMD, "2020 Vision" was a strategy for dealing with conflict, for engaging in coercion, not a strategy for creating cooperation. Its concerns were with how to threaten credibly to take down an opponent's infrastructure and how to overcome his area-denial efforts.

Opposition to "2020 Vision" was most actively centered in N513, N00K's natural rival in strategic planning. To be fair, N513's opposition was less bureaucratic than intellectual. N513 and its head during this period, Commander Joseph Bouchard, felt that "2020 Vision" failed to give sufficient attention to the real strengths of naval power—the enormous maneuverability of naval forces, their freedom from foreign political constraints, their sustainability, and their contribution to shaping the peacetime diplomatic environment and to responding to a range of humanitarian, political, and military crises—and that it overstated the likely impact of massed precision attacks. Initially, N513's alternative vision was expressed in the form of critiques of "2020 Vision." Ultimately, though, as support for "2020 Vision" waned, N513 was commissioned to produce its own document. Its mandate, however, was not to produce a "vision" statement (which might give the impression that the Navy was moving away from "Forward . . . from the Sea") but to generate an "operational concept."

The "Navy Operational Concept" (NOC) produced by N513 in early 1997 stressed that

> operations in peacetime and crisis to maintain regional economic and political stability are traditional roles of the Navy–Marine Corps team. . . . Our hallmark is forward-deployed forces with the highest possible readiness and capability to transition instantly from peace to crisis to conflict. This flexibility positions us to fight and win early, or to contain conflict. More importantly, our presence may prevent conflict altogether. By any standard or measure, peace is cheaper than war.[40]

The NOC returned to the concept of "expeditionary operations" first suggested in ". . . From the Sea" as the intellectual centerpiece for understanding how the Navy would execute its littoral strategy.

> Expeditionary operations . . . are a potent and cost-effective alternative to power projection from the continental United States and are suited ideally for the many contingencies that can be deterred or quickly handled by forward-deployed forces. Expeditionary operations complement, enable and

dramatically enhance the effectiveness of continental power-projection forces when a larger response is needed.[41]

Where "2020 Vision" had focused on what naval power might accomplish in wartime, the NOC focused on the stabilizing value of "being there" in peacetime. Bouchard was explicit about the liberal-internationalist ideology inherent in his account of the role played by sustained forward naval presence.

> The Navy's role in peacetime engagement is to project American influence and power abroad in support of U.S. efforts to shape the security environment in ways that promote regional economic and political stability. Stability fosters a sense of security in which national economies, free trade practices, and democracies can flourish. Democratic states, especially those with growing economies and strong trade ties, are less likely to threaten our interests and more likely to cooperate with the United States. This stability and cooperation, which our peacetime engagement promotes, assists in meeting security threats and promoting free trade and sustainable development.[42]

Where "2020 Vision" focused on tiers of targets, the NOC offered a vision of enhanced cooperation and strengthened international regimes.

> Our global presence ensures freedom of navigation on international trade routes and supports U.S. efforts to bring excessive maritime claims into compliance with the international law of the sea. When disaster strikes, we provide humanitarian assistance, showing American compassion in action. Our forward deployments always include a wide range of diplomatic activities, such as: sending Sailors and Marines ashore as representatives of the American people; bringing foreign visitors onto sovereign U.S. naval vessels; and carrying out a wide range of community relations activities. These efforts promote American democratic ideals abroad, enhance mutual respect and understanding with the peoples of other countries, and demonstrate U.S. support for friendly governments. Our forces support U.S. diplomatic efforts aimed at shaping the security environment, such as improving relations with former adversaries or reducing tensions with potential adversaries.[43]

Obviously, the NOC could not ignore the more violent side of the Navy's duties. But, the NOC argued, the deterrent impact of naval forward presence derived not so much from the particular capabilities resident in the forward force but from the implicit threat of the full might of America. "We deter by putting potent combat power where it cannot be ignored, and by serving as a highly visible symbol of the overwhelming force the United States can deploy to defeat aggression." The unique contribution of naval power to national strategy was its political and military flexibility, not its firepower. Politically,

> operating in international waters, our forces are sovereign extensions of our nation, free of the political constraints that can hamper land-based forces. We put the right capability in the right place at the right time. We possess the unique capability of responding to ambiguous warning that either would not justify costly deployments from the continental United States, or might be insufficient to persuade nations in the region to host U.S. forces on their soil. When a visible presence might be provocative or foreclose U.S. military options, we can position submarines covertly to provide on-scene surveillance capabilities and firepower. Rotational deployments allow us to maintain our forward posture indefinitely.[44]

Militarily, the range of options provided by forward naval forces was their strength during crises—the same forces could send Marines ashore, evacuate noncombatants, enforce no-fly or no-sail zones, escort shipping, or launch air or missile strikes. In combination with the maneuverability of naval forces, this flexibility provided the capacity to frustrate a potential aggressor:

> We make it exceedingly difficult for an adversary to target us and deny him the option of pre-emption by keeping our forces dispersed and moving, by operating unpredictably or covertly, and by employing deception. The wide range of options we provide for immediate response to aggression leaves a potential aggressor uncertain of the intended course of action. This uncertainty keeps him off balance, disrupting his ability to formulate a coherent campaign plan and eroding confidence in his ability to effectively execute operation plans.[45]

In wartime, forward presence meant that naval forces could disrupt an aggressor's plans and frustrate his efforts to achieve a fait accompli. In addition, naval forces would be "critical for enabling the joint campaign. We ensure access to the theater for forces surging from the United States by supporting coalition forces to keep them in the fight, by seizing or defending shore bases for land-based forces, and by extending our defensive systems over early-arriving U.S. joint forces ashore."[46]

In deliberate contrast to "2020 Vision," the NOC was also careful to stress that "in some tactical situations, such as operations on urban terrain, a SEAL or Marine with a sniper rifle may be the optimum precision weapon," and that the Navy

> will be a full partner in developing new amphibious warfare concepts and capabilities for implementing the Marine Corps concept Operational Maneuver From the Sea (OMFTS). . . . We will provide enhanced naval fires, force protection, command and control, surveillance and reconnaissance, and logistics support for Marines ashore—enabling the high-tempo operations envisioned by OMFTS.[47]

Interestingly, while the NOC was briefed to and approved by the Navy's top leadership, and unlike "2020 Vision" was signed out by the CNO, its release was handled without any fanfare: distribution was on the Internet, and no "glossy" was prepared. Far from reflecting doubts about the content of the NOC, however, this low-key approach was meant to underscore the consistency of Navy policy and to dispel any concerns that the NOC represented a change in direction or new intellectual departure.

"Forward . . . from the Sea: Anytime, Anywhere"

In the wake of the Quadrennial Defense Review, the Navy again reaffirmed its commitment to its littoral strategy and to the liberal-internationalist vision of foreign policy and to the transoceanic-countermilitary image of war on which that strategy rested. Underscoring and publicly confirming the continuity in Navy thinking, the Department of the Navy's 1998 Posture Statement—issued jointly by Secretary of the Navy John Dalton, the CNO (Admiral Jay Johnson), and the Commandant of the Marine Corps (General Charles Krulak)—was titled "Forward . . . from the Sea: Anytime, Anywhere."

Like the NOC and earlier white papers, "Forward . . . from the Sea: Anytime, Anywhere" was premised on the assumption that the role of the U.S. military would be to support the spread of liberal institutions, such as democracy and the free market, around the globe. At the same time, however, it accepted the Marine Corps' concept of "chaos" and at least some of the Corps' pessimism about building a peaceful world order:

> We live in a complex and ever-changing world. The growth during this decade of democracies and free market economies is most encouraging. Yet nationalism, economic inequities, and ethnic tensions remain a fact of life and challenge us with disorder—and sometimes chaos. As both positive and negative changes take shape, the United States has become what some call the "indispensible nation"—the only nation with the technological capability and acknowledged benevolent objectives to ensure regional stability.[48]

This chaos and disorder, and the threat posed to the spread of democracy and liberal values, represented the principal challenge to American security, not some peer competitor. The Posture Statement went on to reiterate both the American national interest in supporting a liberal international order and the role of American naval power in this mission: "Naval forces project U.S. influence and power abroad in ways that promote regional economic and political stability, which in turn serves as a foundation for prosperity."[49] Now explicitly linking the littoral strategy to the new National Military Strategy of "Shape, Respond, Prepare," the 1998 Posture Statement reprised five familiar themes about the role of naval power in supporting a liberal-internationalist foreign policy.

First, "Forward . . . from the Sea: Anytime, Anywhere" reasserted the centrality of forward presence across the spectrum of conflict—in shaping the peacetime environment, responding to crises, and preparing to counter aggression. Second, it equated forward presence with *naval* forward presence, suggesting that constraints on the deployment or use of American forces on the sovereign territory of allies would mean that forward deployments would, in general, necessarily be sea based. It reasoned that

> shaping and responding require presence—maintaining forward-deployed combat-ready naval forces. Being "on scene" matters! It is and will remain a distinctly naval contribution to peacetime engagement. As sovereign extensions of our nation, naval forces can move freely across the international seas and be brought to bear quickly when needed. . . . Operating in international waters and unfettered by the constraints of sovereignty, naval forces are typically on scene or the first to arrive in response to a crisis. The inherent flexibility of naval forces allows a minor crisis or conflict to be resolved quickly by on-scene forces. During more complex scenarios, naval forces provide the joint force commander with the full range of options tailored for the specific situation. From these strategic locations, naval forces shape the battlespace for future operations.[50]

Third, while noting the role of naval power in warfighting, the Posture Statement emphasized that the unique Navy contribution to U.S. security efforts was the ability of naval forces to shape the peacetime environment and respond to crises short of, or prior to, war. The document detailed the wide range of peacetime and crisis "shape" and "respond" missions conducted by naval forces.

> Our forces . . . participate in a complete range of shaping activities—from deterrence to coalition building—establishing new friendships and strengthening existing ones during port visits around the world. These visits promote stability, build confidence, and establish important military-to-military

> relationships. In addition, port visits provide an opportunity to demonstrate good will toward local communities, further promoting democratic ideals. . . . Each exercise, large or small, directly contributes to successful coalition building. Credible coalitions play a key role in deterring aggression and controlling crises. . . . Routine naval deployments signal both friend and foe of our commitment to peace and stability in the region. This demonstrated ability to respond rapidly to crises—and to fight and win should deterrence fail—offers a clear warning that aggression cannot succeed. Moreover, the ability of the forward-deployed forces to protect local allies and secure access ashore provide [*sic*] a guarantee that the full might of our joint forces can be brought to bear.[51]

Fourth, even while stressing the Navy's unique capability to shape the peace and respond to challenges short of war, the Posture Statement was careful to underscore Navy's endorsement of jointness in warfighting. Without backing away from the position that Navy–Marine Corps activities were inherently joint, the Posture Statement emphasized that "the Navy and Marine Corps also can integrate forces into any joint task force or allied coalition quickly."[52] Jointness would not relegate the Navy to subordinate roles, however. In the first place, even while recognizing that "in those cases where aggression is not contained immediately . . . by swiftly responding naval forces" the Army and Air Force would be involved, the Posture Statement sought to dispel any impression that the Navy's role in a land battle would be limited to providing logistics.[53] The document emphasized the Navy's participation in actual combat and its ability to provide key command and control for joint operations.

> Naval operations are critical elements of the joint campaign. We deliver precision naval fire support— strike, force interdiction, close air support, and shore bombardment. We seize the advantage of being able to operate on and from the sea. Using high-tech information-processing equipment, we achieve superior speed of command by rapidly collecting information, assessing the situation, developing a course of action, and executing the most advantageous option to overwhelm an adversary.[54]

In the second place, in addition to playing a critical role while missiles, bombs, and bullets were flying, the Navy would (presumably unlike the Army or Air Force) be in harm's way both in the critical days and hours before the shooting started and in the weeks, months, and years after it stopped: "When the joint campaign is over, naval forces can remain on scene for long periods to enforce sanctions and guarantee the continuation of regional stability."[55]

Finally, the Posture Statement also repeatedly underscored the remarkable flexibility of naval forces, likening them to a rheostat permitting the National Command Authorities to send carefully calibrated messages and respond in a carefully calibrated fashion—and to leave force levels at a particular setting for indefinite periods of time. The extraordinary range of political and military options inherent in forward-deployed naval forces was also highlighted.

Even while extolling flexibility, however, the Posture Statement reaffirmed the Navy's commitment to traditional force packages—carrier battle groups and amphibious ready groups—and its unwillingness to address the possibility that less capable forces or other force packages might be sufficient to carry out the Navy's forward tasks in peacetime or crisis, let alone wartime.

> The balanced, concentrated striking power of aircraft carrier battle groups and amphibious ready groups lies at the heart of our nation's ability to execute its strategy of peacetime engagement. Their power reassures allies and deters would-be aggressors, even as it demonstrates a unique ability to respond to a full range of crises. . . . The combined capabilities of a carrier battle group and an amphibious ready group offer air, sea, and land power that can be applied across the full spectrum of conflict. . . . This balance and flexibility provides the National Command Authorities (NCA) a range of military options that is truly unique.[56]

Indeed, in the same paragraph it cited a commitment to "innovative thinking [in] preparing us . . . for an uncertain future," the Posture Statement was explicit and emphatic about what would not change—that "we will maintain carrier battle groups and amphibious ready groups forward, shaping the international environment and creating conditions favorable to U.S. interests and global security."[57]

Back to the Sea? Unresolved Difficulties

Despite the Navy's confidence that it is on track and that "the Navy's course for the 21st century set by *Forward . . . From the Sea* has proven to be the right one for executing our critical roles in all three components of the *National Military Strategy* [peacetime engagement, deterrence and conflict prevention, and fight and win] and for conducting the future joint operations envisioned in *Joint Vision 2010*," there are reasons for concern about the Navy's littoral strategy.[58] Two are obvious.

Barring dramatic developments in the external environment or unanticipated and profound shifts in domestic political culture, the liberal-internationalist construction of national security seems likely to dominate American thinking well into the new century.[59] The notion that a stable, peaceful international order is achievable is an attractive one, and at the moment Americans seem unlikely to conclude either that their own well-being can be separated from that of the rest of the world or that they are powerless to effect change.

The transoceanic-countermilitary image of war, however, appears far less robust. Experiences in places like Somalia and Bosnia have two impacts. In the first place, they underscore the ugliness and wearisome unpleasantness of actually trying to control another nation's sovereign territory. In the second place, they make the idea of countermilitary warfare appear ridiculous: when the "enemy" is a mobilized society, not distinctively uniformed and highly disciplined soldiers, it is increasingly difficult to maintain an image of warfare as a clean, surgical interaction between opposing states and their professional soldiers, sailors, and airmen.

Indeed, the tension between liberal internationalism and a transoceanic-countermilitary image of war should be obvious. If American political leaders hold to a liberal-internationalist vision of national security, it is logically necessary for them also to believe that war is an acceptable, albeit unpreferred, tool: the liberal-internationalist vision implies a willingness to intervene, with force if necessary, to protect liberal democratic states and liberal international norms. Given recent experiences, however, if war is conceptualized in transoceanic-countermilitary terms (that is, if it is seen as requiring an intervention in the sovereign affairs of an adversary, and the defeat of his military forces, to achieve political victory), it will probably cease to be regarded as a usable option. The American public's stomach for Somalias and Bosnias appears quite limited. Ultimately, a liberal-internationalist image of national security is thus likely to compel Americans leaders to find some new, more attractive image of war. When they do—when, as in the past, they start assuming that war can be won simply by controlling the high seas or that war is a struggle between entire nations in which direct attacks on society are permitted—the littoral strategy will become a liability for the Navy.

The second and more important reason for beginning to explore alternatives to the littoral strategy, however, is skepticism about its ability to yield the peacetime, crisis, and wartime leverage claimed. The old Scottish verdict "not proven" seems amply earned in this case. It is useful to consider each of these environments—peacetime, crisis, and wartime—and what littoral naval power can reasonably be expected to produce.

In peacetime, the littoral strategy reasons, forward naval presence will encourage societies to take the risk of investing in liberal democratic institutions both at home and internationally. This ability of a forward-operating American navy to project power ashore is assumed to support regional politics by supporting general deterrence—that is, by deterring dissatisfied states from even thinking about changing the status quo through violent means. And it is expected to reassure existing liberal democracies, convincing them that neither accommodation with antidemocratic forces nor unilateral security measures that might trigger a spiral of hostility are necessary. This is an appealing image.

Belief in the peacetime impact of power projected "from the sea," however, is based on faith rather than evidence or analysis. There is no actual evidence that either routine peacetime presence by naval forces or expeditionary naval operations affect the evolution of societies, their support for international law, their general propensity to resort to force to resolve disputes, or their fears that others will.

The lack of evidence in support of a proposition is, of course, not evidence against that proposition; it is simply an absence of evidence. A priori, however, there is substantial reason to doubt the efficacy of littoral projection of naval power in shaping the peacetime environment. What is known, principally from studies of crises (about which more will be said below), regarding decisions to engage in aggression and states' ability to understand or focus on power projected "from the sea" suggests a real danger that states will ignore or underestimate the capabilities inherent in American naval power. Moreover, even if it were shown to be the case that applying naval power "from the sea" has a significant positive impact on the peacetime environment, it would still remain to be demonstrated that it is a cost-effective means of creating that impact— that naval power is less expensive than alternative military means, such as subsidizing regional proxies, or than nonmilitary means, such as fostering trade and development or developing a specialized capacity for humanitarian relief.

In crisis, the forward-deployed capacity to project power "from the sea" is touted as having an immediate deterrent effect—that is, dissuading an adversary who is tentatively considering going to war from following through on that idea. Here we do have some evidence; at very best, however, it must be regarded as offering mixed support for the Navy's advocacy of a littoral approach. A variety of studies of conventional deterrence have been undertaken.[60] While the research questions, underlying theoretical assumptions, and research methods have varied, several general findings emerge.

The principal one is that immediate extended deterrence with conventional means— that is, using threats of conventional response to deter an adversary who is considering aggression against a third party—regularly fails, even in cases where commitments are "clearly defined, repeatedly publicized and defensible, and the committed [gives] every indication of its intentions to defend them by force if necessary."[61] Unlike nuclear deterrence, conventional deterrence does not appear to result in a robust, stable stalemate but in a fluid and competitive strategic interaction that, at best, buys time during which underlying disputes or antagonisms can be resolved. The possession of decisive conventional military superiority and the visible demonstration of a resolve will not necessarily permit the United States to deter attacks on friends and interests.

There are three reasons why immediate extended conventional deterrence is so problematic. First, potential aggressors are sometimes so strongly motivated to challenge the status quo that they are willing to run a high risk, or even the certainty, of paying the less-than-total costs of losing a war. Second, potential aggressors frequently conclude, correctly or incorrectly, that they have developed a military option that has politically or militarily "designed around" the deterrent threat. Third, there is considerable evidence that, particularly when they are under severe domestic stress, potential aggressors are unable to understand or respond rationally to deterrent threats. "Wishful thinking" by leaders who find themselves caught in a difficult situation appears to be an all-too-common pathology.

Further, and more germane to the issue of naval forward presence as a crisis deterrent tool, there is some evidence that because of the general insensitivity of potential aggressors to information, efforts to "signal" resolve through measures such as reinforcing or redeploying forces have limited effectiveness. If force movements are large enough to foreclose particular military options, they may forestall aggression. But as a means of indicating resolve and convincing an aggressor of the credibility of deterrent commitments, they do not generally appear to have an impact.

All of this would seem to provide a reasonable argument against bothering to invest too heavily in forward military forces—or at least against believing that they offer much assurance of guaranteeing regional crisis stability. Ultimately, the key to preventing conflicts seems to be resolution of the underlying issues. At best, conventional deterrent efforts buy time.

On the other hand, there is also some evidence that in some circumstances it is in fact possible to buy time. In particular, having forces in place that can deny potential aggressors a quick victory seems to tend to reinforce deterrence. The historical record suggests that the prospect of quick victory may be an important element in at least some aggressors' calculations: the potential aggressor's belief that he can either score a quick knockout or achieve a limited fait accompli appears to make aggression significantly more attractive.

This offers some grounds for supporting forward naval presence. On the other hand, it also suggests the possibility that the Army is right and that if forward presence is to matter it needs to be on the ground, that an offshore presence of a potent but limited force, with only the implicit threat of surged ground forces, is less likely to have an impact, at least if the potential aggressor has limited goals. It also suggests the possibility that the symbolism of naval forward presence, serving as a reminder of the full weight and power the United States could ultimately bring to bear, may not be that important.

In war, the argument that forward naval forces operating with a littoral strategy can have an important impact in the initial phases of the conflict, thereby preparing the ground for later U.S. successes, is doubtless true. While true, however, it may well be relevant in only a limited range of cases. Most potential conflicts or contingencies involve adversaries who are too small for this effect to matter much. Short of a major regional conflict (MRC), the superiority of U.S. military forces is sufficiently overwhelming that initial setbacks are not likely to be critically important. At the other extreme, in the case of a regional near-peer competitor—a Russia or a China—it is hard to imagine a littoral strategy having much of an impact: the amount of (nonnuclear) power that can be projected from the sea is trivial compared to the size of the adversary's society or military establishment. What is left is a handful of admittedly very important cases: MRCs against such rogue states as Iran, Iraq, and North Korea. What is interesting about these cases, however, is that there are not very many of them; their identity is known; and plans can be made in advance to move large amounts of land power and land-based air power to the theater at relatively short notice. The unique flexibility of naval power is, in these cases, relatively less valuable.

Critics of the littoral strategy are, then, likely to argue that it is difficult to find cases in which a major investment in the capacity to project power from the sea makes sense. A small investment would be sufficient for most Third World contingencies, particularly if the United States does not demand real-time response. Even a large investment would be insufficient to deal with the great powers. And in the case of the medium-sized conflicts, the MRCs, paying for the extra flexibility of naval power may not be cost-effective.

If there is reason for some cautious skepticism about the wisdom of building a navy for its capacity to project power from the sea, then perhaps it is worth thinking about some of the other things that the U.S. Navy does. In particular, it may be worthwhile to rethink the old Mahanian notion of sea power—not because Mahan was some sort of prophet and his ideas have eternal validity but because in the particular circumstances of the early twenty-first century his observations about the importance of the international commons per se may be relevant.

The globalization of energy and food markets, as well as cross-industry trade in industrial goods, makes the sea remarkably important for national well-being, not simply for the well-being of the American nation but for that of most nations. By the middle of the next century, even China will be critically dependent on its access to the ocean. Global naval hegemony—that is, the capacity to exercise control over the world's high seas—thus offers a powerful reason to invest in naval power. At best, control of the world's oceanic highways may convey the power to shape the general evolution of international society. At minimum, it is likely to provide a veto power over many changes in international norms and regimes that the United States dislikes.

Obviously, global naval hegemony does not convey an ability to dictate national policies or to control the social and political development or activities of other states. It is unlikely to offer much useful leverage if the Chinese choose to repeat Tienanmen Square, if there is a coup in Russia, or if Hutus and Tutsis resume killing each other. But then again, no approach to naval power is likely to offer much useful leverage in these cases.

The point is that there are realistic limits to what naval power is likely to provide to a twenty-first-century America, and these may be well short of the goals encompassed within a liberal-internationalist vision of national security. These limits do not mean the United States should cease investing in naval power. They do, however, suggest that U. S. leaders and the U.S. Navy should not mislead themselves into believing that investing in the capacity for littoral warfare will necessarily yield an ability to control social and political developments around the world. Liberal internationalism can generate a dangerous hubris. A naval strategy that panders to the hubris is unlikely in the long run to serve the interests of either the nation or the Navy.

Back to the Future: Sea Power and the American Navy

The Navy's success in navigating the dangerous waters of post–Cold War strategic adjustment should not blind it to the challenges that lie in the immediate future. As the military services struggle to design strategies to support the national one of "engagement and enlargement," as the Navy continues to wrestle with the problem of operationalizing a littoral strategy, and as both the vision of war on which the littoral strategy is based and that strategy's capacity to deliver what it promises are called into question, it may be wise to begin to think about moving Navy strategy back to the sea. A more realistic understanding of what naval power can actually accomplish—what navies do and what necessitates their construction—may well lead the United States to scale back its efforts and to set itself the historically daunting, but under present circumstances modest, goal of oceanic hegemony. Controlling the world common and the global commerce that moves across it may not in itself prevent challenges to peace and liberal democracy, but it offers the potential for considerable influence and leverage, and this, at the present juncture, may be all that can reasonably be expected of naval power.

Moving naval strategy back to the sea implies a way of employing naval power to further the liberal international goals the nation has set itself that is very different from the one envisioned in " . . . From the Sea." With America's entry into the second American century, however, the time seems ripe for another Mahan to explore what this alternative strategic conception would mean for the U. S. Navy.

Notes

1. For a review of this debate and a sophisticated theoretical account of factors that enhance the capacity of military institutions to undertake strategic adjustment see Emily O. Goldman, "Organizations, Ambiguity, and Strategic Adjustment," in Peter Trubowitz, Emily O. Goldman, and Edward Rhodes, eds., *The Politics of Strategic Adjustment: Ideas, Institutions, and Interests* (New York: Columbia Univ. Press, 1998).

2. See Edward A. Smith, Jr., "'. . . From the Sea': The Process of Defining a New Role for Naval Forces in the Post–Cold War World," in Trubowitz, Goldman, and Rhodes, eds.

3. William A. Owens, *High Seas: The Naval Passage to an Uncharted World* (Annapolis, Md.: Naval Institute Press, 1995), p. 4.

4. On the competition between various visions and the cultural forces and dynamic underlying it, see Edward Rhodes, "Constructing

Peace and War: An Analysis of the Power of Ideas to Shape American Military Power," *Millennium*, Spring 1995.

5. On the "clash of cultures," Samuel P. Huntington, "The Clash of Civilizations?" *Foreign Affairs*, Summer 1993, and Huntington, "If Not Civilizations, What?" *Foreign Affairs*, November–December 1993.

6. This vision was perhaps given its most elegant expression by the great liberal-isolationist statesman Charles Evans Hughes. See Hughes, *The Pathway of Peace: Representative Addresses Delivered during His Term as Secretary of State (1921–1925)* (New York: Harper and Brothers, 1925), esp. pp. 3–31 ("The Pathway of Peace," 1923, and "Limitation of Naval Armament," 1921), or David J. Danelski and Joseph S. Tulchin, eds., *The Autobiographical Notes of Charles Evans Hughes* (Cambridge, Mass.: Harvard Univ. Press, 1973), pp. 209–52.

7. For a discussion of the forces leading to an abandonment of the transoceanic-countersocietal image and resulting in the attractiveness of the oceanic-countermilitary one, see Rhodes, *Millennium*.

8. See Robert W. Komer, *Maritime Strategy or Coalition Defense?* (Cambridge, Mass.: Abt Books, 1984).

9. The Maritime Strategy grew out of a diverse set of intellectual efforts in various locations around the Navy. Probably the most important center of activity was OP-603, the strategic concepts branch of the Navy Staff, which developed several influential papers and briefings in the early 1980s spelling out the basic logic of the Maritime Strategy. For the definitive history of the Maritime Strategy, see Peter Swartz, manuscript in preparation. The Maritime Strategy was publicly released as a supplement to the January 1986 issue of the U.S. Naval Institute *Proceedings*, under the signature of the Chief of Naval Operations, James D. Watkins. The most widely cited explication of the strategy is Linton Brooks, "Naval Power and National Security: The Case for the Maritime Strategy," *International Security*, Fall 1986.

10. On the history of the NFCPE, see Smith.

11. Sean O'Keefe, Frank B. Kelso II, and C. E. Mundy, Jr., ". . . From the Sea: Preparing the Naval Service for the 21st Century," Department of the Navy, September 1992. Reprinted in U.S. Naval Institute *Proceedings*,

November 1992, pp. 93–6; this quotation from p. 93.

12. Ibid., p. 94.

13. Ibid., p. 93.

14. "The seeds of conflict will continue to sprout in places where American interests are perceived as vulnerable. The art of managing crises in these areas is delicate and requires the ability to orchestrate the appropriate response and to send precisely tailored diplomatic, economic, and military signals to influence the actions of the adversaries. Naval Forces provide a wide range of crisis response options, most of which have the distinct advantage of being easily reversible. If diplomatic activities resolve the crisis, Naval Forces can withdraw *without* action or build-up ashore." Ibid., p. 94.

15. Ibid., pp. 95–6.

16. John H. Dalton, J. M. Boorda, and Carl E. Mundy, Jr., "Forward . . . from the Sea," Department of the Navy, 1994, p. 1.

17. Ibid., p. 3.

18. Ibid., pp. 7, 8.

19. Ibid., p. 7.

20. Ibid., p. 4.

21. Maj. Gen. Joseph G. Garrett III, USA, "Memorandum for Deputy Director, Strategy and Policy, J-5, Subject: Service Input for the Joint Strategy Review (JSR)," U.S. Army, 3 September 1996, p. 2.

22. Ibid., p. 11.

23. Ibid., p. 4.

24. Ibid., p. 3.

25. Ibid., p. 5.

26. Ibid.

27. Ibid., p. 3.

28. Deputy Chief of Naval Operations (Plans, Policy and Operations), "United States Navy Strategy Review: Report to the Deputy Director for Strategy and Policy (J-5)," U.S. Navy, 29 August 1996, p. 5.

29. Ibid., p. 10.

30. Ibid., pp. 1, 2.

31. Ibid., p. 7.

32. Ibid., pp. 11, 12.

33. Ibid., p. 11.

34. "Beyond 2010: A Marine Perspective," U.S. Marine Corps, n.d., p. 2.

35. Ibid., p. 5.

36. Ibid., p. 7.

37. Ibid., p. 4.

38. Col. Richard M. Meeboer, USAF, "Memorandum for Strategy Division, (J-5), Joint Staff, Attn: Col. Nelson, Subject: Joint Strategy Review (JSR), Air Force Input," U.S. Air Force, 4 September 1996, p. 7.

39. Ibid., p. 9.

40. Jay L. Johnson [Adm., USN], "Forward . . . from the Sea: The Navy Operational Concept," U.S. Navy, March 1997.

41. Ibid.

42. Ibid.

43. Ibid.

44. Ibid.

45. Ibid.

46. Ibid.

47. Ibid.

48. John H. Dalton, J. L. Johnson, and C. C. Krulak, "Department of the Navy 1998 Posture Statement—Forward . . . from the Sea: Anytime, Anywhere," n.d., p. 2.

49. Ibid., p. 5.

50. Ibid., pp. 2–3.

51. Ibid., pp. 6–7.

52. Ibid., p. 3.

53. Ibid., p. 9.

54. Ibid.

55. Ibid.

56. Ibid., pp. 3, 7.

57. Ibid., p. 12.

58. Ibid. More recent versions of the National Military Strategy have revised this tripartite formulation: shape (the environment), respond (to the threats), and prepare (for the future).

59. See Edward Rhodes, "Wilson, Roosevelt, and Defense Policy in the 1990s," *Defense Analysis*, November 1992.

60. See, for example: John Arquilla and Paul K. Davis, *Extended Deterrence, Compellence, and the "Old World Order"* (Santa Monica, Calif.: RAND, 1992); Alexander L. George and Richard Smoke, *Deterrence in American Foreign Policy: Theory and Practice* (New York: Columbia Univ. Press, 1974); Paul K. Huth and Bruce Russett, "What Makes Deterrence Work? Cases from 1900 to 1980," *World Politics*, July 1984; Paul K. Huth, *Extended Deterrence and the Prevention of War* (New Haven, Conn.: Yale Univ. Press, 1988); Robert Jervis, Richard Ned Lebow, and Janice Gross Stein, *Psychology and Deterrence* (Baltimore: Johns Hopkins Univ. Press, 1985); Peter Karsten, Peter D. Howell, and Artis Frances Allen, *Military Threats: A Systematic Historical Analysis of the Determinants of Success* (Westport, Conn.: Greenwood, 1984); Richard Ned Lebow, *Between Peace and War: The Nature of International Crisis* (Baltimore: Johns Hopkins Univ. Press, 1981); Richard Ned Lebow and Janice Gross Stein, *When Does Deterrence Succeed and How Do We Know?* (Ottawa: Canadian Institute for International Peace and Security, 1990); John J. Mearsheimer, *Conventional Deterrence* (Ithaca, N.Y.: Cornell Univ. Press, 1983); Jonathan Shimshoni, *Israel and Conventional Deterrence* (Ithaca, N.Y.: Cornell Univ. Press, 1988); and Barry Wolf, *When the Weak Attack the Strong: Failures of Deterrence* (Santa Monica, Calif.: RAND, 1991). For a summary of this literature see Edward Rhodes, "Review of Empirical Studies of Conventional Deterrence," unpublished, presented at the "Future Navy RMA Roundtable," CNO Executive Panel, Alexandria, Virginia, June 1997.

61. Lebow, p. 211.

CHAPTER EIGHT

The Tyranny of Forward Presence
DANIEL GOURÉ

A specter is haunting U.S. Navy strategic and force planning. It is the specter of forward presence, the continual deployment of Navy and Marine Corps units in waters
adjacent to foreign littorals. Although the Navy speaks of its central purpose as maritime power projection, it is forward presence, particularly in peacetime, that drives
both force structure requirements and operations tempo. The demands placed on both
force structure and operations tempo by the Navy's long-standing commitment to
maintain forward presence in multiple regions have been exacerbated in the past few
years by that institution's desire to extend its area of influence to both littoral waters
and the land beyond. The ever-increasing scope of forward presence exerts a tyrannical
hold on the future of the Navy, a hold that threatens—in an era of constrained defense
budgets and rapidly changing threats—to break the force.

The general argument for forward presence as a cardinal principle of Navy strategic
planning is that "shaping" the international environment is a necessary and appropriate mission for the U.S. military in general, and the Navy in particular.[1] The military is
not alone in believing in the importance of the "shaping" mission. Under various ru-
brics, this impetus was central to the Clinton administration's articulation of national
security policy and national military strategy.[2] Were this only the view of one administration, it could be readily dismissed as international social work.[3] But a growing chorus
of voices in the academic and analytic communities argues that U.S. defense planning
should emphasize "shaping" functions. Some are so bold as to speak of a new role for
U.S. forces in terms of "what can only be termed 'imperial policing.'"[4]

The myth that the world is in dire need of shaping or policing derives from the proposition that with the end of the Cold War the forces that had dampened disorder and
disunity ceased to function. This "chaos theory" increasingly pervades all the services

© 2001 by Daniel Gouré
Naval War College Review, Summer 2001, Vol. 54, No. 3

and the Department of Defense as well, but the Navy and Marine Corps have been among its chief proponents. Here is but one example of the Navy–Marine Corps view:

> Never again will the United States exist in a bipolar world whose nuclear shadow suppressed national-ism and ethnic tensions. The international system, in some respects, reverted to the world our ances-tors knew. A world of disorder. Somalia, Bosnia, Liberia, Haiti, Rwanda, Iraq, and the Taiwan Straits are examples of continuing crises we now face. Some might call this period an age of chaos.[5]

But is this Hobbesian vision real? Has the world reverted in the last decade to a state of nature, from some prior regime of civility, or at least restraint? The Middle East suf-fered four Arab-Israeli wars prior to the end of the Cold War. For decades, Iraq en-gaged in predatory behavior toward its neighbors—producing most notably a ten-year bloodbath with Iran—before deciding to invade Kuwait. India and Pakistan have sev-eral wars to their account, the last in 1971, as well as chronic conflict over Kashmir. The Taiwan Straits is a military problem not because of the end of the Cold War but be-cause of China's arms buildup and the failure of the United States to provide counter-vailing capabilities to Taiwan. The civil and regional wars of Africa are largely consequences of colonization and the rivalries of the Cold War itself.

Many once-fractious parts of the world have become more stable over the past decade. The collapse of the Warsaw Pact and the downfall of the Soviet Union eliminated the major supporter of international terrorism. Thereafter, the inability of Russia to pro-vide cheap conventional weapons to client states also reduced regional arms races dra-matically. Lack of arms may have reduced as well the aggressive tendency of such former client states as Syria, Libya, Iraq, and Iran. One can point even to recent events on the Korean Peninsula as a direct, albeit delayed, result of Pyongyang's loss of its Soviet godfather.

Where problems have arisen, it is not clear that the end of the Cold War was the cata-lytic event. It is difficult, for instance, to establish a correlation between the end of the Cold War and the rise of militant Islam. Further, events in Indonesia have had less to do with the rise and fall of superpowers than with the consequences of the Asian eco-nomic crisis (during which, it must be noted, the Treasury Department did more to maintain stability than all the U.S. forces deployed to the region).

Current military planning has somewhat tempered its earlier "Boschian" vision of global chaos, asserting now that it is the uncertainty of our time and the difficulty of predicting the future security environment that necessitates a strategy of power projec-tion based on forward presence.[6] The fault, in that view, lies not in the unstable nature of the external world but in our inability to forecast the future accurately. For plan-ning purposes, uncertainty may be as good as chaos. In some respects it is even better, since—as the services' planning documents note—it requires that the military maintain capabilities to address all threats.

This sense of chaos, or even mere uncertainty, masks what is really happening: a re-structuring of the international environment, the creation of a new international system.[7] We know from history that such restructuring is long, complex, and often quite messy. Wherever we look, in each of the critical regions of the world, the character of the relations among the dominant powers has yet to be firmly set, much less put on a course toward stable, positive, and peaceful relations. Western Europe is waiting to see if a closer union, and with it an incipient common security and defense identity, can be effected. Nato expansion is confronting the question of Russia's legitimate security interests in Eastern Europe. China's role in East Asia is being defined by Beijing—witness the 1999 military maneuvers and missile launches against Taiwan—in ways that must make all of its neighbors nervous; how China acts will determine to a large extent the behavior of others in the region. The relationship between India and Pakistan is as tense as it has ever been; increasingly, both states see the need to reach out to other powers of the Middle East and Asia in order to strengthen their positions in their own rivalry. Finally, the future of the political and security relationships in the Persian Gulf is frozen, and it will be as long as Iraq and Iran remain pariah states and the United States is required to maintain a military presence in the area.

Historically, the creation of new international orders has been dominated by major economic and military powers. This current period of evolution appears to be no different. In prior periods of reorganization, emerging powers have sought ways to shift regional and even global power balances in their favor, provoking similar behavior by their adversaries. (It is in this light that we need to look with some concern at current Russian and Chinese efforts to forge a new strategic alliance.)

Certain regions will be most important in the development of the new international order. For future U.S. policy, three regions are of vital importance: Europe, from the Atlantic to Russia's borders; the Pacific Rim, from Korea through Southeast Asia; and South Asia and the Persian Gulf. Those regions have three things that set them apart from the rest of the world. First, they contain the overwhelming predominance of global wealth, economic activity, and technological investments. Second, they are the loci of vital U.S. allies and of economic interests that must be protected. Third, they each border on one or more of the emerging potential competitor states.

The United States is the sole global power; it has interests in every region of the world and vital interests in each of them.[8] Thus, while it is difficult to identify where confrontations will arise, the sheer breadth and scope of U.S. interests abroad provide more than a few reasons that this nation may find itself at basic odds with local adversaries. Indeed, at least one major study of U.S. foreign policy in the next century argues that the foremost U.S. interest in Asia and Europe is to prevent the domination of those regions by adversarial powers.[9] Therefore, the United States could find itself in confrontations with rising powers as it seeks to preserve regional balances of power or American access. This would be particularly likely should, as has been the case in the past, a powerful regional state threaten U.S. allies. The United States is likely to be the only nation that can provide sufficient military support to enable these allies to deter or, if necessary, defeat such an adversary.

It is true that the post–Cold War world has demonstrated a degree of disorderliness. But it can hardly be said that the world has entered a period of mounting chaos. Nor can it be claimed that U.S. decision makers and planners are paralyzed by uncertainty. They continue to make decisions and set priorities on force structure, regional deployments, and future acquisitions with a great deal of self-assurance. The chaos/uncertainty argument, then, serves largely as a means of defending the military against the increasingly evident need to make hard choices with respect to current missions and future capabilities. For the Navy, the validity of the doctrine of forward presence represents one of those hard choices.

Should the Navy Maintain a Strategy of Forward Presence?

It is not clear that the U.S. military should focus its planning and force-building around forward presence, much less "imperial policing." The idea that military forces can shape the political environment in regions in which they are deployed has become fashionable as a result of the rise of an issues-based approach to national security policy.[10] Many of these issues are sociopolitical in nature, and their solutions fall, broadly speaking, under the heading of "shaping." The trend toward employing military forces for political purposes has been given additional impetus by the activism of the regional commanders in chief (such as those of Pacific Command or Central Command), which has grown as the power of the State Department and U.S. ambassadors to conduct foreign policy has declined.[11] (One of the potential consequences of their use of forward-deployed forces for political purposes was highlighted by the USS *Cole* incident.)

It is for these reasons, then, that the U.S. military is increasingly focused on and driven by the demands of peacetime and crisis forward presence. The problem of maintaining forward presence has been a crucial factor, for instance, in the U.S. Air Force's creation of a new organization centered on ten aerospace expeditionary forces. The U.S. Army is undergoing its own transformation, seeking to become more responsive and deployable. Each of the services is investing in capabilities to make rapid forward presence easier to establish, whether for major conflicts or smaller contingencies.

In particular, and without question, forward presence has served the Navy well. Forward presence provides a defensible rationale for force sizing, a matter of particular importance in the absence of a threat.[12] In any case, the Navy functions best when it is under way, and as long as it is steaming, it might as well do so where it might be needed.

The idea of forward presence, however, is for the Navy more than a bureaucratic convenience; it is an article of faith. According to the Navy's own *Strategic Planning Guidance*, "By remaining forward, combat-credible naval expeditionary forces guarantee that the landward reach of U.S. influence is present to favorably shape the international environment." In the Navy's view, forward-deployed naval forces discourage challenges to U.S. interests, deter would-be aggressors, and, should deterrence fail, provide means for a timely response. For these reasons, the Navy argues, it could play a new and unique role in U.S. national security. But for this to be true, forward presence has to be the Navy's central mission.[13]

For a number of reasons, tying the future of the Navy to forward presence is problematic. The concept of "shaping" the international environment is fuzzy at best. Too often it has extended well beyond traditional notions of security to involve, inter alia, attempts to influence the internal politics of failing states, efforts to address almost intractable socioeconomic problems, and engagement in what are classic policing functions. Looked at this way, Navy combat forces seem to have little relevance.[14] The forces that would seem to be most useful in the social-work and policing dimensions of forward presence are those generally classed as "combat support" or "combat service support" (e.g., engineer, military police, logistical, and medical units).

The term "forward presence" too is subject to interpretation and competing definitions. In its narrow sense, the emphasis is on *forward*—it simply means the deployment of forces in proximity to locations of interest to U.S. security and foreign policy. A broader definition, focusing on the word *presence*, suggests more complex and political purposes, for which presence generally needs to be nearly continuous and highly visible—requirements that can limit both the flexibility and the combat effectiveness of the forces engaged.

Leaving aside for the moment the question of what constitutes a combat-credible force, it is fair to ask what evidence there is that naval forward presence helps to shape the international environment. One can acknowledge that military forces can perform tasks that are essentially political in nature, such as demonstrating resolve and commitment. The objective of these tasks is different from that of forward presence, as narrowly defined above.

Advocates of forward presence as an instrument of U.S. foreign policy must acknowledge that there is no empirical evidence to support their case. This is particularly true for naval forward presence. While various theories have been propounded as to the relationship between the pursuit of national objectives, the protection of regional interests, the suppression of sources of regional instability, and forward presence, none has any real data to support it.[15] It has been possible to show in certain instances some relationship between the ebb and flow of economic indicators and the deployment of U.S. forces; however, these cases involve the deployment of forces after crises or conflicts have started.[16] Such analyses have not been able to demonstrate the usefulness of peace-time forward presence as a mechanism for preventing conflicts and shaping regional environments. As one analyst (in fact, an advocate of naval power) noted a few years ago, "The interesting fact is that there is virtually little or no evidence, analysis and rigorous examination on which to make a fair and objective assessment of the benefits, costs, advantages and downsides of presence. . . . [T]he record is at best ambiguous regarding the utility, benefits and disadvantages of naval presence."[17]

Even the projection of maritime power may not serve to shape the environment or resolve a regional crisis. The history of the U.S. presence in the Persian Gulf in the 1980s—including Operation EARNEST WILL, the ill-fated attempt to protect oil shipments by reflagging foreign-registry tankers—does not support the thesis that naval forward presence exercises a positive influence on regional dynamics. Similarly, it is considered self-evident in Navy circles that the deployment of two aircraft carriers to the Taiwan Straits region ended the 1996 crisis. At least one post-incident assessment suggests otherwise.[18]

In addition to the shaping function, the Navy asserts, forward presence provides unique operational advantages. The Navy makes a strong case that such deployments are critical enablers of joint warfare, through a combination of sea control and maritime power projection; for instance, where land bases are not available, naval forces can become alternative bases. Naval power-projection capabilities, in this view, are likely to be less vulnerable to adversary attack than land bases. Even here, however, the other services have attempted to make cases that forward presence can be accomplished in other ways and with different means.[19]

The land-versus-sea-base argument has been going on for a long time, with no resolution in sight. It is sufficient here to point out that the fact that naval forward presence may be needed if land bases are not available does not make it the preferred solution. Indeed, when the stakes are sufficiently grave or vital interests and allies are threatened, it is unlikely that U.S. political and military leaders will rely solely on naval forward presence. To put it bluntly, if land bases are necessary, they will be found or even seized. This is an often-overlooked lesson of the Gulf War and the Kosovo campaign. In this connection, the Navy itself speaks of its role as that of an enabler, suggesting that it is the responsibility of the other services—those that require land basing—to win a war. In that light, it is not clear that allies will find the simple presence of naval units offshore adequate. U.S. "boots on the ground" have reassured allies for some fifty years as indications that the United States is willing to share equally in the risks of resisting aggression.

At the very minimum, the Navy needs to rethink how it describes the forward-presence mission.[20] Justifying forward presence in terms of the ability to shape the international environment raises questions of how relevant the current Navy force structure is to that purpose. Moreover, it risks promising more than the Navy can deliver, at least in terms of demonstrable impact. Also, because forward presence is tied to a particular national security strategy, it may be rendered less relevant if the new administration formulates a new, more restrained strategy.

It is, then, difficult to see continuous, peacetime forward presence as anything other than a vehicle for defending the Navy's desired force structure. The political rationale is weak at best, and holding on to it may undermine the Navy's case for more capable forces in the future. One naval officer appears to have recognized the danger in a recent article: "If . . . naval forward presence forces have but small roles in crisis response and contingencies, such forces are luxuries that may have some relevance in peacetime diplomacy but little usefulness in crisis and war. This is not an impression that bodes well for the future of a military service."[21]

Can the Navy Maintain a Strategy of Forward Presence?

Even if it were obvious that forward presence is an important tool of U.S. national security strategy, there are reasons to believe that it will not be possible to continue it for long. Forward presence places inordinate and, in the current budgetary environment, unsustainable physical demands on the Navy. Some fixed and substantial number of ships is necessary to maintain a fraction of them on station continually. For every ship deployed, the U.S. Navy requires between three and five more in rotation: steaming to or from the deployment area; in overhaul; in port for leave and repair; and "working up" in local training exercises. All that in turn translates into a minimum required budget. It is clear that the Navy will not have a large enough budget, and thus not enough ships. Vice Admiral Edmund Giambastiani was reported to have pegged the Navy–Marine Corps annual procurement budget at between twenty-eight and thirty-four billion dollars annually, far above the twenty-two-billion average for the past decade.[22] The lower procurement number translates into reduced ship construction and, inevitably, a navy of fewer than three hundred ships. Even if additional funds and an adequate number of ships were available, changes to the threat environments in regions where forward naval presence is now practiced raise questions as to its wisdom.

All naval forces are subject to the terrible tyranny of distance. It takes time for ships to
sail from their home ports to deployment areas. Nowhere are the distances to be traveled greater than in the Pacific. Whereas it typically takes a U.S. warship about eleven
days to travel from the East Coast to its assigned station in the Mediterranean, the same
deployment can take up to twenty days from the West Coast of the United States to the
littoral waters of the Asian landmass.

No other navy is so tyrannized by its strategy and geography as that of the United
States. Every other naval power is concerned largely with the protection of its own
coastlines and nearby waters. Only the United States is confronted with the need to
project naval power eight to ten thousand miles to areas of concern. The farther away
a deployment area is from home ports, the more ships are required in order that a
given number can be continually present. Hence a strategy that emphasizes forward
presence inevitably puts additional strain on an already-overstretched U.S. Navy.

From a force of nearly six hundred ships in the late 1980s, the Navy has been reduced
to a little over three hundred ships today, of which approximately 45 percent must be
under way in order to meet current peacetime responsibilities. This places enormous
strain not only on the ships but on the men and women who serve aboard them. At the
same time, because of reduced funds for shipbuilding, the average age of the Navy's
vessels is increasing; accordingly, breakdowns become more frequent, maintenance
costs rise, and availability rates decline. However valuable forward presence may be in
the Pentagon's internecine budget battles, it can impose intolerable stress on a service
that is asked to perform missions for which it is underequipped. When forward presence becomes a burden to the very service that is its chief proponent, it is time to rethink the whole proposition.

The Navy understands the problem. In testimony before the House of Representatives in
2000, Vice Admiral Conrad Lautenbacher, Deputy Chief of Naval Operations, declared
that "it is no secret that our current resources of 316 ships are fully deployed and in many
cases stretched thin to meet the growing national security demands."[23] This is not merely
the view from headquarters. Admiral Dennis McGinn, commander of the Third Fleet,
stated before Congress in February 2000 that "force structure throughout the Navy is
such that an increased commitment anywhere necessitates reduction of operations somewhere else, or a quality of life impact due to increased operating tempo."[24] The commander
of the U.S. Fifth Fleet, operating in the Arabian Sea and Persian Gulf, said it best:

> Although I am receiving the necessary forces to meet Fifth Fleet obligations, the fleet is stretched and I
> am uncertain how much longer the Navy can continue to juggle forces to meet the varied regional re-
> quirements, including Fifth Fleet's. I am uncertain that we have the surge capability to meet a major
> theater contingency, or theater war. Eventually, the increased operational tempo on our fewer and
> fewer ships will take its toll on their availability and readiness.[25]

The reality is that numbers matter. The U.S. Navy is critically short of ships; it does not have enough to maintain a full-time, combat-credible naval presence in regions of interest to the U.S. and provide the necessary surge capability for crisis or war. As a result of recent events like Kosovo, for which the western Pacific was stripped of its aircraft carrier, public and congressional attention has been focused on the inadequacy of the Navy's inventory of carriers. Further, the Joint Chiefs of Staff have published a study concluding that the nation requires sixty-eight attack submarines instead of the fifty that have been allowed. A recent surface combatant study concludes that the Navy requires up to 139 multimission warships in order to satisfy the full range of requirements and carry out day-to-day operations; instead, the Navy has been allowed only 116. At least a quarter of its surface combatants are aging frigates and older destroyers that lack offensive and defensive capabilities essential to a twenty-first-century navy. Speaking of the lack of surface combatants, one senior naval officer has been quoted as saying, "We know we are broken. We are running our ships into the ground, our missions are expanding and our force structure is being driven down to 116 surface ships. We have to address it before we hit the precipice."[26]

Unfortunately, without significantly higher defense budgets, there is no possibility that the Navy will be able to acquire the ships and submarines it needs to maintain its current forward presence posture. It is already evident that U.S. defense spending is well short of what will be required to maintain the existing force structure. The United States must be willing to spend on average 4 percent of its gross domestic product (GDP) to support fully the force recommended by the Quadrennial Defense Review over the next twenty years, fiscal years (FY) 2001–20. In fact, however, based on the current FY 2002 budget submission to Congress, defense spending will fall from 2.9 percent of GDP in FY 2000 to 2.4 percent in FY 2010, and to 2 percent in 2020.[27]

The Congressional Budget Office reports that the Defense Department is faced with annual budget shortfalls of fifty-two to seventy-seven billion dollars. General Henry Shelton, chairman of the Joint Chiefs of Staff, testified before Congress in October 2000 that the military services had estimated that they will need at least $48.5 billion more each year. The Secretary of the Air Force, F. Whitten Peters, asserted in a recent interview that the U.S. military needed some $100 billion over current spending levels in order to replace aging equipment and maintain or improve operational readiness.[28] Unless real annual defense spending is increased well above the current $310 billion at some time during this decade, the president and Congress will be left with little choice but to make additional personnel cuts, force structure reductions, and base closures.

The Navy will suffer severely if such projections, and others, of budgetary shortfalls are even approximately accurate. A recent Navy study warned that procurement was short some eighty-five billion dollars for the period 2008–20, with the shipbuilding budget likely to be underfunded by some four billion annually, and naval aviation by $3.3 billion.[29] These shortfalls could result in a Navy one-third to one-half its present size by the year 2010.

If the force cannot be recapitalized, perhaps it can be modernized or transformed, thereby avoiding the problem of finding the necessary additional funds. A number of analytic and political writers have advocated "skipping generations" in procurement in order to focus attention and resources on revolutionary capabilities. Unhappily, the idea of skipping a generation is a fantasy. There is an illusion among its advocates that the current force will last the additional twenty-odd years while the transformation takes place. In fact, however, the funds necessary to support a transformation can be freed up only if current forces and near-term acquisitions are sharply reduced. Reducing forces and acquisitions now will only make the conduct of current operations, including forward presence, more difficult. Moreover, reducing the acquisitions will seriously damage the defense industrial base, on which the services will have to rely for the production of next-generation equipment.

Budgetary strictures also constrain the fielding of the advanced capabilities forward-deployed forces will need if they are to be combat credible and survivable. The Navy acknowledges that the threat to its forward-deployed forces is serious and likely to grow substantially worse over the next few decades.[30] This means that combatants built for the Cold War are increasingly vulnerable, particularly in littoral waters. The Navy will need to invest in a host of new technologies enhancing both the offensive and defensive power of the fleet; otherwise, forward presence will be not merely an expensive conceit but a truly dangerous fetish. Yet it is not clear that either the technology or the resources will be available. The demand that the Navy operate forward in peacetime, then, exerts a perverse effect, forcing on the Navy an expensive modernization/transformation effort that may in the end prove unsuccessful, if only due to a lack of funds.

It must also be recognized that even if transformation is possible, it will take decades to complete. As a result, today's Navy will be required to execute the forward-presence strategy ten and even twenty years into the future. If, as is argued by advocates of transformation, today's Navy will be the wrong force with which to maintain forward presence or contest littoral waters, it seems obvious that the problem is not with the force but with the demand that the Navy continue to base its strategy on forward presence. The Navy must seek ways other than slavish obedience to the tyranny of forward presence to pursue its strategic objectives and support national security.

There remains a final question. Facing a growing littoral threat, depending on large "Cold War era" ships and submarines, and recognizing the effort by some potential adversaries to acquire "green" and even "blue-water" capabilities, why does the Navy continue to emphasize forward presence? It would seem reckless, to say the least, to continue to pursue a demanding strategy with declining resources of the wrong type. Moreover, it would seem to be a waste of the single advantage that the U.S. Navy possesses and that will remain uncontested for decades to come: its ability to dominate the open oceans.

Operating in close-in waters would appear to provide littoral adversaries with an unacceptable advantage. The desire of potential adversaries to contest the U.S. Navy for control of these waters suggests that it would be foolhardy for the Navy to sail into that trap.

The Future of Forward Presence

The future of forward presence, then, appears uncertain at best. The American people's patience with the idea that the United States can shape an international environment to suit its sensibilities appears to be wearing thin. A more judicious approach to the application of military power in the service of foreign policy will inevitably lead to a reduced requirement for forward presence. Where peacetime forward presence is required, naval forces may not be able to provide it more effectively than other kinds of forces. It is possible that policy makers and the public alike will look for more "bang for their presence buck."

The Navy acknowledges that if forward-deployed forces are to play useful roles in peacetime or crisis, they must possess credible combat power. It is not clear how this can be accomplished in the face of the emerging threat. The proliferation of asymmetric and anti-access capabilities may threaten the survivability of forward-deployed naval forces. This problem is particularly acute for traditional surface platforms. Efforts to address the emerging vulnerability of forward-deployed naval forces by changing the character of naval systems and developing new concepts of operations may compromise the combat capability of such forces. To the extent that enhanced survivability must be acquired at the expense of offensive capabilities, it would seem to undercut the basic rationale for forward presence.

Finally, if forward-deployed capabilities can be maintained only at the expense of the ability to control the broad oceans, it will have proven to be a bad decision. At present there are no threats to the U.S. Navy in the open oceans, and this will be the case for the next several decades. However, a force built over the next ten or twenty years for forward presence and littoral combat will have to meet whatever threats emerge in the "shallow seas" for many decades beyond. Increased competition between the United States and rising regional powers could result in a challenge to the U.S. Navy's mastery of the open oceans, or at least one ocean. Such a challenge could come soon enough to necessitate reconsideration of the present policy of optimizing naval forces for the forward-presence mission.

Notes

1. Edward A. Kolodziej, "Leveraging Strategic Assets to Enhance International Security: Opportunities for a Hesitant Hegemon," in Pelham Boyer and Robert Wood, eds., *Strategic Transformation and Naval Power in the 21st Century* (Newport, R.I.: Naval War College Press, 1997), pp. 137–66.

2. *National Security Strategy* (Washington, D.C.: U.S. Govt. Print. Off., 1996); and William Perry, "National Security in an Age of Hope," *Foreign Affairs*, November–December 1996, pp. 64–79.

3. Michael Mandelbaum, "Foreign Policy as Social Work," *Foreign Affairs*, January–February 1996, pp. 16–32.

4. Eliot A. Cohen, "Defending America in the Twenty-First Century," *Foreign Affairs*; and Mackubin Thomas Owens, "The Price of the Pax Americana," *Wall Street Journal*, 18 October 2000, p. 26.

5. Charles C. Krulak and Jay L. Johnson, "A Forward Presence in a Violent World," *Washington Post*, 25 November 1996, p. A28.

6. See, for example, Chief of Naval Operations (N3/5), *Navy Strategic Planning Guidance with Long Range Planning Objectives*, April 2000, available at www.hq.navy.mil/n3n5/files/NSPG2000.pdf.

7. John Ikenberry, "The Myth of Post–Cold War Chaos," *Foreign Affairs*, May–June 1996, pp. 79–91.

8. The Commission on America's National Interest, *America's National Interests* (Washington, D.C.: U.S. Govt. Print. Off., July 1996).

9. Zbigniew Brzezinski, Lee Hamilton, and Richard Lugar, *Foreign Policy into the 21st Century: The U.S. Leadership Challenge* (Washington, D.C.: Center for Strategic and International Studies, September 1996).

10. Stephen A. Cambone, *A New Structure for National Security Policy Planning* (Washington, D.C.: Center for Strategic and International Studies, 1998).

11. Dana Priest, "An Engagement in Ten Time Zones: Zinni Crosses C. Asia, Holding Hands, Building Trust," *Washington Post*, 29 September 2000, p. A1.

12. On this point see Sam J. Tangredi [Capt., USN], "The Rise and Fall of Naval Forward Presence," U.S. Naval Institute *Proceedings*, May 2000, pp. 28–33.

13. *Strategic Planning Guidance*, p. 19. See in general Edward Rhodes, " '. . . From the Sea' and Back Again: Naval Power in National Strategy in the Second American Century," in Boyer and Wood, eds., pp. 307–54. An updated version appears in the *Naval War College Review* 52, no. 2 (Spring 1999), pp. 13–54.

14. For a nuanced examination of the limitations of naval forces in this role, see Edward Rhodes et al., "Forward Presence and Engagement: Historical Insights into the Problem of 'Shaping,'" *Naval War College Review* 52, no. 1 (Winter 2000), pp. 25–61.

15. Philip A. Dur [RAdm., USN], "Presence: Forward, Ready, Engaged," U.S. Naval Institute *Proceedings*, June 1994.

16. Dov S. Zakheim et al., *The Political and Economic Implications of Global Naval Presence* (Arlington, Va.: System Planning Corp., 1996).

17. Harlan Ullman, "Power, Politics, Perceptions and Presence: What's It All About?" in *Naval Forward Presence: Present Status, Future Prospect*, ed. Daniel Gouré, conference report (Washington, D.C.: Center for Strategic and International Studies, November 1997), p. 42.

18. One is Douglas Porch, "The Taiwan Straits Crisis of 1996: Strategic Implications for the U.S. Navy," *Naval War College Review* 52, no. 3 (Summer 1999), pp. 15–48.

19. Tangredi, pp. 30–1.

20. Ibid., pp. 31–2.

21. Ibid., p. 30.

22. Scott C. Truver, "For Change (U.S. Navy Program Review)," *Jane's Defense Weekly*, 4 April 2001, p. 23.

23. House Armed Services Committee on Shipbuilding, Statement of Conrad C. Lautenbacher, Vice Admiral, U.S. Navy, Deputy Chief of Naval Operations, Resources, Warfare Requirements and Assessments, before the Subcommittee on Procurement, 106th Cong., 1st sess., 29 February 2000.

24. House Armed Services Committee, Statement of Dennis V. McGinn, Vice Admiral, U.S. Navy, Commander Third Fleet, before

the Subcommittee on Procurement, 106th
Cong., 1st sess., 29 February 2000.

25. House Armed Services Committee, Statement of Charles W. Moore, Jr., Vice Admiral,
U.S. Navy, before the Subcommittee on Procurement, 106th Cong., 1st sess., 29 February 2000.

26. Robert Holzer, "U.S. Navy Hopes to Expand
Fleet," *Defense News*, 31 January 2000, p. 1.

27. See Daniel Gouré and Jeffrey Ranney,
Averting the Defense Train Wreck in the New

Millennium (Washington, D.C.: Center for
Strategic and International Studies, 1999).

28. "Official: Military Budget Needs Extra $100
Billion," *Washington Times*, 27 October 2000,
p. 13.

29. Robert Holzer, "Navy Paper Outlines $85
Billion Dollar Shortfall on Fiscal Horizon,"
Defense News, 13 November 2000, p. 3.

30. *Navy Strategic Planning Guidance*, pp. 5–14.

CHAPTER NINE

Naval Power for a New American Century
ROGER W. BARNETT

The vicious, unprecedented attacks on the United States on 11 September 2001 by terrorist extremists served to bring into sharp focus two important new factors on the global security scene. First, the United States experienced a sudden, shocking loss of homeland sanctuary. Sanctuary is another way of portraying what is usually referred to as national security. Sanctuary is the place where one feels secure. The central objective of security policy, and the reason for laws and their enforcers, is to allow citizens to enjoy their freedoms within the security of a sanctuary.

Sanctuary is not confined to fixed locations; for example, it follows U.S. citizens and armed forces wherever they go. The bombings of the U.S. Marine barracks in Beirut in 1983, the U.S. Air Force barracks at Khobar Towers in Saudi Arabia in 1996, U.S. embassies in Kenya and Tanzania in 1998, and the USS *Cole* in 2000 violated the sanctuary the United States normally provides over its federal employees and military forces worldwide. Any or all of these events might have been labeled an "act of war," but since "act of war" is not a defined term of art but a political concept, politicians opted not to proceed down the path that leads to a declared war. Those brutal attacks, moreover, were directed against U.S. government employees who were at the time within another state's sovereign territorial responsibility. The 11 September attacks differed in two key aspects: they indiscriminately targeted civilians, and those civilians were located within the U.S. homeland.

The second factor was the demonstration of the devolution of control of very powerful weapons to individuals who were not associated directly with national governments. Heretofore, with only a few exceptions, weapons of mass destruction (WMD) have been exclusively under the control of governmental leaders. On 11 September, as it has been since, it was demonstrated that traditional WMD (biologicals) and other weapons

---

© 2002 by Roger W. Barnett
Naval War College Review, Winter 2002, Vol. 55, No. 1

of mass destruction (large civil airliners loaded with fuel) can be employed by other than central governments.

The placement of WMD into the hands of terrorists rather than governments has momentous security policy implications for all states. Most important, reliance on deterrence will necessarily have to be supplanted by reliance on protection in the form of active and passive defenses. Reestablishing sanctuary for U.S. citizens will require new emphasis on homeland security, an office with that vital responsibility having been established by President G. W. Bush only ten days after the 11 September attacks.

This change in U.S. core security objectives will be accompanied by an extension of the U.S. commitment to global security and political stability. There will continue to be objectives to be served and tasks to be accomplished beyond the purely defensive ones dictated by increased homeland security emphasis. For the most part, these international tasks will involve assisting friends to shore up their homeland sanctuaries, and penetrating the sanctuary that adversaries seek from U.S. military operations. Past objectives centering on preventing or defeating territorial aggression will be replaced by expeditionary operations to deny sanctuary to those who would harm the United States or its vital interests. That was what the operations against the Taliban and al-Qaida in Afghanistan were all about.

These new core security objectives—underwriting homeland sanctuary, helping others to create and sustain sanctuaries, and preventing successful use of sanctuary by adversaries—will have a powerful impact on the ways and means to fulfil them. Those ways and means will come burdened by their own set of associated risks.

When the decision is made to use or threaten the use of military force in pursuit of strategic goals, *doctrines* and *strategies* define the ways, and *military* forces the means. *Risks* articulate the closeness or lack of fit between ends, ways, and means. If the ends sought are too ambitious for the means available, or if the ways necessary to attain them involve the possibility of significant loss for marginal gain, the ends, ways, and means are not in harmony, and the risks must be assessed as high. Sometimes high risks must be accepted, but often decision makers have a poor understanding of the magnitude of the risks or of the consequences of the actions they are contemplating. In the framework of these relationships, this article will discuss the available ways in which naval power can contribute to the accomplishment of the new strategic ends, the naval means to effect the strategies, and the kinds of risks that will have to be accommodated. It will be argued that the U.S. Navy's participation in the ways to accomplish the ends sought are, in fact, limited in number, and that if sufficient resources are not forthcoming to undergird the optimal strategy, high risks will ensue.

Ways

Doctrines and *strategies* comprise the ways, the "hows," by which military force is employed or threatened. They are closely related. Doctrine says, in essence, "All things being equal, this is how we would prefer to operate"; however, it is unspecific as to time, place, or adversary. Strategies, in contrast, recognize the key factors that are never "equal." Strategies deal with concrete opponents in particular places at specific times. How one operates, doctrinally or strategically, has but two operational components: offense and defense. These are tightly interwoven, and because they cannot be entirely separated, they also cannot be prioritized. In order to succeed, a military force must be able to operate on both the offensive and defensive, concurrently and well.

All this is little more than a truism, yet it exposes the conceptual shallowness of the approach of the Joint Chiefs of Staff documents *Joint Vision 2010* and, more recently, *Joint Vision 2020*. Those documents set forth four operational concepts: dominant maneuver, full-dimensional protection, precision engagement, and focused logistics. In that sense they represent little more than a restatement of the eternal verity noted earlier—ways for the application of military force consist of offense (precision engagement) and defense (full-dimensional protection). Support (focused logistics) and maneuver (dominant maneuver), however, are misplaced in this conceptual framework; neither support nor maneuver is ever undertaken for its own sake but only in order to optimize offense or defense.

Maneuver in itself makes no independent contribution to success. It is maneuver combined with attack or the threat of attack or maneuver, combined with defense, that works to produce the desired effect. While Muhammad Ali characterized his fighting style as "Float like a butterfly, sting like a bee," a perceptive defense analyst, probably Edward Luttwak, observed that the results of maneuver might well be, "Float like a butterfly, sting like a *butterfly*." It is not the "float" that makes the difference but the "sting." No choice can be made between maneuver and "fires" (broadly, campaign-level attacks); they are not binary opposites. Because maneuver is *relational*, one maneuvers for the purpose of rendering the offense, the defense, or both, more effective.[1] Similarly, support provides logistical depth to the offense or the defense. One is left with the straightforward understanding that warfare, the application of military force, is composed of offense and defense enhanced by maneuver and support. This is not very satisfying. One must delve, therefore, in greater detail into the levels of warfare at which specific approaches can be identified.

Strategies for the Employment of Naval Forces

With regard to the employment of naval power, six discrete strategies have historically been adopted by states: fleet battle, blockade, commerce raiding, fleet-in-being,
coastal defense, and maritime power projection.[2]

Each of these strategy choices involves a different blend of offense and defense, under-
written in various degrees by maneuver and support. Moreover, as often as not, the
strategies are not pursued separately but combined or pursued sequentially—sometimes even concurrently—during the course of a conflict. States with large, powerful
navies have typically opted for the more offensively oriented battle, blockade, and
power projection, while states less well endowed with naval power have selected one or
more of the remaining three.

The contributions that naval forces make to the overall military strategies of the states
they serve have value only insofar as they can influence political processes, which invariably take place on land. To sink an enemy fleet in isolation from an effect ashore—
even a long-term, indirect effect—is to have accomplished nothing. Blockades that fail
to alter policy are impotent. Power projection that does not succeed in deflecting the
actions or intentions of an adversary is squandered.

Historically, belligerents had difficulty in directly attacking enemy centers of gravity
(or coming to grips with the sources of enemy power); strategies for the employment
of naval forces have typically taken extended periods of time to exert their effects.[3] Decisive battles among fleets have been few and far between, and their impacts have sometimes taken years to be felt. Blockades (nowadays, "embargoes") tend to be notoriously
slow in acting. Power projection, therefore, the most direct expression of naval power, has
come to be emphasized. Note that there is a positive relationship between the effectiveness of a strategy and the degree to which the adversary's sanctuary is threatened. The
emphasis on power projection can also be seen as a by-product of the atrophy of many
naval fleets. The lack of opposition to the establishment of sea control has permitted the
few large and powerful navies to reorient their focuses in a landward direction.

The United States today has no adversary fleets to engage, nor may it reasonably expect
to for the time being. Commerce raiding is incompatible with achieving U.S. objectives.
"Fleet in being" strategies have historically been used by weak navies for purposes of
deterrence or defensive response. For more than a century the United States has been
the preeminent practitioner of "forward presence"—employing naval forces away from
its homeland to deter adversaries, to reassure allies and friends, and to shorten the time
for crisis response. This could be considered a different form of a "fleet in being" strategy, which the United States undertook in expanded fashion after World War II.

Increased participation in the homeland defense mission will involve the employment of ships as a sea-based adjunct to national missile–defense, and probably also to extend ballistic missile defense umbrellas over the territories of friends and allies. In addition, there will have to be an increase in U.S. coastal surveillance and reconnaissance, and in patrol capability. Antismuggling, anti-infiltration, and ship inspection functions at the more than 350 American ports will tax current and programmed U.S. Coast Guard assets significantly. Unquestionably, the number of units assigned to these tasks will have to increase, and the extra burden will have to be shouldered by the Navy—given the Coast Guard's size and breadth of assigned duties, which include major devotion to at-sea public safety and rescue, interdiction of maritime drug trafficking, and protection of American fisheries. The requirement here will be for air reconnaissance and surveillance, and for numbers of small ships, minimally armed. One advantage enjoyed by the United States that, in general, is not shared among its allies is that most U.S. ports (except those close to Mexico or the Caribbean islands) can be approached only by capable, seagoing vessels. The threat of infiltration or smuggling by means of submarines, while it cannot be ruled out entirely, appears unlikely and small enough not to devote tailored resources to it.

Dimensions of Military Force

From another perspective, "ways" address how to meld the three dimensions of the application of military force—*space, time,* and *intensity.* Examination of these dimensions provides insights into how naval forces can be optimally employed in the future to secure American security objectives.

The key characteristic that will be shared among the dimensions of military force in the future is *nonlinearity.* In space—that is, the geographic dimension of strategy—nonlinearity exists when few lines can be perceived in the battle area that describe or organize opposing forces. Such linear constructs as the forward edge of the battlefield, forward line of troops, fire support coordination line, and even the entire notions of front, rear, and flanks are the result of drawing lines in the battlespace. But forces in the future battlespace cannot be expected to array themselves in lines; attempts to visualize the battlespace in linear terms seem already anachronistic at best. As a consequence, geography and force positioning relative to geographic features will have far less impact on operations in the future, but there is a major exception to this generalization. When the strategy involves protecting targets that are geographically fixed—national infrastructure, for example—the battlespace will be rigidly linear. Nonlinearity will apply for the most part to offensive operations, and it is strongly related to sanctuary, because movement is one of the most effective ways to establish and sustain sanctuary.

In the time dimension, linearity manifested itself in the battlespace as *sequential opera-tions*. One was obliged to perform one action before another could be undertaken. Tac-tical success was a prerequisite to operational or strategic efforts. Forces were required to be synchronized in time, and plans typically were prepared with time-phased branches and sequels—actions that took place successively in time. Today and foreseeably, how-ever, many actions will, by preference, be performed simultaneously—in parallel, not in sequence—which will render moot many notions associated with linear, sequential operations.

Nonlinearity exists also with respect to *intensity,* to the extent that small actions can pro-duce completely disproportionate effects. Systems that have significant feedback mecha-nisms tend to react in this non-Newtonian way. Outcomes, because they might bear little linear relationship to inputs, can thus produce elements of shock and surprise.[4]

In nonlinear situations, particular aspects of place, time, and intensity cannot be fac-tored out and then reassembled. The ability to disaggregate and then reintegrate at will—called "additivity" or "superposition"—does not exist in nonlinear systems: "The heart of the matter is that the system's variables cannot be effectively isolated from each other or from their context; linearization is not possible, because dynamic interaction is one of the system's defining characteristics."[5]

Nonlinearities compress, or flatten, the levels of warfare—tactical, operational, and strategic. When geography interposes no impediment to addressing strategic targets di-rectly, when time does not require a sequence of actions to achieve success, when small (tactical) actions can have effects of great (strategic) consequence, and when variables cannot be isolated, the classic levels of warfare lose much of their distinctiveness. On operations and planning, the impact of these trends toward nonlinearity is significant. Many of the precepts of the Joint Operational Planning and Execution System (JOPES) are brought into question. Indeed, current operations and planning systems seem inca-pable of performing well under such conditions.

Yet, all of these nonlinearities have been characteristic of warfare at sea throughout his-tory. Few true "lines" have ever delineated or organized the maritime battlespace—not even the "sea lines of communication" about which some observers of naval matters have written metaphorically, and the "sea-lanes" along which the German navy in two world wars sought to interdict the transoceanic passage of forces and supplies. Naval strategists have long recognized that sea communication is most effectively interdicted at its termini, underscoring the point that the open sea provides much better sanctuary than geographically fixed ports. If ports of embarkation or debarkation can be closed, neither commerce nor seaborne reinforcement or resupply can flow. Thus are the "sea-lanes" rendered irrelevant. Only when ports cannot be cut off does attacking shipping at sea become necessary.

Naval warfare, since the advent of the aircraft and the submarine, has been truly three-dimensional in ways that other forms of warfare have not. An adversary's forces were never to be located across the battlespace on the other side of the "front lines." They could be virtually anywhere, even below the surface. In addition, in the maritime battlespace all targets are moving. In land warfare maneuver is a variable, an option; in the maritime battlespace, maneuver is a constant—a fact of life.[6]

Naval commanders and strategists have known for many decades that in such an environment—a nonlinear, three-dimensional battlespace in which maneuver is a constant rather than a variable—the most difficult problem is *finding the adversary*. This point brings us to two insights about warfare at sea. First, as mentioned above, sea-lanes are most effectively interdicted at their ends, not along their length. Secondly, most naval battles throughout history have occurred within the sight of land, where ships can more easily be located—thus, of course, the importance of maritime choke points.

Tracking an adversary once found is orders of magnitude easier than finding it, and putting a weapon on target is easier still. Of course, this explains why in the maritime environment submarines and aircraft have been exceptionally difficult adversaries; both enjoy a powerful comparative advantage over surface forces in their ability to create and sustain sanctuary for themselves and deny it to their foes.

The historical characteristics of the maritime battlespace have now begun to typify as well the landward battlespaces that U.S. forces can anticipate in the future. Wherever they might be, adversary forces can no longer be expected to be arrayed in lines, for lines confer few of the advantages they once did, either for defense or for the offensive massing of forces. Adversaries will employ all the dimensions of warfare to both offensive and defensive advantage, and they will endeavor not to present stationary targets—which afford no sanctuary, for they can now be attacked with great precision from long ranges. Potential adversaries already understand that finding the *right* target is the cardinal challenge for present and future forces. They will attempt to ensure that their forces cannot be found, identified, located, tracked, or attacked. They are seeking, in other words, to establish sanctuaries. Distance offers sanctuary, as does darkness, and as do stealth, secure locations such as caves or the depths of the seas, bad weather, and passive and active defenses—armor or anti-missile defenses, for example. Factors that increase the difficulty of finding targets aid and abet sanctuary.

Mobile Scud launchers in DESERT STORM, the ensuing years of severe targeting difficulties in Iraq, and the targeting fiascoes in the Kosovo conflict have offered only early glimpses of what will be a migration ashore of maritime characteristics, the land battlespace too will be nonlinear and three-dimensional, and all important targets will either move or be obscured by deception. Of course, adversaries will attempt to attack targets for which sanctuary is very difficult to provide—large, fixed, valuable nodes of national infrastructure will be prime.

Access

The key concept for conducting expeditionary operations is *access*—the aggregated ability to deny sanctuary. Given access, targets can be selected, located, identified, tracked, and attacked (or threatened) to produce the desired effects;[7] without it, they cannot be. If a target can be selected but not located, one does not have access to it. If it can be selected and located but not identified, access has been stymied. If it can be selected, located, identified, and tracked but no attack can be delivered, access has not been achieved. Access does not require an actual attack. A credible threat to deliver a weapon or an attack of another form (computer network attack, for example) suffices to consummate access.

The kind of access suggested here might be thought of as instrumental access. That is, it is more than access to infrastructure located in a geographic area—such as air bases or staging points for army equipment. It is also more than just "being there." Having established such access, forces can undertake a variety of tasks. Access is prerequisite to power projection (striking or raiding targets on the land with explosives or with troops), blockade and quarantine, rescue and assistance, most types of information operations, and to essentially every conceivable operation in war or "military operations other than war."[8]

Access is vital, because most operational and strategic-level targets will be located on land. Operational-level targets are those that if successfully attacked result in changing the course or outcome of campaigns or major operations; strategic targets, by comparison, involve the course or outcome of the war. Conceivably, with the demise of battle fleets (and the unlikelihood of their resurrection), the only strategic or operational targets that it will be possible in the future to encounter at sea or in littoral waters will be ballistic missile-launching submarines and a state's commerce moved by ship.

As Colin Gray has written, "Very prominent among the distinctions of U.S. superpower was, and remains, its unique global military reach. *That global reach is maritime in character for any operation with dimensions beyond those of a raid.*"[9] The end of "reach" is access, and (aside from raids) that access must have duration, a time dimension. Access is attained by reaching across one or more of the physical realms: sea, space, cyberspace, land, and air. Naval forces emphasize, in their attempts to secure access, those realms that are politically uncontrolled. The high seas, space, cyberspace, and the air above the high seas are free for all to use essentially without restriction, and they provide realms through which access to adversaries can be gained.[10] Figure 1 illustrates the relationships.

FIGURE 1

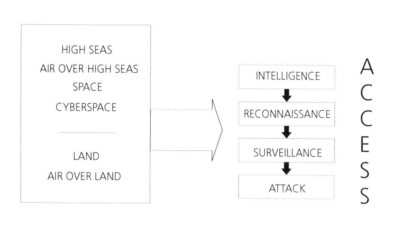

The use of the politically uncontrolled realms emphasized by naval forces incurs only minimal cost. The remaining realms—land, and air over land—are politically controlled, and costs are exacted for their use, whether they are controlled by friends, adversaries, or neutrals. The price might be monetary or political, or it might be in terms of casualties. But any use of those realms invariably involves payment.

Access constitutes the strategic and technical dimensions of targeting. But targeting includes a third dimension—the political. Once access has been gained, considerations that are essentially political surge to the forefront. First, there is the question of rules of engagement. Are the selected targets legitimate under the laws of armed conflict and in terms of the engagement policy? Then comes an assessment of collateral effects and unintended consequences. Will attacking the target result in unacceptable collateral damage, or can unintended consequences be foreseen? Next, one must consider fratricide. What is the risk to friendly forces? Targeting must focus on platform selection. Is a precision weapon or a "dumb" bomb the right attack weapon? Should one use a cruise missile or an aircraft to attack the target? Attack prioritization is an important part of targeting. What should be the priority in which targets are attacked, and why? Also, what will be the domestic political implications, if any, of the attack under consideration? Finally, attack timing must be considered. How does the proposed attack, and the target to be struck, mesh with the overall plan? What should be the interval between attacks? Should targets be struck simultaneously? All these decisions lie beyond the requirement to assure access through intelligence, reconnaissance, surveillance, and arraying the means of attack within range of the prospective target. None of these decisions, however, is pertinent in the absence of access.

Naval forces can work to gain access to strategic and operational targets ashore, but because they have little control over the targeting constraints that might be imposed, their effectiveness will be negatively affected by those constraints. Adherence to them directly increases the risks of failure. Of course, few of those constraints affect the operations of adversaries; thus, their effect is both negative and strongly asymmetric.

The subject of asymmetric warfare has basked in the limelight in recent years, without much rigor attending either its meaning or its impact. In general, it conveys the idea of adversaries taking advantage of one's weaknesses while emphasizing their own strengths. A clearer, tighter understanding of asymmetric warfare would focus on actions that adversaries can take against which the United States and its allies have no direct counters in kind. As examples one can cite terrorism but also hostage taking, siting one's weapons at or near protected targets (such as hospitals or religious shrines), using human shields, and conducting chemical and biological warfare. In this sense, the spawning ground of asymmetric warfare is in the realm of actions the United States cannot or will not take in its own defense. The battlespace is tilted by the constraints the United States places on its own use of force; asymmetric warfare describes an adversary's ability and willingness to take advantage of that unlevel field.

Anti-access

The "flip side" of access is anti-access. Adversaries, of course, will seek to deny U.S. forces access to potential targets. In their attempts to discourage U.S. forces from gaining access they will use the same physical realms as the United States does to gain it, and they will face similar technical and strategic challenges, the central one being how to find the right target. For these reasons, adversaries will seek to increase the effective size of their defensive battlespace (to conceal their vulnerabilities) and to decrease the effective size of their offensive battlespace—to confine the attacker to a well defined killing zone.

"We're clearly moving to the point where it's going to be possible to track all ships every moment of the day and night. As it becomes easier and easier to find ships, they become more and more subject to unexpected attack."[11] This prediction dates from 1982, but it accurately describes the beliefs of many contemporary defense analysts. The assumption persists that modern intelligence-gathering systems of adversaries, coupled with longer-range and more accurate weapons, will aggravate the dangers to those who would approach their territory from the sea. In this regard, one analyst asserts, "It can hardly be imagined, given the state of current designs, that ships will be able to fulfill mission profiles and cope with naval antiship missile threats after about 2005."[12] An Air Force study weighs in with the claim that "in the 21st Century it will be possible to find, fix, or track and target anything that moves on the surface of the earth."[13] In other words, there will be no sanctuaries.

However technology reduces it, the difficulty of locating the right target in the battle-space will remain. As one perceptive observer notes, "You may look at the map and see flags stuck in at different points and consider that the results will be uncertain, but when you get out on the sea with its vast distances, its storms and mists, and with night coming on, and all the uncertainties which exist, you cannot possibly expect that the kind of conditions which would be appropriate to the movements of armies have any application to the haphazard conditions of war at sea."[14] One fundamental reason for this difficulty is recognized by sailors—the curvature of the earth.

Another reason is that those who appreciate the central difficulties of a maritime battlespace also recognize a corollary implied above—that forces operating in a very large, spherical, nonlinear, three-dimensional battlespace in which all targets are moving will take every precaution to ensure that they cannot be detected; if detected, not identified; if identified, not tracked; if tracked, not attacked; and if attacked, not hit. Even if the Air Force claim is fulfilled—which would require, at a minimum, a large constellation of active space sensors and extensive command and control arrangements—forces at sea can thwart access by breaking the adversary's intelligence, reconnaissance, surveillance, command and control, and attack chain. If any link (and surveillance is just one of them) is broken, the chain fails. Accordingly, in the battle-space of the future, as in the maritime battlespace of the past, the survivability of a force can be significantly improved by offensive operations designed to attack the adversary's eyes and brains: his capabilities for command, control, communications, computers, intelligence, surveillance, and reconnaissance.

If offensive anti-access methods are ineffective or for some reason cannot be employed, defensive methods to thwart access can be found in operations security, deception, and active and passive defenses. Of these, operations security and deception are comparatively cheap and can be very effective. If the attacker does not know where one's forces are, or what they are, or if he cannot identify or track them, his odds for a successful attack on them are greatly diminished. Counters—active, passive, and computer network defenses—to such antiaccess measures are difficult and expensive but clearly necessary.

Of interest, deterrence is the last line of defense, and a comparatively weak one. Deterrence comes into effect if access cannot be prevented in other ways. States historically have sought to deter attacks from long-range nuclear-tipped missiles and by terrorists, for example, because other forms of defense against them have great difficulty denying access reliably. Figure 2 illustrates anti-access.

FIGURE 2

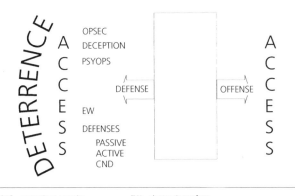

OPSEC—operations security   EW—electronic warfare
PYSOPS—psychological operations   CND—computer network defense

Means

Given the ends to be sought and a sense of the ways that might be used to attain them, what means should be developed and devoted to the requisite missions? A key component of new means being developed by the U.S. Navy is that of network-centric warfare. The Chief of Naval Operations in the spring of 1997 asserted, "For us, it's a fundamental shift from what we call platform-centric warfare to something we call network-centric warfare."[15] This revealed a fresh appreciation that the Navy had to focus not on the material instruments of the order of battle—what the Navy *is* (ships, aircraft, and weapons)—but on what the Navy can accomplish. Network-centric warfare draws its strength and its effectiveness from the power of the network, from what naval platforms and a host of other joint and combined contributors can achieve in concert with one another. The power to prevail is grounded in the ability not to hoard but to share information and act on it.

Network-centric warfare pivots on the establishment and maintenance of a common operational picture and on the decentralization of execution. The common operational picture is a function of the networks available to the warfighter. Conceptually, networks link together sensors, a command and control grid, and the ability to engage the adversary. Using the concepts of "smart push" and "warrior pull," the networks—underlain by a "global information grid"—will provide evaluated, formated, and analyzed information in the form the commander needs. Information that meets certain parameters (such as high-stress time requirements) is "pushed" to the commander without his asking for it. Other information will be available to commanders on demand, if they "pull" it.

In the future, most data collection, processing, analysis, and storage for network-centric warfare will not be organic to the naval force at sea. It will be accomplished off board. For the inputs that undergird information superiority, at-sea commanders will be, as never before, dependent on capabilities that lie beyond, perhaps well beyond, their direct control. Sensors, for example, might be space-based; they might include AWACS or J-STARS aircraft* under operational control of another commander; or they might be unmanned aerial or underwater vehicles. In such situations, shipboard sensors will be employed sparingly and, except in unusual occasions, primarily in self-defense. Ships, aircraft, and even ground—Army or Marine—units ashore will act as nodes in the networks. Some will appear on the engagement network, as ordnance deliverers, others on the sensor network, as collectors of data.

The networks are not reserved exclusively to naval forces. They are, and should be, shared by joint or combined forces that contribute to operations. If naval forces are first on the scene, the networks will effect a convenient, smooth, seamless, and comprehensive enlargement of the scale of operations as new units and kinds of forces arrive. Reliance on off-the-shelf civilian "plug-and-play" technologies should ameliorate interoperability problems among joint and combined forces in the future.

Actions will be undertaken in a decentralized fashion. Forces will self-synchronize from the bottom up. In many cases this will be necessary, because the on-scene forces will have both the best tactical picture and the ability to act quickly; speed will be of the essence in such situations.[16] Self-synchronization is enabled by doctrine (supplemented by the commander's intent and mission orders), by a common situational awareness, and by coordination among the forces involved. Thus, forces must be doctrinally prepared to react to situations they recognize, coordinating (if permitted by the commander's intent in a particular case) among themselves to accomplish the task at hand with no additional control or guidance from above. At the tactical level, this is but a small extension to the "command by negation" doctrine exercised by naval forces for over two decades. Whether self-synchronization is possible, or even desirable, above the tactical level has yet to be determined.

In brief, superiority in all operating domains will be required for success in future operations; in order to establish that superiority, U.S. military forces must be prepared to fight and win in every realm. One can opt not to operate effectively in a particular

---

* AWACS—Airborne Warning and Control System; J-STARS—Joint Surveillance and Target Attack Radar System.

domain, but to do so cedes that domain to potential adversaries without a fight and jeopardizes the attainment of security objectives.

What kinds of platforms will be optimal? It seems clear that with most sensing and data-processing functions moved ashore, platforms can be much less complex. If they can be individually simpler, they can be smaller and more sparingly manned. This translates directly into lower operating costs, which means in turn that more numerous forces can be acquired for the same procurement funding.

Aircraft carriers can be very useful to the exercise of naval power. If land bases are far from the scene or unavailable, carriers might well be the only way to bring tactical airpower to bear. Whether or not highly capable conventional-take-off-and-landing aircraft will be required in the future is more questionable, however, especially for carrier operations in defensive roles. If the need for high-performance, dogfighting aircraft subsides, it will be possible for carriers to be smaller—likely much smaller—than they are today.

The value of submarines will lie in power projection operations and will pivot on whether they can perform as fully functioning nodes on the network. If they can maintain connectivity at an acceptable level, a place for them will be easy to justify. They might, for example, provide survivable magazines for a large number of land-attack weapons. If they cannot be integrated into the network-centric framework, however, they will be viewed as an expensive, highly specialized force useful only for a narrow range of tasks such as prearranged strikes, antisubmarine warfare, and covert insertions of special operations forces.

In the future security environment, numbers will be important. Greater numbers allow naval forces to be in more places at once without overstretch. Second, they mean shorter average transit times to reach areas that need attention. Third, the power of networks is an exponential function of the number of networked nodes—more ships and aircraft, more nodes, more networked power. Finally, larger inventories of ships and aircraft of less individual value will reduce reluctance to place them at risk.

The inventory of naval ships has been declining steadily over the past decade, the reduction amounting to 46 percent from 1989 to 2000. The combination of increasing personnel and operating expenses, growing ship and aircraft unit costs, and declining budgets has squeezed ship procurement. As a result, ship force levels are approaching historical prewar lows. Figure 3 depicts the situation graphically.

Of consequence, ships have high unit costs and last a long time. Of concern, naval inventories must be maintained in peacetime. Once a conflict begins, it is too late to build a fleet. Henry Kaiser constructed fifty escort carriers in 1943–44, but today

FIGURE 3
Ship Force Levels, U.S. Navy

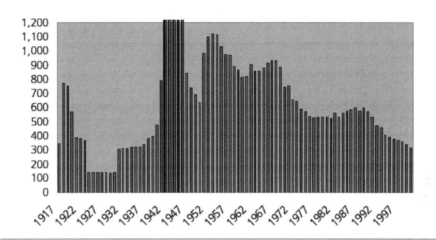

neither time nor U.S. industrial capacity would permit anything approximating that feat. "Whether a democratic government will have the foresight, the keen sensitiveness to national position and credit, the willingness to ensure its prosperity by adequate outpouring of money in times of peace, all of which are necessary for military preparation," warned Alfred Thayer Mahan in 1890, "is yet an open question."[17] It still is.

Naval forces are routinely deployed forward, assigned to the Sixth Fleet (Mediterranean), Seventh Fleet (western Pacific), and Fifth Fleet (Persian Gulf). There are barely three hundred ships in the deploying force; that means fewer than one hundred will be on deployment across the three fleet areas at any one time. Some ships will probably be near where a crisis erupts, but at most they will have to steam on the order of a thousand miles. At a speed of advance of sixteen knots, that will take almost three days. It is of serious concern, therefore, when projections by the Secretary of the Navy result in a ship total of 286 by the year 2007.[18]

Speed matters as well. Arguably, the potential for adversaries to act very quickly and present the United States with faits accomplis has increased and will probably become more acute over time. For a forward-deployed naval force the numbers of ships and aircraft is intimately related to speed. Smaller fleets result in less geographic coverage and longer response times.

A greatly increased role in homeland defense or defense of friends and allies from ballistic missiles, should that come to pass, will be met by ambivalence in the Navy. On the one hand, it constitutes a high-profile strategic mission for the Navy and will probably justify construction of more Aegis-equipped ships. On the other hand, it does not resonate well in U.S. Navy culture, for the positioning of the ships would be essentially fixed, depriving them of their most vital survival asset, mobility. Coastal defense of landward targets from the sea has not historically been in favor in the Navy; the tasks will be wholly defensive; and the mission is one essentially of garrisoning rather than of expeditionary operations.

Risks

Like the selection of ends, ways, and means, the assumption of risks is necessary in combat operations, for "there is no zero-risk situation in war. The willingness to run a calculated risk and to absorb some damage is essential. In sum, heroes run risks. Smart heroes calculate the risks and take steps to shift the odds more in their favor. Those who avoid risks stay home."[19]

Risks are one measure of the fit between ends, ways, and means. If one believes that desired ends cannot be attained, operations assume high risk. In the abstract it is not possible to foretell where the fault lies. It might be that the ends are too ambitious, that the ways are insufficient, or that the means cannot produce the desired effects. It might be that the ends do not justify the risks. That was the reason for the U.S. withdrawal in 1993–94 from Somalia—there was insufficient U.S. interest to justify the loss of eighteen service members. This episode has often been cited as reflecting a U.S. unwillingness to take casualties, which some strategists argue will be a determining factor: "The prospect of high casualties, which can rapidly undermine domestic support for any military operation, is the key political constraint when decisions must be made on which forces to deploy in a crisis, and at what levels."[20] Official U.S. Army doctrine states, "The American people expect decisive victory and abhor unnecessary casualties."[21] The degree of reluctance prompted by casualty estimates, however, is not absolute. It is closely correlated to a perceived necessity to undertake a particular operation. If the operation is deemed vital or necessary to U.S. security, tolerance of casualties will be commensurately high; to the extent the operation is considered discretionary, that tolerance will be low.

Risk determination is related closely to damage assessment. In determining whether attacks on a radar site have been effective, one asks, does the fact that it is no longer radiating indicate that it has been so damaged that it cannot radiate? If a tank company has been attacked, how does one determine its residual combat power? Such appraisals tend to be difficult to make. The advent of weapons that are more precise but carry less destructive power, and of information operations (in particular, computer network attack), renders damage assessment even more problematic.

In future operations, especially information operations, however, the desired effect of military action should be *neutralization:* rendering enemies' actions ineffective, negating their hostile intentions, thwarting their objectives. Similarly, an analyst of the future battlespace writes:

> All of this also will require discerning new and different "measures of effectiveness" for the application of force, that go beyond traditional "battle damage assessment." . . . This implies an "effect-based attack" designed to *manipulate* the enemy, rather than a "target-based attack" designed to destroy. In turn, this could enable commanders to distinguish—at their will—between inflicting lethality and achieving effectiveness.[22]

If this is an accurate rendering, assessing neutralization should be simpler and less ambiguous than the more doctrinal measures such as *destroy, neutralize, suppress, eliminate, disable, degrade, render ineffective, delay,* or *attrite.*[23]

In any event, risks tend to be difficult to assess accurately. One must be specific about the risks being discussed and as to what underlying factors determine risks. One must also appreciate that it is in the adversary's interest to make risk assessment as difficult as possible. Saddam Hussein made obvious attempts at this several times prior to and during DESERT STORM, and he has done so since.

Recently, an analytical tool has been promulgated to assist commanders in assessing and managing risks. "Operational risk management" requires staffs to set forth methodically all recognized hazards of an operation and then translate those hazards into risks by analyzing the severity of the consequences of each hazard in light of its probability. Once the high risks have been identified—those with severe potential consequences and high probability—measures are considered to mitigate, or manage, them. While qualitative and often difficult, this method does offer the commander a more structured and systematic tool than mere guesswork.[24]

To Remain and Persevere

Sinking an enemy fleet, conducting blockades and embargoes, and threatening sea-based attacks are all to no avail if they fail to alter adversaries' actions or intentions. Historically, navies have been able to influence events on land indirectly, because only with great difficulty or after prolonged periods of time could they place an opponent's sanctuary in jeopardy. Now, however, with the free use of the sea, the air over the sea, space, and cyberspace; with the power of information superiority enabled by networking; with long-range precision weapons; with the development of abundant and affordable new sensors; and with the techniques of information warfare, navies are becoming able, as never before, to penetrate adversary sanctuaries and influence events ashore rapidly, directly, and decisively.

The "Maritime Strategy" of the 1980s began a naval realignment process that continues today. It emphasized that the objective of seapower was no longer to defeat opposing fleets but to affect opponents' actions on land, where political processes transpire. The Maritime Strategy called for defending allied transoceanic shipping as far forward as possible and for applying power to the flanks of the Soviet Union in order to relieve pressure on the continental center, the inter-German border. In the 1990s, with the demise of the Soviet Union and the Warsaw Treaty Organization, the threat to U.S. forces in deep waters subsided, and a new naval strategic vision, set forth in the white paper ". . . From the Sea," steered attention to the littorals, the green waters of the world. The 1990s also witnessed the shrinking of the U.S. military and a concomitant reduction in the size of the fleet.

Over time, the battlespace in military operations has become more and more nonlinear with respect to time, space, and intensity. Having been accustomed for centuries to battlespaces that are nonlinear and three-dimensional, and in which all targets are moving, naval forces are particularly well suited to understand and thrive in this environment. The key to future operations is *access*—because once access can be reliably secured, enemy sanctuaries can be compromised and objectives can be attained.

Unquestionably, naval forces will be required concurrently to deal with antiaccess efforts of adversaries. Because the fundamental challenge—for both sides—is to find the right target, operations security and deception will have greater leverage in the future, alongside active and passive defenses. Because information superiority must underwrite targeting efforts, information warfare in all its manifestations will become more and more important.

Naval ships should become smaller, and inventories of them should increase if the U.S. Navy is to continue to be highly effective. Most sensing and information processing functions will be accomplished off board, allowing platforms to be less complex and more numerous for a given procurement expenditure.

Questions remain regarding whether the right targets to vitiate adversary sanctuaries can be identified, whether they can be attacked effectively once they are identified, whether the effectiveness of attacks can be confidently assessed, whether decision makers are willing to assume the risks that might be necessary to approach a hostile shore or to engage adversary forces on the high seas, and whether self-imposed constraints will so reduce the degrees of freedom of U.S. forces as to render them powerless. The central contribution of naval forces is to be there to open the door, quickly and effectively, once these difficult questions have been resolved, and to remain and persevere for as long as it takes to secure national objectives.

Notes

1. This is what distinguishes *maneuver* from *movement*. Maneuver is undertaken relative to adversaries in order to place at risk their centers of gravity or critical weaknesses, or to strengthen one's own defenses vis-à-vis enemy capability.

2. "Maritime power projection—Power projection in and from the maritime environment, including a broad spectrum of offensive military operations to destroy enemy forces or logistic support or to prevent enemy forces from approaching within enemy weapons' range of friendly forces. Maritime power projection may be accomplished by amphibious assault operations, attack of targets ashore, or support of sea control operations." *Department of Defense Dictionary of Military and Associated Terms*, Joint Publication 1-02 (Washington, D.C.: Joint Staff, 23 March 1994, amended through 15 April 1998).

3. One of the themes of Colin S. Gray, *The Leverage of Sea Power: The Strategic Advantage of Navies in War* (New York: Free Press, 1992).

4. See, for example, David S. Alberts, and Thomas J. Czerwinski, eds., *Complexity, Global Politics, and National Security* (Washington, D.C.: National Defense Univ. Press, 1997); Barry D. Watts, *Clausewitzian Friction and Future War*, McNair Paper 52 (Washington, D.C.: Institute for National Strategic Studies, October 1996), pp. 106–7; and Harlan K. Ullman and James P. Wade, *Shock and Awe: Achieving Rapid Dominance* (Washington, D.C.: National Defense Univ. Press, 1996).

5. Alan Beyerchen, "Clausewitz, Nonlinearity and the Unpredictability of War," *International Security*, Winter 1992, pp. 59–90.

6. See Wayne P. Hughes, "Naval Maneuver Warfare," *Naval War College Review* 50, no. 3 (Summer 1997), pp. 25–49.

7. "Selection" of targets lies at the intersection of intelligence and policy. Selection, in this sense, distinguishes what is a target and what is not, and which targets can produce the desired effects if successfully attacked or threatened. Selection will rely heavily on the ability to collect, process, evaluate, and disseminate large quantities of information—on information superiority. While the great difficulty of selecting the "right" target should not be underestimated, it is not pivotal to this analysis.

8. The contemporary image of information operations is that it comprises computer network attack and defense. In fact, however, it is much larger, encompassing not only those subjects but deception, psychological operations, electronic warfare, operational deception, operational security, some types of physical destruction, and even, on occasion, public affairs.

9. Colin S. Gray, "Sea Power for Containment," in *Navies and Global Defense: Theories and Strategy*, ed. Keith Neilson and Elizabeth Jane Errington (Westport, Conn.: Praeger, 1995), p. 204. [Emphasis supplied.]

10. The "high seas" denotes those areas that are beyond the agreed twelve-mile "territorial seas" and other controlled areas (such as archipelagic seas) provided for in the United Nations Convention on the Law of the Sea.

11. Steven Strasser, with David C. Martin, James Doyle, Mary Lord, and John J. Lindsay, "Are Big Warships Doomed?" *Newsweek*, 17 May 1982, "News/Alnews," LexisNexis.

12. Erbil Serter, "Warship Designs for the 21st Century," *International Defense Review*, Quarterly Report (Jane's Information Group, 1 December 1997), p. 3, LexisNexis.

13. U.S. Air Force, *Global Engagement: A Vision for the 21st Century Air Force*, 1996, available at www.af-future. hq.af.mil/21/indext.htm, 2 December 1998.

14. Winston Churchill, *The Gathering Storm* (Boston: Houghton Mifflin, 1948), p. 601.

15. Remarks delivered by Admiral Jay L. Johnson, USN, Chief of Naval Operations, to the U.S. Naval Institute, Annapolis, Maryland, 23 April 1997.

16. "Most images of war are linked to destroying an enemy, controlling resources, maintaining sovereignty, and rearranging territory. Yet wars are won or lost, begun and ended, and conducted in time as well as space, with time normally the more important factor." Grant T. Hammond, *Joint Force Quarterly*, Spring 1994, p. 9.

17. Alfred Thayer Mahan, *The Influence of Sea Power upon History: 1660–1783* (New York: Hill and Wang, 1957), p. 58.

18. As reported in "Navy Gives Rumsfeld FY-03 Budget to Buy 'Only' Five Ships, 81 Aircraft," *Inside the Navy*, 3 December 2001, p. 1.

19. H. Dwight Lyons, Jr., Eleanor A. Baker, Sabrina R. Edlow, and David A. Perin, *The Mine Threat: Show Stoppers or Speed Bumps?* (Alexandria, Va.: Center for Naval Analyses, 1993), p. 19.

20. Edward N. Luttwak, "A Post-Heroic Military Policy," *Foreign Affairs*, July–August 1996, p. 36.

21. U.S. Defense Dept., *Operations*, Field Manual 100-5 (Washington, D.C.: Dept. of the Army, June 1993), pp. 1–3.

22. Douglas H. Dearth, "Imperatives of Information Operations and Information Warfare," in *Cyberwar 2.0: Myths, Mysteries, and Reality,* ed. Alan D. Campen and Douglas H. Dearth (Fairfax, Va.: AFCEA International Press, 1998), p. 396.

23. Rudy T. Veit, *Joint Targeting: Improving the Playbook, Communications, and Teamwork,* Strategy Research Project (Carlisle Barracks, Pa.: U.S. Army War College, 1996), p. 26.

24. For the U.S. Navy and Marine Corps, the governing instruction for the process of operational risk management is Opnav [Navy Staff] Instruction 3500.39 / Marine Corps Order 3500.27, 3 April 1997.

PART THREE

Naval Transformation

CHAPTER TEN

Transforming the U.S. Armed Forces
Rhetoric or Reality?

THOMAS G. MAHNKEN

The leadership of the Defense Department has enthusiastically endorsed the proposition that the growth and diffusion of stealth, precision, and information technology will drastically alter the character and conduct of future wars, yielding a revolution in military affairs. President George W. Bush campaigned on a pledge to transform the U.S. armed forces by "skipping a generation" of technology. A month after assuming office, he promised in a speech at the Norfolk Naval Base to "move beyond marginal improvements to harness new technologies that will support a new strategy." He called for the development of ground forces that are lighter, more mobile, and more lethal, as well as manned and unmanned air forces capable of striking across the globe with precision.[1]

Secretary of Defense Donald Rumsfeld stated during his confirmation hearings that his central challenge would be to "bring the American military successfully into the 21st century."[2] Soon after assuming office, Rumsfeld commissioned Andrew W. Marshall, the Pentagon's premier strategic thinker, to conduct a fundamental review of American strategy and force requirements. The review reportedly recommended that the Defense Department emphasize forces capable of fighting and winning wars in Asia, with its vast distances and sparse infrastructure, in the face of increasingly challenging threats.[3]

Speaking at the U.S. Naval Academy in May 2001, President Bush called for "a future force that is defined less by size and more by mobility and swiftness, one that is easier to deploy and sustain, one that relies more heavily on stealth, precision weaponry, and information technologies." He also committed himself "to fostering a military culture where intelligent risk-taking and forward thinking are rewarded, not dreaded," and to "ensuring that visionary leaders who take risks are recognized and promoted."[4]

© 2001 by Thomas G. Mahnken
Naval War College Review, Summer 2001, Vol. 54, No. 3

The U.S. armed forces themselves have embraced—at least rhetorically—the need to transform so as to meet the demands of information-age warfare. They have fielded new capabilities, such as stealth and precision strike, and explored novel approaches to combat, such as network-centric warfare and effects-based operations. Nevertheless, significant organizational barriers to the adoption of new technology, doctrine, and organizations exist. The services have been particularly reluctant to take measures that are disruptive of service culture, such as shifting away from traditional platforms and toward new weapon systems, concepts, and organizations. The Army's attempts to field a medium-weight ground force, the Navy's development of network-centric warfare, and the Air Force's experience with unmanned air vehicles illustrate such difficulties. In each case, efforts at transformation have faced opposition from service traditionalists who perceive threats in new ways of war. For the Defense Department to succeed in transforming the U.S. armed forces, it must both reallocate resources and nurture new constituencies.

The Character of War in the Information Age

Recent years have witnessed the rapid growth and diffusion of information technology. It is radically changing the structure of advanced economies, the nature of politics, and the shape of society. It is also shifting the ways in which wars are fought. What many refer to as the emerging revolution in military affairs (RMA) is merely the military manifestation of the information revolution. The shape, scope, and strategic impact of the revolution is uncertain. Still, the experience of recent conflicts, together with trends in the development of technology, suggests changes in the conduct of war on land, at sea, and in the air, as well as the growing use of space and the information spectrum for military operations.

One trend that is already apparent is the ability to achieve new levels of military effectiveness by networking together disparate sensors, weapons, and command-and-control systems. Rapid advances in information and related technologies already allow military forces to detect, identify, and track a far greater number of targets over a larger area for a longer time than ever before. Increasingly powerful information-processing and communication systems offer the ability to distribute this data more quickly and effectively. The result is a dramatic improvement in the quantity and quality of information that modern military organizations can collect, process, and disseminate. In the future, as in the past, forces that can secure a superior understanding of their own dispositions, those of their adversaries, and the features of the battlefield will be at a considerable advantage.[5]

In a number of instances, the U.S. armed forces have attempted to explore how improvements in situational awareness can increase combat effectiveness. From September 1993 to September 1994, for example, the U.S. Air Force conducted an experiment that pitted eighteen F-15Cs equipped with Joint Tactical Information Distribution System (JTIDS) terminals against unmodified F-15s. JTIDS provided a datalink that allowed each modified F-15 to share its sensor and threat data with all the others. Their unmodified opponents were supported by E-3A Airborne Warning and Control System (AWACS) aircraft but could share information only by voice radio. The enhanced situational awareness provided by JTIDS allowed the modified F-15s to achieve an exchange ratio that was in their favor by a factor of around 2.6.[6]

The increasing use of information technology portends a significant shift in the balance between offense and defense, fire and maneuver, and space and time. Militaries that harness the information revolution are already at a marked advantage in comparison to those that do not. The Gulf War hinted at the battlefield advantages that accrue to armed forces that capitalize on stealth, information, and precision weaponry. Nato's air war over Serbia stands out as another demonstration of at least the tactical effectiveness of advanced military technology.

The integration of information technology into military forces is also changing the relationship between fire and maneuver. Networking long-range sensors and weapons allows us to concentrate fire from dispersed platforms on a common set of targets. The U.S. Navy, for example, has examined the "Ring of Fire," a concept for focusing dispersed naval fire on shore-based targets.[7] Networking thus allows the potential massing of effects without massing forces. It could also reduce vulnerability by denying an adversary the ability to target forces with his own long-range strike systems, while increasing the tempo of military operations by reducing the delay between observation and action.[8] By operating faster than adversaries, a networked force may effectively deny them battlefield options.[9] These trends favor networked forces that are small, agile, and stealthy over hierarchical organizations that are large, slow, and nonstealthy. Should the U.S. armed forces exploit these trends, the United States will gain increased tactical, operational, and—potentially—strategic leverage over potential adversaries.

While the United States currently enjoys a considerable lead in exploiting the information revolution, it is hardly alone in attempting to do so. Indeed, the list of militaries interested in information-age warfare is long and growing. Some may develop strategies to deny foes the ability to project power into their spheres of influence.[10] Others may challenge the United States in space or the information spectrum. Moreover, their ability to do such things is growing. The director of the Defense Intelligence Agency, for example, has testified that Russia and China, as well as other smaller states and nonstate actors, are pursuing capabilities to disrupt, degrade, or defeat American space systems.[11] Similarly, one recent article assessed that twenty-three nations have the ability to launch information-warfare attacks.[12] Failure to meet such threats could lead to a military that is increasingly irrelevant to the types of wars that the United States will fight.

Past revolutions in warfare have changed not only the character and conduct of combat but also the shape of the organizations that wage war. The emergence of new ways of war has altered the importance of existing services, and combat arms triggered the rise of new elites and eclipsed previously dominant ones. During the first half of the twentieth century, for example, naval aviation assumed a central role in war at sea. As the aircraft carrier displaced the battleship as the centerpiece of modern navies, naval aviators challenged the traditional dominance of surface warfare officers. During the same period, the advent of land-based aircraft created new elites within armies and eventually spawned new military services. Armored forces usurped the roles of cavalry in armies across the globe. The information revolution portends similar organizational turbulence as the character of war on land, at sea, and in the air changes and as combat spreads to space and the information spectrum.

The U.S. Armed Forces and the Emerging RMA

The Department of Defense has declared its recognition of the need to change radically the structure of the U.S. armed forces in order to embrace the information revolution. The 1997 Quadrennial Defense Review committed the department to transforming its forces. As then–Secretary of Defense William Cohen put it:

> The information revolution is creating a Revolution in Military Affairs that will fundamentally change the way U.S. forces fight. We must exploit these and other technologies to dominate in battle. Our template for seizing on these technologies and ensuring military dominance is Joint Vision 2010, the plan set forth by the Chairman of the Joint Chiefs of Staff for military operations of the future.[13]

The congressionally mandated National Defense Panel argued even more strongly in favor of the need to transform U.S. forces. The panel's report urged the Defense Department to "undertake a broad transformation of its military and national security structures, operational concepts and equipment, and . . . key business processes," including procurement reform.[14] It recommended, among other things, that the department accord the highest priority to a transformation strategy designed to prepare the United States to confront the new and very different threats of the twenty-first century. It also argued that the department should place greater emphasis on experimenting with a variety of systems, operational concepts, and force structures.

In 1998, the secretary of defense and the chairman of the Joint Chiefs of Staff designated U.S. Joint Forces Command (or JFCOM, formerly Atlantic Command) as the Defense Department's executive agent for joint experimentation.[15] Since assuming this responsibility, JFCOM has explored the concept of "rapid decisive operations," including attacks against critical, mobile targets—a mission that places a premium on nearly simultaneous sensor-to-shooter data flows and high-speed, long-range weapons.[16] The command plans to hold large-scale exercises to test new operational concepts in 2002 and 2004.

Beyond such initiatives, however, the Defense Department has yet to implement its announced commitment to transform its forces. The American armed forces today look much the same as they did ten years ago, only smaller. They have emphasized improving their ability to accomplish current tasks over exploring new ways of war. Similarly, most major acquisition programs of the last decade have represented incremental improvements to current systems. The services have fielded relatively few new weapon systems; of these, only a tiny fraction, such as the B-2 stealth bomber, could have major impacts on the conduct of war.[17]

Advocates of transformation point to the need to shift from a force based upon major weapon systems to one based upon networks. They argue that precision-guided weapons, platforms to collect enormous amounts of information about the enemy, and command and control systems to direct one's own forces will play increasingly important roles in warfare. While the services have invested increasing amounts of money in information technology, budget data on major acquisition programs suggest that the U.S. military services continue to have strongly platform-centric approaches to procurement. More than 75 percent of the Department of the Navy's major-acquisition budget for fiscal year 2002 is committed to large, traditional platforms—for instance, a new class of submarine (SSN 774), carrier-based aircraft (the F/A-18E/F), various surface ships (DDG 51 and LPD 17), and the tilt-rotor V-22 for the Marine Corps. U.S. Army and Air Force programs show comparable emphases upon platforms.[18]

Rhetoric about transformation has yet to be reflected in weapons the services acquire, let alone the way they acquire weapons. The Army's attempts to transform itself into a medium-weight force, the Navy's experimentation with network-centric warfare, and the Air Force's investment in unmanned combat vehicles all illustrate the difficulties associated with exploring new approaches to combat.

The U.S. Army and the Medium-Weight Force

The Army faces the challenge of transforming itself from a tank-heavy force designed to protect Western Europe from the armored columns of the Warsaw Pact to one capable of responding to contingencies worldwide on short notice. Operation ALLIED FORCE, Nato's war against Serbia, highlighted the Army's lack of units that are light enough to move quickly yet heavy enough to strike hard. The experience prodded the Army chief of staff, General Eric Shinseki, to launch an effort to reconfigure the Army into a more mobile yet still lethal force. In October 1999 he announced a goal of transforming the service into a "medium- weight" force capable of deploying a five-thousand-man brigade anywhere in the world within ninety-six hours. As he put it, "We must provide early-entry forces that can operate jointly, without access to fixed forward bases, but we still need the power to slug it out and win decisively."[19] He designated two brigades at Fort Lewis, Washington, as test beds for exploring new concepts and organizations. These units have traded in their tracked M1A1 Abrams tanks and M2 Bradley fighting vehicles for wheeled LAV III infantry fighting vehicles leased from Canada. They are also examining innovative new tactics and organizations. In November 2000, the Army awarded a four-billion-dollar contract to build the "Interim Armored Vehicle," a new generation of light, wheeled vehicles with which to equip the new medium-weight units.

A key element of the Army's transformation is the Future Combat System, a network of light—and possibly unmanned—vehicles that would replace tanks and self-propelled artillery in medium-weight units. Planners intend that the new vehicle will weigh no more than twenty tons (compared to the seventy-ton M1 Abrams), so that it can be transported aboard the Air Force's most numerous transport aircraft, the C-130. Because it will lack the armor to slug it out with enemy tanks, its effectiveness will depend on its ability to identify and engage enemy forces before they can engage it.[20] The Army's plan for the Future Combat System is quite ambitious: the service plans to choose a design before Shinseki leaves office in 2003; production is to begin in 2010; and the system is to be fielded by 2012. The General Accounting Office has, however, expressed concern that key technologies may not mature quickly enough to meet such a timetable.[21]

The Army's transformation plan is not without its detractors. The merits of a medium-weight force composed of wheeled vehicles remains to be demonstrated. Moreover, the prospect of a medium-weight force threatens the traditional emphasis upon armor as the centerpiece of ground combat, a notion that has defined the service for the past six decades. Indeed, it challenges the very definition and purpose of armored units. It is therefore hardly surprising that both active-duty and retired armor officers and enlisted men have been vocal in their opposition to the replacement of the tank with lighter wheeled vehicles. Many are particularly uncomfortable with the prospect of trading their heavily armored tanks for more vulnerable, if more mobile, vehicles.[22]

Nor is it certain that the Army will maintain its current course. This is not the first time that the Army has attempted to transform itself. Indeed, it has examined the structure and organization of its combat units on twelve separate occasions over the last sixty years, accumulating a track record that is at best mixed.[23] It remains to be seen whether the current effort will survive General Shinseki's retirement.

The U.S. Navy and Network-centric Warfare

The U.S. Navy faces the challenge of transforming itself from a fleet designed to fight in the open ocean to one that can dominate the littorals and project power ashore. Like the other services, it must also define its roles in space and cyberspace. To carry out these tasks, the Navy has sought to link weapon, sensor, and command and control systems— that is, to wage network-centric warfare. The Marine Corps, for its part, is exploring new methods of power projection and attempting to come to grips with the challenges associated with military operations in urban terrain.

The Navy's track record of innovation is checkered. The demise of the Arsenal Ship highlights the barriers to innovation within the service. The Arsenal Ship, a vessel built to commercial standards and manned by a small crew, would have packed enough fire-power to stop an armored column. Despite enjoying the support of Admiral William Owens (the vice chairman of the Joint Chiefs of Staff), Admiral Jeremy M. Boorda (the Chief of Naval Operations), and General Charles Krulak (the Commandant of the Marine Corps); the program lacked institutional support within the Navy. Critics raised questions about the utility and effectiveness of the ship. In addition, the ship lacked a constituency within the Navy. Indeed, it appeared to threaten a number of constituencies inside and outside the Navy. Some surface warfare officers and aviators saw it as a threat to the aircraft carrier, while submariners saw it as stealing a mission they themselves wanted. Still others disliked the idea that the Arsenal Ship's considerable firepower could be at the disposal of a ground commander. These communities attempted to undermine the case for the Arsenal Ship. Indeed, Admiral Boorda was forced to move the program from the Navy to the Defense Advanced Research Projects Agency in an attempt to preserve it. The ship's opponents were aided by people in industry and Congress who had stakes in the status quo. As one former congressional aide put it, the Arsenal Ship "was a threat to the carrier, and that was a threat to Newport News Shipbuilding. And that, in turn, was a threat to the Virginia [congressional] delegation."[24] In November 1997 the Navy killed the program, which a year earlier it had declared one of its highest priorities, due to "insufficient funds."

At a deeper level, it appears that the Arsenal Ship challenged the Navy's traditional notion of command. The vessel was essentially a truck designed to bring ordnance within firing range of targets. It would have lacked the sensors to target its own weapons, and it would have possessed only a minimal self-defense capability. Officers who had for years aspired to command destroyers, cruisers, and aircraft carriers likely did not relish the thought of becoming truck drivers.

Nonetheless, in recent years the Navy has begun exploring concepts that would replace large platforms with a network of smaller and less vulnerable systems. The Navy

Warfare Development Command (in Newport, Rhode Island) and the Naval Postgraduate School (in Monterey, California), for example, have examined STREETFIGHTER—a family of small platforms designed to gain and sustain access to the littoral region in the face of a strong resistance, or "access denial"—as well as CORSAIR, a small aircraft carrier.[25] Further, the Navy Warfare Development Command, stimulated by the performance of HMAS *Jervis Bay* in East Timor, is exploring the use of fast catamarans to deploy and sustain amphibious forces. Other Navy innovators have proposed converting *Ohio*-class SSBNs to carry special operations forces and large numbers of land-attack cruise missiles.

Such ideas have predictably drawn fire from officers who see them as a threat to existing surface ship programs. STREETFIGHTER in particular represents a challenge to the Navy's current approach to force structure, which emphasizes a relatively small number of large, highly capable ships.[26] Rather than conducting rigorous analysis of the benefits and limitations of such platforms, STREETFIGHTER's detractors have tended to engage in ad hominem attacks. Vice Admiral Dan Murphy, the commander of the Sixth Fleet, was remarkably blunt in his criticism of STREETFIGHTER: It is "a wild idea. . . . There is nothing behind it. There is no analysis. You know, [Vice Admiral Cebrowski] dreamed up a bumper sticker, but in fact what he is talking about, to go into the littorals to get into the tough situation, to fight your way through and deliver power is exactly what we are doing [with DD 21]."[27] More recently, big-ship admirals have begun deriding STREETFIGHTER vessels. As one admiral put it, "If the next major naval battle is fought in [Newport's] Narragansett Bay, Streetfighters will be decisive."[28]

Nor have the Development Command's efforts influenced the Navy's acquisition plans in any concrete way. Navy programs are currently dominated by incremental improvements to existing surface ships and aircraft. The service has yet to allocate any funds to procuring small, highly maneuverable ships such as STREETFIGHTER. Nor is that situation likely to change in the near future. In 2006, the Navy plans to begin building the CVX, a new aircraft carrier. It is therefore not surprising that the Defense Department's top strategist has chided the Navy for failure to field experimental platforms.[29]

The U.S. Air Force and Unmanned Air Vehicles

The Air Force, a service historically defined by the technology of manned aircraft and dominated by fighter pilots, now faces the challenge of unmanned aerial vehicles, as well as military operations in space and cyberspace. In each case, the dominance of fighter pilots within the service has stymied innovation.

Rhetorically, at least, the Air Force sees itself in the vanguard of the RMA. As one recent article proclaimed triumphantly, "During the past decade, the U.S. Air Force has undergone a major transformation—a series of revolutionary changes so profound they have altered the face of modern warfare."[30] It has been a world leader in the development of stealth, precision-guided munitions, and the use of space to support military operations. As the official Air Force report on Operation ALLIED FORCE put it:

> The air war over Serbia showed that the Air Force has embraced the RMA—not only in its acquisition strategies for emerging technologies, but in the way it used those technologies during this conflict. . . . The United States Air Force . . . showed that it is a leader in the revolution in military affairs by leveraging new concepts to support future joint and coalition efforts. . . . The air war over Serbia offered airmen a glimpse of the future, one in which political leaders turned quickly to the choice of aerospace power to secure the [Nato] Alliance's security interests without resorting to more costly and hazardous alternatives that would have exposed more men and materiel to the ravages of war.[31]

Like the other services, the Air Force has begun to adapt conceptually and organizationally to the needs of the new security environment. It has reorganized itself into "expeditionary air forces" to project and sustain combat power more efficiently. It has also developed the "Global Strike Task Force" concept, as a way of countering an adversary's strategy for denying access to a combat theater.[32] Along with the Navy, it is exploring such innovative concepts as "effects-based operations," an idea that endeavors to link explicitly the application of military force to strategic objectives.

In fact, and notwithstanding its innovative concepts, the Air Force has as a whole been slow to embrace new ways of war. The hurdles it has faced in integrating unmanned airborne vehicles (UAVs) into its force posture are illustrative.

The service has, at least superficially, welcomed unmanned vehicles. It currently operates two squadrons of RQ-1A Predator medium-altitude-and-endurance UAVs. Controlled by ground-based operators, these aircraft transmit electro-optical, infrared, and synthetic-aperture-radar imagery via satellite to ground stations in the United States or the theater of operations. It is also acquiring the RQ-4 Global Hawk, a high-altitude, long-endurance unmanned airborne vehicle designed to fly 12,500 nautical miles at an altitude of up to sixty-five thousand feet and remain aloft for thirty-six to forty-two hours. Advocates of the system argue that it is capable of replacing the venerable U-2 reconnaissance aircraft. The Air Force has formed a UAV Battle Lab to explore a number of novel operational concepts for the employment of unmanned vehicles. Perhaps more telling is the fact that in 1997 the Air Force awarded a UAV operator the Aerial Achievement Medal—roughly on a par in prestige with the Air Medal—for safely landing a damaged UAV at the Mostar air base in Bosnia-Herzegovina.

Last fall, the Air Force rolled out the first prototype "unmanned combat air vehicle" (UCAV), the X-45A. The aircraft, to be controlled by a ground-based operator, is designed to fly as high as forty thousand feet, have a thousand-mile range, and carry twelve miniature bombs.[33] Its primary mission will be to attack enemy air-defense sites and pave the way for manned aircraft. The Air Force has also tested a weaponized version of the Predator as a rudimentary unmanned combat air vehicle.

Support for unmanned vehicles within the Air Force has, however, been lukewarm. The service's modernization focus is upon a new generation of manned, short-range fighters to replace its existing ones; unmanned vehicles (and manned bombers as well) are being shortchanged. For comparison, the Air Force plans to spend nearly seventy billion dollars on the F-22 fighter aircraft and (along with the Navy and Marine Corps) at least two hundred billion more on the Joint Strike Fighter; the UCAV budget stands at a mere $126 million.[34] In response to perceived foot-dragging on the part of the Air Force, Congress has passed legislation requiring that one-third of the nation's deep-strike capability be unmanned by 2010.[35]

The cultural barriers against embracing unmanned vehicles are substantial. UAVs have been in use for decades, but the Air Force has yet to exploit them fully. Over the past two decades, the Defense Department has spent two billion dollars on unmanned airborne vehicles—roughly the cost of a single B-2 bomber, one-tenth the money it spends on manned combat aircraft in a single year. As a result, UAV technology remains far short of its potential.[36] Indeed, in 1993 Congress created the Defense Airborne Reconnaissance Office to manage unmanned-vehicle programs after unsuccessfully prodding the Pentagon to take them more seriously. The Air Force formed its UAV squadrons only after the Army threatened to take the mission—and the associated resources—away from it.

The pilot culture that dominates the Air Force is another obstacle. While Air Force UAV operators must be pilots, tours with UAV squadrons are designated as nonflying assignments and are thus less than desirable. As an incentive for serving two years with a Predator squadron, the Air Force has been obliged to give pilots the subsequent opportunity to fly a new type of aircraft, which would improve their career chances.[37]

The emergence of UAVs and UCAVs has created growing tension between pilots and supporters of unmanned systems. Many pilots see the UCAV as a threat. As one officer put it, no one "has ever succeeded in picking up a woman in a bar by saying he commanded a wing of drones."[38] While humorous, such sentiment illustrates the barriers to adopting new approaches to combat. This situation is analogous to that in the 1950s, when the advent of intercontinental ballistic missiles threatened the manned-bomber community.

What Is to Be Done?

The services have so far failed to match the rhetoric of transformation with action. While each claims to embrace new ways of war, none has yet demonstrated a sustained

commitment to fundamental change. Nothing shows this more clearly than their acquisition budgets. Service funding is still dominated by incremental improvements to
traditional systems; radically new technology, doctrine, and organizations have received
smaller resources. None of this should be surprising. Large bureaucracies such as the
U.S. armed forces are designed to minimize uncertainty, including that brought on by
large-scale change. And new is not always better. Yet the U.S. armed forces face the imperative of adapting to the new and different challenges the United States will face in
coming years. Should they fail to do so, they could find themselves becoming increasingly irrelevant.

It would be wrong to view the services as uniformly opposed to fundamental change.
Rather, each service is split between traditionalists and elements who are enthusiastic
about new ways of war. One recent survey of the U.S. officer corps revealed significant
splits over the character and conduct of future wars as well as over the urgency of
change.[39] The Defense Department needs to identify and nurture forward-looking constituencies. The starting point should be an intellectual map of the services, one that
identifies and locates both support for and opposition to new mission areas. Such a
map could assist the Defense Department's leadership in channeling resources to
those portions of the services that are most enthusiastic about emerging warfare areas.
It could also assist the department in evaluating the adequacy of military career paths.

The Defense Department also needs to devote additional resources to experimentation.
In particular, the services should advance from the stage of war-gaming innovative concepts to acquiring small numbers of the weapon systems involved and developing concepts and organizations for their use. The Navy, for example, should purchase a
squadron of STREETFIGHTERs to form an operational test bed for network-centric warfare. The Marines, for their part, should establish experimental units dedicated to projecting power in the face of capable access-denial defenses and to conducting military
operations in urban terrain.

More generally, the Defense Department should begin redistributing resources away
from legacy systems of declining utility and toward new ways of war. The Pentagon
should scale back or cancel weapons that are heavy or have limited mobility, highly de-
tectable signatures, and limited range; it should increase funding for long-range precision strike, stealth, and C4ISR* systems. The department should also increase
substantially the funds it devotes to research and development.

Today's defense budget is split fairly equally between the services. While such an arrangement minimizes interservice friction, it is not particularly conducive to innovation. Indeed, there is a strong argument to be made that interservice competition can

* Command, control, communications, computers, intelligence, surveillance, and reconnaissance.

be an engine of change. One way to promote innovation would be to force the services to compete for funds based upon their ability to meet current and anticipated operational and strategic challenges. These challenges would include the need to assure access to regions of critical importance to the United States; gain and maintain information and space superiority; protect against nuclear, biological, chemical, and information attack; and conduct military operations in urban terrain. In order to ensure that the American armed forces meet these emerging challenges, the secretary of defense should set aside a significant portion of the military's procurement budget for innovative programs.

The service secretaries are a potentially powerful but generally underutilized constituency for change. They have it within their power—through control of promotion boards and officer assignments—to have enduring impacts on their services. They should wield this power to ensure that officers associated with emerging warfare areas, such as space and information warfare, enjoy opportunities to rise to senior leadership positions.

The United States leads the world in many of the technologies that are driving the information revolution, as well as many of the weapons that the revolution has spawned. Transforming the armed forces will require the Defense Department not only to continue to acquire advanced weapons but to develop the organizations and doctrine needed to employ them effectively. That attempts to do so have encountered resistance is not surprising. Change is by definition a disruptive process, one that creates winners and losers. Still, the U.S. armed forces must change radically—adding new capabilities and shedding old ones—if they are to meet the challenges of the emerging security environment.

Notes

1. David E. Sanger, "Bush Details Plan to Focus Military on New Weaponry," *New York Times*, 14 February 2001, p. 1.

2. Jim Garamone, "Rumsfeld Details DoD Goals, Objectives in Testimony," *Defense Link*, www.defenselink.mil/news/Jan2000/n01122001_20010125.html.

3. Michael R. Gordon, "Pentagon Review Puts Emphasis on Long-Range Arms in Pacific," *New York Times*, 17 May 2001, p. 1.

4. "Remarks by the President at the U.S. Naval Academy Commencement, May 25, 2001," available at www.whitehouse.gov/news/releases/2001/05/text/20010525-1.html.

5. See Thomas G. Mahnken and Barry D. Watts, "What the Gulf War Can (and Cannot) Tell Us about the Future of Warfare," *International Security*, Fall 1997.

6. John Garstka, "Network Centric Warfare: An Overview of Emerging Theory," *Phalanx*, December 2000, www.mors.org/Pubs/phalanx/dec00/feature.htm.

7. See "Fleet Battle Experiment Bravo," www.nwdc.navy.mil/Products/FBE/bravo.bravo.htm.

8. James R. FitzSimonds [Capt., USN], "The Cultural Challenge of Information

Technology," *Naval War College Review* 51, no. 3 (Summer 1998), p. 10.

9. Arthur K. Cebrowski [Vice Adm., USN] and John H. Garstka, "Network-Centric Warfare: Its Origins and Future," U.S. Naval Institute *Proceedings*, January 1998, pp. 28–35.

10. See Thomas G. Mahnken, "Deny U.S. Access?" U.S. Naval Institute *Proceedings*, September 1998.

11. Bill Gertz, "Space Seen as Battlefield of Future," *Washington Times*, 8 February 2001, p. 1.

12. Lisa Hoffman, "U.S. Opened Cyber-War during Kosovo Fight," *Washington Times*, 24 October 1999, p. C1.

13. William S. Cohen, *Report of the Quadrennial Defense Review* (Washington, D.C.: U.S. Defense Dept., 1997), p. iv.

14. National Defense Panel, *Transforming Defense: National Security in the 21st Century* (Washington, D.C.: U.S. Govt. Print. Off., December 1997).

15. Office of the Assistant Secretary of Defense (Public Affairs), "Atlantic Command Designated Executive Agent for Joint Warfighting Experimentation," News Release 252-98, 21 May 1998, www.defenselink.mil/news/May1998/b05211998_bt252-98.html.

16. Jim Garamone, "Joint Forces Command to Test Revolutionary Combat Concept," *Defense Link*, 8 May 2000, www.defenselink.mil/news/May2000/n05082000_200005082.html.

17. Tom Donnelly, "Revolution? What Revolution?" *Jane's Defence Weekly*, 7 June 2000, pp. 22–7.

18. U.S. Defense Dept., *AR&A/AM: Selected Acquisition Report* [hereafter SAR] (Washington, D.C.: Office of the Under Secretary of Defense [Acquisition, Technology, and Logistics], 14 November 2001), summary tables.

19. Jason Sherman, "Dream Work," *Armed Forces Journal International*, May 2000, p. 25.

20. Ibid., p. 28.

21. "GAO Draft Report: Objective Force Schedule May Be Too Aggressive," *Inside the Army*, 19 February 2001, p. 1.

22. Sydney J. Freedberg, "The New-Model Army," *National Journal*, 3 June 2000, p. 1750; and Richard J. Newman, "After the Tank," *U.S. News & World Report*, 18 September 2000.

23. Combat Studies Institute, "History of Transformation," *Military Review*, May–June 2000, pp. 17–29.

24. Thomas E. Ricks and Anne Marie Squeo, "Why the Pentagon Is Often Slow to Pursue Promising Weapons," *Wall Street Journal*, 12 October 1999.

25. For STREETFIGHTER, see Arthur K. Cebrowski [Vice Adm., USN] and Wayne P. Hughes [Capt., USN (Ret.)], "Rebalancing the Fleet," U.S. Naval Institute *Proceedings*, November 1999, pp. 31–4.

26. Greg Jaffe, "Debate Surrounding Small Ships Poses Fundamental Questions for U.S. Navy," *Wall Street Journal*, 11 July 2001, p. 1.

27. "Murphy Slams 'Street Fighter,' Navy Distances Itself from Comments," *Inside the Navy*, 18 October 1999, p. 3.

28. Paul Bedard, "Washington Whispers," *U.S. News & World Report*, 9 October 2000, p. 8.

29. Robert Holzer, "Top U.S. Military Strategist Faults Navy Innovation," *Defense News*, 12 February 2001, p. 1.

30. John G. Roos, "Effects-Based Operations," *Armed Forces Journal International*, March 2001, p. 66.

31. Headquarters, U.S. Air Force, *Initial Report, the Air War over Serbia: Aerospace Power in Operation Allied Force* (Washington, D.C.: Dept. of the Air Force, 2000), pp. 48–9.

32. Frank Wolfe, "Jumper Lays Out Future CONOPS for Global Strike Task Force," *Defense Daily*, 20 February 2001, p. 5.

33. Dave Moniz, "Pilotless Bombers to Be Tested Next Year," *USA Today*, 21 August 2000, p. 8.

34. Richard J. Newman, "Taking the Pilot Out of the Cockpit," *U.S. News & World Report*, 18 September 2000, p. 23.

35. George C. Wilson, "A Chairman Pushes Unmanned Warfare," *National Journal*, 4 March 2000, p. 718.

36. Ricks and Squeo, "Why the Pentagon Is Often Slow."

37. Ed Timms, "Unmanned Aircraft Earning Wings over Balkans," *Dallas Morning News*, 25 October 1999, p. 1.

38. Paul Richter, "Pilotless Plane Pushes Envelope for U.S. Defense," *Los Angeles Times*, 14 May 2000, p. A1.

39. See Thomas G. Mahnken, "Innovation in the U.S. Armed Forces: How Optimistic Should We Be?" unpublished manuscript, December 2000.

CHAPTER ELEVEN

Network-centric Warfare
What's the Point?
EDWARD A. SMITH, JR.

What *is* network-centric warfare? What's the point? Many attempts to answer these questions emphasize the "network" and the new technologies used to create more effective sensor and communications architectures. These architectures, it is argued, will enable us to create and exploit a common situational awareness, increase our speed of command, and "get inside the enemy's OODA [observe, orient, decide, and act] loop."[1] Yet such descriptions of technologies and capabilities can leave us asking the same questions: What is it? Just what does it bring to warfare? Why is it so critical to America's future military power that we must give up other capabilities to buy it?

These questions highlight the need for a warfare-centered working concept of network-centric operations. Such conceptual work can help us both recognize the potential in networking and discern its limits and limitations. It also can provide a fundamental understanding of the role of network-centric operations on the battlefield and across the spectrum from peace through war. An evolving working concept is, in short, the first step in designing a network-centric "navy after next."

Using technology to multiply the impact of military forces seems almost axiomatic. The problem is in identifying which technological combinations hold the most potential. Information technology is one obvious force multiplier, but what we really face are three concurrent technological revolutions.[2]

The first is in *sensor technology*. The sensor revolution is twofold: one movement toward sensors able to achieve near-real-time surveillance over vast areas, and another toward smaller, cheaper, more numerous sensors that can be netted to detect, locate, identify, and track targets. Together, these trends can produce systems that will provide the quantity and quality of data needed to create a "situational awareness" that is "global in scope and precise in detail."[3] The second revolution is in *information technology.* The information revolution will bring the geometric increase in computing power necessary to process, collate, and analyze this vast quantity of sensor data, and it will provide means to distribute information to any recipient or "shooter" anywhere in the world at near-real-time speeds. The third is in *weapons technology.* The weapons revolution is a matter of increasing numbers of precise munitions by reducing costs. It, like the sensor revolution, is twofold. Better streams of targeting data can permit a "dumbing down" of expensive guidance packages, while new designs, electronics, "lean" manufacturing, and mass production can decrease the cost for a given level of accuracy and capability.[4]

In the coming decade, these revolutions will interact and multiply each other's impacts and create a kaleidoscope of potential synergies that will change the character of war as we know it.[5] These revolutions and this change in how we think about war have come to be embodied in the idea of network-centric operations.

Network-centric Operations

The first step in creating a working concept for network-centric operations is identifying the key changes that grow from the triple technological revolution. One change, clearly, is the increased precision and speed that may now be possible in military operations. Speed and precision make it feasible to exploit specific battlefield opportunities and operate at a pace calculated to overwhelm an enemy's capacity to respond. They also offer a highly agile force, able to change from one rapid, precise operation to another at will and able to compress complex targeting processes to fit the nearly real-time dimensions of the battlefield. These emerging possibilities signal changes in how we wage war.

The leading network-centric proponents explain the impact of network-centric warfare in this manner. In traditional military operations, a mission is assigned and planned, forces are generated, and operations are executed to concentrate power on an objective. This is a highly coordinated, "stepped" cycle: periods of relative inaction, during which forces are generated and actions coordinated (the flat part of the step) alternate with periods of action, when combat power is applied (the vertical part). However, if forces were networked to create near-real-time situational awareness (see figure 1), we could act continuously. We would no longer need to pause before deciding on further action; the information and coordination needed would already be there. Moreover, shared awareness would permit a flattened, decentralized command structure, with decisions made at the lowest practical level of command—a "self-synchronization" that would permit us to reclaim "lost combat power." Then, as we train and organize to optimize these capabilities, the pace of these semi-independent operations would accelerate further to permit a new "speed of command." This description makes clear that network-centric operations are really about optimizing combat power—that is, *combat efficiency.*

FIGURE 1
Self-Synchronization and Speed of Command

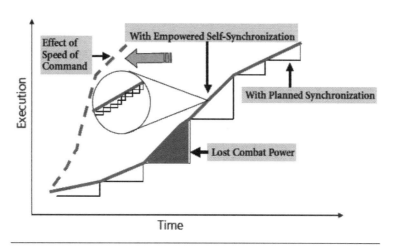

Vice Adm. A. K. Cebrowski, "New Sciences and Warfare," 21 September 1998.

While equating accelerated, self-synchronized operations to increased combat efficiency makes intuitive sense, it needs further explanation. One approach is to look at the above-mentioned "steps" in the context of the well known work of Colonel John Boyd, U.S. Air Force, but treating OODA loops as a succession of linear cycles overlaid on the steps.[6] Boyd's "observe," "orient," and "decide" phases then would equate to the flat part of a step, while the "act" phase would be the vertical. Plotted on axes of time (x) versus cumulative application of military force (y), the steps become OODA cycles, with each "act" adding to the total of the military force applied (see figure 2).

This construct of a *combat cycle* brings us to look not just at decision making but also at the parallel process of generating combat power. For example, the "observe" process includes both the decision to observe certain activities and the physical actions needed to acquire the intelligence, surveillance, and targeting data and then transmit it to the right people or systems. New sensor and information technologies can compress this process significantly, but there is a limit to how much. To optimize the impact of precision, we need more than sensor-based awareness; we need to identify specific vulnerabilities, and to do that we need to know the enemy. Such knowledge draws on sensor information—and will be subject to some time compression as a result—but it also depends on regional expertise and on intelligence databases developed long before the battle begins. Thus, the new sensors and information technology can

FIGURE 2
OODA Cycle

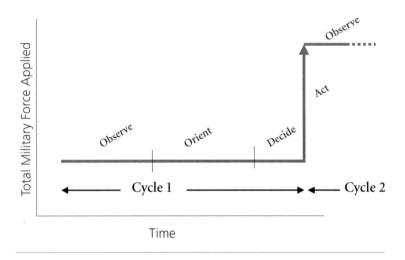

shorten the cycle only to the degree that long-term collection and analysis are already available on the net.

A similar limit emerges in the combined "orient and decide" phase.[7] Better awareness helps us avoid mistakes and use assets more efficiently, but we must still complete a set of physical actions to generate military power. We may have to move an aircraft carrier into range of the objective, plan and brief a mission, fuel and arm aircraft, and launch them. We may also have to deliver follow-on air strikes to achieve an objective. The pace of these actions is determined by the physical capabilities of systems and people; a carrier can move only so fast, and flight deck operations can be hurried along only so much. "Efficiency" here is as much a function of how we organize, train, and equip our forces as it is of information flows. The same is true of the "act" phase. Once in the air, aircraft must proceed toward the target and then—at a time dependent on the speed and range of the weapons used and the distance they must travel—launch their ordnance.

To increase combat efficiency, therefore, we must accelerate both parts of the combat cycle, the OODA cycle and the process of generating combat power. A strike-sortie-generation demonstration conducted by USS *Nimitz* (CVN 68) in 1997 is a good example of how these two elements come together.[8] *Nimitz* used only a rudimentary network to aid targeting and decision making, but it then focused on optimizing the operations of the carrier and the air wing to make better use of the increased information that the network made available. For this demonstration, among other things,

Nimitz added pilots to its air wing, introduced new high-speed cyclical operations, and relied on accompanying missile ships for air defense.[9] The result was a fourfold increase in sorties over a four-day period. Arming each aircraft with multiple precision weapons, each of which could reliably destroy an aim point, further multiplied the effect. The battle group thus established a faster, more efficient power-generation cycle, one that produced—when combined with networks' ability to identify the "targets that count" in commensurate numbers—an order-of-magnitude increase in the group's combat efficiency.

This is significant for several reasons. First, the *Nimitz* operation shows that using better equipment, organization, training, and information can shorten power-generation cycles and thus take advantage of network-centric speed and awareness. However, it also indicates that the time required for power generation varies with equipment, training, and organization; that in turn suggests that dissimilar military forces have power-generation cycles of radically different lengths. For example, the length of *Nimitz*'s cycle would differ from that of a squad of SEALs (Navy special operations forces) inserted from a submarine, a cruiser firing Tomahawk land-attack missiles, a squad of Marines in a firefight, or bombers operating from bases in the continental United States.

In a traditional battle, the commander manages the complex interaction among different combat cycles by so coordinating units that their respective "act" phases strike the enemy at the same time or in some prescribed sequence. The more diverse the forces, the greater the coordination problem.[10] The entire effort is held hostage to the speed of the slowest combat cycle, all other units being deliberately kept from achieving their optimum operational tempos so as to mass effects or be mutually supportive. This forgoes additional cycles that might have been applied by quicker-paced forces, and as a result, less power is applied overall (see figure 3). In short, by optimizing mass, we minimize efficiency.

Here is where agility becomes important. Precision and speed permit us to reduce cycle length and thereby increase the pace of operations, but they are insufficient by themselves to create a warfare revolution—or prevent it from backfiring. To deal with changes in the enemy threat or take advantage of emerging battlefield opportunities, we must be able *both* to conduct rapid, semi-independent operations *and* to mass forces and effects as required. We must be able to change the mode, direction, and objectives of our actions, just as much as we need to bring speed and precision to targeting.

This agility and the speed and precision it exploits all derive from the amalgam of information, sensors, and communications that constitutes the "information backplane" of network-centric operations. The network permits us to undertake more actions in a given time, to focus those actions better, and to act and react faster and with more certainty. Yet, these

FIGURE 3
Coordinated Attack . . . Then What?

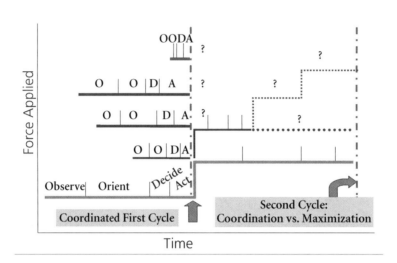

attributes—better, faster, more—still add up to little more than a more efficient form of attrition. How do we make the leap to a level of efficiency that would permit us to break enemies' wills rather than simply grind down their means of waging war?

Effects-based Operations

While increasing the number of aim points struck, the volume of fire generated, or the damage inflicted remains a critical, irreducible core of what military forces do, it is only the first step toward combat efficiency. The real payoff in network-centric operations is foreshortening combat by causing the enemy to yield long before his means to resist have been exhausted, or long before additional friendly forces might be expected to arrive in the crisis area. This efficiency revolves around the ability of network-centric forces to undertake precise *effects-based operations*, that is, outcome-oriented activity focused on enemy behavior. The objective of these operations is psychological rather than physical. Hence, they are focused on the enemy's decision-making process and ability to take action in some coherent manner—especially "getting inside his OODA loop" and inducing or exploiting chaos. The knowledge, precision, speed, and agility brought by network-centric operations constitute the price of admission into this realm.

"Getting Inside OODA Loops"

In our OODA-cycle diagram, any "act" or application of combat power can be seen in two ways. From the perspective of straightforward attrition, it is an effort that attacks, destroys, or in some way degrades the enemy capability to wage war or sustain it. Yet, that same "act" is also a stimulus that enemies "observe" and factor into their decision-making processes. The more significant the action, the greater effect it will have on decisions. This "effect" is a function not solely of how much we destroy but of what and how we attack. If the stimulus is significant enough, the effect may be to force enemies to reconsider their courses of action and, perhaps, begin their decision-making cycles all over again. That is to say, we would disrupt their OODA loops. A succession of such stimuli might not only disrupt a foe's OODA loop but even create a condition of "lock-out," in which the enemy can no longer react coherently (see figure 4).

The requirements for such effects-based operations are stringent. If we were concerned only with attrition, improvement in efficiency would require only increases in the size and frequency of our attacks—that is, the total quantity of power applied. Breaking the will, in contrast, requires putting the right forces on the right vulnerabilities at the right times so as to produce some particular effect. To make matters more difficult, this needs to be done not just to a single enemy OODA cycle, as in a one-on-one fighter engagement, but against the multiple and interacting OODA cycles of different enemy units and forces, which are operating simultaneously at the tactical, operational, and strategic levels of conflict.

A pointed, if serendipitous, example of such a disruption occurred in the battle of Midway in June 1942. Intelligence derived from the breaking of Japanese codes enabled the Americans to anticipate the Japanese attack, detect enemy carriers before their own

FIGURE 4
Interaction between OODA Cycles

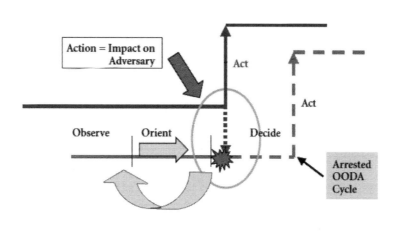

were found, and launch an attack first. When the Japanese commander received word of an American carrier in the area—just before he was attacked by carrier-based torpedo planes—he reconsidered a planned attack on Midway, reoriented his effort, and ordered his aircraft rearmed for fleet action. Then, as his planes were being rearmed and his combat air patrol aircraft were engaged in low-level intercepts of American torpedo planes, the dive-bomber element of the disjointed American attack (in figure 5, the second dotted arrow) struck, catching the Japanese carriers with their decks full of planes and bombs.[11] What happened in the next minutes ended the Japanese attack on Midway and was the turning point in the Pacific War. In effect, the sighting of one ship and a tactically ineffective torpedo-plane attack had collectively, and fortuitously, a decisive impact on the enemy OODA cycle: they occurred at just the right time and forced the Japanese to begin anew. The challenge for network-centric operations is to repeat this effect reliably, predictably, and at will. How do we do that?

If we compare the Japanese and American combat cycles at the time of the torpedo attack, it becomes evident that the cycles were out of phase with each other. Had they been in phase, American and Japanese strikes would have passed each other in the air

FIGURE 5
Midway

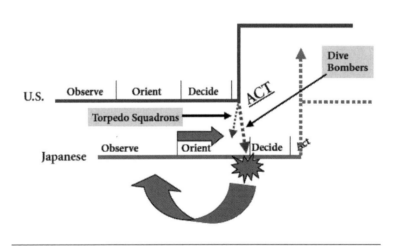

and struck empty decks on both sides, without the disastrous consequences for the Japanese—but possibly dire ones for the smaller force of American carriers. But thanks to its intelligence coup, the American side completed its observation, orientation, and decision phases in time for its air-strike "act" to hit the Japanese when they were most vulnerable and before they could initiate a fleet action. The American success rested partly on careful preparation—the intelligence, reconnaissance, and early launch of aircraft—and in part on the serendipity of the poorly (in terms of the plan) coordinated arrival of their strike elements over the target.

To emulate Midway, we must measure the enemy OODA cycle correctly and then coordinate our actions to occur at exactly the right times. This requires not only the "battlespace awareness" that in 1942 enabled the American fleet to launch its strikes first but also knowledge of the enemy necessary to identify and exploit critical junctures.[12] We must then be able to sustain controlled, high-tempo operations. There is a problem here: intelligence simply will not yield such knowledge of the enemy reliably, consistently, or at all levels.[13] How then might network-centric operations enable us to bring about another Midway?

One solution is to multiply the number of opportunities to repeat the Midway serendipity. The more frequent the stimulus, the greater the chance a strike will occur at the right time to obtain the desired effect on the enemy decision-making process. Shortening the length of our overall combat cycle (see figure 6) would multiply the number of impacts on an adversary's decision making over a given period and increase the likelihood of striking at the "right time" to disrupt the adversary's cycle. But as we have noted, the power-generation side of the combat cycle can be compressed only so much.

Another approach would be to build on "self-synchronization" and "shared situational awareness" to launch smaller, more numerous operations, each of which could generate

FIGURE 6
Compression of Time

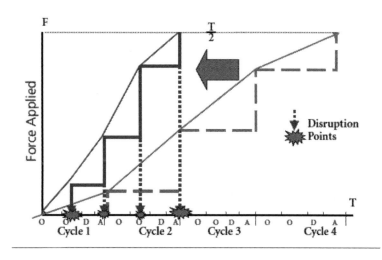

a stimulus sufficient to affect the adversary's OODA cycles.[14] The length of the individual unit combat cycles might remain the same, but they could be staggered, overlapped, so as to produce a rapid succession of stimuli. This approach has an obvious limitation: the more we diminish the size of our individual actions, the more vulnerable each will be to defeat in detail. However, with better awareness and better knowledge of the enemy, we can hope to anticipate enemy actions and optimize forces for disruptive effect or for mutual support (see figure 7).

Finally, we could multiply the number of cycles but also compress the time needed to execute each cycle. In essence, we would use our network-centric capability to liberate individual forces to operate at their respective optimum combat cycles and by so doing increase the number of OODA cycles we execute. Ideally, the stimuli can be made numerous enough to overwhelm enemies with new developments, forcing them continually to revisit decisions, redirect efforts, and pause for observations, even to the point that they cannot ever take action.

This suggests an analogy very different from that of Midway. Instead of thrusting a rapier into the OODA cycle at precisely the critical time, we could unleash something akin to a swarm of bees. Even if no single unit has a decisive impact, the overall effect might be to leave the victim swinging helplessly at attackers coming from all directions, unable to mount any coherent defense save retreat. In essence, we would provide so many stimuli that adversaries could no longer act coherently but must constantly recycle: "Does the act that just struck me invalidate the assumptions upon which my

FIGURE 7
Multiple Overlapping Cycles

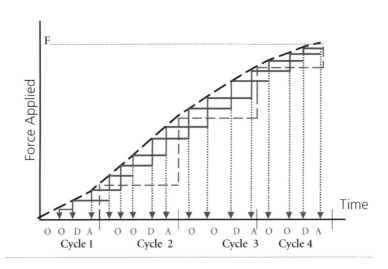

currently intended course of action rests? Does it demand a redirection of my effort? Will an additional attack come, and will it force me into revisiting my plans yet again?" The result would be lockout.

This "swarm" approach poses new challenges. How do we coordinate the swarm so as to achieve concrete military objectives beyond simply interfering— perhaps without success—in the enemy decision-making loop? How do we know when to mass forces or effects so as to avoid their being destroyed one by one? How do we assess the effectiveness of our efforts and then feed the results of these assessments into the next round of "orient," "decide," and "act" phases? Will enemies *know* they have been defeated and cease to resist, or simply continue to swat at the attacks until they can no longer do so—that is, continue a blind attrition war? To be effective, the "swarm" would need to work toward a unified set of military objectives, under a single commander's intent, whereas to achieve sufficiently brief cycle times, its individual elements must be largely self-contained and self-coordinated. In short, our forces would need to become self-synchronized and self-adaptive—but those are key capacities we hope to draw from network-centric operations.

Exploiting Chaos

The principle of chaos in warfare is not new.[15] Clausewitz talks in terms of exploiting the fog and friction of war to drive the enemy into a rout—that is, into a state of chaos.[16] Recent writings on "chaos theory" have drawn a comparison between the concept of chaos in physical systems and its application to warfare.[17] The boundary region between chaos and order is particularly significant, because small inputs or changes in system parameters there can have very large impacts, even causing entire systems to collapse. In military operations, this would equate to creating situations in which relatively small applications of power at the right time have highly disproportionate and potentially decisive impacts. This is particularly significant for expeditionary warfare and forward presence, in that it suggests that a relatively small forward force might exploit chaos to offset what it lacks in numbers.

How do we define this boundary region in militarily useful ways? A simple approach is to define the edge of chaos in terms of the intensity of the operations, specifically the pace and the scale and scope of operations, which can be plotted along the x and y axes of a coordinate scale. We can understand intuitively that the more we increase the pace of our operations (x), the more difficult they will be to manage. Similarly, the greater the scope and scale of our operations (y), the more difficult they will be to control. By extension, we can surmise that at some point along the x axis lies an operation so rapid that we cannot coordinate it, and that somewhere on the y axis is an operation (such as a global thermonuclear war) of such size or scope that we lose control of our forces; beyond either of these points we lapse into chaos ourselves (see figure 8). These two points represent transitions from order into chaos. Figuratively, then, a line drawn between these two points is the *edge of chaos*—it defines the limit of our control, and it contains all order-to-chaos transition points.

In this context, *chaos* encompasses all military operations that are so rapid or of such scale as to be uncontrollable and that are, therefore, unfocused and incoherent, such as a rout on a battlefield—"every man for himself."[18] The opposite is *order*—military operations whose scale, scope, and pace permit them to be controlled, coordinated, and focused on given objectives. Historically, when armies and navies have met in battle, at least one tactical objective has been to drive the enemy force from order into chaos. How can we identify and exploit this operational boundary?

FIGURE 8
Defining the Edge of Chaos

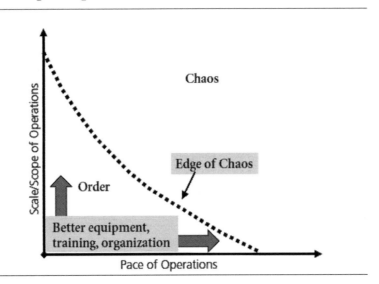

One factor is that the edge of chaos is not fixed. It changes constantly. As the *Nimitz* demonstration underlined, a highly trained and organized force using sophisticated equipment can operate safely at a pace and scale of operations that would push a less well-trained and equipped force into chaos. Better equipment, training, and organization, then, enable us to drive our transition points farther out along the x and y axes and thereby define new edges of chaos. This also means that the edge of chaos varies from one force to the next, as each comprises different units, differently equipped, manned, trained, and organized. Opposing forces in any battle are therefore likely to have their own, quite different, edges of chaos. These two edges of chaos define three zones. Zone 1 (see figure 9) is the zone of chaos—all the combinations of scale, scope, and pace that neither side would be able to manage. Zone 2 defines a complex, asymmetric region in which the better equipped and trained force can coordinate operations but the other cannot. In Zone 3 is the realm in which both sides can operate comfortably—the zone of order.

By definition, neither side can operate successfully in Zone 1, and neither derives any advantage from operating in a way that permits its enemy an orderly and focused response (Zone 3).[19] In contrast, the boundary region, Zone 2, offers the disproportionate impacts predicted by chaos theory. It is a regime of inherent asymmetry, in which the less capable side can neither respond in kind nor fail to respond (and be pummeled into submission or confined to preplanned actions, unresponsive to the situation).[20] This can be carried another step. If one side is consistently able to operate beyond the other's edge of chaos, it can induce a state of despair in which further resistance is, or at least appears to be, futile. Focusing precisely on vulnerabilities most likely to drive the enemy into chaos can accelerate this process.

Self-Synchronization and Asymmetric Warfare

This all leads us to self-synchronized operations, of which a good historical example is the 1805 battle of Trafalgar, in which Admiral Horatio Nelson destroyed the combined French and Spanish fleets. The crux of the action was Nelson's bold movement to break through the French-Spanish battle line in two places and then concentrate his forces on

FIGURE 9
Operations on the Edge of Chaos

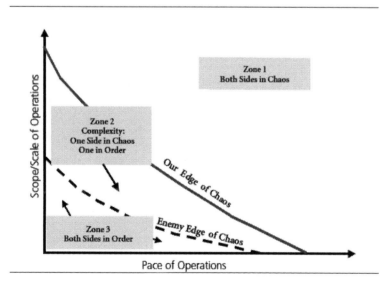

bite-sized portions of it. The basis for success in so risky an undertaking was what could be described as a "cerebral network" among Nelson and his ship captains, his "band of brothers." That network had been formed by more than eight years of combat operations together; Nelson was confident that all of his subordinates would perceive a developing situation in the same way—that is, that they would have a shared situational awareness.[21] He was equally sure that his commanders not only understood his intent but would exploit aggressively any opening in the enemy line accordingly and carry out mutually supportive actions without further direction. For that reason, Nelson could limit his final directive before the battle to the inspiring, but otherwise not very helpful, reminder that "England expects every man to do his duty." Nothing more was needed. The commanders knew what to do.

This contrasted sharply with the situation of the opposing commander, Admiral Villeneuve. His force was larger and in many ways technologically superior, but it lacked any semblance of the cerebral networking Nelson had forged. The French ship captains and subordinate commanders had spent most of the war blockaded in port. They distrusted Villeneuve, even as Villeneuve distrusted his own judgment. Added to this was the problem of coordinating with a Spanish fleet, with which the French had never before operated. The best Villeneuve could do was to form his ships into a conventional eighteenth-century line of battle, foreseeing an engagement in which two ordered, parallel battle lines would pound each other until most of the ships of one side or the other struck their colors, blew up, or sank. When Nelson refused battle on these terms and instead broke through the French-Spanish line, the pace of operation that he thereby forced on the French and Spanish immediately exceeded their ability to cope and invalidated their numerical superiority. Villeneuve largely lost control of his forces and with it the ability to fight a coherent battle. In such conditions his ships, though they fought bravely, could only contribute to the general chaos; a substantial proportion never entered the battle at all.

Network-centric operations can, after a fashion, replicate the cerebral networking of Nelson's band of brothers without the eight years of combat preparation and without the slow tempo of battle at sea that facilitated situational awareness in the early nineteenth century. However, there is a hitch: What would happen if one side's edge of chaos did not lie entirely on one side of the other's but crossed it (figure 10), producing a *second* asymmetric zone, in which the advantages were reversed?

This reversal points to a dangerously misleading assumption underlying much thinking today about the "revolution of military affairs": that the United States will always be technologically superior and thus fight faster and better. In reality, tempo of operations is not solely a function of technology; it is also a function of the centralization of

FIGURE 10
Intersecting Edges of Chaos

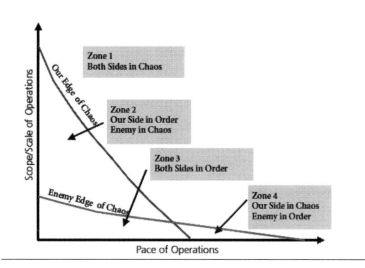

command. One can choose to trade centralized control for speed and scope of operations. This may forgo some of the ability to mass effects on a specific objective, but if the effect sought derives from the pace and scope of the attacks rather than from the amount of destruction, or from a cumulative impact rather than specific actions, then this trade-off may be acceptable. In other words, one could confront a technologically superior enemy by creating a new asymmetric zone in which small, decentralized units could operate successfully but in which an opponent using large formations under centralized control could not respond coherently.

The importance of this fourth zone is even more evident if we plot the respective edges of chaos on a graph with three axes (figure 11)—one for pace, one for scale, and a separate orthogonal axis for scope. This presentation highlights two aspects of decentralization: forces can be broken into smaller, self-synchronized units, and they can be dispersed over a wide area to make coordinated and timely response by the other side more difficult. These points correspond rather closely to Maoist theory of guerrilla warfare. Guerrillas use dispersed formations so small that they cannot be targeted effectively by heavier government forces. These bands then conduct many small raids, so rapidly that the raiders are gone before opposing forces can be brought to bear. Since the desired effect, attrition of an opponent's will, depends more on pace and scope than on damage to specific targets, control can remain highly decentralized. This was the essential problem the United States confronted in Vietnam.

FIGURE 11
Edge of Chaos—Three Axes

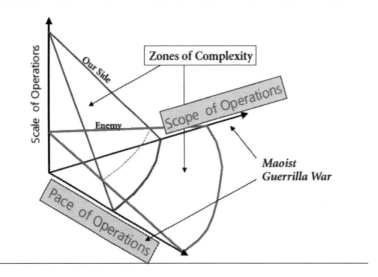

These examples imply a new understanding of chaos—that chaos need not mean solely loss of control over one's forces. It could also mean a situation in which the size of forces and delays in generating and using them consistently prevent one side from accomplishing its objectives. How do network-centric operations address this low-tech asymmetry? One way is based on the knowledge and situational awareness brought to bear by the network. If the guerrillas' actions can be anticipated or instantly detected and responded to, much of what they gain by dispersing and decentralizing can be negated. In effect, networking permits the high-tech side to move its edge of chaos out from the x and z axes of the diagram until decentralization no longer confers any advantage on the guerrillas. Also, whereas by decentralization guerrillas or urban fighters opt for increasing the number and decreasing the size of their operations, a network-centric force might do the same—for example, by resorting to a ground war of small units aided by superior situational awareness. Alternatively, it could increase its pace, using the network to manage high-speed, complex operations. In each case, networking combined with self-synchronization enables forces to operate as a "self-adjusting complex adaptive system" while retaining the ability to mass superior effects at will.

A Reality Check

As we gradually build a working concept of network-centric operations, we need to bear in mind some commonsense caveats. Networking is not a universal solution to warfare problems, nor will it change the nature of war. Older forms of warfare are likely to persist alongside the new. Speed will be critical to our success, but numbers and endurance will still count. Situational awareness will multiply our power, but knowing the enemy will be more important than ever. Above all, intelligent adversaries will respond, and the more successful our concept of network-centric operations becomes, the more asymmetrical their responses are likely to be.

But it is not our objective in developing a working concept to provide all the answers. It is simply to identify combinations of new thinking and new things that offer *better* answers to our warfare needs, on as many levels of war as possible, and over as wide a portion of the spectrum of conflict as possible. The measure of our success will be not the quality of the networking or the quantity of firepower we can bring to bear but the effect that networking enables us to have on our would-be enemies in peace and in war.

Notes

1. Observe, Orient, Decide, Act—a cycle used by Colonel John R. Boyd, U.S. Air Force, to characterize fighter engagements and since then applied to the decision-making process in general. See John R. Boyd, *A Discourse on Winning and Losing* (Maxwell AFB, Ala.: Air Univ. Press, August 1987).

2. Walter Morrow, "Technology for a Naval Revolution in Military Affairs," Second Navy RMA Round Table, Science Applications International Corporation, Tysons Corner, Virginia, 4 June 1997.

3. Ibid.

4. This trend is already evident in the falling unit-price of the Navy Tomahawk cruise missile, from $1.2 million ten years ago to less than $700,000 in 1998, to possibly $300,000 or less before the decade is out—a roughly 50 percent drop every ten years. Daniel Murphy [Rear Adm., USN], "Surface Warfare," Navy RMA Round Table.

5. The situation is analogous to the triple revolution in guns, armor, and propulsion that marked warship design between 1862 and 1910—that is, from the commissioning of the USS *Monitor* to the first launch of an aircraft from a U.S. Navy ship. That threefold advance induced a period of trial and error that produced in turn such rapid change in warship design that new units were obsolete within a few years of entering service. It also brought forth Alfred Thayer Mahan and a fundamental rethinking of what navies could do.

6. Boyd.

7. In Boyd's tactical engagement loop, "orient" and "decide" are separated into two phases; however, this distinction becomes problematic in more complex operations, especially at the operational and strategic levels of war. As used here, the "orient" and "decide" phases are considered together, as collectively defining the time necessary to generate the right force to achieve the right effects.

8. The results of the *Nimitz* demonstration are detailed in a two-volume CNA study: Angelyn Jewell et al., *USS* Nimitz *and Carrier Airwing Surge Demonstration* (Alexandria, Va.: Center for Naval Analyses, 1998).

9. In the *Nimitz* case, the air wing was composed of low-maintenance, quick-turnaround F/A-18s, which could readily fly five or more sorties per day. The carrier air wing started with intense "flex-deck" operations but soon discovered that the flight deck became unworkable; the "edge of chaos" had been reached. It therefore switched to an aggressive concept of cyclical operations that enabled the wing to launch more aircraft while maintaining better order on the flight deck. Interview with Rear Adm. John Nathman, USN, Commander, *Nimitz* Battle Group, Pentagon, 11 February 1999.

10. The problem is especially bad in coalition operations, governed as they are by multiple national rules of engagement.

11. For the Japanese decision process and force-generation cycle at Midway, see Dallas W. Isom, "The Battle of Midway: Why the Japanese Lost," *Naval War College Review* 53, no. 3 (Summer 2000), pp. 60–100, esp. pp. 72ff.

12. In the Midway example, because the U.S. and Japanese forces were very alike, their OODA cycles would have been roughly similar. In a conflict between two dissimilar forces, that would not be the case, making the adversary's OODA cycle much more difficult to predict.

13. However good the surveillance picture or "battlespace awareness" we generate, the ultimate determinant of the speed and direction of the enemy decision-making cycle is the enemy. Sufficiently fine-grained knowledge of the enemy arises not from sensor data but from analysis based in large part on human-intelligence reporting—which is necessarily sporadic. We cannot, therefore, depend on having the intelligence when we need it or, indeed, on collecting the needed data at all.

14. Note that in each case the total amount of force applied remains constant and that what varies is the way in which that force is applied.

15. The idea of inducing chaos will hardly be a new concept to ground forces, for whom the fundamental challenge is to control very large numbers of "actors" in battle. In the ground context, "breaking the enemy's will to resist" equates to causing the enemy to disintegrate into panicked flight. While this understanding remains operative, the focus of the chaos sought here lies at the operational, even the strategic, level rather than the battlefield.

16. Barry Watts, *Clausewitzian Friction and Future War* (Washington, D.C.: National Defense Univ. Press, 1996), pp. 105ff.

17. Major Glenn James, U.S. Air Force, uses the example of a water faucet that drips with annoying regularity. As the flow of water is increased, the frequency of the drip rises but the regularity remains. However, when the flow is quickened even minutely beyond some definable rate, the drops no longer have time to form, and the drip changes abruptly to a sporadic—that is, chaotic—flow. The very minor increase in flow has caused the physical system to become chaotic. Glenn James, *Chaos Theory: The Essentials for Military Applications*, Newport Paper 10 (Newport, R.I.: Naval War College, 1997), pp. 15–6.

18. It is worth making a distinction here between tactical-level chaos that induces the enemy to take flight and strategic-level chaos that induces irrational behavior by a power with nuclear weapons. Between these two extremes lies a realm in which "shock and awe" can achieve specific effects calculated to support political and military objectives. However, implicit in the idea of effects is a risk-versus-gain calculus that applies to chaos as much as to other effects.

19. In the strategic nuclear confrontation of the Cold War, it was necessary to operate in this zone of order to avoid the risk of an irrational act or an uncontrolled escalation.

20. An example arose in the October 1973 Arab-Israeli War. The Egyptian army's "edge of chaos" was far inside that of the Israelis. Therefore, the Egyptians were forced to resort to a scripted preemptive campaign. That gave them an initial success in crossing the Suez Canal but left them largely incapable of responding to Israeli counteraction.

21. The two fleets took more than three hours to close. This allowed ample time for the commanders to observe the enemy line and any gaps in it that they might exploit. The cerebral networking provided a common understanding of how such gaps might be exploited and of how ships might provide mutual support and exploit any further opportunities.

CHAPTER TWELVE

Transforming the Navy
Punching a Feather Bed?

PETER J. DOMBROWSKI AND ANDREW L. ROSS

> *To change anything in the Na-a-vy is like punching a feather bed. You punch it with your right and you punch it with your left until you are finally exhausted, and then you find the damn bed just as it was before you started punching.*
>
> Franklin D. Roosevelt

The Bush administration has made military transformation a central defense and national security objective.[1] It came into office declaring its commitment to profound, potentially radical military change. Even while engaged in the global war on terror, preparing to go to war against and then fighting one rogue state, and deterring another, the U.S. military has been pressed to remake itself. Indeed, the threat of terrorism is said to demonstrate the need for transformation, and a possible war in Southwest Asia has been viewed by some as an opportunity to showcase the military's emerging transformational capabilities. While deployed across multiple theaters, the armed forces are to develop a coherent view of the future and to begin implementing the technological, doctrinal, and organizational changes necessary to meet future warfighting requirements. Moreover, this is to be done in a budget environment in which, despite dramatically increased defense spending, flexibility is limited by current operating expenses. By any standard, this is a tall order. Yet civilian officials in the Department of Defense continue to push the military to think more creatively and move more quickly. Individuals, programs, and services thought to stand in the way of building the "military after next" have been taken to task.[2]

The Navy claims that its challenges are particularly difficult. The fleet has shrunk. It is likely to shrink still further before it grows. Programmed recapitalization and modernization are thought to exceed the resources expected to be available. Operational requirements have dictated more frequent, and longer, deployments. Operating tempo has spiked. The fleet and resources are stretched thin. Is now the time to transform, to introduce new platforms and force the naval acquisition system and the naval industrial base to adopt new business practices and achieve greater economies? For transformation proponents, the answer is a resounding "Yes."

Of course, some within the Navy had begun to think about the next Navy and even the Navy after next well before Governor George W. Bush was selected to be president. Over the last decade, the concept of network-centric warfare, which calls for a profound "shift from platform-centric operations to Network Centric Operations," gained gradual, if often grudging, acceptance.[3] Network-centric warfare, in the form of "ForceNet," is at the heart of "Sea Power 21," which was introduced in 2002 as the Navy's transformation vision. ForceNet is the integrating agent of SP-21's "Sea Strike," "Sea Shield," and "Sea Basing," which are to increase the Navy's capacity to strike deeply and sustain joint operations even in the absence of land bases, as well as to help protect both the American homeland and U.S. allies and friends against ballistic missiles and other threats. Intended as a comprehensive guide to naval transformation, Sea Power 21 also reflects an appreciation of the long-term demands of waging the war on terror and combating weapons of mass destruction, as well as of how the Bush administration is likely to employ military power.

We present here a four-part, interim assessment of the Navy's ongoing transformation project.[4] First, we provide the context for our assessment with a review of the administration's approach to transformation. Second, we describe Sea Power 21 and its network-centric-warfare underpinnings. In the third section we examine whether the Navy's vision of its future is indeed transformational and the extent to which the Navy is progressing toward its vision's promise. We conclude by evaluating the prospects for Navy transformation and by asking whether the force envisioned by Sea Power 21 will meet the nation's national security requirements in the coming decades.

The Transformation Imperative

An array of joint and service transformation visions had been developed even before the Bush administration took office. *Joint Vision 2020*, like *Joint Vision 2010* before it, foresees a military able to dominate the full spectrum of military operations, from low-intensity conflict to major theater wars. Information superiority is to be the underpinning of "dominant maneuver," "precision engagement," "focused logistics," and "full-dimensional protection."[5] U.S. forces are expected to prevail over any and all military challengers by moving more quickly, hitting harder and more precisely, and when necessary, sustaining operations longer than potential adversaries.

Not only the Navy but the Army, Air Force, and Marine Corps have developed transformation visions. The Army's transformation project promises to deliver an "Objective Force" with a Future Combat System that will be responsive, deployable, agile, versatile, lethal, survivable, and sustainable.[6] The Air Force's *Vision 2020* promises "Global Vigilance, Reach and Power" through a full-spectrum aerospace force to control and exploit not only the air but also space.[7] Air Force assets are to be able "to find, fix, assess, track, target, and engage any object of military significance on or above the surface of the Earth in near real time."[8] *Marine Corps Strategy 21* and the Corps's "Operational Maneuver from the Sea" doctrine promise scalable, interoperable expeditionary forces at a high level of readiness.[9]

Since each service is attempting to exploit the opportunities presented by modern information technologies and is responding to the overarching guidance provided in such documents as *Joint Vision 2020* and the *National Military Strategy,* there are many commonalities across the individual visions. Each service claims, to one degree or another, to be expeditionary; even the Army is lightening its forces, in order to increase mobility and sustainability. Each vision also focuses on the ability to strike adversaries with a variety of weapons; no potential target anywhere in any environment—land, sea, air, space, or cyberspace—will not, in the end, be vulnerable to U.S. forces. Strike operations are to be enabled by "information dominance"—which, reduced to its essentials, means improving the intelligence available to all echelons, but especially shooters. A premium is placed on precision, speed, agility, flexibility, adaptability, and connectivity. Operations are to be conducted in parallel rather than sequentially. All of the services genuflect before the requirements for jointness and interoperability.

In 2001, the stakes were raised. A new administration took office proclaiming its commitment to transformation. Military transformation had emerged as an article of faith for the Bush team during the presidential campaign. In his September 1999 Citadel speech, then-Governor Bush called for "creating the military of the next century," seizing the opportunity "created by a revolution in the technology of war," moving beyond "marginal improvements," "skipping 'a generation of technology,'" and encouraging "a new spirit of innovation."[10]

In remarks at the Joint Forces Command in February 2001, the new president returned to the themes of his Citadel address:

> We are witnessing a revolution in the technology [of] war. Power is increasingly defined not by size, but by mobility and swiftness. Advantage increasingly comes from information. . . . Our goal is to move beyond marginal improvements to harness new technologies that will support a new strategy. . . . On land, heavy forces will be lighter. Our light forces will be more lethal. . . . In the air, we'll be able to strike across the world with pinpoint accuracy, using both aircraft and unmanned systems. On the oceans, we'll connect information and weapons in new ways, maximizing our ability to project power over land.[11]

Upon assuming office, the new secretary of defense, Donald Rumsfeld, moved quickly to initiate the "comprehensive review" of military strategy, structure, and procurement priorities promised by President Bush. Andrew W. Marshall, the director of net assessment and a longtime proponent of transformation, was tapped to lead a wide-ranging review of U.S. defense strategy.[12] Additional teams were formed to focus on transformation, conventional forces, nuclear forces, missile defense, space, crisis response, acquisition reform, and quality of life, among other issues.[13] An Office of Force Transformation, led by Vice Admiral Arthur K. Cebrowski, USN (Ret.), a leading advocate of network-centric warfare, was established. The services were directed by the Office of the Secretary of Defense (OSD) to develop transformation roadmaps. A Defense Transformation Guidance document was developed to accompany OSD's Defense Planning Guidance. These and other initiatives clearly signaled the importance of far-reaching military innovation to the Bush team.

The administration's commitment to transformation was formalized in the Defense Department's September 2001 *Quadrennial Defense Review* report. Even in the wake of the attacks of 11 September and the onset of the global war on terror, the secretary of defense continued to emphasize the importance of "the transformation of U.S. forces, capabilities, and institutions."[14] Transformation was once again proclaimed to be "at the heart" of the administration's "new strategic approach."[15] Indeed, a renewed sense of urgency was conveyed: "Transformation is not a goal for tomorrow, but an endeavor that must be embraced in earnest *today*."[16] Four transformation pillars—joint operations; experimentation; intelligence, surveillance, and reconnaissance (ISR); and research and development and selective recapitalization—and a set of "six critical operational goals" were identified.[17]

Under Secretary of Defense (Acquisition, Technology and Logistics) Pete Aldridge has remarked that "transformation is a loose concept."[18] Yet administration officials have attempted to pin down the meaning of "transformation." The most prominent dimensions of transformation—technology, doctrine, and organization—were evident in the characterization of transformation provided in the 2001 Quadrennial Defense Review (QDR) report:[19]

> Transformation results from the exploitation of *new approaches to operational concepts and capabilities*, the use of old and new technologies, and *new forms of organization* that more effectively anticipate new or still emerging strategic and operational challenges and opportunities and that *render previous methods of conducting war obsolete or subordinate*. Transformation can involve *fundamental change in the form of military operations*, as well as potential change in their scale. It can encompass the *displacement of one form of war with another*, such as *fundamental change in the ways war is waged* in the air, on land and at sea. It can also involve the *emergence of new kinds of war*, such as armed conflict in new dimensions of the battle space.[20]

The administration's characterization of transformation suggests that remaking the armed forces requires more than routine, sustaining innovation. As the 2002 *Annual Report* explicitly recognized, transformation entails "discontinuous change," not merely the incremental change typical of modernization.[21] Risks are to be taken.[22] Transformation is to result in fundamentally new, rather than merely improved, technologies and weapons systems, doctrines, and operational concepts. Revolutionary rather than evolutionary change is the objective.[23] Marginal improvements in capabilities are to be rejected in favor of leaps ahead.[24] As indicated by the QDR's use of language evocative of a "revolution in military affairs," its discussion of transformation's "social" dimensions, its recognition of the necessity for "fundamental changes . . . in organizational culture and behavior," and the military's palpable concern about the administration's transformation agenda, the stage has been set for disruptive innovation.[25]

Even in the face of the military's increased responsibilities for homeland security, the demands of Operation ENDURING FREEDOM, the complexities of the broader global war on terror, and preparations for and then war against Iraq, the transformation imperative has remained among the highest priorities of the Bush administration.[26] The September 2002 National Security Strategy, for example, called for transforming the U.S. armed forces and other national security institutions to maintain and enhance American primacy.[27] The Bush administration, seemingly, has repudiated the Clinton administration's approach to transformation and embraced the approach of the 1997 National Defense Panel, which recommended "transforming the armed forces into a very different kind of military from that which exists today," for according "the highest priority to executing a transformation strategy," and for accelerating transformation.[28] Against this backdrop, the U.S. Navy and the other armed services have struggled to turn such nascent concepts as network-centric warfare from abstract exercises in strategic thinking into full-fledged transformation plans.

The Navy Transformation Vision

Publicly unveiled by the Chief of Naval Operations, Admiral Vernon Clark, at the Naval War College in June 2002, "Sea Power 21" is the most complete, and recent, depiction of the Navy's transformation vision.[29] It is a successor to . . . *From the Sea* and *Forward . . . from the Sea,* post–Cold War visions that profoundly reoriented the Navy away from blue-water fleet-on-fleet engagements to projecting power ashore in the littorals.[30] Sea Power 21, however, is focused as much on *how* the Navy will fight in the future as on *where* it will fight. The offensive Sea Strike, defensive Sea Shield, and facilitating Sea Basing capabilities it calls for are to be integrated by ForceNet, which is to "network" the future Navy's formidable capabilities. The inspiration for Sea Power 21's emphasis on the force-multiplying, potentially transforming, effects of connectivity and networking is network-centric warfare, a concept of future warfare long advocated by former Naval War College president Vice Admiral Cebrowski.[31] In the form of ForceNet, network-centric warfare is embedded in Sea Power 21's vision of how the Navy will "organize, integrate, and transform."[32]

Network-centric Warfare

For its proponents, network-centric warfare is the emerging vision of the future of war.[33] It is a vision driven by a particular understanding of the transformation of modern society from the industrial age to a postindustrial, or information, age at the beginning of the twenty-first century.[34] Advances in information technologies that have resulted in widespread socioeconomic changes are expected to revolutionize the conduct, if not the nature, of war.[35] In particular, the increasing use of networks for organizing human activities is touted as a means for reshaping the way American forces train, organize, equip, and fight.[36]

In brief, networks harness the power of geographically dispersed nodes (whether personal computers, delivery trucks, or warships) by linking them together into networks (such as the World Wide Web) that allow for the extremely rapid, high-volume transmission of digitized data (multimedia). Networking has the potential to increase exponentially the capabilities of individual nodes or groups of nodes and to render the use of resources more efficient. In theory, networked nodes have access not only to their own resident capabilities but also, more importantly, to capabilities distributed across the network. The loss of a networked node need not be crippling; in a robust network, its functions can and will be assumed by other nodes. Since networked nodes can share information efficiently, they can be designed individually as relatively simple, low-cost adjuncts to the network itself.[37]

The Navy and the other services have been developing, individually if not jointly, the capabilities for network-centric operations (NCO).[38] In a draft capstone concept paper, the Navy Warfare Development Command identified four NCO "pillars," or supporting concepts: information and knowledge advantage, effects-based operations, assured access, and "forward sea-based forces" (see figure 1).[39]

The benefits of NCO to be provided by the pillars of information and knowledge advantage and effects-based operations include speed of command, self-synchronization, advanced targeting, and greater tactical stability.[40] Netted sensors are to provide shooters and commanders with "unmatched awareness of the battle space."[41] Within the battle space, war fighters are to be able to "self-synchronize" their activities to fulfill a commander's intent by drawing upon a shared "rule set—or doctrine," as well as a common operational picture (COP).[42] Self-synchronization is accomplished by devolving

FIGURE 1

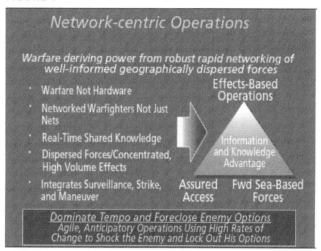

Source: NWDC, Network Centric Operations, p. ii.

decision making downward to the lowest appropriate level, thus allowing war fighters to respond directly and quickly to tactical, operational, and even strategic challenges. "Fires" (munitions delivery) are to be employed in a framework of effects-based operations rather than of attrition-based warfare. Precision-guided munitions in conjunction with advanced ISR capabilities will allow targets to be hit with greater economy—simultaneously rather than sequentially—greatly increasing the possibility of imposing disproportionate effects, particularly psychological ones, on the adversary. Tactical operations may thus achieve strategic objectives.

By geographically dispersing sensors, shooters, and their supporting infrastructure within an overarching network, U.S. forces will be able to achieve greater tactical stability—a favorable balance between survivability and combat power.[43] Fires, rather than forces, will be massed, and they will be delivered from beyond visual range. Ideally, effects-based operations, fueled by information and knowledge superiority, will enable U.S. forces to "lock in success and lock out enemy solutions."[44] Smaller, lighter, faster, less complex, and less expensive nodes (i.e., platforms) linked by interoperable, highly redundant, self-healing networks will present adversaries with fewer high-value targets and improve the robustness of operations against a determined foe.

Implicitly at least, NCO is a joint vision that harnesses capabilities from all services; it is applicable to warfare on land, air, or sea.[45] That it is a Navy concept with naval origins, however, is evident in the two pillars that are more distinctly maritime: assured access and forward-deployed sea forces. "Assured access" refers to the ability of the U.S. armed forces to gain entry to and use both overseas infrastructure, such as ports and

airfields, and the battle space itself, even when confronted by a capable and active adversary.[46] No sanctuary is to be ceded to the opponent. It is the job of the Navy and the
Marine Corps to enable and ensure access by follow-on elements of the Air Force and
the Army—the heavier forces necessary to fight and win major theater wars. The Navy
accomplishes this through the combat capabilities inherent in its forward-deployed
presence assets (i.e., the ability to operate in the littoral). Since sea-based forces "do not
rely on permissive access to foreign shore installations that may be withdrawn or cur-
tailed," they "furnish an assured infrastructure for additional joint forces."[47]

The most robust form of NCW also features a wide variety of nodes (or platforms)
that are to be smaller, lighter, faster, or less complex than current platforms. Unmanned
vehicles, for instance, are to deploy sensors or serve as sensors, communications relays,
and weapons platforms. In the view of its strongest advocates, NCW requires innovative design concepts such as small littoral combatants (a concept formerly known as
"Streetfighter"), fast lift, and small-deck aircraft carriers. According to their logic, fulfilling the ultimate promise of network-centric operations requires less complex and
less expensive network-tailored nodes/platforms that will facilitate self-synchronization
and "swarming" tactics and increase tactical survivability.[48] Complexity is to be located
on the web rather than on the node; the expensive platform nodes that populate the
legacy force will be displaced by simpler, less expensive ones. In today's Navy, platforms
are networked via, for instance, the Cooperative Engagement Capability (CEC) and IT-21.
In the network-centric Navy of the future, nodes will be tailored to network requirements from their earliest conception.

Sea Power 21

Network-centric warfare, in the form of ForceNet, is "the 'glue' that binds together" Sea
Power 21's "three fundamental concepts": Sea Strike, Sea Shield, and Sea Basing.[49] Integrated by ForceNet, the offensive and defensive capabilities of Sea Strike and Sea Shield
and the operational autonomy of Sea Basing are to provide "unprecedented maritime
power"—nothing less than "decisive warfighting capabilities from the sea."[50] The development of these capabilities will be supported by three additional elements of Sea
Power 21: "Sea Trial's" innovation processes, "Sea Warrior's" investment in people, and
"Sea Enterprise's" improved business practices. SP-21 is driven not by the asymmetrical
challenges posed by regional or transnational threats but by a concerted effort to exploit
(and thereby help preserve) the asymmetry inherent in U.S. technological preeminence;[51]
accordingly, it is to provide "powerful warfighting capabilities" that "will ensure our joint
force dominates the unified battle space of the 21st century."[52]

The core operational concepts of Sea Strike, Sea Shield, and Sea Basing, the "operational construct and architectural framework" of ForceNet, and the three supporting

concepts had all appeared earlier in the Department of the Navy's *Naval Transformation Roadmap.*[53] Beginning in June 2002, these concepts took the form of "Sea Power 21" in a series of speeches and articles by the Chief of Naval Operations and other flag and general officers.[54] Sea Power 21 represents a concerted effort to market as transformational the future capabilities sought by the Navy's leadership, civilian and military alike. The array of capabilities envisioned by the NTR and SP-21, which are to be developed in a phased process from 2002–2020, are depicted in table 1.[55]

TABLE 1
*The NTR's and SP-21's Transformational
Warfighting Capabilities*

Sea Strike
- Persistent intelligence, surveillance, and reconnaissance
- Time-sensitive strike
- Offensive information operations
- Ship-to-objective maneuver
- Covert strike

Sea Shield
- Homeland defense
- Sea/littoral superiority
- Theater air and missile defense
- Force entry enabling

Sea Basing
- Enhanced afloat positioning of joint assets
- Accelerated deployment and employment time

ForceNet
- Expeditionary, multitiered sensor and weapons grid
- Distributed, collaborative command and control
- Dynamic, multipath, and survivable networks
- Adaptive/automated decision aids
- Human-centric integration

Source: *Naval Transformation Roadmap: Power and Access . . . from the Sea* (Washington, D.C.: Dept. of the Navy, 2002); and Admiral Vern Clark, U.S. Navy, "Sea Power 21: Projecting Decisive Capabilities," U.S. Naval Institute *Proceedings* (October 2002), pp. 32–41.

With the promulgation of the Naval Transformation Roadmap and Sea Power 21 in 2002, network-centric concepts, in the form of ForceNet, are for the first time firmly embedded in the official version of naval transformation. It remains to be seen, however, whether naval transformation will fulfill the overarching vision of transformation suggested by *Joint Vision 2020* and the Bush administration's defense planning documents.

Evaluating Naval Transformation

There are two ways to assess the Navy's transformation enterprise. First, it can be evaluated against transformation objectives articulated by President Bush and the members of his national security team. In effect, this approach uses a measure external to the Navy. Second, Navy transformation can be assessed in terms of how well the Navy has implemented to date its own concepts. This approach measures internal progress toward the Navy's stated objectives.

We argue here that although the Navy has made progress toward developing a coherent transformation vision over the past decade, there are gaps between the administration's stated objectives and the Navy's transformation enterprise. As for the overall prospects for transformation, a definitive judgment cannot yet be rendered; much depends on how well the Navy supports the headline goals of Sea Power 21 and NCW over time. It is difficult to evaluate the implementation of the Navy's vision, because the effort cannot be expected to bear fruit for another ten years or more. However, there are already signs that as a result of budgetary, bureaucratic, and political impediments to transformation, implementation is lagging and will continue to lag.

Does Naval Transformation Measure Up?

Judged against the expectations created by the president and his defense team, the naval transformation enterprise will fall short, even *if*—and this is a big if—it is fully implemented in the coming decades. Transformation advocates within OSD, including the Office of Force Transformation, believe that transformation is a matter of discontinuous, even "revolutionary," change. Yet while neither the next Navy (of 2010) nor the Navy after next (of 2020) will look exactly like today's Navy, they will be quite recognizable. With a few important exceptions, operational capabilities are unlikely to have been transformed; instead, capabilities resident in the current Navy will have been improved.

The Navy advertises Sea Power 21 as a "new operational construct."[56] Yet much of Sea Power 21 is a repackaging of familiar ideas. The Navy has long possessed offensive, defensive, and presence capabilities. Although relabeled "Sea Strike," "Sea Shield," and "Sea Basing," those capabilities will continue to be enhanced, or modernized; they are unlikely to be revolutionized. The "new operational construct" essentially calls for routine, sustaining modernization.[57]

A similar judgment can be rendered against network-centric operations. At the most basic level, the desirability of the kinds of information and knowledge advantages touted by NCO is not new. Military commanders since time immemorial have sought more and better information.[58] As for effects-based operations, the Navy, indeed all branches of the military, have often sought to destroy targets with an eye to the reactions of enemy forces and political decision makers. Was not strategic bombing in World War II intended to break the will of the English, German, and Japanese citizenries? Assured access is not a novel idea either. The Navy has long provided battlespace access for other components of the total force; did it not make it possible for the Marines and Army to island-hop across the Pacific? The Navy has also long been the provider of "forward sea-based forces."[59] Dominating the tempo of war and foreclosing adversary options is also a traditional warfighting objective. How all of this is achieved will certainly be improved, but it is not clear that the Navy will be revolutionized.

Neither is the Navy new to the information age. ForceNet builds upon existing Navy information technology capabilities and programs.[60] Few if any of the envisioned capabilities entail skipping a generation of technology; if anything, even with the advent of spiral development, Navy information technologies will continue to lag behind those of the civilian IT sector. Indeed, existing plans from the Navy–Marine Corps Intranet (NMCI) to CEC, the Naval Fires Network (NFN), and the Expeditionary Sensor Grid (ESG) will incorporate and build upon existing networks to enhance future connectivity. Sustaining innovation is likely to continue to be the norm. Tellingly, the performance metrics of the nodes, or platforms, and networks envisioned by NCW and NCO require less discontinuous and disruptive innovation than sustaining innovation.[61]

The sense of urgency attached to transformation by the president is little evident in the NTR and other Navy planning documents. For the Navy, it seems that thus far transformation means business as usual—incremental, evolutionary changes in both capabilities and the doctrine necessary to employ those capabilities. There is no evident generation-skipping. The NTR, in particular, features rampant incrementalism. It calls for "more effectively" utilizing and exploiting assets; for enhancing, increasing, improving (sometimes significantly), and leveraging existing capabilities while accelerating certain current programs. Risk taking is also difficult to detect; indeed, the Navy has remained steadfastly risk averse.

The evolution since the mid-1990s of the Navy's plans for a future carrier is instructive. Initially, with what was "CVX," the Navy took an ambitious, clean-sheet design approach that may well have resulted in the skipping of a generation, a leap ahead. Due to budgetary constraints and reluctance to assume technological risks, that approach was scaled back with the shift to "CVNX," a distinctly evolutionary program intended to yield a *next-generation* carrier. By most accounts, it was only pressure from OSD for a "CVN-21" incorporating a range of emerging technologies that prevented the Navy's next carrier from being merely a slightly improved *Nimitz*-class carrier. Just how transformational the Navy's next carrier will actually be is an open question. The point is that the Navy reached ahead as far as it did only because it was pushed by OSD.

Some analysts have speculated that Navy programs might be vulnerable after the cancellation of the Army's Crusader artillery system. But few Navy programs have been canceled to free up resources for transformation.[62] Instead, such existing programs as the Joint Strike Fighter are billed as transformational. Further, the alignment of programs and resources with the Navy transformation vision and roadmap is far from seamless. Programs remain platform-centric rather than network-centric.[63] In the course of his remarks at Ship Tech 2003, Rear Admiral Jay Cohen, Chief of Naval Research, characterized SP-21 and the NTR as "ship-centric." Science and technology, and research and development, programs remain focused more on near-term technology transition to the fleet than on the long-term basic S&T/R&D that may be required for true transformation. Routine modernization and the recapitalization of legacy systems appear to overshadow programs that could yield disruptive innovation.[64]

Navy transformation to date is thus a rather modest enterprise. It is difficult to distinguish from modernization. It emphasizes sustaining innovation and incremental, evolutionary change. At best, it amounts to "modernization plus." Barring unforeseen developments, the Navy will continue to do what it does now, only better. The Navy's transformation enterprise does not live up to the expectations created by the Bush defense team; Sea Power 21 is unlikely to result in transformation.

It must be acknowledged, however, that the Navy's measured, incremental, evolutionary approach to transformation is actually not entirely out of sync with OSD's approach. The urgency attached to transformation, the emphasis on discontinuous—even disruptive—change, evident in the QDR, the 2002 *Annual Report*, and elsewhere is not absolute. Administration officials recognize that transformation is a long-term process, that its promise will be fully realized only with the passage of time.[65] "Today's challenges" must be addressed even while the military is transforming for the future; future readiness is not to be ensured at the expense of current readiness.[66] Prudence and balance are ever the watchwords: "It would be imprudent to transform the entire force all at once. A balance must be struck between the need to meet current threats while transforming the force over time."[67] This approach, which much resembles that of the Clinton administration, is unlikely to result in a rush to transformation by the Navy—or any of the other services.

Modernization Plus

Each of Sea Power 21's major foci provide possible exceptions to the argument that current plans for Navy transformation do not measure up. Several initiatives particularly deserve attention.

Sea Strike. A range of strike platforms have been portrayed as "undergoing a revolution in capability."[68] For instance, SSGNs—Trident ballistic-missile submarines converted to attack boats, carrying cruise missiles and unmanned vehicles and deploying special-operations forces—will have Arsenal Ship–like capabilities; indeed, they will be even more stealthy than the Arsenal Ship would have been. SSGNs will also bolster the Navy's existing cruise-missile launch capability (if not the number of cruise missiles available for launch). Why four SSGNs should be regarded as transformational, however, is not evident.

The DD(X) destroyer, CG(X) cruiser, and Littoral Combat Ship (LCS) have also been characterized as revolutionary.[69] This "Surface Combatant Family of Ships," however, may be no more a radical departure than the aforementioned CVN(X). That DD(X) is being designed as a multimission *land-attack* destroyer is in line with the Navy's post–Cold War reorientation from blue water to the littoral. As for the LCS, given the vehement reaction to the concept of a Streetfighter when it was introduced, it is no less noteworthy that the Navy is not only proceeding with the program but is seriously considering alternative hull designs, some of which are of foreign origin.[70] Yet the mix of surface combatant capabilities represented by this family of ships inspires a sense of *déjà vu.* As two retired admirals have pointed out, "The Family of Ships is really a 21st-century version of the high-low mix of the 1970s."[71] This reincarnated high-low mix may be undermined by two of the problems that doomed the earlier attempt: at the low end, cost growth; at the high end, inability to procure the number of platforms required to make the mix work. The Navy has not yet escaped the tyranny of resource constraints.

Many transformation proponents have highlighted the potentially revolutionary impact of unmanned vehicles on military operations from reconnaissance to strike. Sea Strike envisions a future battle space populated by an array of unmanned vehicles—aerial, surface, and subsurface. Yet the Navy's unmanned-vehicle programs appear to lag behind Air Force, Army, and Marine counterparts. This is especially true for unmanned aerial vehicles (UAVs). According to one recent report, there are fourteen separate Navy unmanned-vehicle programs. Seven are UAVs; of those, five are being used, or will be used, in very limited numbers for testing, training, or developmental training; the other two (Northrop Grumman's Pegasus and Boeing's X-45) are largely funded by the Defense Advanced Research Agency and are not projected to see naval service until 2015. As for Global Hawk, a now well-known UAV that was first rushed into operation for the Afghanistan campaign, the Navy plans to purchase only two systems, one in 2005 and one in 2007.[72] The Navy has also sought a hundred million dollars to upgrade a Pioneer system that dates back to the mid-1980s. By contrast the U.S. Air Force, Army, and Marine Corps have deployed relatively new, relatively capable UAVs even as they continue to test and evaluate next-generation systems.

Perhaps this is unfair. After all, there is something to the claim that operating UAVs in a maritime environment poses challenges not faced by ground-based systems. Launch and recovery of ship-based naval UAVs, for example, presents serious technical challenges. Finding space to store, maintain, and operate UAVs on vessels not originally designed to host them can be problematical. Moreover, if the Navy is able to field reconnaissance variants of either the Pegasus or the X-45 by 2015 as planned, the service will actually be on track to meet the needs of the Navy after next.

Even though the utility of UAVs has become increasingly clear over the past two decades, the Navy has been slow to recognize their value. It has pursued unmanned aerial vehicles only in fits and starts. Representatives of one major UAV manufacturer told one of the authors that they "hated" doing business with the Navy, because it spent so much time researching operational requirements and testing existing systems. They doubted that the Navy would ever actually field a system.[73] The Fire Scout vertical-take-off-and-landing UAV program, whatever its specific merits, seems representative; after an initial investment the Navy pulled back from production in early 2002, all but terminating the program, and began thinking once again about new UAV designs and concepts. Then, early in 2003, Fire Scout was reinvigorated.[74]

Even UAV-related developments with regard to one of the Navy's most highly touted near-term transformation programs, the SSGN conversion, may represent less than meets the eye. In the winter of 2003, the Giant Shadow experiment "absolutely validated that UAVs provide a great value, on the tactical and operational level of war, to an SSGN that's operating as . . . an ISR home base," according to the commander of the experiment's joint force maritime component.[75] One element of the overall experiment tested the ability of a land-launched Boeing/Insitu ScanEagle UAV to communicate with the submarine and other naval assets. Yet *Aerospace Daily* quoted the maritime component commander as concluding, "I'd like to pursue a UAV for submarines, although I'm not convinced that [ScanEagle] is it. . . . Its wingspan is too big [and] the launching . . . was sometimes problematic."[76] Modification of the ScanEagle, other competing UAV designs, or the development of a UAV designed specifically to operate from submarines may have to wait, however, given current programming.

Sea Shield. Much of Sea Shield, at least as described in publicly available documents, is not new. It prominently features traditional force protection missions—air defense, mine countermeasures, and antisubmarine warfare programs—and ensuring access to the littoral. Potentially more disruptive, however, are plans to provide theater ballistic missile defense and ballistic missile defense from sea-based platforms. In the words of Admiral Clark,

It [Sea Shield] is about projecting global defensive assurance, projecting defense. . . . Traditionally, naval defense has been concerned with protecting our units or the force, and the sea lines of communication. Tomorrow's navy must of course do all of that, but we must be able to do much more:
projecting defensive technology beyond the task force, providing theatre and strategic defense for the
first time.[77]

In short, the U.S. Navy is preparing to play a central role in defending the homeland
not against the seaborne invasions of old but ballistic missiles armed with weapons of
mass destruction.[78] The Navy's sea-based "Mid-Course" system is expressly intended to
protect population areas from ballistic missile threats. Navy assets committed to this
homeland defense mission become "strategic" in the same sense that the fleet's ballistic
missile submarines (SSBNs) have been strategic.[79] Also like SSBNs, they are unlikely to
be available for other missions.

Although the long-term effects of this aspect of Sea Shield on the Navy remain to be
seen, stationing a picket line of ships to track and intercept ballistic missiles aimed at
the American homeland or an allied population center may very well change the culture of the service. Rather than engaging the enemy fleet on the high seas or striking
enemy forces in the littoral or far inland, Navy officers and enlisted personnel will be
asked to wait and respond to an attack. Taken to the extreme, crews onboard ships dedicated to missile defense will be akin to missile launch officers sitting in silos waiting
for the balloon to go up.[80]

Sea Basing. Since 11 September 2001 it has become apparent that the United States
may be involved in conflicts of longer duration than at any time since the Vietnam War.
Future operations in failed or failing states, for example, may require it to commit
forces for years rather than months. Access to bases in neighboring countries will not
always be readily available; neutral states and even a few allies have been reluctant to
grant the U.S. military unrestricted access to facilities or overflight rights at various
points during the war on terror and during preparations for a potential invasion of Iraq.
More of the same can be expected in the future. As a result the United States may increasingly rely on sea-based forces to conduct strike operations and support ground forces.

Sea Power 21's emphasis on sea basing has reinvigorated discussions about the need for
mobile offshore bases (MOBs) that have continued since Admiral William Owens first
raised the idea in the mid-1990s.[81] Thus, for example, some planners want next-generation
Maritime Prepositioning Force (Future), or MPF(F), vessels to have "the ability to se-
lectively onload and offload military gear at sea."[82] One concrete means to accomplish
sea basing that differs somewhat from the MOB concept involves combining the Joint
Command and Control Ship, or JCC(X), with the MPF(F) program.

Although, again, it is too early to know what form Sea Basing will take as it moves beyond
the concept development stage, some form of a MOB could provide a transformational

capability. At least for some missions and finite periods of time, they would free American forces from the tyranny of land bases. They would also tie the Navy still more closely to its Marine and Army counterparts, placing it in a distinctly supporting role and making it joint in a way envisioned only in rhetoric today.

ForceNet. The claim that the range of Sea Strike, Sea Shield, and Sea Basing capabilities are indeed transformational rests largely on ForceNet. ForceNet was presented in the Naval Transformation Roadmap as the Navy's framework for implementing network-centric warfare.[83] Originally developed by the Chief of Naval Operations' Strategic Studies Group, it has been billed variously as putting the "warfare" in network-centric warfare and as "the next generation of NCW." According to Admiral Clark, ForceNet is the plan for making NCW an "operational reality": it will integrate "warriors, sensors, command and control, platforms, and weapons into a networked, distributed combat force."[84] This planned network of networks and system of systems is expected to be the information-technology backbone of information-age naval warfare. Today the ForceNet concept serves as an umbrella both for existing programs such as the NMCI, IT-21, CEC, and NFN and for major future programs such as the ESG and the Expeditionary Command and Control, Communications, Computers, and Combat Systems Grid (EC5G)(see figure 2).

It is the connectivity and synergy to be provided by such efforts that is intended to be the source of any transformation brought about by SP-21's core operational concepts. Sea Strike's time-sensitive strike;[85] offensive information operations from the

FIGURE 2
The EC5G: A Notional Depiction

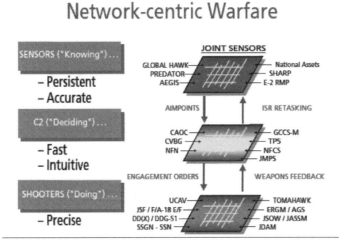

Source: *Chief of Naval Operations HQWeb,*
ucso2.hq.navy.mil/n7/webbas01.nsf/(wwwebpage)/webbase.htm.

sea, shared situational awareness, simultaneous strike, and sensor fusion; Sea Shield's layered theater air and missile defense;[86] the common air, surface, and underwater picture;[87] forward homeland defense;[88] Sea Basing's distributed and networked platforms;[89] and the interoperability touted by SP-21 generally—all are to be either provided or enabled by ForceNet. The weight of Navy transformation rests on ForceNet. Unless its promises are realized, the potential of platforms such as CVN(X), DD(X), CG(X), LCS, and SSGNs; unmanned aerial, surface, and undersea vehicles; and combat force structures such as "expeditionary strike groups" and missile-defense surface action groups will not be fully exploited.

A principal "enabling element" of ForceNet is the planned set of information, sensor, and engagement grids capable of linking all elements of the network with each other and with the wider information "back plane" that constitutes the World Wide Web and Defense Department–specific networks. This is not a single network but a network of networks, "a global grid of multiple, interoperable, overlapping sensor, engagement, and command nets."[90] The success of ForceNet requires the development, procurement, and deployment of large numbers of more capable sensors to populate the sensor grid and provide a common operational picture.

Among existing programs, as illustrated in figure 3, the Cooperative Engagement Capability, IT-21, the Radar Modernization Program (RMP), the Web Centric Anti-Submarine Warfare Net (WeCAN), and the Navy–Marine Corps Intranet will help the Navy evolve further toward the ability to conduct network-centric operations.[91] A critical step is the deployment of a multitiered—space, air, surface/ground and undersea—expeditionary sensor grid combining, among other things, invasive sensing systems, unmanned

FIGURE 3
The Information Grid: Detailed View

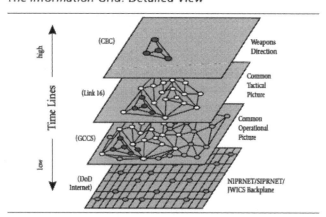

Source: Jim Eagle's Web Page, Operations Department, Naval Postgraduate School, Monterey, California, spica.or.nps.navy.mil/netusw/CebrowskiNetWar/sld005.htm.

platforms, massively distributed information systems, and computer network attack and defense capabilities.[92] At its simplest, the ESG is a "toolbox of sensors and networks necessary to build . . . real-time battlespace awareness."[93]

A network-centric future has implications for the Navy's doctrine, organization, and relationship with the other services. In 1998, the Navy Warfare Development Command was stood up as an institutional champion for innovation. It was specifically tasked to develop new concepts of operations and new doctrine. In addition to NCO, it is developing operational concepts for Sea Strike, Sea Shield, and Sea Basing. Also in development are a range of supporting and functional concepts for informational operations, homeland defense, theater air and missile defense, future naval fires, high-speed lift, and the Littoral Combat Ship. Whether the impact of these new operational concepts and doctrine will be transformational remains to be seen. But the Navy will not transform without them.

In addition to the establishment of the Navy Warfare Development Command, there have been a number of other organizational initiatives. Under Admiral Clark, NWDC itself has been subordinated to the Commander, U.S. Fleet Forces Command (CFFC), Sea Trial's designated lead agent, to coordinate experimentation programs. To facilitate integrated platform and network planning, the Navy Staff's N6 and N7 codes have been merged under a new Deputy Chief of Naval Operations for Warfare Requirements and Programs, who was designated the director of ForceNet. Information operations have been added to the list of major warfare areas, and the Naval Network Warfare Command has been established to coordinate information technology and information operations activities.[94] None of these initiatives, however, yet poses a serious challenge to the dominance of the Navy's platform-centric baronies.

The shift to a network-centric force could have profound implications for the Navy's relationship with its sister services. ForceNet and its NCW/NCO foundation assume a high level of jointness and interoperability. The language of jointness and interoperability actually suffuses all of Sea Power 21. Sea Strike's operational capabilities are to be employed in joint campaigns; Sea Shield is to provide protection for the joint force; and Sea Basing is to support joint operations. The promise of jointness has serious implications for the implementation of ForceNet. If jointness is to be taken seriously and the advantages of connectivity and integration are to be exploited fully, all of the military's offensive and defensive capabilities, not just the Navy's, must be networked. A common operational picture, for instance, is not really common unless it is shared by the Air Force and the Army as well as by the Navy and the Marine Corps. The difficulties of ensuring a common operational picture should not be underestimated, however. How is it to be achieved? Should the services pursue separate but coordinated capabilities? If so, can they be confident that the resulting systems will mesh to form an integrated system of systems with the seamless connectivity required for a joint COP? Or should the approach be joint from the start, with system acquisition assumed by the Joint Staff or Joint Forces Command and the services required to tailor their new platforms to joint NCW requirements? There is an undeniable logic to the joint acquisition of joint capabilities. That logic is particularly compelling in the case of the network capabilities that are at the heart of the sought-after transformation. The jointness required to realize fully NCW's potential may be profoundly transformational. A truly joint Navy would be a transformed Navy. But that does not appear to be the transformation the Navy has in mind.

Is the Lack of Transformation a Problem?

Thus far, what passes for transformation within the Navy is less revolutionary than official rhetoric suggests. Even under a best-case scenario—where most if not all of the Navy embraces current transformation initiatives, the resources necessary to implement transformation are readily available, and the technological challenges inherent in developing new capabilities are met—it is difficult to avoid concluding that the Navy after next will be a modernized version of the existing fleet. It is possible that over time the accumulation of small-bore changes will yield a force that deserves to be characterized as transformed. However, the prospects for discontinuous, disruptive change appear slim.

Programs billed as transformational will add important capabilities to the Navy. The Navy's abilities to collect and share information, sustain operations, operate in a more stealthy fashion, and directly contribute to the defense of the American homeland will improve. But these capabilities are unlikely to provide the virtual "lockout" of competitor options envisioned by proponents of transformation. Nor will they prevent adversaries from devising asymmetric strategies for countering U.S. naval power. But they may further ongoing changes in the organization of the Navy, its culture, and perhaps even the nature of the officers and enlisted men and women serving their country.

Is the lack of real transformation a problem?[95] Not especially. In our view, no compelling strategic rationale for transformation has yet been articulated. Transformation that equates to a revolution in military affairs is not required for the maintenance and extension of either U.S. military dominance specifically or American primacy generally. Nor is it a requirement for fighting and winning the global war on terror. Generic capabilities designed to meet generic threats (as in capabilities-based planning) or old threats pumped up for a new millennium (as in threat-based planning against a North Korean foe) in the service of force protection will suffice in the absence of a clear and present danger on the order of that posed by the former Soviet Union.

According to the NTR, the objective of naval transformation is "to achieve a broad, sustained and decisive military competitive advantage over existing or potential adversaries."[96] The Navy, however, already possesses that competitive advantage. It is the world's preeminent naval force. It already exercises virtually unchallenged command of the seas and possesses unrivaled power projection capabilities. There is nobody in the rearview mirror. At worst, the Navy will face asymmetric challenges in the littoral and perhaps the emergence of a regional competitor, such as China. While these are difficult challenges, there seems little reason to think that they constitute a "competitive challenge" to the dominance of the U.S. Navy. That preserving and extending its preeminence requires "substantially extending boundaries of necessary military competencies and . . . discovering fundamentally new approaches to military operations"[97] remains to be demonstrated. What future challengers require that the Navy embrace fundamentally new approaches that challenge it to reinvent itself?

The Navy that will gradually emerge from the naval transformation enterprise will be well suited to carry out the roles and missions implied by the evolving U.S. grand strategy initiated by the Clinton administration and more fully, and bluntly, articulated by its successor. The Navy will be better equipped to strike terrorists and rogue states posing either conventional or WMD threats to the American homeland, installations abroad, or allies. It will contribute to both active and passive defense against ballistic missile threats. And it will operate more jointly than in the past and with a high level of connectivity.

Civilian officials in the Department of Defense intent on transformation may indeed feel that attempting to change the Navy (and the rest of the military) is like punching a pillow. But the Navy's modernization-plus approach is likely to provide the nation with the capabilities required for the future.

Notes

1. Epigraph as quoted in Richard H. Kohn, "The Erosion of Civilian Control of the Military in the United States Today," *Naval War College Review* 55, no. 3 (Summer 2002), p. 20.

2. Paul Bracken, "The Military after Next," *Washington Quarterly* 16, no. 4 (Autumn 1993), pp. 157–74.

3. Navy Warfare Development Command [hereafter NWDC], *Network Centric Operations: A Capstone Concept for Naval Operations in the Information Age* (Newport, R.I.: NWDC, draft dated 19 June 2001), p. 1.

4. We write not as transformation advocates but as analysts of the transformation phenomenon.

5. *Joint Vision 2020* is available at www.dtic .mil/jv2020/.

6. For the Army's Vision and Army Transformation, go to www.army.mil/armyvision. For a useful overview of Army transformation issues see Edward F. Bruner, *Army Transformation and Modernization: Overview and Issues for Congress*, RS20787 (Washington, D.C.: Congressional Research Service,

Library of Congress [hereafter CRS], 4 April 2001).

7. The U.S. Air Force *Vision 2020* can be found at www.af.mil/vision/.

8. From *The Aerospace Force: Defending America in the 21st Century*, p. iii, at www.af.mil/lib/taf.pdf. An overview of Air Force transformation issues is provided by Christopher Bolkom, *Air Force Transformation and Modernization: Overview and Issues for Congress*, RS20787 (Washington, D.C.: CRS, 1 June 2001).

9. James L. Jones [Gen., USMC], *Marine Corps Strategy 21* (Washington, D.C.: Dept. of the Navy, Headquarters U.S. Marine Corps, 3 November 2000), available at www.usmc.mil/templateml.nsf/25241abbb036b230852569c4004eff0e/$FILE/strategy.pdf. See also *Expeditionary Maneuver Warfare: Marine Corps Capstone Concept* (Washington, D.C.: Dept. of the Navy, Headquarters Marine Corps, 10 November 2001), available at 192.156.19.109/emw.pdf.

10. Governor George W. Bush, "A Period of Consequences," address delivered at The Citadel, South Carolina, 23 September 1999.

11. "Excerpts from Bush's Remarks on the Military," *New York Times*, 14 February 2001, p. A26. Also available at www.whitehouse.gov/news/releases/print/20010213-1.html.

12. Thomas E. Ricks, "Pentagon Study May Bring Big Shake-Up: Unconventional Defense Thinker Conducting Review," *Washington Post*, 9 February 2001.

13. See William M. Arkin, "Rumsfeld Top-to-Bottom Review Evolves," *Defense Daily*, 16 April 2001.

14. *Quadrennial Defense Review* [hereafter *QDR*] *Report* (Washington, D.C.: Dept. of Defense, 30 September 2001), p. iv.

15. Ibid., p. 16.

16. Ibid., p. iv. Emphasis added. In DoD's 2002 *Annual Report to the President and the Congress*, it is explicitly the attacks of 11 September 2001 that lend urgency to transformation. Donald H. Rumsfeld, *Annual Report to the President and the Congress* (Washington, D.C.: Dept. of Defense, 2002), p. 1. On page 67 of the *Annual Report*, at the outset of chapter 6, "Transforming the Force," it is argued that "September 11 made manifest the danger of postponing preparations for the future. We must prepare now to anticipate future surprises and mitigate their effects." Available at www.defenselink.mil/execsec/adr2002/index.htm.

17. *QDR Report*, pp. 30–47.

18. He added (unhelpfully, in our view) that "we are the better for it." E. C. "Pete" Aldridge, Jr. [Under Secretary of Defense (AT&L)], "Technology and National Defense," address to Darpa Tech, 30 July 1992, available at www.acq.osd.mil/usd/new_speeches/peo.doc.

19. On the dimensions of transformation, see Andrew F. Krepinevich, "Calvary to Computer: The Pattern of Military Revolutions," *National Interest*, no. 37 (Fall 1994), pp. 30–42.

20. *QDR Report*, p. 29. Emphasis added.

21. Rumsfeld, *Annual Report*, p. 68.

22. See Donald H. Rumsfeld, "Transforming the Military," *Foreign Affairs* 81, no. 3 (May/June 2002), pp. 20–32.

23. According to Deputy Secretary Paul Wolfowitz, "Our overall goal is to encourage a series of transformations that, in combination, can produce a revolutionary increase in our military capability and redefine how war is fought." Paul Wolfowitz, "Prepared Statement for the Senate Armed Services Committee Hearing on Military Transformation," 9 April 2002, available at *DefenseLink*, www.defenselink.mil/speeches/2002/s20020409-depsecdef2.html.

24. As Under Secretary Aldridge put it, "resources are finite and if we can do better, we will not hesitate to bypass a good program today in favor of a profoundly transformational one tomorrow." Aldridge, "Technology and National Defense."

25. On the importance of the RMA for military transformation see Robert Tomes and Peter Dombrowski, "Arguments for a Renewed RMA Debate," *National Security Studies Quarterly* 7, no. 3 (Summer 2001), pp. 109–22. For the reference to culture and behavior, *QDR Report*, pp. 6, 29. On the distinction between sustaining and disruptive innovation, see Clayton M. Christensen, *The Innovator's Dilemma* (New York: HarperBusiness, 2000).

26. The Bush administration's commitment to transformation may even exceed that exhibited by the military itself. See, for instance, Donald Rumsfeld, remarks as delivered at the National Defense University, Fort McNair, Washington, D.C., 31 January 2002, available at *DefenseLink*, www.defenselink.mil/speeches/

2002/s20020131-secdef.html; "Transforming the Military"; and "A Choice to Transform the Military," *Washington Post*, 16 May 2002, p. 25. See also Wolfowitz, "Prepared Statement for the Senate Armed Services Committee Hearing on Military Transformation."

27. *The National Security Strategy of the United States of America* (Washington, D.C.: White House, September 2002), pp. 29–31. Specifically called for is the development of "assets such as advanced remote sensing, long-range precision strike capabilities, and transformed maneuver and expeditionary forces" (pp. 29–30).

28. National Defense Panel, *Transforming Defense: National Security in the 21st Century*, December 1997, p. iv, available at *Federation of American Scientists*, www.fas.org/man/docs/ndp/toc.htm. On the Clinton administration's "balanced" approach to transformation, see William S. Cohen, *Report of the Quadrennial Defense Review* (Washington, D.C.: Dept. of Defense, May 1997).

29. Vernon Clark [Adm., USN], "Sea Power 21: Operational Concepts for a New Era," remarks delivered at the Current Strategy Forum, Naval War College, Newport, R.I., 12 June 2002.

30. On this reorientation see Jan S. Breemer, "The End of Naval Strategy: Revolutionary Change and the Future of American Naval Power," *Strategic Review* 22, no. 2 (Spring 1994), pp. 40–53; and Edward Rhodes, "'From the Sea' and Back Again: Naval Power in the Second American Century," *Naval War College Review* 52, no. 2 (Spring 1999), pp. 13–54.

31. See Arthur K. Cebrowski [Vice Adm., USN] and John J. Garstka, "Network-centric Warfare: Its Origin and Future," U.S. Naval Institute *Proceedings* (January 1998), pp. 28–35. On NCW see also David S. Alberts, John J. Garstka, and Frederick P. Stein, *Network Centric Warfare: Developing and Leveraging Information Superiority*, 2d ed. (Washington, D.C.: C4ISR Cooperative Research Program, 1999); Committee on Network-Centric Naval Forces, Naval Studies Board, *Network-centric Naval Forces: A Transition Strategy for Enhancing Operational Capabilities* (Washington, D.C.: National Academy Press, 2000); and Edward P. Smith, "Network-centric Warfare: What's the Point?" *Naval War College Review* 54, no. 1 (Winter 2001), pp. 59–75. Admiral Clark was not the first CNO to

embrace transformation and network-centric warfare. In his preface to the April 2000 *Navy Planning Guidance,* then Chief of Naval Operations Adm. Jay L. Johnson wrote of building "a Navy for the Information Age" and its "transformation to a network-centric and knowledge-superior force." Chief of Naval Operations, *Navy Planning Guidance: With Long Range Planning Objectives* (Washington, D.C.: Dept. of the Navy, April 2000), p. 1. Similarly, the Vice Chief of Naval Operations declared, "We are moving away from a platform-centered Navy to one being built around data networks. . . . [O]ur concept of operations will use as its basis an integrated, common network." William J. Fallon, "Fighting to Win in the Littoral and Beyond," *Armed Forces Journal International* (June 2001), pp. 67–68. Dennis McGinn (then a vice admiral) asserted that "investment in networks and sensors is transformational." Quoted in Robert Holzer, "U.S. Navy Mulls Fundamental Shift in Tactics, Funds," *Defense News,* 7 May 2001, p. 1.

32. Vern Clark [Adm., USN], "Sea Power 21: Projecting Decisive Joint Capabilities," U.S. Naval Institute *Proceedings,* October 2002, p. 33.

33. The account of network-centric warfare provided here draws upon Peter J. Dombrowski, Eugene Gholz, and Andrew L. Ross, *Military Transformation and the Defense Industry after Next: The Defense-Industrial Implications of Network-Centric Warfare* (Newport, R.I.: Strategic Research Department, Center for Naval Warfare Studies, U.S. Naval War College, September 2002).

34. For serious treatments of the forces at work see Daniel Bell, *The Coming of Post-Industrial Society: A Venture in Social Forecasting* (New York: Basic Books, 1999), and Manuel Castells, *The Rise of the Network Society,* 2d ed. (Oxford: Blackwell, 2000). For popular treatments, see Thomas L. Friedman, *The Lexus and the Olive Tree: Understanding Globalization* (New York: Farrar, Straus, and Giroux, 1999), and James Gleick, *Faster: The Acceleration of Just About Everything* (New York: Pantheon, 1999). Works that have received far more attention in military circles than they deserve include Kevin Kelly, *New Rules for the New Economy: 10 Radical Strategies for a Connected World* (New York: Viking, 1998); Alvin Toffler, *The Third Wave* (New York: William Morrow, 1980); Alvin Toffler, *Powershift: Knowledge, Wealth, and*

Violence at the Edge of the 21st Century (New York: Bantam Books, 1990); and Alvin Toffler and Heidi Toffler, *Creating a New Civilization: The Politics of the Third Wave* (Atlanta: Turner, 1995).

35. See John Arquilla and David Ronfeldt, eds., *In Athena's Camp: Preparing for Conflict in the Information Age* (Santa Monica, Calif.: RAND, 1997); Eliot A. Cohen, "A Revolution in Warfare," *Foreign Affairs* 75, no. 2 (March/April, 1996), pp. 37–54; Victor A. DeMarines, with David Lehman and John Quilty, "Exploiting the Internet Revolution," in *Keeping the Edge: Managing Defense for the Future,* ed. Ashton B. Carter and John P. White (Cambridge, Mass., and Stanford, Calif.: Preventive Defense Project, 2000), pp. 61–102; Joseph S. Nye, Jr., and William A. Owens, "America's Information Edge," *Foreign Affairs* 75, no. 2 (March/April 1996), pp. 20–36; and Bill Owens, with Ed Offley, *Lifting the Fog of War* (New York: Farrar, Straus and Giroux, 2000). For a more popular account see Alvin Toffler and Heidi Toffler, *War and Anti-War: Making Sense of Today's Global Chaos* (New York: Warner, 1993).

36. See, for example, Cebrowski and Garstka, "Network-Centric Warfare," and Alberts, Garstka, and Stein, *Network Centric Warfare,* esp. pp. 15–23. A useful discussion of NCW/NCO is provided by Scott C. Truver, "Tomorrow's U.S. Fleet," *U.S. Naval Institute Proceedings* (March 2001), pp. 102–10. For a comparison of U.S. and Swedish versions of NCW see Nick Cook, "Network-centric Warfare: The New Face of C4I," *Interavia* (February 2001), pp. 37–39. Cautionary notes are provided by Thomas P. M. Barnett, "The Seven Deadly Sins of Network-centric Warfare," *U.S. Naval Institute Proceedings* (January 1999), pp. 36–39; Richard J. Harknett and the JCISS Study Group, "The Risks of a Networked Military," *Orbis* 44, no. 1 (Winter 2000), pp. 127–43; Milan Vego, "Net-centric Is Not Decisive," *U.S. Naval Institute Proceedings* (January 2003), pp. 52–57; and Franklin Spinney, "What Revolution in Military Affairs?" *Defense Week*, 23 April 2001.

37. Not all nodes, of course, are created equal. Some are more complex and, therefore, more expensive than others. The point is that networked nodes should be simpler and lower in cost than stand-alone nodes.

38. There is no real consensus among its proponents about precisely what NCW is or entails. Its proponents charitably view NCW as a dynamic, living, evolving concept. Skeptics are more inclined to characterize NCW as a moving target, riddled with ambiguities and informed by dubious analogies. In a definition attributed to John Garstka, NCW is "warfare which harnesses information technologies in the form of global sensor, connectivity, and engagement grids to achieve a common operational picture that will lead to self-synchronization, massed effects, and the desired lock-out of a given enemy's courses of action." See Robert Odell, Bruce Wald, Lyntis Beard, with Jack Batzler and Michael Loescher, *Taking Forward the Navy's Network-Centric Warfare Concept: Final Report*, CRM 99-42.10 (Alexandria, Va.: Center for Naval Analyses, May 1999), p. 11. The Naval Studies Board's Committee on Network-centric Naval Forces defined network-centric operations as "military operations that exploit state-of-the-art information and networking technology to integrate widely dispersed human decision makers, situational and targeting sensors, and forces and weapons into a highly adaptive, comprehensive system to achieve unprecedented mission effectiveness." Committee on Network-centric Naval Forces, Naval Studies Board, *Network-Centric Naval Forces*, p. 12. NWDC has described NCO as "deriving power from the rapid and robust networking of well-informed, geographically dispersed war fighters. They create overpowering tempo and a precise, agile style of maneuver warfare." NWDC, *Network Centric Operations*.

39. NWDC, *Network Centric Operations*.

40. On information and knowledge advantage see www.nwdc.navy.mil/Concepts/IKA.asp. On effects-based operations see www.nwdc.navy.mil/Concepts/EBO.asp.

41. Quoted in Truver, "Tomorrow's U.S. Fleet," p. 103.

42. For "rule set," NWDC, *Network Centric Operations*, p. 9.

43. Ibid., p. 11.

44. Ibid., p. 10.

45. The joint aspects of NCW are highlighted in John J. Garstka, "Network Centric Warfare: An Overview of Emerging Theory," available at www.mors.org/Pubs/phalanx/dec00/

feature.htm; John G. Roos, "An All-Encompassing Grid," *Armed Forces Journal International* (January 2001), pp. 26–35; Hunter Keeter, "Cebrowski: Joint Philosophy Fosters Network Centric Warfare," *Defense Daily*, 12 April 2002, p. 8; and Fred P. Stein, "Observations on the Emergence of Network Centric Warfare," available at www.dodccrp .org/steinncw.htm and as "Information Paper: Observations on the Emergence of Network-Centric Warfare" at www.dtic.mil/ jcs/j6/education/warfare.html.

46. NWDC, *Network Centric Operations,* p. 10.

47. Ibid., pp. 4–5.

48. On swarming, see Joseph E. Skinner [Cdr., USN], "Swarm the Littorals," U.S. Naval Institute *Proceedings* (March 2001), pp. 88–91.

49. Clark, "Sea Power 21: Projecting Decisive Joint Capabilities," pp. 33, 37. Alternative visions of naval transformation are provided by Robert O. Work [Col., USMC (Ret.)], *The Challenge of Maritime Transformation: Is Bigger Better?* (Washington, D.C.: Center for Strategic and Budgetary Assessments, 2002); and Andrew F. Krepinevich, Jr., *A New Navy for a New Era* (Washington, D.C.: Center for Strategic and Budgetary Assessments, May 1996).

50. Clark, "Sea Power 21: Projecting Decisive Joint Capabilities," p. 41.

51. Particularly information technologies and systems integration capabilities.

52. Clark, "Sea Power 21: Projecting Decisive Joint Capabilities," p. 41.

53. *Naval Transformation Roadmap: Power and Access . . . from the Sea* (Washington, D.C.: Dept. of the Navy, 2002).

54. See, particularly, Clark, "Sea Power 21: Operational Concepts for a New Era," and "Sea Power 21: Projecting Decisive Joint Capabilities"; Mike Bucchi [Vice Adm., USN], and Mike Mullen [Vice Adm., USN], "Sea Shield: Projecting Global Defensive Assurance," U.S. Naval Institute *Proceedings* (November 2002), pp. 56–59; Cutler Dawson [Vice Adm., USN] and John Nathman [Vice Adm., USN], "Sea Strike: Projecting Persistent, Responsive, and Precise Power," U.S. Naval Institute *Proceedings* (December 2002), pp. 54–58; Charles W. Moore, Jr. [Vice Adm., USN] and Edward Hanlon, Jr. [Lt. Gen., USMC], "Sea Basing: Operational Independence for a New Century," U.S. Naval Institute *Proceedings* (

January 2003), pp. 80–85; Richard W. Mayo [Vice Adm., USN], and John Nathman [Vice Adm., USN], "ForceNet: Turning Information into Power," U.S. Naval Institute *Proceedings* (February 2003), pp. 42–46.

55. During the first phase, 2002–2004, the focus will be on improving networks, sensors, people, and weapons, with networks and sensors the highest priorities. People and infrastructure will be accorded highest priority during the second stage, 2004–2010, and platform and infrastructure improvements are to be added to the agenda. Platform and infrastructure improvements join the list of high priority efforts during the third stage, 2010–2020. See Gopal Ratnam, "New Office to Drive U.S. Navy Transformation," *Defense News*, 8–14 April 2002, p. 6.

56. Clark, "Sea Power 21: Operational Concepts for a New Era."

57. Some commentators have even suggested that the version of transformation advanced in Sea Power 21 amounts to little more than employing "sea" as an adjective in a series of bumper stickers.

58. John Keegan, *The Mask of Command* (New York: Viking, 1987).

59. "A permanent Mediterranean squadron was established in 1815 to keep the Barbary pirates in check." Walter Russell Mead, *Special Providence: American Foreign Policy and How It Changed the World* (New York: Knopf, 2001), p. 26.

60. See Ronald O'Rourke, *Navy Network-centric Warfare Concept: Key Programs and Issues for Congress*, RS20557 (Washington, D.C.: CRS, 6 June 2001).

61. See Peter J. Dombrowski, Eugene Gholz, and Andrew L. Ross, "Selling Transformation: The Defense Industrial Sources of Sustaining and Disruptive Innovation," *Orbis* 46, no. 3 (Summer 2002), pp. 523–36.

62. Although in a technical sense DD-21 was canceled, it seems clear that much of the preparation for DD-21 has merged directly into the DD(X) program.

63. It may be that even in a network-centric Navy spending on future programs will remain platform-centric. But the balance between spending on network-centric programs and platform-centric programs should shift in favor of the former more than it has thus far.

64. Transformation does not require that all navy programs be revolutionary, discontinuous, and disruptive. But the Bush administration's characterization of transformation suggests that the balance between routine, sustaining innovation and potentially discontinuous, disruptive innovation should shift in favor of the latter more than it has thus far.

65. *QDR Report*, p. v; and Rumsfeld, *Annual Report*, p. 22.

66. *QDR Report*, p. 10.

67. *QDR Report*, p. 16. Also, on pp. 47–48: "This transformation will be conducted in a timely but prudent manner. In particular, prudence dictates that those legacy forces critical to DoD's ability to defeat current threats must be sustained as transformation occurs. . . . DoD must overcome trends of the past to sustain a balanced defense program that maintains near-term readiness without mortgaging the long-term capabilities of the force."

68. Dawson and Nathman, "Sea Strike," p. 56.

69. Charles Hamilton [Rear Adm., USN] and Donald Loren [Rear Adm., USN], "It's All in the Family," U.S. Naval Institute *Proceedings* (August 2002), pp. 68–70.

70. However, recent designs for the Littoral Combat Ship look less like the "Streetfighters" (which were to have fought in "swarms") proposed by Vice Admiral Cebrowski than like modern frigates.

71. Henry C. Mustin [Vice Adm., USN (Ret.)] and Douglas J. Katz [Vice Adm., USN (Ret.)], "All Ahead Flank for LCS," U.S. Naval Institute *Proceedings* (February 2003), p. 32.

72. All data from David Brown, "Battle Bots," *Navy Times*, 3 February 2003, pp. 14–16.

73. Author interview, June 2002.

74. Christopher J. Castelli and Jason Ma, "In Reversal, Navy Praises Fire Scout UAV, May Buy Improved Versions," *Inside Defense.com*, 20 January 2003.

75. Jefferson Morris, "UAVs Prove Value to Submarines in 'Giant Shadow' Experiment, Captain Says," *Aerospace Daily*, 30 January 2003.

76. Ibid.

77. Vernon Clark [Adm., USN], "Remarks," 2002 Naval-Industry R&D Partnership Conference, Washington, D.C., 15 August 2002,

available at www.chinfor.navy.mil/navpalib/cno/speeches/clark-rdpc02.txt.

78. On the role of the Navy, see Rodney P. Rempt [Rear Adm., USN], "Using the Oceans for Missile Defense," address, 8 January 2002, available at www.nwc.navy.mil/pres/speeches/rotary.htm#top.

79. We are indebted to our colleague Timothy Somes for this insight.

80. For a useful historical perspective, see Joseph F. Bouchard, "Guarding the Cold War Ramparts: The U.S. Navy's Role in Continental Air Defense," *Naval War College Review* 52, no. 3 (Summer 1999), pp. 111–35.

81. Christopher J. Castelli, "DOD Panel Mulls Seabasing Ideas, including Mobile Offshore Bases," *Inside the Navy*, 18 November 2002. On the mounting opposition to MOBs, see Pat Towell, "'Mobile Offshore Base' Proposal Has Slew of Powerful Opponents," *Congressional Quarterly Weekly* (15 February 2003), p. 382.

82. Christopher J. Castelli, "Navy Envisions MPF(F) Multimission Sea Bases for DJC2 and Special Ops," *Inside the Navy*, 17 June 2002.

83. *Naval Transformation Roadmap*, p. 5. ForceNet was rendered as "FORCEnet" in the NTR. For useful reportage on ForceNet see Gopal Ratnam, "New Office to Drive U.S. Navy Transformation," *Defense News*, 8–14 April 2002, p. 6; and Gail Kaufman and Gopal Ratnam, "U.S. Navy Releases Broad Transformation Outline," *Defense News*, 15–21 April 2002, p. 8.

84. "We have been talking about network-centric warfare for a decade, and ForceNet will be the Navy's plan to make it an operational reality." Clark, "Sea Power 21: Projecting Decisive Joint Capabilities," p. 34. As Mayo and Nathman, "ForceNet," put it, "ForceNet implements the theory of network-centric warfare" (p. 43).

85. With promises of "sensor-to-shooter closure . . . measured in seconds, instead of hours or minutes." Dawson and Nathman, "Sea Strike," p. 54.

86. With its "single integrated air picture." Bucchi and Mullen, "Sea Shield," p. 57.

87. Which is to ensure "battlespace dominance on, above, and below the sea," and access to the littorals. Ibid., p. 58.

88. Which requires "expanded sensor coverage," "increased situational awareness by networking," and "sharing information with other services and agencies." Ibid., p. 59.

89. Which are to enable the joint force to maintain operational autonomy and exploit the maneuver space of the sea. Moore and Hanlon, "Sea Basing."

90. Ibid., p. 6.

91. Background on CEC, IT-21, and NMCI is provided in Ronald O'Rourke, *Navy Network-Centric Warfare Concept*. On IT-21 see J. Cutler Dawson, Jr., James M. Fordice, and Gregory M. Harris, "The IT-21 Advantage," U.S. Naval Institute *Proceedings* (December 1999), pp. 28–32. For Admiral Clark, Chief of Naval Operations, the NMCI is "the gateway to transformation." See Dept. of the Navy, *Electronic Business Strategic Plan 2001–2002*, available at www.ec.navsup.navy.mil _eb/strategic_plan_toc.asp.

92. NWDC, *Expeditionary Sensor Grid*, undated brief, p. 4. See also Robert Holzer, "Massive Sensor Grid May Reshape U.S. Navy Tactics," *Defense News*, 14 May 2001, pp. 1, 4; and

Catherine MacRae, "Services, DARPA Doing Early Research on 'Expeditionary Sensor Grid,'" *Inside the Pentagon*, 21 June 2001.

93. NWDC, *The Expeditionary Sensor Grid: Gaining Real-Time Battlespace Awareness in Support of Information and Knowledge Advantage*, post-workshop draft, 19 June 2001, p. 3.

94. Previously, there had been a Director of Space, Information Warfare, Command and Control (N6) and a DCNO, Warfare Requirements and Programs (N7).

95. We do not here attempt to provide an explanation of why the Navy's transformation enterprise falls short of the expectations created by the Bush defense team. That would require another article. In the meantime, see the following insightful piece: Thomas G. Mahnken, "Transforming the U.S. Armed Forces: Rhetoric or Reality?" *Naval War College Review* 54, no. 3 (Summer 2001), pp. 85–99.

96. *Naval Transformation Roadmap*, p. 6.

97. Ibid.

CHAPTER THIRTEEN

Building the Future Fleet
Show Us the Analysis!

ERIC J. LABS

Since 11 September 2001, the U.S. defense budget has risen by about 25 percent, after factoring out inflation. The reasons for such an increase are numerous: simultaneously fighting wars in both Afghanistan and Iraq, increases in military pay and benefits, and more money for some major weapons programs. In this same time period, money devoted to building the Navy's ships has only bounced around. In fiscal year 2001, the Navy spent $12 billion on ships. The President's request for ships in 2005 is $11 billion. Why might this be the case?

- First, while Navy officials may be doing an excellent job explaining why the United States needs a navy, they are not doing a good job explaining why it needs the navy they say it needs.

- Second, both numbers of ships and their capabilities matter when measuring or justifying the need for naval power.

- Third, the Navy's transformation vision, Sea Power 21, does not resolve those issues.

- Fourth, as a result, the Navy may find itself constrained to execute its long-term ship-building program with budgets no greater than today's levels.

The Navy Must Provide a Better Explanation for Its Ship Programs

The U.S. Navy is doing a great job explaining why the United States must have a Navy, but not such a good job explaining why it needs either a 375-ship fleet, or even to maintain its current 295-ship fleet. For example, in many presentations on military transformation or the future security environment, Navy officials illustrate the paths and avenues of the world's oceangoing commerce, or the distribution of the world's population. Their point is to demonstrate how more and more of the world's economic activity crosses the oceans—hence the need for the United States to maintain an active

military presence around the world to ensure the freedom of the seas. They also observe that 80 percent of the world's population lives in the littorals; therefore the Navy
must focus on and be able to operate in the world's coastal regions because with the demise of the Soviet threat, that is where the action will be. The fact that most of the
world's population lives in coastal regions was true twenty years ago and 200 years ago.

In 1992, the U.S. Navy in its first post–Cold War vision statement, . . . *From the Sea,*
emphasized the importance of refocusing its attention from blue-water sea control to
littoral operations. Twelve years later, redefining the spread of economic globalization
or the sea-oriented distribution of the world's population provided little help to anyone trying to determine "how much Navy do we really need?" Over the past decade, the
Navy has proposed at various times a fleet composed of 300, 310, 346, or 360 ships. The
latest number is now "around 375."

The Navy's justification for the 375-ship fleet rests on a sequence of key concepts articulated in the Defense Planning Guidance (DPG) and the Navy's response to meet it.
The DPG states that U.S. military strategy must defend the homeland, deter aggression
in four theaters, swiftly defeat aggression in two, and win decisively in one. This has
been dubbed the 1-4-2-1, or simply 4-2-1, strategy. In response, the Navy developed its
Global Concept of Operations (Global Conops), which redistributes the fleet to create
expeditionary strike groups out of amphibious ready groups, surface combatants, and
submarines. Today's nineteen strike groups include twelve carrier battle groups and
seven surface action groups. The thirty-seven strike groups of the Global Conops include those formations as well as the twelve expeditionary strike groups, two additional
surface action groups, and the four SSGNs, each of which constitutes its own "group."
To carry out this concept of operations, the Navy has stated, it would require about 375
ships. This is the official justification so stated in the report submitted to Congress last
year. It is also found in the Navy's vision statement, "Sea Power 21," the cornerstone article written by the Chief of Naval Operations, Admiral Vern Clark.[1]

Yet the Navy does not explicitly answer the question of how or why those capabilities in
those quantities will achieve the strategy articulated in the DPG. Why are thirty-seven
strike groups the right number? Why not forty-five or thirty? The Navy prefers to talk
about capabilities and those capabilities are quite impressive, but why are 375 ships
needed? Is the Navy arguing that 375 ships are necessary for deterrence in four theaters
but that three hundred ships would not be able to do the same in the future? Are 375
ships necessary to swiftly defeat in two theaters, or win decisively in one? As I will demonstrate, the Navy's wartime requirement for ships appears to be less than 375. Recent
history and any comparison with the naval forces of the world suggest that one decisive
victory is more than covered by today's 295-ship Navy. So, if 375 ships are necessary to

swiftly defeat in two theaters, then that has not been made explicit. Of course, one could criticize my argument by saying that the Navy can already do all the jobs asked of it by the Defense Planning Guidance with its existing fleet, but the nation assumes some "risk" in doing so. However, one can then immediately ask how that risk is being measured. Are U.S. national security or vital interests at stake? Or only some minor interest? How is the reduction of risk being related to by the capabilities of different fleet sizes?

Both Numbers and Capabilities

Let me now turn directly to the numbers versus capabilities question. While some contend that the service needs more ships, others argue that the emphasis should be on fleet capabilities. For example, during his first tour as Secretary of the Navy, Gordon England stated that "it is capabilities, not numbers that matter . . . our 300 ships are far more potent than [was] our 600-ship Navy."[2] At the same time, Admiral Clark maintains that the Navy needs about 375 ships to do all things asked of it, adding, "You can only be in one place at one time with one ship and so numbers do matter. Numbers do have a quality all their own."[3] Those public statements indicate a tension among Navy officials over whether the service should emphasize the issue of numbers or capabilities. Capabilities measure the actual ability of the Navy to do certain missions or tasks. However, as Admiral Clark indicated, quantity also plays a role in this. One could build the most expensive, most capable warship the world has ever seen, and still it will be in one place at one time. Thus the proper question is a combination of both concepts: What capabilities does the U.S. Navy need and in what quantity?

Consider the ongoing debate over how many expeditionary strike groups are required. A year ago the Navy's answer was twelve, but according to officials, the answer may now be eight because of Sea Swap (the Navy's experiment with rotating crews every six months to a forward deployed ship); the number of groups will make about the same contribution to forward presence as twelve.[4] That is an interesting point on several levels.

On one hand, just two or three years ago, the Navy argued that rotating crews to forward deployed ships would be too difficult—the challenges in both maintenance and training were considered by many as too great. Despite earlier pessimism, however, the Navy did not in the end stop considering, experimenting with, and pushing new methods of operations. Sea Swap is still an experiment only on surface combatants, although Navy officials have declared it "successful." Thus the Navy may be embracing Sea Swap with more zeal than is warranted at this stage. It has already indicated that it is planning—or at least justifying—reductions in major portions of the force structure based on the Sea Swap experiment.

Yet in the absence of a clear understanding of the Navy's peacetime and wartime requirements for amphibious ships and expeditionary strike groups, proposing to cut the
force structure based on the Sea Swap experiments is raising issues and concerns in
Congress, particularly among members who represent shipbuilding states.[5] Sea Swap
only helps by providing more overseas presence with the existing number of ships or
the same amount of presence with fewer numbers of ships. Sea Swap does not create
more wartime capability but actually reduces it by a little or a lot depending on how it
is used. If the size of the force structure in question remains the same, Sea Swap reduces wartime capability a little because no ships are preparing to go on deployment
(to relieve the forward deployed ship) or have returned from deployment (after reliev-
ing the forward deployed ship). Wartime capability is greatly reduced if cuts in the
force structure follow its implementation. Wartime capability is still determined by the
number of ships—actual, physical hulls—in the fleet. Thus one could argue that if Sea
Swap permits the Navy to reduce its number of ships, it may also help provide deterrence in four theaters since it enables presence, yet it weakens the Navy's ability to
swiftly defeat adversaries in two theaters because it reduces wartime capability.

Reducing the number of ships via Sea Swap, in categories that have an excess relative to
wartime requirements would be prudent. However, the Navy should clearly explain
what its wartime requirements are and why. Until this recent debate over the number of
expeditionary strike groups, both the Marines and the Navy had wartime requirements
for amphibious lift ships that were greater than the existing amphibious lift force. The
long-standing Marine Corps requirement for amphibious lift is to have enough ships to
carry 3.0 Marine expeditionary brigades. Long viewed as unaffordable, the Navy and
the Marine Corps in the 1990s accepted that the Navy's "fiscally constrained" requirement for amphibious lift would be 2.5 Marine expeditionary brigades. Currently, the
Navy has enough amphibious ships to lift 1.9 Marine expeditionary brigades. Cutting
to eight expeditionary strike groups on the basis of Sea Swap would be, in short, a major change to long-standing wartime force planning.

Consider another example, the DD(X). Navy and industry briefings on the DD(X), of
which there have been many over the past few years, make the case for why we need the
DD(X). The ship will have an integrated power system, growth potential for new and
innovative weapons, dramatic signature reduction in order to make the ship very
stealthy, and long-range guns. Such capabilities, should they prove successful, would be
very impressive and a valuable addition to the fleet. What is lacking in those briefings,
however, is a case for how many of these ships the Navy should buy, and why. Do we
need six DD(X)s or twenty-four? In 2003, the Navy's Global Conops brief stated it
needed sixteen: one for each of the twelve expeditionary strike groups and then an additional four for wartime surge. Three months later, the Navy submitted to Congress a

report on shipbuilding requirements over the next thirty years.[6] It proposed a force of twenty-four DD(X)s. Does that imply two DD(X)s for each ESG? If so, why two? (It requested one just three months earlier.) Perhaps sixteen are now needed because there might be only eight expeditionary strike groups. What is the justification for all these numbers? Is there analysis behind them? Should analysis matter? In June 2004, John Young, the Assistant Secretary of the Navy for Acquisition, acknowledged that the Navy would probably end up with between thirteen and nineteen ships.[7] He went on to add that the Navy is studying various "scenarios" to determine the right number. Yet the DD(X) program has been under way, in one form or another, since the mid-1990s, and the Navy is asking for the first ship authorization in fiscal year 2005. Why has the Navy not yet finished the analysis needed to determine how many of those ships are needed? The DD(X) appears largely oriented to providing long-range fire support from the sea, a capability the Navy currently lacks. The scenarios for it, however, seem fairly predictable and, therefore, so should the size of the DD(X) force.

Let us consider another well known example of this problem—requirements for the littoral combat ship. In 2000, the Navy sent a thirty-year shipbuilding report to the Congress. Nowhere in that report did it make mention of a need for small, fast surface combatants to maintain sea control in the world's coastal regions, nor was there mention in the 2001 Quadrennial Defense Review Report. By 2002, however, the Navy was discussing widely the need for such a craft, and by 2003, the Chief of Naval Operations, Admiral Clark, was describing the LCS as his "most transformational program and number one budget priority."[8] He stated a need for thirty to sixty of these vessels. In May 2003, the Navy sent a new long-range shipbuilding program to Congress that called for fifty-six LCSs. No analysis had been prepared ahead of time to determine whether the LCS was the right ship for the missions the Navy wanted, and the characteristics and capabilities of the ship had not been established. Later Admiral John Nathman, who was then Deputy Chief of Naval Operations for Warfare Requirements and Programs (N6/N7), stated in testimony that most of the analysis done to support the LCS program was done after the Navy made the decision to go forward with the program.[9] What, then, was the basis for requiring fifty-six LCSs?

In addition, senior officials have stated that Sea Swap could also affect the LCS program. In June 2004, Admiral Nathman, now the Vice Chief of Naval Operations–designate, stated that perhaps they needed only forty to fifty LCSs. He argued that crew swapping could yield a "smaller procurement objective for LCS."[10] According to the Navy, the primary missions of the LCSs are defeating anti-access threats, such as hunting for diesel electric submarines, countering swarms of small boats, and clearing mine fields. Those wartime missions are unlikely to be undertaken except in an imminent crisis or wartime environment. For a ship designed and built for wartime missions, why should the procurement objective change if crew swapping is used? The wartime requirement for ships is based on the number of hulls—something Sea Swap, as stated earlier, does not address. What, then, is the wartime requirement for LCSs? It does not appear to be fifty-six, or applying Sea Swap would not matter. Finally, the Navy also states that the LCS may take on additional missions, such as safeguarding the sea lanes, as a second-order task after the anti-access missions. Because that is more of a presence mission, Sea Swap would improve the ability of the LCS force to do that job.

Finally, even as the numbers of DD(X)s (and other types of ships) changed over the course of the past two years, the 375-ship number remained essentially the same, potentially adding to the confusion regarding what the Navy needs. Such confusion may be affecting the funding and implementation of the Navy's shipbuilding program. In the 2005 Department of Defense authorization bill, the House Armed Services Committee acted to cut construction money from the DD(X) and LCS programs in order to delay them for one year. The House Appropriations Committee cut both DD(X) and LHA(R) funding, and criticized the Navy for its lack of analysis and detailed explanations for what it was doing. The Committee stated that it

> . . . remains deeply troubled by the lack of stability in the Navy's shipbuilding program. . . . Programs justified to Congress in terms of mission requirements in one year's budget are removed from the next. . . . The Committee further notes that documentation submitted with budgetary proposals is often lacking in specifics regarding total program requirement (number of ships to be constructed), total program cost, and detailed expenditure plans. This lack of information makes it difficult for Congress to weigh options for funding programs throughout the Department of Defense. Furthermore, it obscures the impact of current decisions on future budgetary requirements. [11]

Sea Power 21 Is Not Helping

The Navy's vision statement, Sea Power 21, makes a good case for having in the tool kit all the capabilities it mentions, such as Sea Shield, Sea Strike, and Sea Basing. Sea Shield describes all of the capabilities that will be brought to bear to defend the fleet—or elements of it—from attack. They include missile and air defense provided by surface ships and the planes of an aircraft carrier, as well as anti-access threats posed by quiet conventional submarines, small boats, and mines. Sea Strike focuses on the offensive power of the fleet, to include the striking power of surface combatants (either with missiles or gunfire support), submarines, aircraft carriers, or the Marines disembarking from amphibious ships. Sea Basing refers to the Navy's and Marine Corps's plans to conduct military operations with battalion and brigade-sized forces ashore, supported logistically almost entirely from the sea. [12]

Nevertheless, Sea Power 21 provides no guidance that would help anyone understand how much is needed. It lays out in detail the changes and capabilities the Navy requires, including all of the major programs the Navy is now pursuing: CVN-21, DD(X), CG(X), LCS, *Virginia*-class attack submarines, SSGNs, LPD-17, LHA(R), MPF(F), etc. No discussion of the quantities required for those programs, however, is included. This is somewhat understandable. It is often easier to explain and thus justify the capabilities a particular weapons program brings to the fight than to sort out how many of them are necessary. Without additional justification for the quantities of major platforms the Navy desires, other factors may play a more important role in determining the size of the future fleet.

Resource Constraints

Budgets will play a key role in determining the U.S. military's force structure, including that of the Navy. No matter how much money is available, there are always demands for more spending on an increasing range of goods and services. Thus Navy shipbuilding programs are competing with other demands within the Department of the Navy, the demands of other services, and those of domestic programs, be they social security, the environment, industry subsidies, or tax cuts. National strategy and force structure are always developed within that budgetary context. After all, if strategy (and thus force structure) could be developed unconstrained by budgets, a strategy would be unnecessary—the trade-offs and balances between competing priorities inherent in a strategy would not need to be made.

Future budgets may thus force hard choices on the Navy. From 1990 to the present, the Navy's shipbuilding program was underfunded by about $50 billion simply to maintain today's 295-ship fleet. If the force goal was 375 ships, shipbuilding would be underfunded by more than $100 billion. Hence if those hard choices must be made, either by the Navy, the Department of Defense, or Congress, a clear explanation of the wartime and peacetime requirements of the fleet would be valuable. In some ways, the Navy is a victim of its own success. It no longer has the Soviet navy to plan or size its fleet against. Today, the U.S. Navy could defeat any naval power on the planet within a short period of time. While that may be a blessing at sea, it can be a burden in Washington, D.C. Answering the question of what capabilities the Navy needs, in what quantities, *and why* may make the difference in determining whether it ends up with a fleet that is substantially larger, or smaller, than the one it has now. Right now, the service's strategy, vision, and analysis do not appear to have succeeded in producing a convincing answer. This is not to say that good answers will guarantee a larger fleet. But the long-term fiscal future suggests that with the baby boomers beginning to retire and the demand for resources by Social Security and Medicare costs rising dramatically, the lack of a strong justification will increasingly look like taking a knife to a gunfight.

Notes

1. Admiral Vern Clark, "Sea Power 21: Projecting Decisive Joint Capabilities," U.S. Naval Institute *Proceedings* (October 2002), p. 38.

2. Gopal Ratnam, "U.S. Navy Wrestles with Fleet Size, Abilities," *Defense News,* 1 July 2003, p. 4.

3. "Interview with Chief of Naval Operations Admiral Vern Clark," *Sea Power* (October 2002).

4. Christopher J. Castelli, "Navy Wants to Cut Number of Strike Groups, Slash LPD-17 Shipbuilding," *Inside the Navy,* 26 April 2004.

5. Castelli, "Navy Wants to Cut Number of Strike Groups."

6. Director of Surface Warfare (OPNAV N76), *A Report to Congress on Annual Long-Range Plan for the Construction of Naval Vessels* (13 May 2003).

7. Maline Brown, "Young Acknowledges Navy to Curtail DD(X) Buy, Accelerate Cruiser," *Inside the Navy,* 21 June 2004.

8. Quoted in Scott Truver, "Navy Plans to Develop LCS Fleet with 'Lightning Speed,'" *Sea Power* (May 2003), p. 15.

9. Jason Ma, "Admiral: Most LCS Requirement Analysis Done after Decision to Build," *Inside the Navy,* 14 April 2003.

10. Dave Ahearn, "Adm. Nathman Says Perhaps Just 40 to 50 LCSs Required," *Defense Today,* 24 June 2004.

11. Quoted in the House Appropriations Report, June 2004, pp. 164–65.

12. See Clark, "Sea Power 21." For the supporting articles on the individual concepts, see Vice Admiral Mike Bucchi, "Sea Shield: Projecting Global Defensive Assurance," U.S. Naval Institute *Proceedings* (November 2002); Vice Admiral Cutler Dawson, "Sea Strike: Projecting Persistent, Responsive, and Precise Power, U.S. Naval Institute *Proceedings* (December 2002); Vice Admiral Charles Moore, Jr., and Lieutenant General Edward Hanlon, Jr., "Sea Basing: Operational Independence for a New Century," U.S. Naval Institute *Proceedings* (January 2003).

CHAPTER FOURTEEN

Transformation and the Navy's Tough Choices Ahead
What Are the Options for Policy Makers?
RONALD O'ROURKE

After a decade of making painful choices and implementing wrenching changes, it now seems that policy makers face another set of potentially far-reaching decisions concerning the future of the Navy. These new decisions, which are driven in large part by a significant apparent mismatch between current programs and potential resources, could significantly affect the structure and capabilities of the Navy over the next twenty years or more. Some of the most significant of the new choices concern the concept of military transformation: What does it mean for the Navy? What might be involved in implementing it?

There are many ways to explore this issue. This article begins by focusing on the balance between program goals and potentially available resources. It then presents four general options for future U.S. naval forces that arise from this balance. The discussion concludes by examining possible elements of a strategy for policy makers to implement the fourth and least-defined of these options—the transformation of U.S. naval forces in a manner more rapid and extensive than now planned.

Where We Are: The Balance between Programs and Resources

Policy makers cannot develop or assess options for future naval forces until they first assess where the Navy currently stands, and from a programs-versus-resources perspective, the first thing to be said about the current situation is that the Navy's current programs collectively appear to be significantly larger than its budget.

Take, for example, just one portion of that budget—the shipbuilding account, which is intended to support the currently planned fleet of about 310 ships. (This figure includes fifty-five attack submarines, up from fifty in the 1997 Quadrennial Defense Review.) The shipbuilding account currently provides an average of about $7.9 billion per year for actual procurement of new ships and procures a mix of about 7.5 ships per year (see figures 1 and 2). Increasing the ship-procurement rate to about 8.7 ships per year—the steady-state rate for a 310-ship Navy—and adjusting the mix of ships procured to reflect the planned mix of ships in the 310-ship plan would require the shipbuilding account to be increased by about two billion dollars per year. A bit less than four billion dollars in additional funding per year would be needed to achieve and maintain a procurement rate of 10.2 ships per year, which is what would be needed after fiscal year (FY) 2005 to work off the backlog of deferred ship procurement that has accumulated relative to the steady-state rate since fiscal 1993. About five billion dollars in additional funds per year might be needed to adjust the mix of these 10.2 ships to compensate for the fact that the ships procured since the early 1990s have included a less-than-proportionate share of submarines, which are more expensive than most other types of ships.[1]

FIGURE 1
Annual Funding for Ship Procurement
For 310-ship Navy, in bil. of $FY01

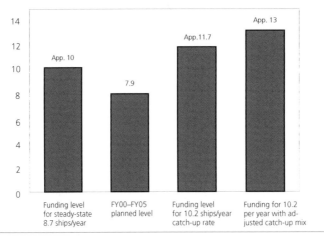

Prepared by Ronald O'Rourke, November 2000

That would be two billion to five billion dollars in additional required funding per year—for just one of the Navy's appropriation accounts. Other individual Navy accounts would not require nearly as much additional money to fund fully, but it appears that several program areas could easily absorb increases of from several hundred million dollars to more than a billion dollars a year if the programs in these areas were to be more fully funded.

FIGURE 2
Ship Procurement for 310-Ship Navy
Average annual number procured

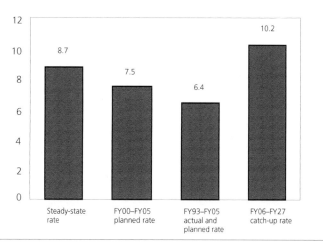

Prepared by Ronald O'Rourke, November 2000

The "Procurement, Marine Corps" account, for example, has a steady-state funding requirement of about $1.2 billion a year. The FY 2001 budget returns this account to about that level, but because this account was funded at about one-half of that level for several years, the Marine Corps states that it must now increase this account to about $1.8 billion a year—an additional six hundred million dollars for each of the next several years. Similar things could be said for the Navy's aircraft procurement, weapon procurement, and research and development (R&D) accounts, and the accounts relating to readiness, maintenance of real property, and housing.

When one adds up the increases for all these areas, including shipbuilding, the total funding differential could be ten billion or more dollars per year, depending on how robustly the current programs of the Department of the Navy (DoN) are funded (figure 3). A recent Congressional Budget Office report puts the figure at seventeen billion dollars per year.[2] This considerable difference between what it would take to fund fully the Navy's programs and its current budget "top line" is a central feature of the Navy's current situation.

The Center for Strategic and International Studies, in Washington, D.C., last year published an updated analysis of what it calls the "coming train wreck" between defense program goals and available resources.[3] The title of this analysis has made the train-wreck metaphor a well-established phrase in debates over future defense spending. This

FIGURE 3
Annual DoN Funding Shortfall
Billions of FY 2000 dollars
Average planned funding for FY01–FY05 (bottom) and additional
amount needed to reach sustaining level (top)

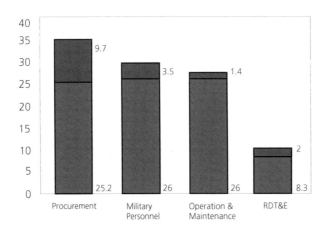

Prepared by Ronald O'Rourke, November 2000
Data taken from CBO report, *Budgeting for Naval Forces* (October 2000), table 5.

metaphor, however, may not be the best one, because it suggests that the conflict between programs and resources is still ahead, that the services have not yet felt its effects, and that these effects, when they arrive, will come all at once, in a cataclysmic way.

The conflict between program goals and available resources, however, is already with us. It has been growing incrementally for the last several years, and the tensions that have built up over that time have already begun to outstrip the Navy's strategies to generate internal budget savings, as well as the service's other temporary coping measures.

As a result of the tension between program goals and available resources, Navy programs have undergone a succession of cutbacks and reductions in recent years. The cumulative effects of these reductions are difficult to discern unless one stands back and assesses them in their entirety—which sometimes can be hard for military officers to do, since their career paths often move them from one job to the next every two or three years. Rather than a train wreck, then, it might be better to think of the effects of the imbalance between goals and resources as akin to gradual oxygen deprivation: it happens slowly, its effects build up over time, and the victim is likely not to be fully aware of what is happening. But in the end, if not alleviated or at least well managed, it can be just as fatal as a train wreck.

A second feature of the Navy's current situation is that in the midst of this growing tension between programs and resources, there are proposals for increasing the Navy's force structure from the current 318 or so ships to about 360 ships, so that the fleet can better meet the demands being placed on it, particularly for maintaining desired levels of forward deployments, without placing an undue burden on the Navy's personnel and equipment. Such an increase in force structure would clearly require substantially more additional funding than would be required to fund fully the current 310-ship program.

A third important feature of the Navy's current situation is that since the middle of 1999 there has been an increased focus in debates over future U.S. defense spending on the "revolution in military affairs" and on "defense transformation." The theme of transformation was featured prominently in the Defense Department's presentations of its proposed defense plan to Congress in early 2000, and in statements on defense policy that year by both sides in the presidential campaign.

Where We Might Go from Here: Four General Options

Given this situation—the programs/resources imbalance, the proposals for increasing force structure, and increased interest in defense transformation—four general options for future U.S. naval forces can be sketched out:

- The first of these options would stay on today's path: it would maintain today's collection of programs and today's level of resources. It is, in effect, the baseline option.

- The second option would maintain today's programs but seek the additional resources needed to fund them fully—the ten billion (or more) additional dollars per year mentioned earlier.

- The third option is force-structure expansion toward a fleet of something like 360 ships. This option would maintain today's collection of programs in expanded form and would require an even larger amount of money to achieve.

- The fourth option is transformation, which would involve changing the current mix of programs. It could be implemented at various resource levels, but since it is not usually spoken of today in connection with large net increases in total resources, it can be associated here with today's levels of resources or something a bit higher.

First Notional Option—Stay on the Current Path

Choosing the first option would mean continuing the various strategies now being pursued to generate internal budget savings that would in turn be applied to currently underfunded priorities, including modernization. These include familiar measures like regionalization of bases and of maintenance; competitive sourcing and privatization; "smart ship," "smart work," and "smart base" initiatives; and also acquisition reform measures, such as multiyear procurement, commercial-off-the-shelf (COTS) procurement, and using cost as an independent variable (CAIV) in the design of new systems.[4] This approach would also continue to balance, as well as possible, near-term readiness against longer-term modernization. It would seek to protect core procurement programs, the readiness of deployed forces, and selected R&D efforts leading toward a moderate, gradual evolution of the force.

In theory, the internal savings produced by this strategy might be enough to finance an increase in procurement rates approaching steady-state replacement levels. This plan, however, depends on certain key, and rather optimistic, assumptions: that the money-saving strategies will be implemented as planned, that they will generate the projected amounts of savings within a certain amount of time, and that no unexpected needs for increased expenditures will arise—that there will be no more financial shocks to the system.

This strategy appears to be a fragile one in that its success requires all these factors to work out as planners hope. The experience of the last several years, in fact, suggests that there is a good chance that one or more of these assumptions will not pan out. Some strategies for saving money may be only partially implemented; some even of those that are fully implemented may not produce hoped-for results; and unexpected financial demands could well arise.

If matters did not work out as planned, the result would be an intensification of the challenges that the Navy now faces in trying to make ends meet. This strategy carries a high risk of producing, over time, a gradual erosion in force structure, an erosion that would begin when today's ships begin to retire in large numbers after 2010 and particularly after 2020. The fleet could fall below the current level of about 318 ships, and then below three hundred ships, as the consequences of fifteen or twenty years of deferred procurement begin to manifest themselves. This would lead to a corresponding reduction in the number of ships that could be deployed forward at any one time. Similar effects would become manifest in aircraft inventories. In general, there would be pressure on the Navy's ability to maintain required levels of readiness, with the burden for this task falling increasingly on the backs of Navy personnel. Also, there would be limited or spotty modernization; in place of new designs and new production, there would be significant reliance on modified designs, upgrades, and service-life extensions.

With regard to the potential for reduced forward-deployed operations, the nation could respond to such a state of affairs in a number of ways. It could simply accept reduced levels of forward-deployed forces, which could require choosing to maintain higher levels of presence in one region at the expense of presence in another, reducing the number of ships sent to each region, or reducing the fraction of the year that ships are deployed to various regions.

Alternatively, the nation could seek to maintain higher levels of forward-deployed naval forces by increasing the number of ships that are "forward homeported" in overseas operating areas. This would raise all of the traditional issues associated with forward-homeported ships, including the need for host-nation acceptance; the possibility of host-nation restrictions on how the ships are used; the risk of becoming excessively tied politically to one region at the expense of others; the issue of how and where these ships are to be maintained; and the risk—the severity of which would depend on the host nation involved—of being evicted and seeing calculations made on the assumption of forward homeporting upset.

Finally, the nation could respond by seeking greater efforts from allies and friends in support of maintaining regional security. This option, however, would depend not just on the willingness of those allies and friends to take on this responsibility but on their capability to do so as well. For naval forces, capability is a significant consideration, since U.S. naval forces include platforms and systems (and resulting capabilities) that are rare in or absent from the naval forces of U.S. allies and friends, including carrier-based fixed-wing aircraft, nuclear-powered attack submarines, surface combatants with highly capable area-air-defense systems, land-attack cruise missiles, and substantial amphibious assault forces.

Optimistically, this first option would result in a fleet of about the size of today's, with some amount of modernization. Less optimistically, the fleet would have fewer ships than it does today, and the amount of modernization could be meager. Either way, but particularly in the less optimistic scenario, this option raises issues regarding both numerical and qualitative sufficiency for carrying out potential missions fifteen or twenty years from now.

Second Notional Option: Fully Fund the Current Plan

Pursuing the second option—fully funding the currently planned 310-ship force—would involve continuing the same money-saving measures described under the first option while seeking the additional resources needed to fund today's collection of programs more completely. These additional resources could come from an increase in the defense budget top line or an increase in the Navy's share of the top line.

It is not clear whether the next administration will support an increase in the defense budget so large that the Department of the Navy's proportionate share of that increase would amount to ten (or more) billion dollars per year. While both presidential campaigns spoke in favor of maintaining a strong defense, neither committed itself specifically to an increase of this size. Moreover, the new administration will face numerous competing federal budget priorities, such as shoring up Social Security; financing new domestic program initiatives in areas such as education, health care, and the environment; granting tax reduction; and carrying out debt reduction. In light of these competing federal budget priorities, substantial growth in the defense top line, while possible, is by no means certain.

The alternative of increasing the Department of the Navy's share of the Defense Department's top line has been mentioned regularly for many years now. The experience of the past several years, however, suggests that mutually offsetting forces in the Pentagon tend to make such shifts difficult to achieve. All the services will likely ask the new administration for more funding, and all of them will bring well developed arguments to bear. In practice, each service's efforts have tended to cancel out those of the others.

If the division of the defense budget changes, moreover, it might not be in the Navy's favor. The Army is now pursuing a force transformation, and policy makers on Capitol Hill, at least, have reacted very supportively to this initiative. On this basis, one might argue that the most likely beneficiary of a defense-budget reallocation would be the Army rather than the Department of the Navy.

If the Navy were to obtain enough new money to fund fully today's programs, then compared to the first option, force structure would be more stable, there would be less pressure on readiness, and there would be somewhat more modernization. Current levels of presence could be maintained, and there would be less need for compensatory measures like forward homeporting or increased reliance on allies. Whether this force would be sufficient numerically and qualitatively for tomorrow's forward requirements, however, would still be in question. If the Navy did not succeed in obtaining all the additional needed resources, the outcome would be more like that of the first option, and the adequacy of the force numerically and qualitatively would be more problematic.

Third Notional Option: Expand the Force Structure

The third option of increasing the Navy's force structure toward 360 ships and maintaining today's collection of programs in expanded form would be pursued like the second, except that the amount of additional resources to be sought would be substantially greater. The question of an increased defense top line or an increased Department of the Navy share would arise again, but in more intensified form.

This option offers a fairly wide array of potential outcomes, depending on how much additional funding the Navy secured. If the Navy obtained most or all of what it asks for, the Navy could over time build itself up toward the 360-ship figure. Forward deployments could be expanded from present levels. Numerical sufficiency would be less of an issue, or no problem at all, but qualitative sufficiency might still be an open question, particularly if the new money were devoted primarily to acquisition of current systems rather than development of new ones. If, however, the Department of the Navy did not receive a large increase in resources, the outcome could be more like that of the second option or the first, depending on the amount it did manage to obtain.

Fourth Notional Option: Transformation

The fourth notional option is transformation beyond that which is already reflected in the Department of the Navy's plans. This option would involve altering today's mix of programs and implementing this altered mix at a level of funding about equal to or a bit higher than today's level.

In discussing this fourth option, it should be noted that, in debates over future U.S. defense spending, the term "transformation" is currently being used in two basic ways. The Defense Department and supporters of current defense plans often use transformation to refer to measures to change U.S. military forces that are already incorporated into the current Five-Year Defense Program, and to such long-range Defense Department conceptual documents as *Vision 2020*. This is the kind of transformation to which the Defense Department referred when it presented its proposed fiscal 2001 budget to Congress in early 2000. For naval forces, these measures include, among other things, current plans for implementing network-centric warfare in the fleet. It is an implicit feature of the three general options discussed above.

Those who believe present Defense Department efforts to implement transformation are inadequate use the term transformation in a different way—to refer to measures that would change U.S. military forces more rapidly or extensively than now planned by the department. This is the kind of transformation referred to under the fourth general option discussed here.

Although there has been much discussion of this more ambitious kind of transformation since the early 1990s, and particularly over the last year or two, it is still not clearly defined in terms of program content or cost. In relation to naval forces, it is typically characterized simply by citing specific proposals, such as STREETFIGHTER, the Arsenal Ship, or the conversion of Trident ballistic-missile submarines (SSBNs) to an SSGN configuration, carrying cruise missiles.

In general, however, it might be fair to say that this kind of transformation can be contrasted from the first kind—the kind reflected in the other three options—as involving different platforms and systems, different operational concepts, and a greater emphasis on long-term investments (as opposed to nearer-term programs). Its advocates argue that this kind of transformation is a means to produce, for a given amount of resources, a force more effective against future threats than one that would result from funding and implementing today's collection of programs.

The Fourth Option: Implementing Transformation

A major question facing policy makers and others who support or are interested in this kind of transformation is how to make it happen. What measures, in other words, could policy makers consider taking (or encouraging others to take) to implement this second kind of transformation? The following are some candidate measures that might form the core of a strategy for transforming U.S. naval forces.

Signaling. One measure to consider in beginning a transformation process would be to make clear to people both outside and inside the naval community that transformation has become an important Department of the Navy priority, even the top priority. Signaling to outsiders is important in terms of winning support for any effort, particularly from Congress. The support that the U.S. Army received in congressional markups of the fiscal 2001 defense budget for its own transformation program is a good example. Signaling to members of the naval community would be equally important, because it would alert them to the facts that they may need to alter the focus of their efforts and that the current distribution of resources may change.

RDT&E. A second item would be to expand research, development, testing, and evaluation efforts so as to include a greater emphasis on "clean-sheet" designs and prototyping. This is likely to require a substantial increase in the RDT&E account—even more than what would be needed to fund more fully current research and development programs—particularly for developing new designs and building and testing prototypes. Instead of adding perhaps several hundred million or a billion dollars to the Navy's RDT&E account (as under the second option discussed earlier), pursuing a transformation strategy might involve adding some multiple of this amount—perhaps two or three times as much.

Experimentation. A third need—one that is often mentioned in connection with transformation—is greater use of experimentation. This could include the establishment of standing experimental forces to supplement the experimentation that can be carried out by general-purpose forces.

These first three items come quickly to mind and are frequently mentioned in discussions of transformation strategies. There are additional measures, however, that can be considered, some of which are less frequently mentioned.

Reassurance. One of these would be to reassure platform communities (that is, the major sectors of the service closely involved with either surface ships, submarines, or aircraft) as well as program managers and contractors that transformation does not represent a mortal threat to their organizational well-being. Institutions, like individuals, tend to prefer stability and continuity over instability and discontinuity. Transformation carries with it the prospect of the latter and thus tends to elicit defensive reactions from people and organizations. The likelihood of swift and vigorous defensive reactions may well have been increased by several years of defense downsizing, which has encouraged institutions and individuals to focus more intensely on self-preservation. Years of program cutbacks and cancellations have encouraged a strong inclination toward "circling the wagons" and defending programs and priorities that have survived earlier reductions.

If transformation is to succeed, incentives would need to be changed so that individuals would know that they can succeed and advance in a transformative environment, and so that businesses would be confident of maintaining their profitability. Program managers' success should not be measured solely by their ability to carry forward procurement programs that were designed years ago if those programs are no longer appropriate, but rather on their ability to recognize where change may be needed and to move quickly to restructure the efforts.

Keeping NCW in Perspective. A fifth potential initiative would be not only to emphasize network-centric warfare but set it in context, in terms of its place in the intended transformation. Much excitement has been generated by network-centric warfare, and for good reason. But in the midst of this enthusiasm, there is a potential for simply equating transformation with network-centric warfare and letting it go at that. That would be a mistake, for although network-centric warfare is essential to transformation, a comprehensive transformation would involve other changes as well.

Right now, the Navy is essentially superimposing network-centric capabilities onto its existing force architecture. This will clearly increase Navy capabilities; but network-centric warfare, which fundamentally alters the relationships between different elements of a force, makes possible wholly new naval force architectures that can differ from today's fleet design. Indeed, exploiting the full potential of network-centric warfare may actually demand a change in the current force architecture. Simply applying it as a veneer over today's force architecture will limit the benefits it produces.

At a time when funds for the development and procurement of new designs are limited, there is a temptation to use network-centric warfare as a rationale for not investing in platforms and systems that could contribute to a new and different force architecture. Misapplying the concept of NCW in this manner would result in missed opportunities. Network-centric warfare will help a great deal, but transformation does not begin and end there.

Force Architectures. The Navy does not show much evidence, at least to outside observers, of having done very much work for years in the area of alternative force architectures. The last completed major effort that was publicized outside the Navy may have been a project conducted by Captain Clark "Corky" Graham at the Naval Surface Warfare Center at Carderock, Maryland, in 1989–92. This architecture focused on a large, modular ship that went by various names, including "carrier dock multimission" and "carrier of large objects," the objects being such things as aircraft, smaller scout/fighter ships, and amphibious forces.[5]

Instead of alternative force architectures, the focus in recent years appears to have been primarily on designing new platforms and systems for the current fleet concept. But with the Navy becoming ever more networked, and with the capabilities of individual platforms increasingly becoming functions of their places in that network, the need for paying more attention to the design of the overall force is becoming increasingly urgent. Just as the designer of a ship should seek to optimize the total ship (rather than its individual systems or components), the need now appears to be to optimize the architecture of the entire naval force rather than simply the designs of the individual platforms that make it up.

There are several new platform and system concepts now on the table, but their merits and limitations will be less and less easy to identify and evaluate except in the context of a larger force architecture. If the focus remains on designing individual new platforms without parallel work on revised architectures, the result is likely to be a perpetuation of the current architecture, producing only next-generation versions of today's platforms and allowing change only through linear descent—stovepipe evolution, if you will.

It might turn out that a further elaboration of today's force architecture is the right approach to meeting tomorrow's operational needs. But this cannot be known with any confidence if the issue is not explored, and there is little evidence of such exploration in recent years. One hears references to a future "system of systems," but the tendency is to consider this metasystem as a by-product of individual platform and program development—something that will emerge and evolve passively, from the bottom up. Such an approach could overlook many of the opportunities that a more consciously designed "system of systems" could offer for increasing fleet capabilities. To achieve not just any system of systems but the best one will require not just bottom-up evolution but top-down concept generation as well.

One current example of focusing on optimizing the entire force architecture and approaching fleet modernization from the top down is the U.S. Coast Guard's DEEP-WATER acquisition project. This project, which aims at replacing a large portion of the Coast Guard's current deep-water-capable assets, is deliberately seeking to avoid a simple one-for-one replacement of cutter classes and aircraft types. Instead, it focuses on identifying the most cost-effective force architecture—that is, the optimum combination of surface platforms, air platforms, C4ISR* systems, and logistics systems—that technology now permits. The program would then procure the elements of this architecture in an integrated fashion.

This is an ambitious project for the Coast Guard, and that service faces several challenges in implementing it successfully. Parts of what the Coast Guard is attempting may not be appropriate or practical for the Navy to consider. Even so, it is worth examining for the lessons it can provide for thinking about future naval force architectures and for achieving them.

What might a transformed naval force architecture include? Elements that are frequently mentioned include a greater reliance on unmanned vehicles (including autonomous vehicles), increased use of distributed sensor networks, and new kinds of ships.

The possibilities for ships are quite diverse. In comparison to current designs, they could have larger and more varied payloads; they could be much more modular; they could be significantly smaller, or significantly larger; they could have much higher maximum speeds; and they could take advantage of nontraditional hull forms. They could be hybrid ships, mixing, say, the functions of an aircraft carrier and surface combatant, or a surface combatant and an amphibious ship. They could be "mother ships," deploying large numbers of smaller ships and unmanned platforms; they could be mobile offshore bases rather than ships at all. They could be derived from commercial designs. All these things have been proposed at one time or another.

An effective strategy to develop alternative force architectures might have three primary aspects. First, it could involve parallel efforts by multiple groups. Alternative force architectures could take various shapes, and the most promising candidates are likely to be discovered more quickly if a number of groups try independently to find them. These groups could be recruited from a variety of settings—the fleet, the platform communities, government laboratories, industry, universities, and think tanks. Each kind of group would have different strengths and limitations. For example, a group whose members are drawn from one of the Navy's platform communities might create architectures that expanded the capabilities of that platform in ways that other groups

* C4ISR stands for command, control, communications, computers, intelligence, surveillance, and reconnaissance.

might not think of; on the other hand, however, it would understandably be disinclined to propose an architecture that downplayed or eliminated that platform.

Similarly, an industry group might have a better understanding of how to apply cutting--edge technologies, particularly from the commercial arena, to create new force architectures. It might be less bound by force-design traditions than people working within Navy offices, and it would be likely to have a keener appreciation for producibility considerations. But a group whose members were drawn from the "widget" industry could not be expected to advance an architecture, whatever its merits, that did not require widgets.

A second potential element of an effort to generate alternative naval force architectures would be a greater use of simulation-based design as applied to the entire force rather than individual ships. The nation cannot afford to build new architectures for experimental purposes, and the Navy could sift through the many possibilities more quickly through intensive modeling and assessment.

Lastly, developing new force architectures should not be thought of as a one-time exercise but as a continuing effort, so that it can incorporate new developments and the contributions of new participants.

Operational Concepts. The need for new operational concepts is frequently discussed in connection with transformation. Much of this discussion concerns proposed operational concepts for warfighting and crisis response operations, and this part of the discussion does not need to be further elaborated here. The discussion of new operational concepts, however, arguably should not stop with warfighting and crisis-response operations, because it can also include consideration of new concepts for how to maintain normal forward-deployment and presence operations. A key goal here would be to identify concepts that can reduce the Navy's current "station-keeping multipliers"—the numbers of ships of given kinds needed to keep one such ship on station in an overseas operating area. These multipliers are considerably higher than people often assume. Although it has often been asserted with conviction over the years, even by admirals, that it takes three Navy ships to keep one on station, the actual station-keeping multipliers for Navy ships are in fact more like five to one, or six to one for ships homeported in the continental United States—the exact numbers depending on the category of ship in question, the specific overseas operating area involved, and (for deployments to the Persian Gulf/Indian Ocean region) whether the ship is homeported on the East or West Coast.[6]

In the post–Cold War era, these station-keeping multipliers have been used extensively to justify Navy force levels. Indeed, for several years now the Navy's force-structure requirements have been based primarily on the number of ships necessary to maintain established levels of presence overseas, and only secondarily on warfighting needs.

Although these station-keeping multipliers are effective force-level justifiers, they also reflect a high operational-cycle "overhead"—the fact that the Navy must procure a large number of expensive platforms to keep a fraction of them deployed on station at any one time. Reducing the multiplier might permit a smaller number of ships to maintain a given level of presence. Frequently mentioned strategies for accomplishing this include double-crewing ships and scheduling long-duration deployments coupled with crew rotation, as was envisaged for the Arsenal Ship. Even after taking into account the additional costs of such measures—for additional crews, more shore-based training facilities, and shorter ship-service lives—this approach might produce net savings that could be devoted to research and development or acquisition.

Measures like these to reduce station-keeping multipliers could be applied only insofar as they did not leave the fleet with insufficient forces for warfighting. They also raise serious issues concerning maintenance, training, and crews' sense of "ownership" of the ships they serve on—which can contribute to the efforts they make on behalf of their ships. These issues are by no means trivial and may prove difficult to resolve. But that should not disqualify them from consideration as potential components of transformation.

The Acquisition System. If much of this is to be accomplished, significant changes might need to be made to the Defense Department acquisition system, particularly in terms of how proposed systems are evaluated and justified. One potential change would be to reduce the emphasis the system puts on replacing specific capabilities that are now being provided by systems approaching retirement age. This approach encourages decisions in favor of replacing older systems with new-generation versions of the same things—a replacement-in-kind strategy that leads to force modernization by linear descent and to a consequent perpetuation of the current force architecture. Instead, the acquisition system could be broadened to accept justification of proposed systems in terms of how they make sense within a future force architecture, irrespective of whether they exactly replace the capabilities of systems being retired, and even if they would result in overlaps of capabilities with other systems that are still years away from retirement.

If transformation is to involve greater use of prototypes, then the acquisition system might need to be changed so that the large up-front design costs associated with developing prototypes can be justified more in terms of their demonstrative (as opposed to purely operational) benefits. In addition, if transformation would mean frequent design changes during production, and frequent modification or restructuring of programs, then the acquisition system would need to be changed so that the assessed cost-effectiveness of proposed systems is not dependent on completing lengthy production runs of stable designs.

Finally, if transformation were to include increased use of experimentation, the acquisition system arguably should be changed to reduce its current emphasis on avoiding test failures at all costs on the grounds that such failures are inherently wasteful. This potential kind of waste should be compared to the more subtle forms of waste that can result when the emphasis on avoiding test failures at all costs slows down the replacement of inappropriate or cost-ineffective systems. Just as the Navy is trying to move away from the "zero-defect" mentality in its personnel policies, so too might it consider, in a transformative era, moving away from an acquisition system with a zero-defects orientation. The Navy (and the Defense Department generally) would need to recognize that if transformation is the goal, an absence of mistakes can be evidence of insufficient effort.

The current acquisition system can be viewed as, among other things, a huge system for avoiding errors and apportioning the blame when something goes wrong. A transformed acquisition system would encourage people to take risks when appropriate and protect them from blame or criticism for errors that result from honest efforts to discover something new.

Agile Manufacturing. Lastly, industry, in coordination with government efforts to change the acquisition system, can assist in the transformation process by altering its business model so that its operations are no longer built so much around the concept of executing long production runs of stable designs. Under this new model, profitability in the future would be derived more principally from research and development work, prototyping, and short production runs or longer runs with frequent changes in design. These activities would need to be viewed by industry as a significant and stable source of profits. The idea of operating profitably on the basis of short production runs of frequently changing designs is established in certain commercial industries that must contend with rapid changes in product technology or with frequent shifts in consumer preferences. The practices adopted by these commercial firms may be able to provide lessons in how to accomplish the same thing in defense production.

Moving toward this new business model, which might be called "agile manufacturing," would likely involve the adoption of new production capabilities and processes. Defense firms have already made significant strides in adopting new production capabilities and processes in areas such as "lean" manufacturing (which involves, among other things, the avoidance of tools and jigs that are suitable for producing only one kind of item) and "flexible" manufacturing (which includes systems that can produce various components in small quantities in response to user demands for individual spare parts). Agile manufacturing would build on these improvements to put prototyping, limited production runs, and rapidly changing designs more at the center of a firm's business operations.

These are not the only elements that might be included in a successful transformation strategy, but a strategy that lacked elements like these would be less likely to achieve its goals. Policy makers in the new administration and the 107th Congress may consider what a transformed naval force might look like and whether it would be better than the force that might result from pursuing the three alternative options discussed earlier. Their views on these issues will no doubt vary, but the Navy and the nation will likely benefit from the debate.

Notes

1. For a discussion, see *Statement of Ronald O'Rourke, Specialist in National Defense, Congressional Research Service, before the Senate Armed Services Committee Subcommittee on Seapower Hearing on Ship Procurement and Research and Development Programs,* 2 March 2000, pp. 3–9.

2. U.S. Congress, *Budgeting for Naval Forces: Structuring Tomorrow's Navy at Today's Funding Level* (Washington, D.C.: Congressional Budget Office, October 2000).

3. Daniel Gouré and Jeffrey M. Ranney, *Averting the Defense Train Wreck in the New Millennium* (Washington, D.C.: Center for Strategic and International Studies, in Cooperation with Management Support Technology, Inc., 2000).

4. In an acquisition program using CAIV, goals are set for procurement or total ownership of the system (or both). Industry is given broad flexibility in making system-design tradeoffs to develop a system that meets the government's minimum-performance specifications and offers the most overall system capability for that cost.

5. For published discussions of this concept, see Anne Rumsey, "Navy Plans Look-a-Likes," *Defense Week,* 13 March 1989, p. 3; Robert Holzer, "Navy Floats Revolutionary Ship Design for Future Fleet," *Defense News,* 14 May 1990, pp. 4, 52; Norman Polmar, "Carrying Large Objects," U.S. Naval Institute *Proceedings,* December 1990, pp. 121–2; Edward J. Walsh, "'Alternative Battle Force' Stresses Commonality, Capability," *Sea Power,* February 1991, pp. 33–5; and Michael L. Bosworth, "Fleet Versatility by Distributed Aviation," U.S. Naval Institute *Proceedings,* January 1992, pp. 99–102. See also the "USN's '2030' Plan for Future Fleet," *Sea Power,* April 1992, pp. 79, 82. At one point in the early 1990s, the Advanced Research Projects Agency (ARPA) explored an alternative fleet architecture that included mobile offshore bases and small modular boats. For a discussion, see "ARPA Envisions Future Battle Fleet," *Navy News & Undersea Technology,* 3 October 1994, pp. 3–5.

6. For a discussion, see U.S. Congress, Library of Congress, *Naval Forward Deployments and the Size of the Navy,* by Ronald O'Rourke, CRS Report for Congress 92-803 F, 13 November 1992 (Washington, D.C.: Congressional Research Service, 1992), pp. 13–23. See also U.S. Congress, Library of Congress, *Naval Force-Structure Planning: Breaking Old Habits of Thought,* by Ronald O'Rourke, CRS Report for Congress 93-332 F, 19 March 1993 (Washington, D.C.: Congressional Research Service, 1993), pp. 2–3.

Conclusion

The U.S. Navy will continue to evolve as it has throughout most of its long history with changes in the American political landscape and the evolving strategic consensus. One set of drivers in this evolution comprises information technology and the desire to take advantage of the opportunities provided by improved data processing, advances in tele-communications, the increasing use of robotics, and advanced materials for building naval platforms, among many others. Notwithstanding the long life-cycles of aircraft carriers, ships and aircraft generally have finite and knowable life spans. Standard re-placement and modernization patterns will ensure that the instruments of naval power improve over time. With the Navy's increasing emphasis on naval transformation, the pace of change promises to be even more rapid in the next two decades. Even if more expensive costs and lower procurement budgets allow for fewer new platforms, ad-vanced technologies will change naval capabilities. For example, more accurate and deadly precision-guided munitions for aircraft and extended-range munitions for naval guns will increase the deep-strike capacity of naval forces even if the platforms them-selves age and new, more capable platforms are procured in smaller numbers than orig-inally envisioned.

Another source of the Navy's ongoing evolution is the desire of the service itself to demonstrate its viability as an instrument of national policy. After all, and despite the Navy's long and storied tradition, respected national security analysts continue to pose questions like, "Will Globalization Sink the Navy?"[1] Even the absence of a dominant grand strategy will not inhibit the U.S. Navy from injecting its own "visions" of a strat-egy that supports the national military strategy. Indeed, George Baer has concluded about the Navy's advocacy of "The Maritime Strategy" of the 1980s that "its central failure lay in the fact that the maritime strategy was not fully accepted as the basis for a national policy of sea power. This did not mean all was lost. The Navy had hoped that it could justify major acquisitions for an offensive carrier-and-submarine fleet, and that it did."[2]

The default position of the modern Navy has been to do a little bit of everything. Ships, for example, have rarely been optimized for single missions; rather, they house weapons and systems capable of carrying out a wide range of roles.[3] Although some types of ships have dwindled in number, the Navy has rarely given up missions. Instead it prefers to keep available ships, aircraft, and other assets with a range of capabilities. This general principle is illustrated by the evolution of the submarine force. Nuclear-powered "boomers" armed with ballistic missiles and attack submarines designed to hunt and kill enemy submarines are less in demand now that the Soviet submarine fleet lies rusting on the shores of the Barents Sea. Instead, several SSBN hulls are being converted to SSGNs, capable of striking targets far inland or of inserting special operations personnel to conduct a wide variety of missions ashore.

The U.S. Navy has often been left to its own devices in devising a maritime strategy that supports the national security and military strategies of the United States. Several times since 1945 the service has sought and failed to "gain recognition for the concept [of a maritime strategy] a discrete element of national strategy" or even as the centerpiece of American strategy.[4] By some accounts this is an almost inevitable outgrowth of the natural evolution of U.S. national security concerns from a "continental," to an "oceanic," to what Samuel P. Huntington called a "transoceanic" outlook—"a clearly stated, offensive, strategic concept for applying power against nonnaval, nonmaritime state."[5] The Navy has been less than successful in promoting the maritime view versus continentalist opponents. Why?

In major conflicts against land powers navies are often unable to act decisively ashore without the participation of the other military services. Despite the claims of the Maritime Strategy of the 1980s, which sought to take the offensive against the Soviet Union, and the efforts of the U.S. Navy to conceptualize its role in the post–Cold War world with documents like "Forward . . . from the Sea," the Navy is still struggling to acquire the weapons, platforms, doctrine, and tactics necessary to influence events ashore in any but the smallest contingencies.[6] In fact, technology today actually limits the Navy's impact: naval guns, even with extended-range guided munitions, reach only so far inland; limited numbers of cruise missiles preclude extended engagements; naval aircraft, even with air refueling, remain as yet limited to relatively brief sorties against land targets; and naval task forces can only linger so long in one locale without refueling, refitting, and resting their crews. Innovations have undoubtedly extended this range—concepts like Sea Swap crewing, home porting ships closer to the battle space, and more capable tenders and perhaps sea bases for the fleet, and dockyards abroad—but still limits remain. For all the importance of the Navy's contributions to recent conflicts like the Persian Gulf War, the various Balkans conflicts, the Afghanistan campaign, and the invasion of Iraq, they were ultimately supporting.[7] For these reasons and others related to political and bureaucratic realities, any future effort to promote a new equivalent of the Maritime Strategy, or even a new version relying on "naval forces for rapid power projection" and "more leverage over events ashore than has been possible from the sea in the past" as the key component of national strategy appears unlikely to succeed.[8]

In the future, the Navy will not be free to set its own course without reference to the roles and missions of the other services as it did during the nation's first great naval buildup in the 1890s. Unlike much of American history, when the Navy and War Departments operated as separate fiefdoms, the norm at least since the National Security Act of 1947 and reinforced by the Goldwater-Nichols defense reforms, has been toward joint and combined operations.[9] The Navy itself has recognized this in its rhetoric, if not always in its budget decisions, by emphasizing "jointness" in everything from the network-centric vision of warfare to renewed efforts to qualify more naval officers for joint command through professional military education. Even coalition operations with allies and temporary friends remain a key part of American naval thought. Whether through formal alliances like NATO or informal coalitions of the willing, whether in the Indian Ocean as part of maritime operations in support of the Global War on Terror or in deep-strike missions against Serbia from the Adriatic, the U.S. Navy almost always sails with other navies.

The service, in short, will keep searching for a strategic vision that complements American grand strategy, the capabilities of the other military services, and the emerging national security environment—characterized today by terrorism, "small wars" and, on the horizon, the possibility that a peer or near-peer competitor will arise once again. The Navy will do so not just to protect the American homeland and key allies but to maintain control over the global commons, both a necessity for stable international commerce and an enabler for continued American primacy.

Notes

1. James J. Wirtz, "Will Globalization Sink the Navy?" in *Globalization and Maritime Power*, ed. Sam J. Tangredi (Washington, D.C.: National Defense Univ. Press, 2002).

2. George W. Baer, *One Hundred Years of Sea Power: The U.S. Navy, 1890–1990* (Stanford, Calif.: Stanford Univ. Press, 1994), p. 441.

3. Peter J. Dombrowski, Eugene Gholz, and Andrew L. Ross, *Military Transformation and the Defense Industry after Next: The Defense Industrial Implications of Network-centric Warfare*, Newport Paper 18 (Newport, R.I.: Naval War College Press, 2003), esp. pp. 39–40.

4. Michael E. Palmer, *Origins of the Maritime Strategy: The Development of American Naval Strategy, 1945–1955* (Annapolis, Md.: Naval Institute Press, 1988), p. 87.

5. Ibid., p. 5. See also Huntington's original article: Samuel P. Huntington, "National Policy and the Transoceanic Navy," U.S. Naval Institute *Proceedings* 80 (May 1954), pp. 483–93.

6. For an excellent overview of this "maritime strategy" see John Hattendorf, *The Evolution of the U.S. Navy's Maritime Strategy, 1977–1986,* Newport Paper 19 (Newport, R.I.: Naval War College Press, 2004).

7. For a brief overview see Edward J. Marolda, "The U.S. Navy and the Persian Gulf," www.history.navy.mil/wars/dstorm/ sword-shield.htm/. A more extensive full treatment can be found in Edward J. Marolda and Robert J. Schneller, Jr., *Shield and Sword: The U.S. Navy and the Persian Gulf War* (Annapolis, Md.: Naval Institute Press, 2001).

8. Owen R. Cote, Jr., "Buying '. . . From the Sea': A Defense Budget for a Maritime Strategy," in *Holding the Line: U.S. Defense Alternatives for the Early 21st Century,* ed. Cindy Williams (Cambridge, Mass.: MIT Press 2001), p. 141.

9. On Defense Department organization issues see James R. Locher III, "Has It Worked? The Goldwater-Nichols Reorganization Act" *Naval War College Review* 54, no. 4 (Autumn 2001), pp. 95–116; for a brief summary of the Navy's initial position on Goldwater-Nichols see Baer, *One Hundred Years of Sea Power,* pp. 443–444.

About the Authors

Dr. Roger W. Barnett is professor emeritus at the Naval War College, where until September 2001 he held the Jerry O. Tuttle Military Chair of Information Operations. Retired from the U.S. Navy in the grade of captain, Dr. Barnett was a member of the U.S. delegation to the strategic arms talks with the Soviet Union in 1970–71. He is the author of *Asymmetrical Warfare*, published by Brassey's (U.S.) in 2003.

Dr. Peter Dombrowski is a professor in the Strategic Research Department and editor of the Naval War College Press at the Naval War College. Dr. Dombrowski is the author of over thirty journal articles, book chapters, and government reports. He recently completed an edited volume, *Guns and Butter: The Political Economy of the New International Security Environment* (Lynne Reinner, forthcoming 2005) and a book coauthored with Eugene Gholz, *Buying Transformation: Technological Innovation and the Defense Industry* (forthcoming). He received his BA from Williams College and an MA and PhD from the University of Maryland, College Park.

Dr. Daniel Gouré is vice president of the Lexington Institute, a defense-policy "think tank." Prior to joining Lexington, he was the deputy director of the International Security Program at the Center for Strategic and International Studies, in Washington, D.C. Dr. Gouré earned his PhD at Johns Hopkins University; he has pursued his national security career in government at the U.S. Arms Control and Disarmament Agency and the Office of the Secretary of Defense. Earlier he worked for the Science Applications International Corporation and the System Planning Corporation, among other firms. A frequent lecturer and the author of numerous articles, Dr. Gouré is a coauthor (with Jeffrey Ranney) of *Averting the Defense Train Wreck in the New Millennium* (1999).

Sir Michael Howard, born in London in 1922, earned bachelor's and master's degrees in modern history at Oxford before serving in the British army in World War II (Italian campaign, twice wounded, Military Cross). After the war he taught at King's College, University of London, becoming the institution's first lecturer in war studies, then professor in war studies, and founding the International Institute for Strategic Studies (IISS). In 1968 he became a senior research fellow at All Souls College, Oxford, then Chichele Professor of the History of War, earning a D.Litt. from Oxford in 1977. From 1980 to 1989 he was Regius Professor of Modern History at Oxford, and from 1989 to 1993 he held the Robert A. Lovett chair of Military and Naval History at Yale University. He is today president emeritus of IISS, a fellow of the British Academy, and a foreign corresponding member of the American Academy of Arts and Sciences. Of his many publications, his most recent books are *The First World War: A Very Short Introduction* (2002) and *The Lessons of History* (1991); other especially well known books are *Franco-Prussian War: The German Invasion of France 1870–1871* (1961, 2d rev. ed. 2001), *The Causes of Wars* (1983), and the now-standard English translation (with Peter Paret) of Clausewitz's *On War* (1976). The reprinted article is adapted from a Raymond A. Spruance Lecture delivered at the Naval War College on 17 April 2002.

Dr. Michael Ignatieff is Carr Professor of the Practice of Human Rights and the director of the Carr Center of Human Rights Policy at Harvard University's John F. Kennedy School of Government. Professor Ignatieff earned his doctorate in history from Harvard University and has been a fellow at King's College, Cambridge; l'École des Hautes Études, Paris; and S. Antony's College, Oxford. His recent scholarly books include *Human Rights as Politics and Idolatry* (2001), *The Rights Revolution* (2000), *Virtual War: Kosovo and Beyond* (2000), *The Warrior's Honor: Ethnic War and the Modern Conscience* (U.S. edition 1998), *Isaiah Berlin: A Life* (1998), and *Blood and Belonging: Journeys into the New Nationalism* (U.S. edition 1994). The reprinted article was adapted from a lecture delivered at the Naval War College on 12 November 2002.

Dr. Richard H. Kohn is professor of history and chairman of the Curriculum in Peace, War, and Defense at the University of North Carolina at Chapel Hill. After undergraduate study at Harvard and earning a doctorate at the University of Wisconsin, he taught at City College, City University of New York; Rutgers University–New Brunswick; and at the National and U.S. Army War Colleges. He served as chief of Air Force history and chief historian of the U.S. Air Force, 1981–1991. Most recently he edited (with Peter Feaver*) Soldiers and Civilians: The Civil-Military Gap and American National Security* (2001). The reprinted article is an expansion and update of the Harmon Memorial Lecture in Military History delivered in December 1999 at the U.S. Air Force Academy. Earlier versions were given as lectures at the Army, Air, Naval, Marine Corps, and National War Colleges, the Marine Corps and Air Command and Staff Colleges, the U.S. Military Academy, U.S. Central Command, the Duke University Law School national security law course, the Syracuse University national security management course, the University of North Carolina at Pembroke, and, at the invitation of the Chairman, the Joint Staff. When the reprinted article originally appeared, the author expressed thanks to Andrew J. Bacevich, George A. Billias, Eliot A. Cohen, Peter D. Feaver, Thomas C. Greenwood, Paul Herbert, Peter Karsten, Lynne H. Kohn, and Abigail A. Kohn for criticisms and suggestions, and numerous other friends, colleagues, and officers and civilians in audiences who offered questions and comments. Jonathan Phillips, Erik Riker-Coleman, and Michael Allsep provided indispensable research assistance.

Dr. Eric J. Labs received his doctorate from the Massachusetts Institute of Technology in 1994. For the past ten years, he has worked at the Congressional Budget Office (CBO). He is the Principal Analyst for Naval Forces and Weapons and specializes in procuring, budgeting, and sizing of the forces for the Department of the Navy. He has published several studies under the auspices of the CBO, as well as a number of articles and papers in academic journals and conferences, including the U.S. Naval Institute's *Proceedings* and *Sea Power*. His most recent CBO study is *The Future of the Navy's Amphibious and Maritime Prepositioning Forces* (November 2004). He is currently working on an analysis of the Navy's total ship force structure. In 2001 and 2003, he received the CBO Director's Award for Exceptional Achievement. The views in the reprinted article are those of the author and should not be interpreted as those of the Congressional Budget Office or the U.S. Congress. A shorter version of this essay was first delivered at the June 2004 meeting of the Current Strategy Forum.

Mr. James R. Locher III graduated from the U.S. Military Academy in 1968 and received an M.B.A. from Harvard University. In 1978 he joined the Senate Committee on Armed Services as a professional staff member, leading efforts that resulted in the Goldwater-Nichols Defense Reorganization Act of 1986. In October 1989, President George H. W. Bush appointed him assistant secretary of defense for special operations and low-intensity conflict. Since 1993, he has written, lectured, consulted, and served on commissions related to the organization of the Defense Department. In 2003–2004, Mr. Locher served as chairman of the Defense Reform Commission on Bosnia and Herzegovina. His book *Victory on the Potomac: The Goldwater-Nichols Act Unifies the Pentagon* was published in 2002.

Dr. Thomas G. Mahnken is a professor in the Department of Strategy and Policy of the Naval War College, Newport, Rhode Island. After receiving bachelor's degrees from the University of Southern California and a master's degree from Johns Hopkins University, he participated in the Gulf War Air Power Survey and served in the U.S. Defense Department's Office of Net Assessment. In 1995–96, he was a National Security Fellow at the John M. Olin Institute for Strategic Studies at Harvard University. In 1997 he earned his doctorate from Johns Hopkins. He is a lieutenant in the U.S. Naval Reserve. He is the author of a forthcoming book on intelligence and military innovation, is co-author of volume 5 of the Gulf War Air Power Survey, and has written articles that have appeared in *International Security, Journal of Strategic Studies, Intelligence and National Security,* and *Joint Force Quarterly,* among others.

Mr. Ronald O'Rourke is a Phi Beta Kappa graduate of the Johns Hopkins University, from which he received his BA in international studies, and a valedictorian graduate of the university's Paul Nitze School of Advanced International Studies, where he received his MA in the same field. Since 1984, Mr. O'Rourke has worked as a naval analyst for the Congressional Research Service of the Library of Congress. In that time, Mr. O'Rourke has written numerous reports for Congress on various issues relating to the Navy. He regularly briefs members of Congress and congressional staffers, and he has testified before congressional committees on several occasions. In 1996, Mr. O'Rourke received a Distinguished Service Award from the Library of Congress for his service to Congress on naval issues. He is the author of several journal articles on naval issues and is a past winner of the U.S. Naval Institute's Arleigh Burke essay contest. Mr. O'Rourke has given presentations on Navy-related issues to a variety of audiences in government, industry, and academia.

Dr. Edward Rhodes is dean for the Social and Behavioral Sciences at Rutgers University. A former International Affairs Fellow of the Council on Foreign Relations, he has served in the Strategy and Concepts Branch of the Navy Staff. He is the author of *Power and MADness: The Logic of Nuclear Coercion* (1989), the coauthor (with Jon DiCicco, Sarah Milburn, and Tom Walker) of *Presence, Prevention, and Persuasion: A Historical Analysis of Military Force and Political Influence* (2004), and the coeditor (with Peter Trubowitz and Emily Goldman) of *The Politics and Strategic Adjustment: Ideas, Institutions, and Interests* (1998). An earlier version of this article appeared in *Strategic Transformation and Naval Power in the 21st Century*, ed. Pelham G. Boyer and Robert S. Wood (Newport, R.I.: Naval War College Press, 1998).

Dr. Andrew L. Ross is a research professor in the Strategic Research Department of the Naval War College's Center for Naval Warfare Studies. His work on grand strategy, national security and defense planning, regional security, arms control, weapons proliferation, the international arms market, and defense industries has appeared in numerous journals and books. He is the editor of *The Political Economy of Defense: Issues and Perspectives* (1991) and coeditor of three editions of *Strategy and Force Planning* (1995, 1997, 2000).

Dr. Edward A. Smith Jr. holds an undergraduate degree from Ohio State University and a Ph.D. in international relations from The American University. Before retiring as a captain in the U.S. Navy, he served in combat in Vietnam; on the staffs of Cruiser-Destroyer Group 8 and the Commander in Chief, Atlantic Command and the Supreme Allied Commander Atlantic; in the Office of Naval Intelligence; and on the Chief of Naval Operations Executive Panel. He is now Boeing's Executive Strategist for Effects-Based Operations. His widely used book *Effects-Based Operations,* published by the Department of Defense in 2001, is now in its third printing. He has just completed a second book, *Complexity, Networking, and Effects-Based Operations,* forthcoming in 2005.

Mr. Frank Uhlig Jr. is a sponsored research scholar of the Naval War College. For over twenty years he was an editor and senior editor at the U.S. Naval Institute, where he founded the annual Naval Review. In 1981 Frank Uhlig became the editor of the Naval War College Press (which produces this journal); he retired from that post in September 1993. When the reprinted article originally appeared, the author expressed thanks to Captain Wayne Hughes and Commander Guy Thomas (both cited in the notes) but also to Professor Milan Vego, of the Naval War College's faculty; to Captain Peter Swartz, U.S. Navy (Retired), of the CNA Corporation in Alexandria, Virginia; and to Mr. Robert J. Cressman, of the Naval Historical Center in Washington, D.C.

Dr. Stephen M. Walt is the Robert and Renee Belfer Professor of International Affairs at the John F. Kennedy School of Government at Harvard University. Professor Walt received his doctorate in political science from the University of California, Berkeley. A research fellow at Harvard University, 1981–84, and assistant professor of politics and international affairs at Princeton University from 1984 to 1989, he has also been a resident associate at the Carnegie Endowment for International Peace, a guest scholar at the Brookings Institution, and a professor of political science at the University of Chicago, where he was master of the Social Science Collegiate Division and deputy dean of the Graduate Division of Social Sciences. His *The Origins of Alliances* (1987) received the 1988 Edgar S. Furniss National Security Book Award. Recent publications include *Keeping the World "Off-Balance": Self-Restraint and U.S. Foreign Policy* (2000) and *Revolution and War* (1996). His *Taming American Power: The Global Response to U.S. Primacy* is forthcoming from W. W. Norton in 2005. He is also the author of articles in *Foreign Policy, The National Interest, International Security,* and *Foreign Affairs.*

The Newport Papers

The Atlantic Crises: Britain, Europe, and Parting from the United States, by William Hopkinson (no. 23, May 2005).

China's Nuclear Force Modernization, edited by Lyle J. Goldstein with Andrew S. Erickson (no. 22, April 2005).

Latin American Security Challenges: A Collaborative Inquiry from North and South, edited by Paul D. Taylor (no. 21, 2004).

Global War Game: Second Series, 1984–1988, by Robert Gile (no. 20, 2004).

The Evolution of the U.S. Navy's Maritime Strategy, 1977–1986, by John Hattendorf (no. 19, 2004).

Military Transformation and the Defense Industry after Next: The Defense Industrial Implications of Network-Centric Warfare, by Peter J. Dombrowski, Eugene Gholz, and Andrew L. Ross (no. 18, 2003).

The Limits of Transformation: Officer Attitudes toward the Revolution in Military Affairs, by Thomas G. Mahnken and James R. FitzSimonds (no. 17, 2003).

The Third Battle: Innovation in the U.S. Navy's Silent Cold War Struggle with Soviet Submarines, by Owen R. Cote, Jr. (no. 16, 2003).

International Law and Naval War: The Effect of Marine Safety and Pollution Conventions during International Armed Conflict, by Dr. Sonja Ann Jozef Boelaert-Suominen (no. 15, December 2000).

Theater Ballistic Missile Defense from the Sea: Issues for the Maritime Component Commander, by Commander Charles C. Swicker, U.S. Navy (no. 14, August 1998).

Sailing New Seas, by Admiral J. Paul Reason, U.S. Navy, with David G. Freymann (no. 13, March 1998).

What Color Helmet? Reforming Security Council Peacekeeping Mandates, by Myron H. Nordquist (no. 12, August 1997).

The International Legal Ramifications of United States Counter-Proliferation Strategy: Problems and Prospects, by Frank Gibson Goldman (no. 11, April 1997).

Chaos Theory: The Essentials for Military Applications, by Major Glenn E. James, U.S. Air Force (no. 10, October 1996).

A Doctrine Reader: The Navies of the United States, Great Britain, France, Italy, and Spain, by James J. Tritten and Vice Admiral Luigi Donolo, Italian Navy (Retired) (no. 9, December 1995).

Physics and Metaphysics of Deterrence: The British Approach, by Myron A. Greenberg (no. 8, December 1994).

Mission in the East: The Building of an Army in a Democracy in the New German States, by Colonel Mark E. Victorson, U.S. Army (no. 7, June 1994).

The Burden of Trafalgar: Decisive Battle and Naval Strategic Expectations on the Eve of the First World War, by Jan S. Breemer (no. 6, October 1993).

Beyond Mahan: A Proposal for a U.S. Naval Strategy in the Twenty-First Century, by Colonel Gary W. Anderson, U.S. Marine Corps (no. 5, August 1993).

Global War Game: The First Five Years, by Bud Hay and Bob Gile (no. 4, June 1993).

The "New" Law of the Sea and the Law of Armed Conflict at Sea, by Horace B. Robertson, Jr. (no. 3, October 1992).

Toward a Pax Universalis: A Historical Critique of the National Military Strategy for the 1990s, by Lieutenant Colonel Gary W. Anderson, U.S. Marine Corps (no. 2, April 1992).

"Are We Beasts?" Churchill and the Moral Question of World War II "Area Bombing," by Christopher C. Harmon (no. 1, December 1991).

Newport Papers 4, 10, and from 14 on are available online (Acrobat required) at www.nwc.navy.mil/press/npapers/newpaper.htm.